PSYCHOLOGICAL
AND ETHICAL IDEAS:
WHAT EARLY GREEKS SAY

MNEMOSYNE

BIBLIOTHECA CLASSICA BATAVA

COLLEGERUNT

J.M. BREMER · L.F. JANSSEN · H. PINKSTER

H.W. PLEKET · C.J. RUIJGH · P.H. SCHRIJVERS

BIBLIOTHECAE FASCICULOS EDENDOS CURAVIT

C.J. RUIJGH, KLASSIEK SEMINARIUM, OUDE TURFMARKT 129, AMSTERDAM

SUPPLEMENTUM CENTESIMUM QUADRAGESIMUM QUARTUM

SHIRLEY DARCUS SULLIVAN

PSYCHOLOGICAL AND ETHICAL IDEAS:
WHAT EARLY GREEKS SAY

PSYCHOLOGICAL AND ETHICAL IDEAS

WHAT EARLY GREEKS SAY

BY

SHIRLEY DARCUS SULLIVAN

E.J. BRILL

LEIDEN · NEW YORK · KÖLN

· 1995

The paper in this book meets the guidelines for permanence and durability of the Committee on Production Guidelines for Book Longevity of the Council on Library Resources.

Library of Congress Cataloging-in-Publication Data

Sullivan, Shirley Darcus, 1945-
  Psychological and ethical ideas : what early Greeks say / by
Shirley Darcus Sullivan.
      p.   cm. — (Mnemosyne, bibliotheca classica Batava.
  Supplementum, ISSN 0169-8958 ; 144)
  Includes bibliographical references and indexes.
  ISBN 9004101853 (cloth : alk. paper)
    1. Philosophy, Ancient.   2. Philosophy of mind—Greece—History.
  3. Ethics, Ancient.   4. Classical literature—History and criticism.
  I. Title.   II. Series.
  B187.5.S85   1994
  180—dc20   94-36311
                                                             CIP

Die Deutsche Bibliothek - CIP-Einheitsaufnahme

[Mnemosyne / Supplementum]
Mnemosyne : bibliotheca classica Batava. Supplementum. -
Leiden ; New York ; Köln : Brill.
    Früher Schriftenreihe
144. Sullivan, Shirley Darcus: Psychological and ethical ideas. -
    1995
Sullivan, Shirley Darcus:
Psychological and ethical ideas : what early Greeks say / by
Shirley Darcus Sullivan. - Leiden ; New York ; Köln : Brill,
1995
    (Mnemosyne : Supplementum; 144)
    ISBN 90-04-10185-3

ISSN   0169-8958
ISBN   90 04 10185 3

PRINTED IN THE NETHERLANDS

To the memory of my mother,
Bernice Muriel Darcus,
and my husband,
Richard Douglas Sullivan

sed nil dulcius est bene quam munita tenere
edita doctrina sapientum templa serena

Lucretius, *De rerum natura* 2.7–8.

CONTENTS

PREFACE

This book discusses specific ideas that were prominent in the Archaic Age of Greece (750–440 B.C.). It treats the following ideas: psychological activity, soul, excellence, and justice. It presents sources where these ideas are to be found; it interprets different passages; it gives extensive information on discussions of the ideas in the notes and bibliography. For each idea, it aims to describe the evidence, to suggest an interpretation of it, and to give a composite picture of that idea in the Archaic Age. The book focuses in particular on poets and philosophers of this period, treating both together rather than separately as is usually the case. Although evidence for the ideas chosen is readily available for Homer, for the first time it is presented specifically in this way for other authors of the Archaic Age. Further features of the book are as follows.

Readership

The book is intended for readers who are interested in what the early Greeks have to say about the different ideas mentioned above. Some readers may be acquainted with early Greek literature in the original Greek. Some may know it only in translation. Others may be coming to this material for the first time. With this broad readership in view, the book aims to be essentially introductory in nature. It assumes no previous acquaintance with the authors it treats or their works. It presents all Greek terms in translation (with transliteration provided in some instances). It also presents in the Appendix biographical details of the different poets and philosophers who are discussed, information on their writings, and, for the philosophers, chief points of their teachings.

Range of Subject

The book focuses upon specific ideas of poets and philosophers of the Archaic Age of Greece. For the person unfamiliar with these authors, their number and interests may appear somewhat overwhelming. They

lived at different times and wrote in different genres. They lived in
widely scattered areas, coming both from the western and eastern
Greek world. The Archaic Age of Greece extends approximately from
Homer (mid-eighth century B.C.) to the death of Pindar (c. 440 B.C.).
We shall stay within this period, concentrating on the early epic poets,
the lyric and elegiac poets, and the Presocratic philosophers. In the
case of these last we shall include some discussion of the philosophers Anaxagoras and Democritus even though they lived and wrote
later in the fifth century B.C. Although he lived during the Archaic
Age, we shall not treat Aeschylus, since Greek drama falls outside
the scope of the present study. With this focus on specific ideas over
this extent of time, it becomes impossible to discuss details of all that
the various poets wrote and all that the philosophers thought. For
this reason too general information is given in the Appendix. In the
case of the philosophers a broad picture of their philosophical views
will accompany discussion of the ideas this book treats. Of necessity,
with these philosophers, it will give specific interpretations which may
differ from those offered by others. Since this is so, it will also provide information in the footnotes on studies with different viewpoints.

Approach to Subject

In this work we shall look at what a large number of authors had to
say about psychological activity, soul, excellence, and justice. These
ideas were chosen for the following reasons. First, they allow a focus
upon early Greek individuals, showing how they think, act, and relate to other people and to their universe. The first two ideas, "psychological activity" and "soul", concentrate on the inner nature of
early Greek people. How did they think, feel, or will? How did they
view the life-principle within? The third idea, "excellence", describes
a strong motivating influence in their lives. The fourth idea, "justice", is of major importance as they relate to one another in society
or offer explanations of why the universe functions as it does.

Second, these ideas are prominent in early Greek authors. These
individuals include our two earliest Greek epic poets, Homer and
Hesiod, the Greek lyric and elegiac poets, and the Presocratic philosophers. Selecting from among their poems and other writings, we
shall discuss the earliest appearances of the ideas listed above and
show how they either stayed the same over the course of time or

changed. The book will bring together authors often treated separately by those studying the Archaic Age. By so doing, it will allow a composite view of what was being written about these ideas in both poets and philosophers during this period. We shall see similarities and differences with respect to these ideas in those writing in various genres.

As mentioned above, the book aims to describe what early Greek writers say about certain psychological and ethical ideas. It will present the evidence and offer an interpretation of it. The introductory level of the book will preclude discussion with other scholars about possible approaches to or interpretations of different authors. The complexity of the sub-fields that treat these ideas in detail is fully recognised by the author. It is hoped that the book will instill in the reader a desire to explore these sub-fields in greater depth.

Bibliography, Footnotes, Translations, Structure

The Selected Bibliography will list major studies relevant both to the Archaic Age in general and to the ideas treated in the book. In the footnotes further specialized information will be given on discussions of each specific idea. In some cases the book will reflect these studies, in others not. They will thus direct the interested reader to other sources of information and different points of view. In the bibliography and footnotes the abbreviations of journals are those used by *L'Année philologique*. Authors listed in the bibliography will be mentioned in the notes by name or name and short title only.

The translations of the various passages quoted from the poets and philosophers are my own. In most cases these will be literal translations of the Greek.

Although this book can be read continuously, it may readily lend itself to consultation on one or more specific idea. In light of this possible use of the book, each chapter will form a complete unit in itself with appropriate cross-references provided for points that may have been introduced elsewhere in other chapters. Within chapters too topics (*thumos*, e.g., *phrēn*) will form complete units in themselves with an overview provided at the end of all of them. This structure has led to some repetition but this has been kept, it is hoped, to a minimum. For the reader who wishes to consult the book for a specific author, the index will provide a list of passages discussed. The general index will give a list of items discussed either briefly or at length in the text. These will include not only the major ideas treated in the different chapters but also others that have been introduced.

This book treats psychological and ethical ideas that were of great interest not only to early Greeks but to those of later times as well. As we present the evidence for these ideas and offer an interpretation of them, we hope to show in early Greek literature how people thought and what they highly prized.

Shirley Darcus Sullivan

University of British Columbia
June 1994

ACKNOWLEDGEMENTS

My thanks to the Social Sciences and Research Council of Canada and to the University of British Columbia for grants that aided my research. I thank colleagues who have shown interest in this work. In addition I thank Andrew McCracken for the care and thoughtfulness with which he typed the manuscript. Lastly, I thank the two individuals to whom the book is dedicated for so generously enriching my life with their gifts of wisdom.

*

The maps have been reproduced from: J.M. Robinson (Editor), *An Introduction to Early Greek Philosophy*. Copyright © 1968 by John Mansley Robinson. Reprinted with permission of Houghton Mifflin Company.

CHAPTER ONE

THE NATURE OF THE EVIDENCE

In early Greek poetry and philosophy we find many ideas that were to play a significant role in Greek thought. These ideas, having a long history, would in turn influence the course and development of Western thought. The present study will focus upon some of these ideas, namely psychological activity, soul, excellence, and justice. Generally, different authors did not set out to define one or more of these ideas but in the literature and philosophy they present these ideas are clearly discernible. To clarify what various authors thought about them proves to be both interesting and challenging.

In this chapter we shall describe our method in treating these ideas in early Greek poetry and philosophy. We shall also examine the nature of the evidence we shall encounter. In all instances this evidence has characteristics that greatly affect the study of ideas within it. Some characteristics provide richness of opportunity for discussion of ideas. Others severely limit what can be said about them. Once we have made clear what the evidence is like and how we are going to treat it, we can move on to the ideas themselves.

In treating the ideas listed above, we shall start with the poetry of Homer and Hesiod. Then we shall look in detail at what the lyric and elegiac poets and also the Presocratic philosophers say about them. Basically we shall cover a period called the 'Archaic Age', which is usually conceived of as starting with Homer (mid-eighth century B.C.) and concluding with death of Pindar (440 B.C.). Even though there is some overlapping, it is a period that stands apart from the 'Classical Age' of the fifth century, appropriately so since it has a character distinct from this other period.[1] Many of the characteristics of this Archaic Age will become apparent in the course of our discussion. In our study we shall extend the boundaries of this period somewhat by treating as well the Presocratics Anaxagoras and Democritus (c. 420 B.C.).

---

[1] On the nature of the Archaic Age see Bowra, *Greek Lyric*, *Pindar*, Burn, Burnett, Campbell, *Golden Lyre*, Davison, Fowler, Fränkel, *Dichtung*, *Wege*, Gentili, Jaeger, *Paideia*, Kirkwood, *Greek Monody*, Lefkowitz, *Lives*, Mulroy, Podlecki, *Early Greek Poets*, Thalmann, Treu, Walsh.

In the different chapters we shall discuss the ideas named above
during this expanded period. The origin of these ideas will be briefly
treated. Then their nature in the Archaic Age will be set forth. This
approach will show what the ideas were like during that period. This
information may prove valuable for understanding how their later
appearance was both similar and/or different. Homer and Hesiod
provide ample material for the study of these ideas. We shall, therefore, choose from their works passages that appear most appropriate.
Our evidence from the lyric and elegiac poets and Presocratic philosophers is fragmentary but likewise is often abundant. We shall
again select from them what seems most apt for each discussion. In
all cases our focus will be on the ideas rather than on the particular
poets or philosophers.

In this study we shall make no references to any 'development of
ideas'. We do not assume that any one period of Greek poetry or
philosophy had the 'correct version' of an idea. Over time ideas
emerge, change, and disappear. They are always in nature suited to
their times, especially reflecting the human and social needs that exist
in different periods. Our task will be to discern what manifestation
of an idea occurred when. We shall suggest why this particular
manifestation occurred. As we move through the centuries we shall
note any changes that appear. The ideas we have chosen are ones
that remain greatly important to the Greeks. They do not fade but
they certainly, in some cases, do alter.

As we study early Greek poetry and philosophy, we discover that
ideas may be present for which there is not yet a specific term. The
lack of a word for something does not mean the absence of a concept of that thing within a society. It may be that no precise definition of a concept has yet been worked out but this lack of a definition can occur when a notion is present and simply taken for granted.[2]
A widespread general awareness of the concept may exist. We shall
suggest that this is the case with the Greek notion of 'self', a notion
that already appears to be present in Homer (see chapter 2).

A situation can also occur where a specific term for an idea does
exist but, even though present in some passages, may not necessarily
be found in all passages which treat that idea. We shall see this
happen in Homer with the case of 'justice' (see chapter 5). *Dikē*, the
term for 'justice', occurs in certain contexts but is missing from the

---

[2] On this point see Sullivan, *Psychological Activity*, p. 2 with notes 5 and 6.

opening of the *Odyssey* in which the idea of justice plays a major role. Specific terms and their presence in different passages can very much aid the study of ideas. But a wider perspective is needed than simply studying terminology in the treatment of ideas. In this book we shall attempt to maintain a broad perspective as we consider different ideas.

Homer and Hesiod

As we look at the various ideas, we shall begin with our earliest poets, Homer and Hesiod. But in no sense do these two authors mark the beginning of the poetic tradition among the Greeks. Long had bards and rhapsodes sung songs, weaving together glorious tales of heroes. For centuries, before Homer or Hesiod composed their poems, were such tales told. These tales formed part of an oral tradition of poetry among the Greeks. By the time of Homer (mid-eighth century) and Hesiod (late eighth century) a great reserve of poetic language existed on which poets could draw.

The early Greek stories were passed on in an artificial form of language, largely made up of formulas. These formulas were fitted into epic metre, dactylic hexameter. They were varied in multiple ways depending upon their placement within the lines of poetry. In this oral culture bards would weave together stories, new and old, using the many formulas at hand.[3]

But if we describe Homer and Hesiod as following a long tradition of other poets, who likewise composed stories from a reservoir of formulaic language, do we suggest that their works fail to reveal any individual poetic contribution? In no way. The formulas were

---

[3] On the formulaic nature of Homeric verse see in particular M. Parry, *L'Epithète traditionelle dans Homère*, Paris, 1928 and 'Studies in the Epic Technique of Oral Verse-Making', *HSCP*, 1930, vol. 41, pp. 73–147, 1932, vol. 42, pp. 1–50. Both of these (with the first translated) appear in A. Parry (ed.), *The Making of Homeric Verse*, Oxford, 1971, pp. 1–190, 266–364. See also M.W. Edwards, *Homer and the Oral Tradition. The Formula*, Columbus, Ohio, 1986, J.B. Hainsworth, *The Flexibility of the Homeric Formula*, Oxford, 1968, A.B. Lord, 'Composition by Theme in Homer and Southslavic Epos', *TAPA*, 1951, vol. 82, pp. 71–80, *The Singer of Tales*, Harvard, 1960, D.G. Miller, *Improvisation, Typology, Culture and "The New Orthodoxy": How "Oral" is Homer?*, Washington, 1982. See also bibliography in J.P. Holoka, 'Homer Studies 1971–1977', *CW*, 1979, vol. 73, pp. 65–150 and 'Homer Studies 1978–83', *CW*, 1990, vols 83–4, pp. 89–156, 393–461 and D. Packard and T. Meyers, *A Bibliography of Homeric Scholarship 1930–70*, Malibu, Calif., 1974.

readily available but what the bards did with them was their own achievement. The two poems assigned by long tradition to Homer, the *Iliad* and the *Odyssey*, were recognised in very early times by the Greeks as magnificent creations of a poetic genius. 'Tell us the story of Achilles or Odysseus', people might ask. 'Which version?' 'Homer's, of course' became the usual reply.

Hesiod too drew upon this rich reserve of formulaic language. He wrote in epic metre, using it not to tell a story, as Homer did, but to teach his listeners about justice and the nature of the universe.[4] He does so in his poems the *Works and Days* and the *Theogony*. In his narrative epic, Homer stays in the background: the Muse inspires the song that is sung. In his didactic epics, Hesiod, in contrast, specifically mentions himself and the manner in which the Muses, in a personal encounter, inspired his song. Each poet, drawing from the same fount of poetry, thus very much presents an individual poetic response.

When we examine ideas present in any work, it is very important to establish the ways in which this work may be limited in how it presents these ideas. With regard to early Greek poetry, it is quite apparent that the nature of the poems of Homer and Hesiod, in particular the manner in which they were composed, limits them in several regards.

First, the poems were written in a specific metre that imposed a restricted pattern and range of expression. Second, the repetition of formulas raises the question: to what degree does the poet simply repeat formulas without consciously choosing those in which the words might prove to be especially appropriate for the context? Third, the language that Homer and Hesiod employ had already had, by their time, a long history.[5] How artificial had it become by the eighth century? How 'living' were the words within it? How well did it reflect the spoken language of the time?

---

[4] Recently there has been debate concerning whether Homer or Hesiod was the earlier poet. For persuasive evidence for the traditional order of Homer first see R. Janko, 'The *Iliad* and the Editors: Dictation and Redaction', *CSCA*, 1990, vol. 9, pp. 326–34.

[5] On Homeric language see Fränkel, *Dichtung*, pp. 27–49, I. Morris, 'The Use and Abuse of Homer', *Classical Antiquity*, 1986, vol. 5, pp. 81–138 (with helpful bibliography), G. Nagy, 'Homeric Questions', *TAPA* 1992, vol. 122, pp. 17–60, L.R. Palmer, 'The Language of Homer' in A.J.B. Wace and F.H. Stubbings, *A Companion to Homer*, London, 1962, pp. 75–178, G.P. Shipp, *Studies in the Language of Homer*, Cambridge, 1972, G. Thomas, *Literacy and Orality in Ancient Greece*, Cambridge, 1992,

We see that the poems of Homer and Hesiod are limited by these three factors: metre, repetition of formulas, language. Even though this is the case, it is important to recognise the following points about these limiting factors. First, epic metre, however restrictive, still allows a rich variety of expression. Second, repetition of formulas, even though it is a dominant feature of early epic, none the less requires the poet to make a choice among the available formulas. This choice could well entail sensitivity to the words composing the formulas and their aptness to context.[6] Originally, of course, the words in the formulas must have been conceived as appropriate in themselves. Some importance, therefore, can be given to the appearance of various terms in different contexts. Third, with regard to the artificial nature of epic language and how it may have limited the poems of Homer and Hesiod, we must keep a broad perspective. We simply do not know what the spoken language of the Greeks was like during the time of Homer and Hesiod (eighth century), during the times of the events Homer describes (twelfth century), or before. But we can readily surmise that it did not closely resemble the poetic language of epic. The vocabulary of epic language may have been present in the spoken language but the latter probably had a much wider range of words. The poetic language, having had a long history, probably contained archaic words and phrases no longer in use or considered 'quaint' in nature. Even terms common to both languages probably varied in frequency and perhaps even in meaning.

In this book we shall treat several terms that first appear with a particular meaning in these two poets and then take on different meanings as time passes. We do not know if Homer and Hesiod present a limited view of any of these terms, with their already having a far more important and wider significance in the spoken language of their own time. Nor can we discern whether the opposite was the case: did Homer and Hesiod use a term that was quite rare

---

T.B.L. Webster, 'Language and Thought in Early Greece', *Manchester Literary and Philosophical Society* (=*Manchester Memoirs*), 1952/1953, vol. 94, pp. 17–38. See also A. Heubeck, 'Homeric Studies Today' in *Kleine Schriften*, Erlangen, 1984, and Latacz.

[6] On the influence of M. Parry and Albert Lord and reactions to their views about the oral nature of the Homeric poems see J.P. Holoka, 'Homeric Originality: A Survey', *CW*, 1972/1973, vol. 66, pp. 257–93. See too H. Schwabl, 'Zum Problem der traditionellen Kompositionsformen bei Homer', *WS*, 1986, vol. 99, pp. 39–62. A book that illustrates well the elements of conscious choice of meaning in formulaic poetry is Parry. See also O. Tsagarakis, *Form and Content in Homer*, Weisbaden, 1982, for a similarly less severe approach.

in the spoken tongue? We must, therefore, be cautious in making
any generalizations about uses appearing, disappearing, or changing
as though it would apply to the Greeks as a whole. We can speak
only of what was the case in Homer or Hesiod. We cannot assume
that such was generally so either for the period in which they lived,
or for the period before them. Nor can we assume that, if a term
changed, it did so generally in the times that followed.

Interestingly enough, we can see that the epic language that these
two poets inherited probably itself showed ideas in the process of
change. We necessarily receive in their poems a 'broad view' of an
earlier language in the process of evolving over centuries. At the
same time we encounter a 'narrow view' of language in relation to
what may have been spoken in these poets' own times.

In this book, therefore, with Homer and Hesiod, we shall focus
upon their specific works and how the ideas we are discussing appear in them. When we make comparisons or point out differences,
our frame of reference will ever be the particular poems that we are
studying. This will be especially true in cases where we may look
within these poems at individual characters and their behaviour. In
such instances we are not encountering 'Greeks' in general but specific persons as characterized in a story.

In addition to the limitations described above, the Homeric and
Hesiodic poems are restricted also by the themes they present. Homer
tells us of the adventures of heroes. Hesiod, in one poem, gives advice
to his brother Perses on appropriate and admirable human behaviour;
in the other, he presents a sweeping explanation of where the universe comes from and why it continues in existence. In the treatment of these specific themes, there may be many references to the
ideas that we shall discuss but these ideas do not necessarily 'hold
centre stage'. Lack of mention or discussion of them, therefore, cannot be taken as evidence either for any lack of interest in them or
for the absence of the ideas altogether in their times. This presence
of specific themes in Homer and Hesiod again makes caution necessary in the formulation of any generalization about the frequency of
ideas or their prevalence in a particular period.

Thus far we have pointed out features of the works of Homer and
Hesiod that will affect our discussion of ideas. Both poets had a very
great influence upon the authors who followed them, an influence
that must be kept in mind as we look at the way they in turn discussed the different ideas we are considering.

Lyric and Elegiac Poets

After Homer and Hesiod we shall look at what the lyric and elegiac
poets had to say about the various ideas. In terms of time this group
begins with Archilochus (mid-seventh century) and ends with Bacchylides (mid-fifth century).[7] The Appendix gives a list of these individuals whose poems we shall mention with some details about their
life and work. The lyric and elegiac poets form a group large in
number. They are individuals with varying interests. But looked on
as a group they have much of importance to say about the ideas we
shall treat. We shall refer to different individuals in different chapters according to whether they treat an idea or not.

Just as with Homer and Hesiod, we find with the lyric and elegiac
poets aspects of their poetry that limit its nature as far as the study
of ideas is concerned. First and most important, our evidence for
them is fragmentary. We possess only a portion of what any of them
wrote. This makes caution necessary in formulating any generalizations from the poems we do possess. Again, as with Homer and
Hesiod, our comments about any ideas must be specifically related
to the poems we discuss. The ideas we treat may well have appeared
in many other poems and been presented either in a similar or different light. In every instance we are forced by the fragmentary nature
of the evidence to offer only a limited picture of what any poet might
have thought.

In the case of one poet, however, the situation is the opposite: we
have over 1400 lines of elegy ascribed to Theognis, who lived at the
end of the sixth and beginning of the fifth centuries. Probably only
a portion of these lines belongs to him.[8] For the sake of convenience
this book will refer to Theognis as the author of this large corpus,
with the questionable authorship, however, always a present factor.
With reference to the ideas we are discussing, these verses ascribed
to 'Theognis' may suggest a broader scope of treatment than Theognis
himself in fact presented. This broad treatment may itself prove

---

[7] On the lyric and elegiac poets in general see the following. (Specific studies will
be mentioned in the appropriate footnotes.) Adkins, *Poetic Craft*, Bowra, *Greek Lyric*,
Pindar, Burn, Burnett, Campbell, *Golden Lyre*, *Greek Lyric*, Davison, Fränkel, *Dichtung*,
Wege, Gentili, Gerber, Hudson-Williams, Kirkwood, *Greek Monody*, *Selections*, Lefkowitz,
Lives, *Victory Ode*, Lloyd-Jones, *Greek Epic*, *JHS*, 1973, Marg, Mulroy, Podlecki, *Early
Greek Poets*, Thalmann, Treu, Walsh, West, *Studies*, *Greek Lyric Poetry*, Woodbury.

[8] On the nature of the poetry of Theognis see West, *Studies*.

valuable in shedding light on different ideas but it must be remembered that not all of it may belong to one individual.

A second limiting feature of lyric and elegiac poetry is its composition in a variety of metres. This poetry includes the following types. Elegiac verse was made up of a dactylic hexameter followed by a shorter line called a 'pentameter'. Elegy was often associated with lament and traditionally accompanied by the flute. Iambic verse, closely resembling the rhythm of conversation, was early connected with invective. It later became the metre for dialogue in Greek tragedy and comedy. Personal lyric was often composed of short stanzas in different metres. Choral lyric included much larger poems written in complex metres with matching stanzas (strophe, antistrophe, epode).

The choice of words made by different poets in these types of poetry was clearly greatly affected by different metrical patterns. Consequently some terms, on which we may be focusing, may be absent in certain poems. Since our approach will be a broad one in which we concentrate on ideas as found in a substantial context, this limitation will not prove to be of crucial importance.

Third, as also with Homer and Hesiod, we find in the lyric and elegiac poets the limiting factor of language. Theirs is not the formulaic language of the epic poets, although we may hear echoes of this from time to time. Theirs is, however, the language of poetry. This language is usually a somewhat artificial one with distinctive features. This is especially the case with Pindar and Bacchylides who write elaborate victory odes characterised by conventions of praise.

With regard to lyric and elegiac poetry, the scope and meaning of many terms may have been far different in the spoken language of the day and, then again, it may not. When terms for our ideas appear, therefore, we can note their meaning in specific contexts and ascribe points of view to the particular author using them. But we shall avoid making wider claims about the views of the people living in any poet's time.

Fourth, as likewise with Homer and Hesiod, the lyric and elegiac poets present specific themes. Their interests differ from the epic poets and vary also among themselves. Even when they treat similar topics, these poets may adopt a focus different from earlier authors and from one another. Their interests are wide-ranging and include war, love, politics, and many concerns affecting the individual. As they treat different subjects, they emerge as individuals within their works. Thematic concerns become a limiting factor for the study of ideas, if the ideas chosen are of peripheral and not central interest to the poet. The opposite, of course, can also be true: themes and ideas may coincide. As we look at the ideas we are treating, we shall see both of these possibilities occurring.

As the Appendix illustrates, the number of lyric and elegiac poets is large. When we discuss the ideas of psychological activity, soul, excellence, and justice, we shall not be able to treat all passages where these ideas are mentioned in the various poets. We shall, therefore, make selections, concentrating on those passages that present interesting and important (especially if innovative) treatments.

The Presocratics

With the Presocratics we encounter authors with interests and concerns often different from other authors.[9] As with the lyric and elegiac poets, we meet a group of individuals ranging over a long period. They begin with Thales (late seventh century) and end with Democritus (late fifth century). For convenience we have listed them in the Appendix with their dates and origins. We have also stated whether they wrote in poetry and prose and given chief points of their philosophical views.

In terms of the form in which these individuals write, we find some using poetry and others, prose. For the Presocratics as for other early Greek writers, form and content seem closely related. For certain Presocratics—Xenophanes, Parmenides, Empedocles—poetry was judged the apt vehicle for expressing their understanding of the universe. All write in hexameter verse, using this metre, as Hesiod did, to teach. This form was apparently thought to be appropriate because the source of what they had to say stood outside the range of merely human experience. Xenophanes, himself being a rhapsode, repeated poetry long thought to be inspired by the Muses. Perhaps then for him, when he presented his philosophical ideas about divinity, poetry seemed the most appropriate form. Parmenides refers to

---

[9] On the Presocratics in general see the following. (Works on specific authors will be mentioned in the appropriate footnotes.) Anton and Kustas, Barnes, Capasso, de Martino and Rosati, Dumont, Fränkel, *Dichtung*, von Fritz, *Grundprobleme*, Furley, *Cosmic Problems*, Furly and Allen, Gerber, W.K.C. Guthrie, Hölscher, Hussey, Jaeger, *Theology*, Kirk, Raven, and Schofield, Lloyd, *Magic*, *Methods*, Mansfeld, Mourelatos, *Presocratics*, Prier, Reale, Robb, J.M. Robinson, Sambursky, Shiner and King-Farlow, Stokes, West, *Early Greek Philosophy*, Wright, *Presocratics*.

a goddess as the source of his poem (B 1). Empedocles invokes the Muse to send 'what is right for mortals to hear' (B 3).

The other Presocratics write in prose. For them this form, so closely reflecting spoken language, appeared to be appropriate for the ideas they were expressing. The choice of this form may suggest that, for them, the source of ideas was simply the human mind with its capacity for judging truth. This is not to say that these philosophers denied the presence of a ruling power or of divinity within the universe. Rather, by using prose, they may have wished to show how and to what degree human beings could come to understand that very divinity by using innate instead of inspired abilities. As we shall see in two cases, Heraclitus and Anaxagoras, the human tool proves to be of crucial importance as a link with a cosmic principle itself.

The question of form of literature is important in another way. When individuals are living in the same age and writing in the same form, do we correctly divide them into distinct categories? Why do we have the two groups, 'lyric and elegiac poets' and 'Presocratics'? Do we rightly separate the Presocratics writing in poetry from other early poets doing the same? On the one hand, there are good reasons for separating the two groups. What distinguishes them is the content of their poems, reflecting their interests. The lyric and elegiac poets focus upon concerns affecting the individual. For the first time we encounter the emotional range found in men and women treated in some detail. We also encounter their activities being described as they engage in battle, athletics, personal relationships, and society. The Presocratics, in contrast, focus upon the role of the human being in the cosmos and upon the nature of the universe itself.

But even though this difference in interests is found in these two groups, they none the less, as contemporaries, share some features in common. In the study of ideas, we encounter each using similar language and referring to related topics. True, those Presocratics, who write in prose, may very well use this language in a distinct way. But, not surprisingly, those writing in poetry sometimes resemble the lyric and elegiac poets rather closely.

In this book, as it treats the Archaic Age, it will prove to be a valuable practice to determine what each of these groups has to say about the various ideas. We shall see that both difference and similarity in approach to these ideas sheds light on their nature and scope during this period. The sharing of genre, language, and interests proves to be especially true of one 'elegiac poet', also called 'Presocratic',

Xenophanes. Some of his poems are usually quoted by editors with those of the elegiac poets, others, with those of the Presocratics. This practice seems to be justified by his wide-ranging interests. In our treatment of his poetry we shall, as appropriate, likewise place him with either the elegiac poets or the Presocratics.

Overall, as we treat the Archaic Age, we can see in the lyric and elegiac poets and the Presocratics the presence of a shared intellectual climate. The lines between the two groups, although often clear, can appear on occasion to be rather poorly defined. It will prove to be the case that by treating the two groups together, we can better understand the centuries in which these individuals lived than by isolating the two.

Our evidence for the Presocratics, as with Homer, Hesiod, and the lyric and elegiac poets, reveals limitations when ideas are studied. First, it is fragmentary in nature. The philosophers may have made many other references to the specific ideas or terms that we are treating. From the fragments that we possess, we can see what they have to say about different ideas but we must not assume that we can present a full picture of any idea.

Second, for those Presocratics who write in poetry, we encounter again the limitations imposed by both language and metre. These two probably had a strong impact, especially upon the specific terms that the poets used. Since we are looking at ideas in a broad context, the limiting effect of language and metre may prove of less importance than it otherwise would. But it must be borne in mind.

A third factor that limits Presocratic evidence is its thematic content. As mentioned above, these philosophers are interested in understanding how the universe works and what role the human being plays within it. Some of the ideas we treat will be of crucial importance (psychological activity, soul, justice) but that of excellence will matter less. Again, as with the lyric and elegiac poets, we shall select, as appropriate, fragments from the different thinkers, analyzing in detail those shedding light on our subject.

Features of Style

Two features of the way authors in the Archaic Age write will prove important for our study. First, the poetry is usually 'inspired' verse. Poets to some degree act as a mouthpiece of a divine being or beings, often called the Muse(s). It is not that poets do not bring much skill (*technē*) to their poems. They clearly do both in choice of words and in working out of metre. This proves to be especially true of the complicated verse of the lyric and elegiac poets and the magnificent odes of Pindar. But poetry ever contains wisdom (*sophia*) as well, given as a gift from without.

What we shall see in terms of style is that this early poetry unfolds as it is sung.[10] Poets listen and compose. Often no attempt at 'tightening an argument' or 'modifying order or quantity of detail' is made. What may strike us as a rambling style or one without cohesion is in fact a 'linear style' that presents ideas as poets conceive them and as they themselves 'hear' them under inspiration. This style does not make the poetry less rich. But it sometimes provides its listeners with some challenges for grasping the structure of the poem as a whole.

A second feature of both the poetry and the philosophy of the Archaic Age is that it was written very much for society. This literature assumes the presence of an audience.[11] What we shall see is that these authors often answer questions that the audience may have posed. But they do not present these questions themselves in their poetry. They simply give the answers to such 'unspoken' questions. In Hesiod, for example, we can understand some of the elaborate detail of the *Theogony* in this light. He starts his poem: 'let us begin with the Muses'. The audience may have asked: 'why?' Hesiod proceeds to give a detailed explanation of why such a beginning is appropriate. Much later in the work we find him answering a far more profound question, itself 'unspoken' in the text. 'Why can we assume that Zeus will continue as ruler of the gods?' Hesiod will 'answer' this unspoken question by describing the wives of Zeus and the gifts they impart to him (886 f.). Because of these gifts, Zeus will prove capable of ruling the universe. These brief examples illustrate a common feature of this literature. If, therefore, we look for the questions that the poets seem to be answering, even though they do not state them in their poems, we can often better grasp the course of an argument or the presentation of ideas in a work. This presentation of ideas becomes in some way a dialogue: authors provide the

---

[10] On features of style in the lyric and elegiac poets see especially Bowra, *Greek Lyric Poetry*, Fränkel, *Dichtung*, and Treu.

[11] On this feature of literature in the Archaic Age see especially J.M. Bell, 'Poet and Public in Archaic Greece', Diss., Univ. of Toronto, 1973, and Gentili.

best 'answers' they can to a curious audience. As we treat various selections, we shall show how different poets 'answer' questions of this nature.

Why these Ideas?

In the chapters to follow we shall discuss psychological activity, soul, excellence, and justice. Why this choice of ideas? The Archaic Age provides much literature for study. In terms of time, it covers a broad period. In terms of authors, it possesses many. As stated in the Preface, we selected a particular topic within it: human beings and their range of behaviour. We then focused within this topic, itself broad in nature, on ideas that would allow discussion of several crucial questions relating to human beings. These questions are as follows.

How did people think, feel and will? To answer this question, we shall look at the idea of 'psychological activity'. What principle keeps people alive? What is the destiny of the individual after death? For these two questions, we shall present a treatment of 'soul'. What do human beings value most highly with regard to individual or social behaviour? What makes people excel? For these questions, we shall examine the notion of 'excellence'. What makes human society possible and able to continue? In what sort of universe do human beings live? What ensures that this universe continues to exist? For these questions, we shall look at the idea of 'justice'. The book will conclude with an overview of the ideas discussed.

CHAPTER TWO

PSYCHOLOGICAL ACTIVITY

Background

When we encounter early Greek literature, we may wonder how its authors will speak of thinking, feeling, willing, and other psychological activities. Perhaps, we assume, the situation will be straightforward. The characters will simply say, as we would, 'I think', 'I feel', or 'I intend'. And in fact they do. We may also expect individuals to refer to the 'mind' or 'heart' within themselves as the specific location where they carry on such activities. And such references we also find. But on closer examination, we discover a view of psychological activity within the person quite different from ours, one rich and complicated in nature. A variety of Greek terms indicates the presence of this activity: *noos, phrēn, thumos, kradiē, ētor, kēr,* and *prapis.* No simple term appears to express what we might mean by 'personality' or 'self'.[1] This is not to say that individuals have no concept of 'self' or that they fail to see themselves as separate and individual agents. They clearly do.[2] But what is distinctive in this early literature is that people usually relate psychological activity to the terms listed above. These terms designate 'psychic entities'. People view these entities as independent agents acting within them or as locations where they carry on psychological activity. Person and psychic entities remain always distinct and the person has differing relationships with them.[3]

---

[1] See chapter 3 for a discussion of *psychē*, the term that gradually came to express this idea.

[2] The question of whether a notion of 'self' is to be found in early Greek literature will be discussed more fully in chapter 3. It has received considerable treatment recently. See R. Gaskin, 'Do Homeric Heroes Make Real Decisions', *CQ*, 1990, vol. 40, pp. 1–15, T. Gelzer, 'How to Express Emotions of the Soul and Operations of the Mind in a Language that Has No Words for Them', *CHS*, 1988, vol. 55, pp. 1–49, de Romilly, pp. 23–45, T.G. Rosenmeyer, 'Decision-Making', *Apeiron*, 1990, vol. 23, pp. 187–218, J.-H. Sautel, 'La genèse de l'acte volontaire chez le héros homerique: les syntagmes d'incitation à l'action', *REG*, 1991, vol. 104, pp. 346–66, Schmitt, R.W. Sharples, '"But Why Has My Spirit Spoken with Me Thus?": Homeric Decision-Making', *G. & R.*, 1983, vol. 30, pp. 1–7, and Sullivan, *Psychological Activity*, pp. 1–19 (with further bibliography).

[3] The relationship between person and the *noos, phrēn,* and *thumos* is treated in detail in my studies as follows:

Before analyzing the nature of these entities responsible for psychological activities, we need to make several preliminary points about such activities themselves in early Greek literature. First, in these activities agent and function are not distinguishable. Thus, in any passage, for example, *thumos* can be 'that which thinks', 'thinking' itself, and 'thought'.[4] If we focus simply on the second aspect, function, passages may appear quite accessible and easy to grasp. But the role of agent is also an element in the appearance of these terms and helps to clarify why person and entity remain distinct. The aspect of result likewise is present and similarly aids in clarifying why individuals habitually encounter one of these entities as something separate and distinct within themselves.

Second, in the rich range of language expressing psychological activity, we may be able to establish categories: intellectual, emotional, volitional, and, where appropriate, moral. Sometimes these distinctions are clear and validly applied. But frequently in this early Greek poetry, they are not. Instead, types of activities are often fused and functions blurred.[5] Several elements may be present in verbs expressing such activity. A verb for thinking may include as well aspects of feeling, willing, or reacting. As a consequence, in a passage where such a word occurs, the range of meaning of a psychic term may be very rich.

But if a blurring of function occurs in the description of psychological activity, does it matter which psychic term is used? Are these terms interchangeable? Could one suffice for all such psychic activity? Examination of the terms, it is true, reveals a great overlap in usage. These terms are essentially fluid and versatile in nature. But even though this is the case, they are not simply synonyms nor are they interchangeable. Each displays distinctive characteristics, some

---

Noos in Homer: *SIFC*, 1989, vol. 7, pp. 152–95; in Hesiod: *Glotta*, 1990, vol. 68, pp. 68–85; in the lyric and elegiac poets: *Emerita*, 1989, vol. 57, pp. 129–68; in Pindar and Bacchylides: *Glotta*, 1990, vol. 68, pp. 179–202.

Phrēn in Homer: see *Psychological Activity*; in Hesiod: *Rbph*, 1989, vol. 67, pp. 5–17; in the lyric and elegiac poets: *Glotta*, 1988, vol. 66, pp. 26–61; in Pindar and Bacchylides: *Glotta*, 1989, vol. 67, pp. 148–89.

Thumos in Homer: *IF*, 1980, vol. 85, pp. 135–50; in Hesiod: *Emerita*, 1993, vol. 61, pp. 16–40; in the lyric and elegiac poets: *SIFC*, 1994, vol. 12, and 1995, vol. 13, forthcoming; in Pindar and Bacchylides: *Rbph*, 1993, vol. 71, pp. 46–68.

[4] On this fusion of agent and function see Claus, p. 16, von Fritz, *CP*, 1943, p. 81, Harrison, pp. 67–74, Russo and Simon, pp. 484–85, and Sullivan, *Psychological Activity*, p. 30.

[5] On the fusion of categories see Claus, p. 7, Furley, pp. 2–7, Harrison, pp. 66–7, Jahn, pp. 186–92, and Sullivan, *Psychological Activity*, p. 30.

of which become more and more apparent in different authors. As
pointed out in chapter 1, our study of these terms is limited to and
by our written evidence, itself of a particular, restricted nature. How
broadly these terms were used in the spoken language cannot be
known. But some of the richness of their range of meaning is detect-
able in the literature we have and it is apparent that these terms all
possess distinctive characteristics.

In our discussion thus far we have used the expression 'psychic
entities' with regard to these psychological terms.[6] This description
was chosen for several reasons. It allows the presence or absence of
physical characteristics. 'Psychic' suggests a range of psychological
functions. 'Entities' points to the presence in the person of distinct
seats of psychological activity. The phrase, however, may suggest rather
strongly the notion of agent; in its use, therefore, we shall have to
recall the ambiguity between agent and function mentioned above.
On the whole, this phrase will prove an apt description of these
terms in the authors we study. Even though it may not clarify specifically what they were, it will not distort their nature, especially regarding their relationship to the person in whom they are found.[7]

Because the psychic entities share many common features but also
have distinctive traits, we shall in this chapter first take a brief look
at them in general. We shall then treat three major entities separately (*noos, phrēn, thumos*) and three entities, closely resembling one
another, together (*kradiē, ētor, kēr*). In the case of the three major
entities, this method alone will allow a clarification of their specific
nature. What may be said of one entity is not said of another. This
clarification of how the entities differ appears to be essential for an
understanding of what the early Greeks thought about psychological
activity as a whole.

Let us now discuss these psychic entities in general.[8] Can we look

---

[6] How these terms should be spoken of has been much discussed by scholars.
They have been called, for example, 'organs' (see Onians) or 'analagous to organs'
(see Snell), both emphasizing a concrete nature. On the other hand, they have been
interpreted more abstractly as expressing 'thought' or 'life-force' (see Claus). For
further discussion of approaches see Claus, pp. 1–47, Jahn, pp. 124–81, Sullivan,
Psychological Activity, pp. 1–19. See also R. Padel, *In and Out of the Mind, Greek Images
of the Tragic Self*, Princeton, N.J., 1992, pp. 12–48 for observations on recent studies.

[7] We shall clarify below the relationship of person to each of the psychic terms
we study.

[8] On the absence of *psychē* from this list and its role in the human being, see
chapter 3.

back before the Homeric poems, themselves the blossoming of a rich and long tradition, and suggest how they were viewed? We have, of course, only the evidence of Homer and the *Homeric Hymns*,[9] but certain passages strongly suggest that these entities were physical in nature. In some cases this physical nature is quite apparent; in others, this is less the case, and, in still others it seems to be missing altogether. Of the entities mentioned above, we see *kradiē*, *ētor*, and *kēr* preserving a strongly physical nature. With a wide range of activity, these three none the less function basically as the 'heart', both as physical organ and, in the same way we use the word, as a seat of strong emotion. Into the second category of entities that display physical characteristics less often, we place *phrēn*[10] and *thumos*. In the last category, those showing no physical qualities, we place *noos*.

With respect to these physical characteristics, it would be easy to suppose a chronological change. First the terms designated entities physical in nature and later, entities psychological in nature. But the situation is not so simple. What happens in early Greek thought is that the distinctions between material and immaterial, corporeal and incorporeal are not made to the degree that we make them.[11] There is some perception of difference, but we encounter a continuum of physical and psychological rather than a sharp division between the two. If we describe one end of this continuum as physical, it is at the psychological end of this continuum that the entities we shall discuss seem to be located.

Within the person, these psychic entities display a feature important for any understanding of them. They are very much 'open-fields of energy' which outside forces can affect.[12] They do not have closed or defined boundaries. Instead, they can be increased, lessened, and destroyed by the gods, outside objects, or other people. The person

---

[9] On the *Homeric Hymns*, see details under 'Homer' in Appendix One. Abbreviations of the *Hymns* are listed there.

[10] Another psychic term, *prapis* closely resembles *phrēn* but appears much less often and has a more restricted range of activity. Since it is not a prominent psychic entity, we shall not treat it separately in this chapter. On its nature see S.D. Sullivan, '*Prapides* in Homer', *Glotta*, 1987, vol. 65, pp. 182–93.

[11] On this feature of early Greek thought see Adkins, *From the Many*, pp. 15–27 and R. Renehan, 'On the Greek Origins of the Concepts of Incorporeality and Immateriality', *GRBS*, 1980, vol. 21, pp. 105–38.

[12] This expression was introduced by Fränkel, *Dichtung*, pp. 88–90. See also Adkins, *From the Many*, pp. 25–6, W. Burkert, *Greek Religion, Archaic and Classical*, Oxford, 1985, pp. 121–2, and Harrison, pp. 77–8.

in whom these entities are found looks on them as changeable in nature and vulnerable. Agamemnon explains that he took Briseis from Achilles because Zeus at that moment removed his *phrenes* and placed delusion (*atē*) there instead (*Il.* 19.88, 137). Aphrodite controls 'be-guilement' which 'steals away the *noos* even of one thinking wisely' (*Il.* 14.217). Hesiod speaks of *thumos* 'growing greater' in the gods (*Theog.* 641). The openness of these entities significantly affects how people relate to them within. Individuals do not know what these psychic entities are going to be like from moment to moment.[13]

We turn now to our specific discussion of these psychic entities. We shall see that, however much they share the same psychological range, distinctive features of each appear. We shall see too that these entities are not just parts of a self, itself not yet defined by a single word. Instead they are dominant, and perhaps even domineering, presences within, from which the person remains distinct, observing and responding to them.

Noos

Homeric and Hesiodic Background

Of all psychic entities *noos* perhaps is most important. In the authors we are treating it is found in the uncontracted form '*noos*'; later the contracted form *nous* is common. Homer and Hesiod provide us with our first picture of *noos*.[14] As mentioned in chapter 1, they give us a necessarily limited picture, both because they write in formulaic language and present specific themes. But none the less, in repeating the formulas devised over the centuries by bards, they show us features of *noos*, some of which set it apart from other psychic entities. What is *noos* like? First, it is mentioned over 100 times in the *Iliad*, *Odyssey*, and the *Homeric Hymns* and in Hesiod, twenty-six times. Sec-

---

[13] See especially below on *noos* which is thought to 'change' with each day that comes.

[14] For *noos* in Homer and Hesiod see especially Biraud, Böhme, Bona, Bremmer, Claus, von Fritz, *CP* 1943, Furley, Gelzer (note 2), Harrison, Jahn, Krafft, T. Krischer, '*Noos, noein, noema*', *Glotta*, 1984, vol. 62, pp. 141–49, Larock, Lesher, *Phronesis*, 1981, G. Nagy, 'Sēma and Noēsis: Some Illustrations', *Arthusa*, 1983, vol. 16, pp. 35–55, Onians, Plamböck, Russo and Simon, R. Schotländer, 'Nus als Terminus', *Hermes*, 1929, vol. 64, pp. 228–42, Snell, *Discovery*, *Der Weg*, Sullivan (note 3), Warden.

ond, it is always referred to in the singular, each person having one *noos*. Third, unlike other psychic entities, which show evidence of a physical nature, it does not. Although placed in the chest, in *thumos*, or in *phrēn*, it never itself acts as a location for other psychic entities.

Functioning within the person, *noos* appears to have a particular association with 'inner sight' or 'inner vision'.[15] This association may suggest primarily intellectual activity, but the range of *noos* is much wider. Passages in the early epics show it as a 'way of thinking', exemplifying the attitudes a person has. This 'way of thinking' can involve some form of 'clear sightedness', extremely valuable for the person concerned. It may as well include deliberation or planning needed in some circumstances. It may involve too a 'way of reacting' to a situation. In such a reaction, emotion may be an element. Finally, a 'way of coping' may well be present, itself suggesting a volitional element. All these features, of course, are not clearly apparent in every passage, but emerge from an overview of them.

Let us glance at some descriptions of *noos*. The *noos* of one god emerges very prominently: that of Zeus. Often in different episodes in which he is involved, it is not he who acts, but his *noos*. It can 'revive' Hector (*Il.* 15.242), 'master' Ajax and the Trojans (*Il.* 16.103), and 'stir up' Odysseus (*Od.* 24.164). It 'easily persuades' others and 'knows prophecy' (*H. Her.* 396 and 535). This *noos* is 'always stronger than that of human beings' (*Il.* 16.688). One cannot 'thwart' or 'avoid' it (*Il.* 8.143, *W. & D.* 105), 'steal' or 'elude' it (*Theog.* 613). Sometimes this *noos* proves to be vulnerable. Sleep can lull it (*Il.* 14.252), or Aphrodite can 'lead it astray' (*H. Ven.* 36). Prometheus succeeds in 'deceiving' it (*Theog.* 537). In general, *noos* in the chief Olympian functions as the seat of his thinking, will, and plans, all of which come into effect.

Other passages tell us about *noos* in human beings. At *Il.* 14.62, when the Achaeans are in great difficulty, Nestor says to Agamemnon: 'let us consider how these matters will be, if *noos* will accomplish anything'. This passage suggests the range of *noos*: it signifies the mind that thinks, the process of thinking, and the plan that may be formed. At *Il.* 15.80 its association with inner vision is clearly stated: 'as when the *noos* of a man leaps who, having travelled over much land, thinks

---

[15] This feature of *noos* was pointed out in particular by von Fritz, *CP*, 1943, and has been much discussed. See especially Krischer (note 14), Sullivan (note 3), *SIFC*, 1989, and Warden.

in his wise *phrenes*, "would that I were here or there" and expresses many desires'. *Noos* moves swiftly: it can envision different places and dart from one to another.

In humans the range of *noos* is broader still. With it someone can ponder, contrive, rejoice or beguile; when it is joined with 'counsel' (*boulē*), one can consider, make gifts, or escape from danger.[16] A person is born with *noos* but its source and particular nature may derive from the gods. At *Il*. 13.732 Zeus is described as giving different gifts to different individuals: to one 'he puts good *noos* in the chest, from which many profit and many this person saves, and himself realizes it best'. To be of 'good *noos*' is clearly an advantage. One person does this in particular, Odysseus, whom Zeus describes as 'excelling in *noos*' (*Od*. 1.66).

In both gods and human beings a particular feature of *noos* is prominent: it can be hidden. It can conceal its thoughts, purposes, and plans. This is particularly true in the case of Zeus. Athena at *Od*. 24.474 asks him 'what his *noos* conceals within'. Hesiod says that 'there is no seer among mortals who would know the *noos* of Zeus' (fr. 303.2). Athena tells Achilles not 'to conceal' in his *noos* the cause of his sorrow (*Il*. 1.363). Odysseus with his 'very shrewd *noos*' speaks in one way but keeps his true thoughts and feelings hidden (*Od*. 13.255). Hesiod advises Perses not to let his *noos* 'belie' the friendly behaviour he shows (*W. & D*. 714). *Noos* therefore hides its thoughts or someone in it keeps true thoughts, reactions, or plans hidden. This can be a boon for the individual but a problem for others. This feature of *noos* suggests an important role of it as a seat of what a person truly thinks.

In a well-known passage, *Od*. 18.130–7, Odysseus reveals another essential feature of *noos*: it changes. He says that the human being is a feeble thing who must endure with a 'daring *thumos*' the sorrows the gods send. 'For the *noos* of the human being on earth is such as is the day that the father of humans and gods brings upon them'.[17] An example of the kind of day that the gods can bring appears in *Od*. 17.322 where a 'day of slavery' removes 'half' of a person's 'excellence' (*aretē*). In the current passage the gods can give either 'ex-

---

[16] For specific references see Sullivan as in note 15, pp. 169–70.

[17] On the interpretation of this passage see H. Fränkel, 'Man's "Ephemeros" Nature according to Pindar and Others', *TAPA*, 1946, vol. 77, pp. 131–45 and *Dichtung*, pp. 148–51.

cellence' (133) or 'sorrows' (134). The presence or absence of these gifts strongly affects how a person acts. This passage suggests the wide range of reference *noos* can have, one not restricted to the intellect. *Noos* signifies a person's way of thinking. In this we see intellectual, emotional, and volitional aspects implied. *Noos* in human beings varies with time. It is not static or determined. It may differ from person to person, as Odysseus found in his travels, coming to know 'the *noos* of many people' (*Od.* 1.3).

Not only is the *noos* of human beings variable, so is that of the gods. Hesiod says that in Zeus it 'is different on different occasions, difficult for mortals to discern' (*W. & D.* 483). In the Trojan War Zeus tells the gods to help either side depending on 'where the *noos* of each' is (*Il.* 20.25).

Within the human being *noos* has a vital role.[18] It may be principally the feature that makes humans what they are. The phrase '*noos* is in *phrenes*' describes the presence of consciousness in Hephaestus' handmaidens, made of gold (*Il.* 18.419). This, plus 'speech' and 'strength', allows them to act like living persons. When Circe turns Odysseus' men to swine, their *noos* remains 'firm' (*Od.* 10.240): in their thinking they remain human beings. Animals in Homer do not have *noos*. Nor do the dead except for Teiresias, made wise by the gift of *noos* (*Od.* 10.494).

Noos changes with the day but within the person, during a lifetime, it may have some enduring traits. On the positive side, it can be 'good', 'wise', 'god-fearing', 'sound', 'earnest', and 'fearless'. On the negative side it can be 'evil', 'harsh', 'unseemly', and 'shameless'. When Antilochus behaves badly in the chariot race, he excuses himself by saying that 'a young man's *noos* is rather hasty' (*Il.* 23.590). Odysseus has a *noos* that is 'not subject to enchantment' and thus he resists Circe's magic (*Od.* 10.329). He is also one who 'always wields a *noos* of great shrewdness in his chest' (*Od.* 13.255). This *noos* is responsible for his consistent behaviour of concealing his true thoughts and feelings and of making up various stories as he copes with different crises.

Noos is vulnerable to the action of outside forces and agents. Emotions and deceptions (*atai*) can cause someone to act in a negative way 'outside *noos*' (*Il.* 10.391, 20.133). When *noos* is 'lost', foolish

---

[18] See the full discussion of *noos* in Jahn, pp. 46–123.

behaviour results as when Ares continues fighting despite the wishes of Zeus (*Il.* 15.129). When it is 'confused' in Priam, he is afraid and stands bewildered (*Il.* 24.358). Its 'good' condition is something much desired.

In summary, we may describe *noos* in Homer and Hesiod as a psychic entity with a broad spectrum of activity. Quite often it functions as a seat of a person's deepest attitudes, thoughts, and wishes. *Noos* is a distinct entity within the person strongly affecting how the individual behaves and appears to others.

How do person and *noos* relate? Someone can be described as having a positive relationship to *noos*: 'knowing', 'excelling', or 'not lacking' in it. Or the relationship may be a negative one: 'ineffectual' in it. *Noos* functions frequently as an active agent within the person who none the less can exert some control over it. But even when the person controls *noos*, there seems to be no opposition between the two. Person and *noos* work in harmony. In general *noos* appears to be a valuable psychic entity which the individual wants to function. If it fails to act, or if it 'hides', activity undertaken can prove unsuccessful. A person remains ever distinct from *noos*. This *noos*, 'changing with the day', may prove itself to be a mysterious presence within.

As suggested above, the awareness that individuals in Homeric poems have of a 'self' is not something well-defined. But they clearly recognise psychic entities at work in them. In the case of *noos*, it, more than other psychic entities, acts as a seat of their deepest qualities, showing what they are like.

Lyric and Elegiac Poets

General Picture

Noos as presented in the lyric and elegiac poets is similar in nature in many ways to what it was in Homer, the *Homeric Hymns*, and Hesiod but it functions to an even greater degree as a seat of an individual's deepest qualities. As mentioned in chapter 1, our evidence for these poets is fragmentary, written in restrictive metres, and focusing on specific themes. In the spoken language the range and meaning of *noos* may have been much wider. Even though this is true, we are given within these poems a picture of *noos* that may reflect to some extent the way it was viewed by people in Greece at the time.

The range of meaning of *noos* in these poets can be briefly described as follows.[19] It engages in intellectual, emotional, and volitional activities, especially the first. Its intellectual activity is often associated with 'inner vision' or with a profound grasp of a situation. Speech ideally reflects *noos* and its thoughts but this does not always occur. *Noos* can display different characteristics and some of these may be enduring ones. But *noos* also changes with the 'day' and with the years. It alters as well if outside agents or forces affect it: the gods and wine in particular can influence its nature.

Some of the characteristics *noos* may have within the person are these. It can be 'trustworthy', 'good', 'pure', or, in contrast, 'unjust', 'flighty', and 'harsh'. It can be 'hidden' both from the individual in whom it is found and certainly from others. Behaviour, therefore, may or may not reflect it. On occasion, someone can intentionally conceal *noos* for self-protection. Often *noos* is related to moral activity, especially to justice. The possession of *noos* may be what sets human beings apart from and higher than other living creatures. But we do hear of the *noos* of animals in these poets.[20] Still greater than the human *noos* is that of the gods, which powerfully directs events in human lives.

In these poets we see *noos* functioning as a seat of a someone's deepest qualities. As in Homer and Hesiod, person and *noos* remain distinct. They act in harmony, even when a person controls *noos*. As in Homer and Hesiod too, *noos* seems to be a great treasure, a psychic entity within endowing the person with valuable capabilities.

Specific Passages

There are over 100 instances of *noos* in the lyric and elegiac poets. Three passages illustrate well its nature and range of meaning. At 1163–4 in the elegiac verse ascribed to Theognis we hear:

> eyes, tongue, ears, and *noos* grow
> in the middle of the chest of those who are wise.

The couplet suggests that the wise have special eyes, tongue, and ears, ones located not on the surface but deep within. In the case of *noos* it is described here, as elsewhere, as located in the chest region.[21]

---

[19] On *noos* in the lyric and elegiac poets see von Fritz, *CP*, 1945, Furley, Jarcho, Luck, Marg, Onians, Snell, *Der Weg*, Sullivan (note 3), Treu, and Warden.

[20] These references are: Arch. 185 (fox), and Theog. 580 (bird).

[21] See, e.g., *Il.* 3.63, Hes., *Theog.* 122, Theog. 121, 507, and 898.

The four items mentioned are not static: they take root within and 'grow' there. *Noos* thus, as we have heard before, alters with time, in this case in a positive way.[22]

In those who are 'wise' eyes, tongue, ears, and *noos* work at a deep level. *Noos* functions well with respect to understanding events: it may see within clearly. These lines suggest perhaps as well that the wise keep hidden what they see, say, hear, and think. Once again *noos* has a 'hidden' nature.[23] In it people can conceal their true thoughts and feelings. *Noos* may thus be a problem for others to discern, but a great advantage for its owner. Here, as elsewhere, *noos* is mentioned with the tongue and it may act as the source of what one says.[24]

Our second passage comes from Semonides, living in the late seventh century. He makes a startling claim about *noos* (1.1–8):

> Boy, loud-thundering Zeus holds the outcome
> of all things that are and places it as he wishes.
> But *noos* is not in human beings but, subject to the day,
> they live like grazing animals, knowing in no way
> how the god will bring each thing to completion.
> Hope and confidence nourish us all
> as we ponder the impracticable. Some wait
> for the day to come, others, the turning of the years.

The poem continues, saying that no one fails to believe that 'next year' riches and blessings will be given. But old age, disease, and death in battle may come first. Some die at sea; others choose to die by suicide. No misfortune is lacking and countless evils attend human beings. In the last three lines he gives advice: 'if you trust me,

---

[22] Elsewhere in the lyric and elegiac poets we hear that 'youth and youthful impetuosity' make *noos* 'fickle' (Theog. 629). *Noos* improves during middle age (Sol. 27, Pin., *Pyth.* 5.110) but is harmed by old age (Mim. 5).

[23] Solon says that the '*noos* of the immortals' is ever hidden (17). Theognis speaks of the *noos* of a friend or of citizens being obscure (121, 367). He also praises a 'trustworthy' *noos* which shows consistent behaviour (74, 698). Wine, he suggests, can reveal what *noos* is like (500). Pindar says that an 'upright *noos*' is revealed just as gold is by a touchstone (*Pyth.* 10.68). Such a *noos* may be concealed but, if discovered, is like gold.

[24] Solon says that one is 'best in *noos* and tongue' between the ages of 49 and 63 (27). Theognis elsewhere says that few people are 'stewards of both *noos* and tongue' (1185). At 91 he tells Cyrnus 'who with one tongue holds *noos* in two ways is a terrible companion'. At 365 he advises him 'to curb' his *noos* and let 'gentleness of tongue follow'. Pindar in fr. 213.4 describes his *noos* as being divided in 'speaking the exact truth'.

we would not be in love with our misery nor, holding our *thumos* on evil pains, would we be tormented' (22–4).[25]

Two features of human beings are prominent in these lines. First, they do not have *noos*. Semonides does not mean, of course, that this psychic entity is totally absent in humans but that, in contrast with Zeus, his range of thinking, and his power, what humans have might as well be described as something absent.[26] Zeus and the other gods clearly 'have *noos*'. Elsewhere the lyric and elegiac poets say of the divine *noos* that 'it is hidden from human beings' (Sol. 17), that 'it prevails' (Theog. 202), that 'it knows all things' (Pin., *Pyth.* 3.29), and that it is 'difficult to turn aside' (Bacch. 5.95).

Semonides in his poem describes the divine *noos* as 'holding the outcome of all things'. The term for 'outcome', *telos*, marks the completion of a series of events or of a life. Zeus can see this outcome and impose it. Human beings neither know nor can control the *telos* that awaits their actions. Instead of clearly apprehending events and their significance, humans have only 'hope and confidence', which may cause them to 'consider' actions that prove 'impracticable'. Consequently their attitude becomes one of waiting and hoping, either for the 'day' or the 'years', and the changes these may bring.

A similar view of gods and human beings is found in Theognis 133–42. Humans act without knowing the *telos* of their activities and often the unexpected happens; they are held in the 'limits of helplessness'. 'As human beings we think vain things, knowing nothing. The gods complete all things according to their *noos*' (141–2). The poem of Semonides suggests that it is weakness in *noos* in particular that accounts for this state of human beings.[27]

The second feature of humans in Semonides' poem is that they

---

[25] For a discussion of this poem see A. Carson, 'How Bad a Poem is Semonides Fragment 1?' in Gerber, pp. 61–8, Fränkel, *Dichtung*, pp. 230–1, D.E. Gerber, 'Semonides Fr. 1 West: A Commentary' in Gerber, pp. 125–8, R. Renehan, 'The Early Greek Poets: Some Interpretations', *HSCP*, 1983, vol. 87, pp. 3–11.

[26] This *noos* may resemble that described elsewhere in the lyric and elegiac poets as 'empty' (*koufos*). Solon describes the Athenians as having an 'empty *noos*' when they fail to perceive the ambitious intentions of their leaders (11). Theognis describes someone evil as having the 'empty *noos*' of a small bird (580). He suggests too that wine can put *noos* in this condition (498).

[27] Pindar at *Nem.* 3.42 likewise speaks of a *noos* that is 'ineffectual' (*atelēs*). Solon says that, as one grows older and *noos* is stronger, a person no longer attempts the impossible (27). Other psychic entities likewise are associated with this human condition of not perceiving consequences: *phrēnes* at Theog. 135 and *thumos* in Sim. 8 (on which poem see under *thumos*).

are 'subject to the day'.[28] Just as we heard above in Homer, the day that comes upon people strongly influences them.[29] They live 'like animals, knowing nothing of how the gods will bring each thing to completion'. Here we can see a connection of *noos* with inner vision, in particular of future events and their consequences, and its absence in humans. For Semonides, to be mortal means not to have this capacity but instead to have only 'hope and confidence'.[30] He therefore ends his poem with the advice of not focusing upon misery or pain.

In our third passage from the early poets Pindar gives a different view of *noos*. In the opening lines of *Nem.* 6 he says that the races of human beings and the gods are akin and yet distinct in that the former are 'nothing' but the latter dwell ever in heaven. He then says: 'but none the less in some way we are similar either in great *noos* or nature (*physis*) to the immortals, although we do not know by day or by night to what sort of finishing line fate has written us to run'. Both Semonides and Theognis had contrasted the human with the divine condition in regard to knowledge and found the first sadly lacking. Semonides did so to such an extent that he said *noos* was not even present in human beings. Pindar likewise recognizes the limitations of human knowledge, in particular its inability to see the future. But he nevertheless suggests that there is a continuum between the divine and the human. What links the two is either *noos* or *physis*. Even though limited in its knowledge, *noos* elevates human beings and makes them god-like.

These three passages from Theognis, Semonides, and Pindar have demonstrated certain primary features of *noos*: its importance as a psychic entity, its hidden nature, its vulnerability to change, its limitations. Once again we see its essential role in the human being as seat of thought.

Presocratics

Just as with the lyric and elegiac poets, we encounter fragmentary evidence and specific themes with the Presocratic philosophers. In

---

[28] On this interpretation of the passage see above Fränkel (note 17), Gerber (note 25), pp. 127–8, and Sullivan (note 3), *Emerita*, 1989, p. 135.

[29] A possible restoration of Stes., P. Lille 76 abc 207 reads: 'the gods put in another *noos* for each day'. Once again *noos* appears to change with the day, in this case directly under divine influence.

[30] On the connection of hope with the human condition see too on Sim. 8 (un-

these philosophers we encounter views presented either in poetry or in prose. What we discover in examining *noos* and other psychic entities is that certain features of them emerge prominently. With *noos* its connection with inner vision appears to be of great importance.[31] The Presocratics mention its function in the human being or in the divinity, whose nature they variously describe. The various psychic entities occupy differing positions of importance in relation to the interpretations of the universe that the philosophers present. *Noos* functions prominently in Parmenides and Anaxagoras, the first emphasizing its role in humans, the second, in the ruling principle of the universe. Other philosophers, for whom *noos* may be less crucial, none the less reveal interesting aspects of it. Let us look at this second group first. It includes Xenophanes, Heraclitus, and Empedocles.

Xenophanes of Colophon, living in the sixth and early fifth centuries, criticised traditional views of the gods and introduced some of his own.[32] In his poems he does not approve of anthropomorphism. He attacks Homer and Hesiod for saying that gods are born, that they resemble humans in shape and speech, and that they perform immoral actions (B 11, 14). His own view is that divinity is 'one', unlike mortals in either thought (*noēma*) or form (B 23). This divinity, though different from mortals, nevertheless functions in some ways as they do but in a markedly different and superior manner. Like them, this god 'sees', 'hears', and 'thinks' (*noeō*), not with specific organs of sense perception, but as a 'whole' (B 24). In other words this god is all sight, all hearing, and all thought. We see therefore that some degree of anthropomorphism is still present in Xenophanes' own philosophy as he focuses on these three functions found also in humans.

What this divine thought is concerned with another fragment suggests (B 25): the divinity 'without labour makes all things tremble by

---

der *thumos*). Theognis likewise at 461 urges Cyrnus not to set his *noos* on 'deeds that cannot be accomplished'.

[31] On this aspect of *noos* in the Presocratics see in particular von Fritz, *CP*, 1945.

[32] On Xenophanes see the Appendix and in particular Barnes, vol. 1, pp. 82–99 and 136–51, Dumont, pp. 91–126, A. Finkelberg, 'Studies in Xenophanes', *HSCP*, 1990, vol. 93, pp. 103–67, W.K.C. Guthrie, vol. 1, pp. 360–402, E. von Heitsch, *Die Fragmente Xenophanes*, Zürich, 1983, Hussey, pp. 11–31, Jaeger, *Theology*, pp. 38–54, Kirk, Raven, and Schofield, pp. 163–80, Lesher, *Xenophanes*, McKirahan, pp. 59–68, Mansfeld, pp. 204–29, Robinson, pp. 50–6, Wright, *Presocratics*, pp. 47–52, S. Yonezawa, 'Xenophanes: His Self-Consciousness as a Wise Man and Fr. 34' in Boudouris, pp. 432–40. The recent book of Lesher is particularly valuable for its discussion of the fragments.

the *phrēn* of *noos*. The picture recalls that of Zeus in the *Iliad* (1.528–30) who 'makes Olympus tremble' by his nod. But Xenophanes' god does much more. The expression 'all things' in the Presocratics is used to designate the 'universe'. It is this that the god moves by thinking, in an action that requires no effort.

In describing this 'thinking', Xenophanes mentions two psychic entities, *noos* and *phrēn*. Like other early poets he speaks of this activity in his divinity in terms in which it is also present in human beings. As we shall see below, *phrēn* frequently functions as an instrument. So here it is by *phrēn* that the god makes all things tremble. This *phrēn* in the god relates in a special way to *noos*: it belongs to it.[33] The fragment does not make clear the precise activity of *noos* but it is possible to suppose that this *noos*, like that ascribed to the gods in other early poets (and described above), is a powerful one. Like theirs, it may 'prevail', be 'stronger', be 'unavoidable'; it may perceive the end of actions. It may know all things.[34] Its function may be related to inner vision. What it sees it likely effects. The result, in Xenophanes' view, is movement in the universe. As B 24 said, the whole of this god 'sees', 'hears', and 'thinks'. Divinity's nature is summed up in these functions.

'Thinking' takes place by the *phrēn* of the *noos*: with this thinking the god makes the universe move. In thought (*noēma*) this divinity markedly differs from human beings who in no way have such powers of mind. Yet mortals and divinity share in a common capacity for thought. Xenophanes uses the terms *noos* and *phrēn* to describe the superior thinking of his divinity, terms which likewise designate its presence in humans. *Noos* and *phrēn* function very differently in the divinity. They appear to be closely related to the essential nature of this divine being.

Heraclitus of Ephesus, living at the beginning of the fifth century, was called even in ancient times the 'obscure' because of the riddling statements he made in prose.[35] He mentions *noos* in three fragments.

---

[33] I take 'of *noos*' as indicating that *phrēn* belongs to *noos*. For discussion of this fragment see Barnes, vol. 1, p. 93, S.M. Darcus, 'The *Phrēn* of *Noos* in Xenophanes' God', *SO*, 1978, vol. 53, pp. 25–39, von Fritz, *CP*, 1945, p. 230, W.K.C. Guthrie, vol. 1, p. 374, Hussey, p. 13, Kirk, Raven, and Schofield, pp. 169–71, McKirahan, pp. 63–4, J.M. Robinson, p. 54, Wright, *Presocratics*, p. 49.

[34] Xenophanes says in another fragment, B 18, that divinity could have 'shown all things to mortals' but did not. This suggests it had full knowledge of them.

[35] On Heraclitus see the Appendix and Barnes, vol. 1, pp. 57–81, 127–35, Conche,

In B 104 he impatiently asks where 'the *noos* or *phrēn*' of most people can be when they trust what bards and the mob say. *Noos* and *phrēn* could be seats for the understanding of philosophical considerations such as Heraclitus presents but are not thus utilized by most people. In two other fragments Heraclitus makes it clear that *noos* is related to a grasp of essential truth as he perceives it. In B 40 he says that 'much learning (*polymathiē*) does not teach *noos*. Otherwise it would have taught Hesiod, Pythagoras, or again, Xenophanes or Hecataeus'.[36] Gathering of facts does not give an understanding of their significance. For this a person must 'see' within. It may be this type of function that Heraclitus believes *noos* to have.

In the third fragment, B 114, Heraclitus relates *noos* to his view of the divine principle in the universe.[37] He terms this divinity *logos*. The exact nature of this *logos* is difficult to discern as is so much of Heraclitus' philosophy.[38] It seems that he uses the term to indicate a thought-process having a structured form. On the cosmic level this exists as the divine principle but is present as well in human beings

---

Héraclite, Dumont, pp. 127–87, D. Gallop, 'The Riddles of Heraclitus' in Boudouris, pp. 123–35, W.K.C. Guthrie, vol. 1, 403–92, Hussey, pp. 32–59, Kahn, *Art and Thought*, Kirk, Raven, and Schofield, pp. 181–212, McKirahan, pp. 116–50, Mansfeld, pp. 231–83, Marcovich, D. O'Brien, 'Heraclitus on the Unity of Opposites' in Boudouris, pp. 298–303, Prier, Ramnoux, J.M. Robinson, pp. 87–105, T.M. Robinson, *Heraclitus*, 'Methodology in the Reading of Heraclitus' in Boudouris, pp. 344–52, L. Rossetti, 'About the Disunity of Heraclitus' Thought' in Boudouris , pp. 353–62, D. Sider, 'War, Order and Sense in Heraclitus: Fragment One and the River Fragment' in Boudouris, pp. 363–8, Sullivan in Gerber, pp. 285–301, Wheelwright, Wright, *Presocratics*, pp. 53–75. See also E.N. Roussos, *Heraklit-Bibliographie*, Darmstadt, 1971 and F. de Martino, P. Rosati, L. Rossetti, *Eraclito: Bibliografia 1970–1984, e complementi 1621–1969*, Naples, 1986. The works of Kahn and Robinson are particularly helpful in their treatment of the fragments.

[36] Cf. Democritus B 64: 'many who know much (*polumathees*) do not have *noos*'.

[37] On this fragment see Barnes, vol. 1, pp. 128–32, Conche, *Héraclite*, pp. 217–19, W.K.C. Guthrie, vol. 1, pp. 425–6, Hussey, pp. 39–40, Kahn, *Art and Thought*, pp. 117–18, Kirk, Raven and Schofield, pp. 186–7, 210–12, Marcovich, pp. 91–7, A.P.D. Mourelatos, 'Heraclitus, Fr. 114', *AJP*, 1965, vol. 86, pp. 258–66, T.M. Robinson, pp. 155–6, Wright, *Presocratics*, p. 59.

[38] Much attention has been given to analyzing the nature of this *logos*. For bibliography see Roussos (note 35), pp. 56–64 and de Martino (note 35), p. 172. See also Barnes, vol. 1, pp. 57–60, W.K.C. Guthrie, vol. 1, 419–30, Hussey, pp. 39–41, Kahn, *Art and Thought*, pp. 9–23, Kirk, Raven, and Schofield, pp. 186–8, McKirahan, pp. 133–4, M. Marcovich, 'Heraclitus: Some Characteristics', *ICS*, 1982, vol. 7, pp. 171–88, 'Problems heracliteos', *Emerita*, 1973, vol. 41, pp. 449–73, T.M. Robinson, pp. 181–91, W.J. Verdenius, 'Der Logosbegriff bei Heraklit und Parmenides', *Phronesis*, 1966, vol. 11, pp. 81–98, B. Wisniewski, '*Logos* et *nous* chez Démocrite et Héraclite', *Eos*, 1987, vol. 75, pp. 5–11. Of these the views of Verdenius are particularly perceptive.

as thought reflected in speech. Heraclitus thus imbues the term *logos*, which his listeners would readily assume meant 'speech', with a more profound and universal significance. As the divine principle guiding 'all things' (the universe) and acting as their source, this 'thought process' exists apart from 'all things'. But within 'all things', it is found as a capacity in human beings.

We shall discuss further features of this *logos* in chapters 3 and 5, but one in particular is important here: it is 'common'. In B 2 Heraclitus says: 'it is necessary to follow the common; even though the *logos* is common, the many live as though they possessed an individual method of thinking (*phronesis*)'. Heraclitus thinks that in *logos*, its form and function, the nature of the divine can be grasped. This *logos* is not speech alone, but speech that reflects thinking (*phronesis*). People should concentrate on analyzing how their *logos* works and come to realise that it is not an individual capacity but one shared alike by all people and having therefore profound importance.

In B 114, which mentions *noos*, the first words are: 'speaking with *noos* (*sun nooi*) people must base their strength on what is common (*sunoi*) to all'. Heraclitus plays on the words 'with *noos*' and the 'common', sounding alike as they do in Greek. Speech with *noos* implies strength based on the 'common of all', that is, the *logos*. We see a special role given to *noos*: it appears as the perception or discernment that grasps what *logos* is and leads to a specific form of speech, one that will best reflect the essence of *logos*. Instead of individuals simply uttering disparate words, 'speaking with *noos*' will emphasize what is 'common to all things', the divine principle manifesting itself in them.

Empedocles, like Xenophanes and Heraclitus, briefly mentions *noos*. This philosopher from Sicily, likewise living at the beginning of the fifth century, was especially interested in the changing nature of the universe and the destiny of the soul.[39] In his poems, the *Physics* and the *Purifications*, he makes three references to *noos*, two negative and one positive. In all three *noos* appears very much as an instrument that people can use well or badly. At B 2.8 of the *Physics* he criticizes

---

[39] On Empedocles see the Appendix and Barnes, vol. 2, pp. 3–15, van der Ben, Bollack, Dumont, pp. 319–439, W.K.C. Guthrie, vol. 2, pp. 122–265, Hussey, pp. 69–73, 130–33, Inwood, Kirk, Raven, and Schofield, pp. 280–321, Lambridis, A.A. Long, *CQ*, 1966, H.S. Long, McKirahan, pp. 232–91, Mansfeld, pp. 382–481, D. O'Brien, *Cosmic Cycle*, Prier, J.M. Robinson, pp. 151–73, Wright, *Empedocles*, *Presocratics*, pp. 107–21. The recent studies of Inwood and Wright are particularly useful in their discussion of the fragments.

those who claim to know 'the whole' even though they have perceived 'only a small part of life'. The 'whole' is not to be seen or
heard by human beings nor to be 'grasped with *noos*'. We may have
here an echo of Xenophanes' description of divinity as seeing, hearing, and perceiving as a whole. It can but humans cannot: to understand the 'whole' something more than human *noos* is needed. Some
divine inspiration, such as Empedocles himself received from the Muse,
seems necessary (B 3). In B 136 of the *Purifications*, speaking in the
context of the transmigration of souls, Empedocles urges a cessation
of slaughter of animals. According to his view, the life principle in
animals is a manifestation of a soul on its journey. In this fragment
he says that by 'carelessness of *noos*' people fail to realise that, in
killing living animals, they kill and devour one another. Once again
noos fails to grasp an essential truth.

At B 17.21 of the *Physics* Empedocles presents a positive picture of
noos. He urges the recipient of his poem to 'gaze on Love with *noos*
and not to sit with eyes dazed'.[40] He connects *noos* with inner vision.
It can grasp the significance of Love, one of the divine principles
that Empedocles suggests governs the universe.[41]

Thus far, then, the brief references to *noos* in the Presocratics. As
mentioned above, in two Presocratics *noos* occupies a central role.
First, in Parmenides.[42] This philosopher, living in Elea in South Italy
at the beginning of the fifth century, wrote a poem in hexameter
verse that was to affect profoundly all subsequent philosophical
thought. The term *noos* itself occurs in only three fragments. Two
are from the portion of his poem in which he presents a true picture
of the universe (the 'Way of Truth'), and one is from the portion
which shows the errors that can result from the acceptance of false
premises (the 'Way of Opinion'). Even though we have only three
instances of *noos* itself, elsewhere its function, *noein*, and its expression,

---

[40] Parmenides likewise speaks of 'things absent' to the eyes but 'grasped by *noos*'
(B 4). See below for discussion of this fragment.

[41] Empedocles' view will be discussed more fully in our treatment of *phrēn* below.

[42] On Parmenides see the Appendix and Aubenque, S. Austin, Barnes, vol. 2, pp.
155–99, 296–8, Boehme, Bormann, Cordero, Coxon, Dumont, pp. 233–72, Gallop,
W.K.C. Guthrie, vol. 2, pp. 1–88, Hölscher, Hussey, pp. 78–99, Kirk, Raven, and
Schofield, pp. 239–62, McKirahan, pp. 151–78, Mansfeld, pp. 284–333, Mourelatos,
Route, Owen, Prier, J.M. Robinson, pp. 107–26, Reinhardt, Tarán, Untersteiner,
Verdenius, *Parmenides*, Wright, *Presocratics*, pp. 77–89, W.F. Wyatt, 'The Root of
Parmenides', *HSCP*, 1992, vol. 94, pp. 113–20. The works of Coxon, Gallop, and
Owen are particularly helpful for Parmenides.

noēma, figure prominently.[43] In the 'Way of Truth' Parmenides assigns *noos* a positive role in the search for truth, even though this *noos* can be in error. In B 6 he states:

> but then [I hold you back from this
> road of inquiry] which mortals, knowing nothing
> wander upon, two-headed. For helplessness
> directs the wandering *noos* in their chests.

Instead of understanding that the senses deceive, especially in suggesting that multiplicity exists, mortals accept sense evidence. Parmenides argues, in contrast, that 'all things' can be only one, Being. *Noos* is victim to 'helplessness' if it trusts the senses. It must function independently from them. This fragment suggests that it is *noos* with its capacity for inner vision, for seeing beyond appearances, which makes understanding reality possible. But it cannot be a 'wandering *noos*'.

In another fragment from the 'Way of Truth', B 4, Parmenides explicitly associates *noos* with inner vision. He says:

> but look at things absent, although firmly present to *noos*.
> For being cannot be cut off from clinging to being,
> neither scattered in every way entirely in the cosmos
> nor drawn together.

Things may well be absent to the eyes but *noos* perceives them as 'firmly present'.[44] And what *noos* perceives is that 'all things' are in reality one Being, which in no way can be separated into distinct parts as a many or, as a many, be drawn back together again. Reality is necessarily one.

Although *noos* has this capacity to grasp the true essence of the universe, it often does not. Our third fragment from the 'Way of Opinion' may explain why *noos* can fail to perceive this truth (B 16):

> As is ever the mixture of the straying limbs,
> so *noos* is for human beings; for that which thinks,
> namely the nature of the limbs, is the same thing in each
> and all human beings. What preponderates is thought (*noēma*).

In the lyric and elegiac poets we heard of *noos* changing with the

---

[43] See B 2, 3, 6, 8 (*noein*) and 7, 8, and 16 (*noēma*).

[44] Cf. B 17.21 of Empedocles (discussed above) where *noos* also grasps a truth not seen by the eyes.

'day'. In this fragment from the portion of his poem where the errors of mortals are described, Parmenides says that *noos* varies according to the components of the limbs of the body.[45] What are these components? In this part of his poem he argues that the acceptance of the existence of two principles, light and night, rather than one only, Being, leads to error. If the limbs of the body are assumed to be made up of light and dark, *noos* will reflect their mixture. The acceptance of this mixture will be the source of error for mortals, elsewhere described as 'two-headed' (B 6). *Noos*, if assumed to be as described in B 16, will fail to grasp the true nature of reality.

The second philosopher in whose thought *nous* is central is Anaxagoras.[46] Living in the late fifth century, he falls outside the Archaic Age but we shall look at what he says of *nous* (now spelled in its contracted form). His view of the universe is in stark contrast with that of Parmenides, whose arguments about the nature of Being he was compelled to consider. But unlike Parmenides, Anaxagoras was convinced that sense evidence was trustworthy to some extent in the picture of multiplicity it presented. Consequently, he argued for what can be called 'extreme multiplicity': all natural substances, existing in the form of seeds, were real and indestructible.[47] Never did these substances exist separately but in each seed a 'portion' of each substance was present and no seed could be broken down into its component parts. This structure of the seeds ensured that the 'many' in the universe were real in the way Parmenides argued that Being was. Only Anaxagoras' assumption of difference among the substances posed a problem. Difference suggests that one substance is not another and therefore must not 'be' in some degree because it lacks the quality of the other. Its own being must therefore be limited.

---

[45] For this interpretation of B 16 see Guthrie, vol. 2, pp. 67–9 and Kirk, Raven, and Schofield, p. 262.

[46] On the philosophy of Anaxagoras see the Appendix and Barnes, vol. 2, pp. 16–39, Cleve, Dumont, pp. 617–81, von Fritz, *ABG*, 1964, M. Furth, 'A Philosophical Hero? Anaxagoras and the Eleatics' in *Modern Thinkers and Ancient thinkers*, London, 1993, W.K.C. Guthrie, vol. 2, pp. 266–338, C.H. Kahn, 'The Historical Position of Anaxagoras' in Boudouris, pp. 203–10, Kirk, Raven, and Schofield, pp. 352–84, McKirahan, pp. 196–231, Mansfeld, pp. 482–555, R. Potts, 'Anaxagoras' Cosmogony', *Apeiron*, 1984, vol. 18, pp. 90–6, J.M. Robinson, pp. 175–94, Schofield, Sider, Teodorsson, Wright, *Presocratics*, pp. 123–36. The works of Schofield and Sider are especially useful for Anaxagoras.

[47] On this interpretation of 'all things' and what these include see W.K.C. Guthrie, vol. 2, pp. 285–6, Kirk, Raven, and Schofield, pp. 366–70, and Schofield, pp. 107–21.

But for Anaxagoras the Many, existing as complicated seeds, were all real and acted as the components of the universe. He argued too that a power had organized them into a recognizable order; this power he identified as *nous*. He described this *nous* in four fragments (B 11–14), giving details as follows. '*Nous* is without limit, self-ruled and mixed with no thing, but alone and by itself' (B 12). Thus, in sharp contrast with the seeds composing 'all things' (the universe), which are always in a state of mixture, *nous* is purely and only itself. Further, 'it is the finest and purest of all things, and has all judgement (*gnōmē*) concerning everything and is most powerful' (B 12). Anaxagoras speaks here of the essence of this *nous*, not yet suggesting that it is an immaterial principle but of everything in the universe it is the 'most fine'. Its function is intellectual since it 'judges' everything and its power is unlimited.

But what is this power? What 'judgement' about 'all things' does *nous* have? *Nous* surrounds and permeates them (B 12, 14), even though it never mixes with the substances in the seeds. It knows these seeds (12). Originally it made them revolve in a motion that led to the arrangement they now display (B 12). It set them in order in the past, does so now, and will continue to do so henceforth (B 12). *Nous* thus controls all things in the universe.

We hear further that 'in some things' a portion of *nous*, apart by itself, is found (B 11). We are not sure what these 'some things' are, but it seems clear that human beings have a portion of *nous*: in having it they share in the ruling principle. In what Anaxagoras says of *nous* we have a vivid example of the microcosm/macrocosm principle so often present in the Presocratics. The cosmos as a whole (the macrocosm) is thought to be patterned after the microcosm, usually human beings or, more specifically, one of the capacities they have. The 'large' is assumed to act like the 'small'. Thus Anaxagoras, we may suppose, saw *nous* as a ruling force in himself. He then projected it as the ruling power in the universe as a whole. But in the resultant picture an essential truth emerges. The microcosm in fact reflects the macrocosm, not vice versa. So in Anaxagoras, the microcosm comprises human beings with their *nous*. With it they organize, control, and understand their world. When faced with complicated situations or objects, they can with *nous* make sense of them, solve or arrange them. The macrocosm is the motive force, *nous*. It functions like the human *nous* but on a cosmic level. In the overall picture, the action of the cosmic *nous* is primary. On the small scale, human beings are privileged to share in its nature. This sharing allows them to understand the cosmic *nous* and the universe itself.

Nous thus has a very prominent role in the thought of Anaxagoras. Although it is not called 'divine' in his extant fragments, it functions as a ruling principle, having 'all judgement about everything'. As such it occupies a position of chief importance in the universe.

Overview of Noos

We have looked at *noos* from the time of Homer to the Presocratics. We have seen that it functions as a psychic entity within the individual that carries on various psychological activities. It can be found in gods, human beings, and animals. It appears to be distinct from the person who relates to it in some way. It appears generally not to display physical characteristics; Anaxagoras, however, describes it as 'finest and purest' of all things. It may be located in the chest region but never acts as a location of other psychic entities.

In terms of function, it is associated especially with inner vision or insight. It can grasp reality that the senses fail to perceive. But it is much more than simply a source of inner sight. It can act very much as a seat of the deepest qualities of the individual. It includes a way of thinking or planning that expresses someone's truest wishes and thoughts. To know a person's *noos* is to know what that person actually thinks or feels. But this *noos* can often be hidden both from the individual having it and from others. It also changes with the 'day' or under the influence of outside forces. Age gradually improves and then weakens it.

Among the psychic entities *noos* is perhaps the most valuable. In Zeus and the gods it knows and effects all. In Anaxagoras' view it is the ruling power in the cosmos. In human beings it is often the psychic entity that can discover truth. It may not always function well or be used in an effective way but potentially it puts human beings in a special place in the universe, however far beneath divinity that may be. This psychic entity may be the feature that makes human beings what they are with their special place among 'all things'. It enables them to cope with reality and to grasp its essential nature. If lost or absent, people are foolish; if present and functioning well, people are wise and to be trusted. It is no wonder that *noos* is to be highly valued within and to be sought in others.

Phrēn

Homeric and Hesiodic Background

Our second psychic entity, *phrēn*, differs in many ways from *noos*.[48] In Homer and the *Homeric Hymns* it appears more often than *noos*, occurring over 300 times; in Hesiod it is found twenty-one times. Unlike *noos*, *phrēn* is usually mentioned in the plural. This feature seems closely linked to the physical identity of *phrenes*. By the time of Homer, even though this precise identity seems to have become somewhat obscure, the plural nature of *phrenes* remains prominent. But *phrēn* can appear also in the singular: this use shows that it could be thought of as a single entity. As its physical association became less prominent, this use perhaps became more common. Once again we recall we are dealing with poetry written in a restrictive metre. How *phrēn* appeared in the spoken language may have been quite different.

Unlike *noos*, then, *phrenes* display some physical characteristics. What the physical nature of *phrenes* was has been much discussed.[49] *Phrenes* in certain passages of Homer have been interpreted as the diaphragm, the lungs, the *pericardium*, or as a composite of psychic entities located generally in the chest region. The last suggestion seems most attractive. By the time of Homer the formulas mentioning *phrenes* had been long repeated. The precise physical nature of *phrenes* may not have been known but their association with the chest region continued as well as their generally plural nature.

One role that *phrenes* have in Homer is to act often as the location of other psychic entities. In this feature too they are unlike *noos* which does not function in this way. In *phrenes*, *thumos* is frequently placed, as are *ētor*, *kēr*, and *noos*.[50] Serving as location likewise points to an original physical nature of *phrenes*. It may suggest too a less active role for *phrenes* than is true of the other psychic entities.

---

[48] On *phrēn* in Homer and Hesiod see Biraud, Böhme, Bremmer, Cheyns, *CILL*, 1980, Claus, Furley, Gelzer (note 2), Harrison, S. Ireland and F.L. Steel, '*Phrenes* as an Anatomical Organ in the Works of Homer', *Glotta*, 1975, vol. 53, pp. 183–94, Jahn, Krafft, Larock, Onians, Plamböck, Russo and Simon, Snell, *Discovery*, *Der Weg*, B. Snell, 'Phrenes-Phronēsis', *Glotta*, 1977, vol. 55, pp. 34–64 (= *Der Weg*, pp. 53–90), Sullivan (note 3), Vivante.

[49] For a full discussion see Cheyns, *CILL*, 1980, Jahn, pp. 9–11, 17–18, and Sullivan, *Psychological Activity*, pp. 21–36, with full bibliography of earlier studies.

[50] See Sullivan, *Psychological Activity*, pp. 268–72 for a list of specific passages in Homer and Sullivan (note 3), *Rbph* 1989, p. 17 for Hesiod.

Even though traces of their physical nature are apparent in some passages of Homer, in most cases *phrenes* act, like *noos*, as a psychic entity capable of a range of psychological activities. This range is very broad but perhaps among their functions those that are intellectual appear to predominate. And here again we see a great difference from *noos*. *Phrenes* are not associated with inner vision or a grasp of reality lying outside the range of perception. Instead, they are often connected with pondering, deliberation, and reflection.[51] With them Odysseus can 'devise a greater deed' (*Od.* 11.474)', Telemachus can 'plan a journey' (*Od.* 1.444), and Agamemnon can 'ponder many things' (*Il.* 10.4). In them, when choices become necessary, a person can deliberate about possibilities as Phemius does on one occasion (*Od.* 22.333), and Odysseus frequently does (e.g., *Od.* 4.117, 10.151, 24.235).[52] Often people 'place' things in *phrenes* for consideration (e.g., *Il.* 1.297, 16.444, *Od.* 19.236). Thus Perses is to 'consider' Hesiod's teaching there (*W. & D.* 107, 274). In *phrenes* too individuals 'know' things, 'hide', 'imagine', or 'recognize' them (e.g., *Il.* 12.228, 9.313, *Od.* 1.115, 22.501).

In passages describing the wide intellectual range of *phrenes* one important feature emerges. They function most often within the person as a location of, a means for, or an accompaniment to activity. Thus, they are frequently a place where someone acts, a tool or instrument that a person uses, or they accompany a person in some action, adding their own activity. Therefore we hear that it is in *phrenes* that Zeus 'devises' a sorrowful return for the Greeks and that Achilles devises 'evil deeds' (*Od.* 3.132, *Il.* 21.19). It was by means of *phrenes* that Thersites 'knew' many disorderly words (*Il.* 2.213). With *phrenes* adding their activity, Apollo 'knows' all things well (*H. Mer.* 467).

Noos, we saw, acted frequently as an active agent within the person. Its activity is valuable and much desired. It does not always function well and can unfortunately be hidden, but in general a person wants it to act and co-operates with it. *Phrenes* are different. They are

---

[51] For a list of instances see Sullivan, *Psychological Activity*, pp. 220–35 for Homer and Sullivan (note 3), *Rbph*, 1989, pp. 15–16 for Hesiod.

[52] The question whether Homeric heroes make decisions or not has been much discussed. See discussion in the studies listed above in note 2. However greatly Homeric individuals are influenced by external factors or by inner psychic entities affected by such factors, they still appear to be involved in the process of choice and the resulting action. Like the concept of self, the ability to make choices may not have been something examined or analyzed but simply an ability taken for granted.

subordinate to the person. In intellectual activities they are an important tool to be utilised in different situations. They do not possess a capacity for 'inner vision', that is, for instantly perceiving the correct and accurate solution to problems. But they are concerned with a different range of thought, itself valuable and necessary. When a solution is not obvious or a decision impends, it is with *phrenes* that someone can consider possibilities of action. At the beginning of situations, a person relies on *phrenes* and their activity in order to act or, likewise, in response to situations, in order to cope.[53]

One association that *phrenes* have in particular is with speech. They serve as a source of speech or a place where words are to be considered. They may lead someone to say 'things appropriate' (*Il.* 1.107), or the opposite (*Il.* 17.173). They are the location where sailors are to guard a message (*Od.* 15.445). *Phrenes* are very much involved with how people relate to one another. Thus in the long quarrel between Agamemnon and Achilles, it is *phrenes* that the former blames most often as the source of his errors.

The range of function of *phrenes* is not, however, limited to the intellectual. They are much involved in emotion, again especially as a location, tool, or accompaniment to action. With them a person experiences joy, pain, anger, or fear. It is with 'baneful *phrenes*' that Agamemnon becomes angry with Achilles (*Il.* 1.342), and with 'raging *phrenes*' that Achilles keeps Hector from burial (*Il.* 24.114). In them too someone can hope, desire, or forget.

Like other psychic entities *phrenes* are vulnerable. They are directly affected on some occasions by the person in whom they are found and often by many different outside forces, especially the gods. Negative emotions such as pain, sorrow, and cares can come upon someone in *phrenes*. Love can affect someone there as it does Zeus (*Il.* 14.294). Wine too and trouble affect a person in *phrenes*, as they do Polyphemus (*Od.* 9.362) and Hector (*Il.* 6.355). Agamemnon blames delusion (*atē*) in his *phrenes* as the cause of his taking Briseis (*Il.* 19.88).

Like *noos*, *phrenes* do not engage only in emotional, intellectual, and volitional activities. They are associated as well with moral behaviour. If they are 'good' or 'noble', admirable behaviour results. Thus Penelope 'knows noble *phrenes*' (*Od.* 2.117), and Clytemnestra once 'used good *phrenes*' (*Od.* 3.266). *Phrenes* can sum up the nature of thought

---

[53] For this aspect of *phrenes* see especially Cheyns, *CILL*, 1980.

in a list of qualities: the daughter of Chryses 'is not inferior in form, stature, *phrenes*, or works' (*Il.* 1.115). Negative traits also are found in *phrenes*. Clytemnestra devises the death of Agamemnon in them (*Od.* 11.438), and the suitors fail to show 'regard or pity' with them (*Od.* 14.82). What *phrenes* are inwardly can also differ from exterior behaviour. The *phrenes* of Paris are in contrast to his beauty (*Il.* 3.45). Penelope speaks in one way to the suitors, but devises the trick of the web in her *phrenes* (*Od.* 2.93). *Phrenes* thus can function as a seat of someone's true feelings and be involved in deceptive behaviour.

Gods and human beings use *phrenes* in similar ways. As chief god, Zeus is 'superior in *phrenes*' (*Il.* 13.631), and, like humans, he carries on in them several intellectual activities and likewise experiences there various emotions. In the case of *noos*, its nature in divinities was thought to set them far above human beings; its presence in human beings could bring them somewhat close to the divine. *Phrenes* do not appear to have this importance. Nor are they restricted to gods and humans. We find them present in animals: fawns, wolves, deer, a lion, or beasts dwelling in the forest.[54]

Within human beings *phrenes* with their activity contribute to their being alive and abide as long as they live. If *phrenes* function well, they provide a valuable tool for their owner. In some passages, they are vividly described as 'destroyed', 'missing', or 'absent', but it is not a physical removal from the body that is indicated, only the loss of admirable function. Thus Agamemnon says that Zeus 'removed' his *phrenes* when he decided to take Briseis (*Il.* 19.137). When Polydamas speaks foolishly, the gods are assumed to have 'destroyed' his *phrenes* (*Il.* 12.234). When Achilles keeps refusing to fight, he is described as 'having no *phrenes*' at all (*Il.* 14.141). The dead do not have *phrenes* but Teiresias is the exception: in the underworld his *phrenes* are 'firm' (*Od.* 10.493).

Within gods and human beings, *phrenes* display a number of characteristics. Some of these suggest permanent qualities of them. Zeus' *phrenes* are 'wise' (*Il.* 14.294), Achilles', 'great' (*Il.* 9.184), and Penelope's, 'well-balanced' (*Od.* 18.249). But in other instances they may change. So Agamemnon's *phrenes* become 'black' as the emotion of rage darkens them (*Il.* 1.103). Noble individuals have *phrenes* that can be 'healed' (*Il.* 13.115). Young people have *phrenes* 'floating in the air' and make

---

[54] See *Il.* 4.245, 16.157, *H. Cer.* 175, *Il.* 17.111, and Hes., *W. & D.* 531 respectively.

Menelaus long for the presence of the aged Priam, whose *phrenes* won him fame (*Il.* 3.108, 24.201). Time then may improve *phrenes*.

What is the overall relationship of person and *phrenes*? In general *phrenes* appear to be subordinate to the person. This is true when they function as the location where someone acts or the instrument which someone uses. When *phrenes* act as an accompaniment to a person, they appear to be co-operative. In general, they emerge as a positive psychic entity within the individual. Even though they can adversely affect behaviour when in a negative state, they very often prove to be a useful presence within. Rarely do *phrenes* appear as an independent agent acting in the person. Nor does a person often exercise control over them. These last two features likewise suggest that *phrenes* were generally subordinate and acted in harmony with the person. *Phrenes* and person remain distinct, with the person finding in them a valuable psychic entity for coping with life's circumstances.

Lyric and Elegiac Poets

General Picture

In the lyric and elegiac poets some features of *phrenes* found in Homer, the *Homeric Hymns*, and Hesiod persist but some differences emerge.[55] As stated before, we must always keep in mind the fragmentary nature of this poetry, its rich metrical variation, and the different themes it treats. But even with these limiting factors, we may still note certain distinctive features of *phrēn/phrenes* within it.

When *phrenes* display physical characteristics, they are, as in Homer and Hesiod, best described as a composite of entities located in the chest region. But their physical nature is only occasionally apparent in this poetry. More instances of the singular, *phrēn*, occur than in Homer or Hesiod. This feature may suggest its greater appearance as an active agent in the individual.

As in Homer and Hesiod, *phrenes* are open to many outside influences. Love, pain, poverty, wealth, and wine can affect them. When outside agents act on them, 'beguiling', 'unhinging', or 'conquering' them, the person's behaviour as a whole is greatly influenced. As in Homer and Hesiod too, *phrenes* still function on occasion as the location of other psychic entities, namely *thumos* and *ētor*.

In terms of activity *phrenes* are, as in earlier poets, associated with

---

[55] On *phrēn* in the lyric and elegiac poets see Furley, Jarcho, Luck, Marg, Onians, Snell, *Der Weg*, Sullivan (note 3), and Treu.

a wide range of psychological activities that a person carries on in, by, or with them. They do not appear very often as an independent agent within the individual but this type of activity is increasing. Joined with this increase is a greater control that someone exerts over *phrenes*, perhaps occurring because *phrenes* are more active within. Connected with *phrenes* are the intellectual activities of thinking, pondering, perceiving, taking counsel, and planning. They are associated too with speech, both as a receiver of it and as its origin. They are often involved in emotions, especially those of love, pleasure, and pain. In them too hopes, desires, and fears are to be found.

Frequently in the lyric and elegiac poets *phrenes* function as a seat of someone's qualities. They significantly affect how someone acts, especially with regard to wisdom and justice. A negative state of *phrenes* can lead to reprehensible behaviour. As in Homer, the possibility that *phrenes* may differ in nature from a person's outward behaviour is very real; in such cases they function as the location of a person's true feelings or thoughts. *Phrenes* can vary greatly in nature. They can be 'wise', 'gracious', 'guileless', 'just', or 'noble'. They can also be 'wretched', 'fearful', 'raging', 'crooked', and 'blind'. Such descriptions suggest the degree to which *phrenes* were related to aspects of moral character in the person.

In general, within the person *phrenes* appear as a location of action, an instrument used, or an accompaniment sharing in activity. Person and *phrenes* are not in conflict but act in harmony and co-operation. As in the epic poets, *phrenes* seem to be subordinate to the person. They may be more active than before and we find in Pindar an address to *phrēn* in the vocative, one that is not found earlier in extant poetry.[56] He asks *phrēn* to resist certain desires (*Pae.* 4.50) and it may be that in some circumstances *phrēn* needs resisting. But, in most instances, individual and *phrenes*, remaining distinct, work well together. As in Homer and Hesiod, *phrenes* emerge as the means by which someone copes with situations that arise, serving as a location for thought and possibilities of reaction.

Specific Passages

As with *noos*, there are over 100 instances of *phrēn* in the lyric and elegiac poets. Certain of these give a vivid picture of its function in the person. Archilochus, living in the mid-seventh century, abuses

---

[56] This is in contrast, for example, with *thumos* and *kradiē*, which a person directly speaks to in Homer (e.g., *Il.* 10.534 and 13.784). See below on these entities.

the man who prevented him from marrying his daughter, Neobule.[57]
He says (172):

> Father Lycambes, what sort of thing have you done?
>   Who unhinged your *phrenes*
> with which before you were well-fitted? Now
>   you will appear a great laughing-stock to the citizens.

We do not know what Lycambes has done in this particular poem
but Archilochus thinks it foolish. Before this action, Lycambes was
'well-fitted' with *phrenes*. The image here may suggest a physical aspect of *phrenes*. A person's construction may be positive because it is
built well with regard to *phrenes*. In contrast, we hear in Homer of
someone 'poorly constructed' in *phrenes*: Elpenor falls to his death
from a roof because of this problem (*Od.* 10.533). Lycambes' *phrenes*,
formerly at any rate, contributed positively to his overall structure.

On the other hand, the phrase 'well-fitted in *phrenes*' may point
only to the function of *phrenes*. When Lycambes was such, he thought
well and acted wisely. Other lyric and elegiac poets too associate
phrenes with wise thinking. Phocylides says that it is 'sharper' for planning at night (7). Theognis urges Cyrnus to 'take counsel' with his
'deep *phrēn*' (1051–2) and speaks of 'practical wisdom' (*gnōmē*) being
in *phrenes* (1173). Pindar says that *phrēn* functions in 'counsels' (*Nem.*
1.27).[58]

But as we know too from other sources, *phrenes* can be damaged.
In this case Archilochus speaks of those of Lycambes as 'unhinged'.[59]
They seem somehow to have been 'loosed' from their structure. In
this condition they do not, or cannot, serve Lycambes well.[60] Else-
where in the lyric and elegiac poets we hear of the removal of *phrenes*.
Alcaeus speaks of a 'whirlwind' carrying off *phrenes* completely (336).
Solon describes himself as 'deprived of *thumos* and *phrenes* at the same

---

[57] On Archilochus and his relation to Lycambes see Podlecki, *Early Greek Poets*,
pp. 46–50.

[58] See also *Pae.* 9.34–7 where he likewise speaks of the 'counsels' (*mēdea*) of *phrēn*
and *Nem.* 7.60 where he mentions the 'understanding' of *phrenes* (*sunesis*).

[59] Archilochus at 130 uses this same image of *noos*. The person knocked down by
the gods wanders 'unhinged in *noos*'.

[60] In the lyric and elegiac poets we find other pictures of *phrenes* in a damaged
condition. Archilochus speaks of being 'thunderstruck with wine' in his *phrenes* (120),
Anacreon, of being 'deaf and dumb' in his (421). Theognis speaks of love 'conquering wise *phrenes*' (1388), and poverty harming them (387); Bacchylides says that 'gain'
hurts wise *phrenes* (fr. 1.1). Pindar mentions *phrenes* that are 'blind' (*Pae.* 7 b 18).

time' (33). These passages too suggest the loss of the admirable function of *phrenes*. When *phrenes* function badly, unwise behaviour results. Lycambes will consequently receive ridicule from the citizens because his were 'unhinged'.

In this poem of Archilochus we see the connection of *phrenes* with practical behaviour. In making a certain choice or decision, Lycambes has done something foolish. The psychic entity on which he relied this time failed him, even though before it proved valuable. The role of *phrenes* as instrument or tool used by the individual is thus evident in this poem.

A second passage from early poetry that we shall treat is an Attic scolion. This poem may come from a song book put together in the late sixth or early fifth centuries for those who did not wish to make up their own songs at drinking parties.[61] As number five of this collection (889 in *PMG*), it says:

> Would that it were possible to see what each person is like
> by opening his chest and, having looked at his *noos*,
> to close it up again, and to consider someone
> a friend because of his *phrēn* that is without deceit.

Eustathius, a late commentator on Homer, referring to this scolion, suggests that it came from a fable of Aesop in which Prometheus is criticised for not fashioning gates in the chests of human beings so that their thoughts could be easily examined.[62]

The lines tell us interesting things about *phrēn* and *noos*. Both are located in the chest region. *Noos*, as we heard often above, is hidden and this causes problems in encounters. One meets with *phrēn* but cannot know if it presents a trustworthy expression of what the person is actually thinking.

It may not be. Evidence of friendship that it manifests may not be authentic. There can be a contrast between outer and inner behaviour. Already in Homer we hear Achilles saying that he hates someone 'who hides one thing in his *phrenes* and says another' (*Il.* 9.313).[63]

---

[61] See Bowra, *Greek Lyric*, pp. 360–1, Podlecki, *Early Greek Poets*, pp. 76, 90, and M. van der Valk, 'On the Composition of the Attic Skolia', *Hermes*, 1974, vol. 102, pp. 1–20.

[62] See Eustathius, *Od.* 1574.16. Note similar thoughts expressed in Soph., *Ant.* 707–9, Eur., *Hipp.* 925–31, 983–5, *Med.* 516–19, *Tro.* 662. Aristophanes parodies the lines in *Eccl.* 938–41.

[63] Cf. too *Od.* 2.93, 17.66, and 24.128 where outer behaviour belies what is in *phrenes*.

Theognis in lines 87–92 asks Cyrnus not to love him 'with words' but to hold his '*noos* and *phrenes* in another direction'. He asks that *noos* be 'trustworthy' and 'pure' and that words reflect its nature.[64] In the present scolion we see that *noos* is crucial. *Phrēn* either reflects it or deceives by concealing it.[65]

Noos best expresses a person's true thoughts or feelings, which *phrēn* can either reveal or veil. Elsewhere we hear too of outer behaviour not being in accord with *noos*. Hesiod asks Perses to let his behaviour reflect it (*W. & D.* 714). Solon says that certain people believed that he would speak in a gentle way but actually conceal his true intentions in a 'harsh *noos*' (34).[66] Unfortunately the possibility of observing the *noos* of others is denied us: human behaviour demands caution since *phrēn* may not candidly reflect *noos*.

In further specific passages Pindar gives us interesting evidence about *phrenes*. In *Nem.* 3.59–60, as he describes in general the way human beings should act, he mentions how *phrenes* are to be used:

> It is necessary for us to seek
> with mortal *phrenes*
> what is appropriate from the gods,
> knowing that which is near at hand,
> of what we are in fate.

Human beings are dependent upon the gods and need to seek divine help. Our *phrenes* are mortal but able, it seems, to discover what behaviour is 'appropriate'. Pindar goes on in lines 61–2 to urge his soul (*psychē*) not to 'hasten after immortal life', but to 'exhaust practicable resources'. 'Appropriate actions', it appears, will essentially be those 'which are near at hand', not events of the future that someone cannot control. They will be in accord with what humans are 'in fate'. In nature they will be moral. Later in this ode, Pindar describes himself as 'honouring' the divinity (*daimōn*), that 'encompasses' his *phrenes* and 'heeding' it according to his 'resources' (108).[67]

---

[64] Cf. *Is.* 6.17 where Pindar praises Lampon because his 'tongue is not outside his *phrenes*': the picture suggests honesty and intelligence.

[65] Note in Eur., *Med.* 659–62 the true friend is one who opens the 'bolt of pure *phrenes*'.

[66] Cf. Theog. 74 and 698 where he says that few people have a 'trustworthy *noos*' and 119–28 where he speaks of the difficulties in knowing what the *noos* of others is truly like.

[67] See too Theog. 161–4 where he emphasizes the importance of the effect a *daimōn* can have: even if *phrenes* are wretched, a good *daimōn* can bring success.

He thus puts into practice the behaviour he recommends earlier in the poem.

In this ode of Pindar we see the connection of *phrenes* with pondering or planning.[68] We see it functioning as a tool or instrument used by the person. And we see its association with admirable behaviour. Elsewhere too Pindar speaks often of this third feature. In *Ol.* 7 he tells the story of Tlepolemos who killed his uncle in a fit of rage. He says that 'unnumbered sins (*amplakiai*) hang around human *phrenes*' (24); these sins make a person vulnerable. Whether these invade *phrenes* or are chosen by the individual is not clear but error results. When this happens, *phrenes* are in a negative state. Pindar then says: 'disturbances of *phrenes* caused even a wise man to go astray' (30). This is what happened to Tlepolemos when he committed murder. The wisdom he had did not prevent his action. In these lines we see the association of *phrenes* with negative behaviour.

In the same ode Pindar praises Diagoras because 'he walks straight upon a road that hates pride (*hybris*), knowing clearly what upright *phrenes* from good fathers enjoin' (90–2). He has inherited good *phrenes* and consequently has acted well. His *phrenes* have apparently suggested the approved ways of behaving that Diagoras has accepted and actively pursued.

Earlier in the same ode Pindar mentions an instance where *phrenes* did not lead to proper behaviour. When the Heliadae forgot to bring fire in a sacrifice for Athena and thus neglected to show proper respect, he says: 'there came an obscure cloud of forgetfulness and it drew the straight road of action outside of *phrenes*' (46–7). *Phrenes* prove vulnerable to forgetfulness and cause the people in whom they are found to behave improperly.[69]

Other passages from the lyric and elegiac poets show us an additional feature of *phrenes*: they are associated with love.[70] Earlier in Homer we hear of love 'surrounding' Paris or Zeus in *phrenes* (*Il.* 3.442, 14.294). Love can also 'deceive' *phrenes* (*Od.* 15.421). In these

---

[68] See too above note 58 and fr. 61, *Ol.* 8.24, and *Bacch.* 11, 1–7 where *phrēn* is likewise connected with pondering.

[69] See also the connection of *phrenes* with moral behaviour in several passages of Theognis, namely 65, 387, 429–33, 733, 1008 and elsewhere in Pindar, as, e.g., at *Ol.* 2.57, 8.24, *Pyth.* 4.139, 5.19, *Nem.* 10.12, and *Is.* 3.2–5.

[70] On this subject see A. Carson, *Eros the Bittersweet*, Princeton, 1986, Fränkel, *Dichtung*, pp. 323–4 and S.D. Sullivan, 'Love Influences *Phrenes* in Greek Lyric Poetry', *SO*, 1983, vol. 58, pp. 15–22.

instances love's effect is negative, leading to poor judgement of some kind.

First, in the lyric and elegiac poets, *phrenes* can be directly affected by love. For Archilochus 'desire for love steals tender *phrenes* from his chest' (191). As in other passages when *phrenes* are removed, it is their function that is lost. Sappho likewise gives a negative picture of love's effect on *phrenes*: 'love shook my *phrenes*, just as a wind falling on oaks on a mountain' (47). Love plays havoc with one's thinking. Ibycus too suggests that love, being 'dark and shameless' and acting 'powerfully', deeply disturbs *phrenes* (286). Theognis similarly speaks of Aphrodite 'conquering wise *phrenes*' (1386–9). Bacchylides says that love 'sets *phrenes* aflutter' (fr. 20 B 8).[71] All these passages suggest that love has a shattering influence upon *phrenes*, changing their condition and impairing their function.

Second, *phrenes* can act as a location of love. Sappho says that her *phrēn* 'burns with longing' (48). She likewise describes someone 'being consumed in her delicate *phrēn* with yearning' (96.17). Pindar says that Poseidon, 'conquered in *phrenes* with desire', carried off Pelops (*Ol.* 1.41). He also describes Medea as 'burning in *phrenes*' because of Jason (*Pyth.* 4.218). In these passages love has invaded *phrenes*, filling them with emotion and strongly affecting a person's behaviour.

Third, we see in one passage of Pindar *phrenes* functioning as the accompaniment with which someone loves. Love can so totally fill *phrenes* that it becomes their chief activity. He says of Ixion: 'when he loved Hera with raging *phrenes*' (*Pyth.* 2.26). With such *phrenes* Ixion imagined that love between a goddess and a mortal was possible. Love had clearly distorted his thinking.[72]

These passages about love show *phrenes* having several features we have seen elsewhere. They are vulnerable to outside forces. They act often as location, instrument, or accompaniment. Because love's influence is consistently described as negative, we see that *phrenes* must usually have been associated with valuable or useful modes of thought. Love disturbs their normal functioning and leads to behaviour, not to be described as fully rational.

---

[71] Pindar too speaks of 'different desires' (*erōtes*) 'chafing the *phrenes* of different people' (*Pyth.* 10.59–60). In this case *phrenes* are connected with a seat of longing, which can bring anxiety.

[72] See also the connection of love and *phrenes* in Aesch., *Choeph.* 594–7, and Eur., *Hipp.* 764–5, 1268–71.

These selections from the lyric and elegiac poets illustrate several features of *phrenes*. They are strongly associated with intellectual activity and, if damaged, make someone act foolishly. They can act as a reflection or concealment of what a person is truly thinking. If people hide their real thoughts, *phrenes* can prove 'deceitful'. They can be connected with moral behaviour, both positive and negative. They are much involved in love. Again and again we see *phrenes* acting as an instrument or tool a person can use and a location for useful deliberation within.

Presocratics

In the Presocratics *phrēn* is rarely mentioned except in Empedocles. Again the fragmentary nature of our evidence may be of crucial importance here. In two fragments where it appears in Xenophanes and Heraclitus, it is mentioned with *noos*. We discussed these above and will briefly treat them again here.[73] We shall then treat Empedocles and look also at a fragment of Democritus.

In B 25 Xenophanes describes the divine principle:[74] 'but without labour [the divinity] makes all things tremble by the *phrēn* of *noos*'. As interpreted above, this fragment says that the god moves the universe by thought in effortless action. The phrase '*phrēn* of *noos*' describes this thought, with the genitive being a subjective one.[75] *Phrēn* belongs to *noos* and is subordinate to it. As we have seen so often in Homer, Hesiod, and the lyric and elegiac poets, *phrēn* functions as an instrument used by the divinity.

Associated with inner vision, *noos* in the god may 'see' all things, know and order them. But divinity's thought is more: it includes *phrēn* as well. This *phrēn* perhaps acts as the location of pondering or deliberation in the god. Human beings, like the divinity, share in *phrēn* and *noos*. These two psychic entities in them, of course, do not function in so powerful a way as occurs in the god. With thought the divinity can instill motion into the universe. With their thought human beings can cope with their world and also understand how the universe operates.

---

[73] See above the treatment of the Presocratics in the section on *noos*.

[74] On Xenophanes see bibliography in note 32.

[75] See above note 33 on this interpretation of the expression '*phrēn* of *noos*'.

The divinity differs from humans not only in the scale of thought but also in the relationship existing between *phrēn* and *noos*. We do not hear elsewhere of *phrēn* belonging to *noos*, although *noos* is once found in *phrenes* (*Il.* 18.419). In human beings the two psychic entities are always described as distinct with separate activities. In the Attic drinking song discussed above (889) we saw that *phrēn* might match *noos* in thought or be different from it, deceiving others by not letting *noos*, as seat of a person's true feelings and reactions, be seen. Usually a person acts in, by, or with *phrenes*, finding them a useful tool and a co-operative psychic entity. *Noos* more often acts within humans; it grasps truth and can effect well what it knows. But when *noos* does not act or when it hides, as it often does, people may have to rely on *phrenes*.

In the divinity all is different. *Phrēn* belongs to *noos*, acting apparently under its guidance. The divinity by thinking moves the universe. This thought is so pervasive that the 'whole of the god' thinks (B 24). Xenophanes may suggest that humans are on a continuum with divinity in relation to mental capacity. Humans are far below the divine but share in a similar ability. Perhaps in B 25 Xenophanes suggests what would be the best way for *phrēn* and *noos* to be related: the first should be subordinate to the second and act in accord with it. This ideal relationship may not be possible in human beings but to the degree that it is, it is one to be fostered.

Heraclitus mentions *phrēn* only once when he asks impatiently concerning people who trust what bards and the mob say (B 104): 'where is their *noos* or *phrēn*?'[76] The two psychic entities are mentioned together and clearly could function in a valuable way but fail to do so.

In Empedocles there are seven mentions of *phrēn*, one of these of particular importance because it concerns the nature of the divine.[77] Empedocles teaches that the universe is made up of four elements, earth, air, fire, and water, arranged and ordered by two moving principles, Love and Strife. This is the view he presents in his poem the *Physics*, and it is in this work that six of our references appear. In his second poem, the *Purifications*, he describes the long process of transmigration that the souls of human beings must go through. He

---

[76] For bibliography on Heraclitus see note 35.
[77] On Empedocles and his philosophy see bibliography in note 39.

associates *phrēn* with a grasp of this teaching in one fragment from this poem.[78]

Let us look at this fragment first (B 114).

> My friends, I know that there is truth in the words
> which I shall speak, but very painful and troublesome
> has the entry of belief (*pistis*) into *phrēn*
> been fashioned for human beings

People, it seems, are not open to new ideas, even if they are true. Their *phrēn* resists. Empedocles may have found this to be particularly the case when he introduced the notion of transmigration. In B 114 *phrēn* functions as a seat of understanding for philosophical truths which are to be received by listening. It is through the senses that this information comes. *Phrēn* may ponder this, resist it, and perhaps only slowly accept it.

In the six fragments of the *Physics* we see a similar activity assigned to *phrēn*. In one of these someone is to 'conceal' something 'within a silent *phrēn*' (B 5). Probably Empedocles refers to his teaching which is to be received in silence. Only thus perhaps will the person prove receptive to it. Empedocles realizes that his teachings are obscure. In another fragment (B 15), he says that someone 'wise in such matters would not guess in his *phrenes*' that all life is simply a mingling and separating of the four elements. *Phrenes* here function as an instrument or location that proves inadequate for grasping this truth.

But the situation can be remedied, it seems, by the acceptance of Empedocles' views in a 'silent *phrēn*' (B 5). If they are accepted, the very nature of *phrenes* may alter, as the next fragment shows. In B 17 Empedocles says: 'come, listen to my words, for learning (*mathē*) increases *phrenes*'. Elsewhere we hear of *phrenes* increasing. Pindar (fr. 124 b 11) speaks of wine increasing them, giving people, it seems, an inflated way of thinking. Bacchylides says that wealth has the same effect upon them (1.162). Empedocles refers to the increase of *phrenes* in a positive way. By hearing, a person will come to understand the view of the universe that he presents: this is 'learning' (*mathē*).

We heard above a negative reference to 'much-learning' (*polymathiē*),

---

[78] On the nature of *phrēn* in Empedocles see in particular a discussion of the fragments named in Guthrie, vol. 2, Inwood, Kirk, Raven, and Schofield, Sullivan in *Studi*, and Wright.

.when Heraclitus said that it could not teach *noos* (B 40). With this statement Empedocles would probably have agreed, for we also heard him say that, even though *noos* may grasp the significance of Love as a divine principle (B 17.21), it cannot grasp the whole truth of the universe (B 2.8). If *noos* cannot, *phrēn* perhaps can do so even less. But *phrenes*, through a person's listening, can become filled with learning that is based on sense perception. *Phrenes*, it appears, are connected with pondering or grasping what is heard. This may form a prelude to a deeper experience of what Empedocles is describing, to be discovered perchance with *noos* and with divine inspiration (B 3).

As in B 114, so here in B 17 *phrenes* are connected with information received through hearing. B 114 says that belief comes with difficulty. But if learning is received, a person's understanding in *phrenes* grows greater.

In B 23 Empedocles again speaks of the way all visible things are formed from only a few, the four elements. He urges Pausanias, the recipient of his poems: 'let not deception overcome you in your *phrēn*'. He would do so by believing something else and not listening to Empedocles' account. As in B 17, *phrēn* is involved in understanding a truth, one received by the senses. It could be deceived about it but will not be if Pausanias listens. The account, received by hearing, will bring a correct understanding to *phrēn*.

In B 133 Empedocles says of the divine (*theion*):

> It is not possible to bring this near to us,
> to be perceived by our eyes or to be grasped with the hands,
> by which the broadest path of persuasion
> for human beings leads into *phrēn*.

The divine nature cannot be grasped by the senses even though they provide information that persuades *phrēn* most readily. As in the fragments discussed above, *phrēn* is associated with the interpretation of sense evidence.

In another fragment, B 134, Empedocles describes what the divine nature is like. First he says that it lacks anthropomorphic features. Then he describes it thus: 'it is only a holy, inexpressible *phrēn*, darting through the whole cosmos with its swift thoughts (*phrontides*)'. Empedocles here identifies the divine being with *phrēn*. In doing so, he offers another example of the microcosm/macrocosm principle found in the Presocratics and described above under Anaxagoras. Human beings (the microcosm) have a *phrēn* with a range of intellectual functions and, as Empedocles says, a particular role in responding to sense evidence. Divinity (the macrocosm) is a *phrēn*. For divinity, *phrēn* is of a different, higher nature than that of humans. He calls it 'holy' and 'beyond words to express'.

This divine *phrēn* is also active, 'darting with swift thoughts through the cosmos'. In other authors we have seen *phrēn* function very often as location and instrument of thought. This is how Empedocles too refers to the human *phrēn*. But the divine *phrēn* is described as an active agent, emerging strongly in this role as we have seen it do somewhat in the lyric and elegiac poets. No one else speaks of *phrēn* 'darting', a verb use to describe the motion of the gods in Homer (see, e.g., *Il.* 2.167, 24.121).

Just as Xenophanes' divinity moves 'all things' by thinking, so apparently does that of Empedocles. Because *phrēn* was connected with wide variety in thinking, it may have seemed to Empedocles the appropriate term to describe a divinity responsible for a universe going though many changes. It appears to be the source for the ordered cycle of change that the four elements go through. By thinking different thoughts, this divinity sometimes makes 'all things' into one, at other times into a mixture, and at yet other times into the four separate elements.

We shall conclude this section on the Presocratics by looking at a fragment of Democritus.[79] Living at the end of the fifth century he is outside the Archaic Age but is the last of the Presocratics. With Leucippus he introduced the notions of atoms and space as the true components of the universe. In so doing, the Atomists present a picture of the universe that starkly differs from their predecessors: there is no divine or cosmic principle guiding it. 'All things' are in essence atoms and space. These, by wide variety of combination, make up the vast complexity of the sensible world. Human beings cannot, of course, perceive atoms directly. Democritus, drawing from the argument of Parmenides about Being and all its necessary characteristics, argues forcefully that this Being must exist in the form of many indivisible particles. What separates the particles and allows them to

---

[79] On Democritus and the Atomists see the Appendix and Barnes, vol. 2, pp. 40–75, 257–62, Cole, Dumont, pp. 747–938, Furley, *Two Studies*, W.K.C. Guthrie, vol. 2, pp. 382–502, Hussey, pp. 141–8, Kirk, Raven, and Schofield, pp. 402–33, McKirahan, pp. 303–43, Mansfeld, pp. 556–671, D. O'Brien, *Theories*, J.M. Robinson, pp. 195–236, Wright, *Presocratics*, pp. 137–43.

be more than a single reality is space. This space likewise functions as the setting where the atoms, ever in motion, move about.

In his analysis of the universe, Democritus accepts to some degree the evidence of the senses but he is sceptical about their ability to offer a full explanation of truth.[80] He places in the realm of mere 'opinion' much of what they present (B 7, 9). They do not allow a full grasp of reality, of which the essence is atoms and space (B 8, 10). Human beings are in fact 'separated' from this reality (B 6) and must 'learn' with this separation in mind. Cognition, he suggests, exists in two forms, one based on sense perception and one that goes much more deeply (B 11). The second is to be preferred but may nonetheless depend to some degree on the first.

In fragment B 125 of Democritus we hear of a response that the senses make to *phrēn*: 'wretched *phrēn*, do you take your beliefs (*pisteis*) from us and then overthrow us? Our overthrow is your downfall'. Empedocles in B 114 (discussed above) had said that the 'entry of belief' into the human *phrēn* is difficult. He relates *phrēn* with the pondering of material that was heard. In a similar way in B 125 Democritus associates *phrēn* with the analysis of sense evidence and warns *phrēn* that it should never dissociate itself totally from such evidence. Ideally, it seems, *phrēn* should draw information from the senses, using it in any explanation of reality it may offer. This explanation will have to depend on deeper perception (B 11), it is true, but it will not contradict sense evidence. If *phrēn* ignores what the senses present, its thoughts will fail to be concerned with truth.[81] *Phrēn* functions in this fragment as an active agent. Democritus associates its activity, as do other Presocratics, with a consideration of how the universe works.

Overview of Phrēn

In this section we have examined the nature of *phrenes* in the lyric and elegiac poets and the Presocratic philosophers. As a psychic entity within the person, we see that they differ in many ways from *noos*. In

---

[80] On the theory of knowledge in Democritus see in particular Barnes, vol. 2, pp. 257–62, W.K.C. Guthrie, vol. 2, pp. 454–65, Kirk, Raven, and Schofield, pp. 409–13, McKirahan, pp. 333–7, J.M. Robinson, pp. 201–6.

[81] In another fragment Democritus also mentions *phrēn*. In B 129 he refers to people who 'think divine things with *phrēn*'. The context is unclear but *phrēn* is used here, as so commonly, as an instrument.

the authors discussed *phrenes* display a wide range of activity. Some of their physical characteristics are occasionally still evident. They are usually spoken of in the plural and may have been considered a composite of psychic entities located in the chest region. They themselves serve often as the location of other psychic entities.

Within the person we see that *phrenes* are associated with different psychological activities, including those that are volitional, emotional, and intellectual. The latter predominate and have a particular focus. Unlike *noos* that seems capable of grasping truth with a form of inner vision, *phrenes* are associated more often with pondering or deliberation. They act as an instrument to be used in decisions or uncertainties. We may suspect that, when *noos* was hidden or failed to function, someone had to rely on *phrenes*. In differing and changing circumstances *phrenes* could prove very valuable.

In the individual *phrenes* have a subordinate role. They do not act very often as an active agent, although this aspect begins to emerge more in the lyric and elegiac poets and the Presocratics. Instead, they are an instrument or tool used by a person. They can also provide activity of a co-operative nature. A person and *phrenes* are always distinct but *phrenes* can have a strong influence upon behaviour. If they are 'damaged', the person behaves foolishly. They can be of varying nature or be affected by outside forces: these conditions likewise influence how a person acts. Generally, person and *phrenes* act in harmony, without the two being opposed.

In the lyric and elegiac poets *phrenes* function more prominently as a seat of a person's qualities. In Pindar especially we see them connected with moral behaviour and in several of these poets, with love. In the Presocratics, *phrēn* in human beings is associated with the interpretation of sense evidence and with the understanding of the nature of the universe. In the divinity it can be an instrument that is used, according to Xenophanes, or can be itself the nature of the divine, according to Empedocles.

In general, *phrenes* function as a useful psychic entity within the person. Although perhaps not as crucially important or of such high value as *noos*, they nonetheless make it possible for human beings on many occasions to cope with the circumstances they encounter. Acting in harmony and co-operation with them, *phrenes* are partly responsible for giving humans the intellectual range they both need and enjoy.

Thumos

Homeric and Hesiodic Background

Our third psychic entity, *thumos*, is by far the most prominent of all, appearing over 750 times in Homer and the *Homeric Hymns*. In Hesiod it is mentioned fifty-seven times.[82] Its range of activity is most extensive. Like *noos*, it is often an active agent within the person. Like *phrenes*, it is often too a location, instrument, or accompaniment. More than either of these two psychic entities we have already studied, it functions as a vibrant source of activity within the person. It proves to be a source of energetic action. Someone's behaviour is strongly determined by *thumos*.

Like *noos*, *thumos* appears only in the singular, each individual having just one. But it may have such varied activity that a person may think that there is 'another' *thumos* present within. This happens to Odysseus where he first plans in his *thumos* to kill Polyphemus but then 'another *thumos*' checks him (*Od.* 9.299–302). First *thumos* is a location of one thought, then of another that replaces the first.

In Homer and Hesiod the physical nature of *thumos* is not very evident. Plato (*Cratyl.* 419E) suggests that '*thumos*' is derived from the Greek verb meaning 'to seethe' or 'to rage' (*thuō*). This derivation tells us something of its function but does not clarify its physical nature. For this, various suggestions have been made: the vaporous breath that arises from blood or the quickened breathing connected with emotion.[83] Another view is that *thumos* is a seat of vital energy that can fill a person.[84] This last suggestion seems most attractive,

---

[82] On *thumos* in Homer and Hesiod see Biraud, Böhme, Bremmer, Caswell, Cheyns, *Rbph*, 1983, A. Cheyns, 'Considerations sur les emplois de *thumos* dans Homère, Iliade VII, pp. 67–218', *AC*, 1981, vol. 50, pp. 137–47, Claus, J.G. Diaz, 'Sentido de "thymos" en la Iliade', *Helmantica*, 1976, vol. 27, pp. 121–6, Dihle, 'Totenglaube', Furley, Garland, *BICS*, 1981, Gelzer (note 2), Harrison, Jahn, Krafft, Larock, J.P. Lynch and G.B. Miles, 'In Search of *Thumos*: Toward an Understanding of a Greek Psychological Term', *Prudentia*, 1980, vol. 12, pp. 3–9; Nehring, Onians, Plamböck, Russo and Simon, Schnaufer, Snell, *Discovery*, *Tyrtaios*, *Der Weg*, Sullivan (note 3), Vivante.

[83] For the first suggestion see Böhme, p. 20, Onians, p. 47, and Rüsche, pp. 25–56; for the second, Böhme, p. 23, Furley, *BICS*, 1956, p. 3, Harrison, p. 66, and Redfield, pp. 171–4. For the second cf. also Caswell, who relates *thumos* in particular to 'wind' or 'storm'.

[84] See Biraud, vol. 1, p. 44, Cheyns, *Rbph*, 1983, pp. 32–43, Harrison, pp. 68–9, Lynch and Miles, pp. 5–6, Marg, pp. 43–79, Schnaufer, pp. 180–98.

especially suiting the way *thumos* appears in the epic poetry of Homer and Hesiod. It is a very active entity that spreads its influence out into the individual. Placed like other psychic entities in the chest, it is able to inspire, direct, and guide the person in different situations.

Thumos, it is true, manifests certain features that suggest a physical connotation. It can function, though rarely, as a location of *noos* (*Od.* 14.490) and *kēr* (*Il.* 6.523). It can increase (*Od.* 2.315), grow weak (*Il.* 14.439), or, in contrast to the body, remain strong (*Il.* 19.164). It partakes of food and drink (*Il.* 2.431). But these characteristics are not primary. In most situations *thumos* functions principally as a psychic entity within the person, which engages in psychological activities.

From the many passages where *thumos* is mentioned in Homer, the *Homeric Hymns*, and Hesiod, we shall mention a few to illustrate its broad range of function. What we shall see is that within the person it is an independent agent, a location of psychological activity, a tool, an accompaniment to action, and a direct receiver of actions from without. Outside forces and agents can often affect it as it proves open and vulnerable. We see the person very much heeding *thumos*, sometimes needing to control it, and even talking to it directly.

The emotional activities *thumos* can carry on include joy, pain, anger, desire, fear, courage, love, and hope. As Achilles sits by the shore, he 'delights his *thumos*' with the lyre (*Il.* 9.189). When Diomedes wounds Ares, the god 'grieves in *thumos*' (*Il.* 5.869). Demeter, 'angry in *thumos*', refuses to allow the earth to grow crops until she sees Persephone again (*H. Cer.* 330). Hesiod tells Perses that, if the '*thumos* in his *phrenes* desires wealth', he should work and keep working (*W. & D.* 381). At the end of the *Iliad* Achilles takes the hands of Priam so that the old man might not 'fear in his *thumos*' (*Il.* 24.672). At the sight of Penelope the suitors 'were enchanted with love in their *thumos*' (*Od.* 18.212). As the Trojans fight, the '*thumos* in their breasts hopes' to burn the ships of the Achaeans and to slay the warriors (*Il.* 15.701).

Thumos is mentioned in connection with several intellectual activities. These include pondering, thinking, knowing, deliberation, planning, and perceiving. Often too a person puts things into *thumos* for consideration. Odysseus 'ponders evils in his *thumos*' for the suitors (*Od.* 20.5). Zeus 'thinks about' events in his *thumos* as he watches the battle of Troy (*Il.* 16.646). Athena says that she 'knew in her *thumos*' that Odysseus would return home (*Od.* 13.339). Hermes 'deliberates in *thumos*' how to take Priam safely from Achilles' camp (*Il.* 24.680). Circe tells Odysseus to 'plan in his *thumos*' the course he will take after passing the Sirens (*Od.* 12.58). Telemachus tells Penelope that now that he has grown up he 'perceives and knows in his *thumos*' good and evil (*Od.* 18.228). It is in *thumos* that Hesiod tells Perses to 'consider' the value of the competitive spirit (*W. & D.* 27).

Thumos in particular is involved in decisions that heroes might make.[85] Frequently we hear of a person 'considering in *thumos*' certain choices. Thus Odysseus 'ponders in *thumos* and *phrēn*' whether he should kill the women who are sleeping with the suitors or to let them be (*Od.* 20.10).[86] In Penelope '*thumos* is drawn in two directions' whether to stay at home with Telemachus or to marry one of the suitors (*Od.* 19.524). Sometimes a person speaks to *thumos* and then sums up his thinking by referring to *thumos* speaking back. Thus, at a moment in battle when he is left by himself, Odysseus 'speaks to his great-hearted *thumos*', pondering whether he should flee, yet dreading capture by the enemy if he stays. Then he asks: 'why does my *thumos* discuss these questions with me?' He knows he must stand his ground (*Il.* 11.403–7). We see that *thumos* is the location where possibilities become apparent and that it contributes to the decision that is formed. On occasion a decision is described impersonally: 'it seems good' to a person in *thumos* to perform some action. Thus, at *Od.* 13.154, Zeus describes to Poseidon the way in which 'it seemed best to his *thumos*' for the ship of the Phaeacians to be turned to stone. From among possibilities a certain emerges as 'best to *thumos*' and Zeus makes it known.

The volitional activities *thumos* is associated with include ordering, urging on, allowing, daring, desiring, and being eager for some action. Polyphemus tells Odysseus that he would not spare him unless 'his *thumos* ordered him to' (*Od.* 9.278). Apollo asks Athena why her 'great *thumos* has sent her from Olympus' (*Il.* 7.25). When Andromache asks Hector not to fight, he replies that his '*thumos* does not allow' such cowardly behaviour (*Il.* 6.444). Odysseus is described as one 'in whose *phrenes thumos* was ever daring' (*Il.* 10.232). Telemachus tells Menelaus that 'his *thumos* desires to return home' (*Od.* 15.66). Prometheus, in his deception of Zeus, 'divides an ox with eager *thumos*' (*Theog.* 536).

Thumos is very much connected with the qualities a person displays. This is made especially clear by the adjectives that appear

---

[85] On the presence of decision in Homer see above note 2.
[86] See further in this passage below under *kradiē*. See also Caswell, p. 15.

with it. These adjectives show likewise that *thumos* has a widely varying nature. It can be 'noble', 'gentle', 'dear', 'intrepid', 'unbending',
and 'strong'. It can also be 'foolish', 'flighty', 'much-suffering', and
'evil'. Zeus' *thumos* is ever 'haughty and unbending' (*Il.* 15.94). Achilles' *thumos* is 'mighty', 'great-hearted and furious', and 'of iron' (*Il.* 9.496,
629, 22.357). Penelope has an 'enduring *thumos*' (*Od.* 11.181). The
Bronze race has one that is 'dauntless' (*W. & D.* 147). In some cases
thumos seems in the person to be of an enduring nature. In others it
changes with the situation or with time.

Like other psychic entities, *thumos* is much affected by outside agents
or objects which can alter its nature. Ajax tells Achilles that because
of Briseis 'the gods have put in his chest a *thumos* that is implacable
and evil' (*Il.* 9.636). Iris urges Achilles to let 'reverent awe come to
him in his *thumos*' at the thought that Patroclus' body might be cap-
tured by the Trojans (*Il.* 18.178). Menelaus says that 'pain has come
to his *thumos*' because of the sufferings caused by the loss of Helen
(*Il.* 3.97). Zeus put 'sweet longing in the *thumos*' of Aphrodite so that
she desired to marry Anchises (*H. Ven.* 45). On seeing Hera, Zeus
tells her that 'no love of any goddess or mortal woman had ever
conquered him in his *thumos* in such a way' (*Il.* 14.315). Zeus' *thumos*
is also vulnerable to 'anger' which comes upon him there when he
realizes the deception of Prometheus (*Theog.* 554). 'Helplessness takes
hold of the *thumos*' of Odysseus and his men when Polyphemus begins to eat them (*Od.* 9.295). Athena places 'strength and courage' in
the *thumos* of Telemachus for his new ventures (*Od.* 1.320).

Thumos has a similar range of activity in both gods and human
beings. Nor is it restricted to these. We hear in Homer of the *thumos*
of oxen, swine, horses, wolves, lambs, a hare and a bird. In Hesiod
we encounter the *thumos* of a lion.[87] Some of these passages in Homer
describe the death of an animal in terms of the loss of *thumos*. But
thumos can also refer to the strength of the living animal as in the
case of a wild boar (*Il.* 17.22) and the horses of Achilles (*Il.* 17.451).

In human beings death too is frequently described in terms of the
loss of *thumos*.[88] When *noos* or *phrenes* are described as lost, an absence
of function is indicated. *Thumos* is different: when it is lost, so usually
is life. A bow can remove *thumos* (*Od.* 4.153), as can disease (*Od.*

---

[87] For specific references see Sullivan (note 3), *Emerita*, 1993, on *Theog.* 833.
[88] See references in Caswell, pp. 12–16 and Sullivan as in note 87, pp. 146–7.

11.200), and so most often can an outside agent. Thus Priam fears
that someone 'will deprive him of his *thumos*' (*Il.* 22.68).

But the loss is not always permanent. *Thumos* can depart in a swoon
and return again. Andromache faints at the sight of the dead Hector: her *psychē* departs, but on recovery it is her '*thumos* that is gathered into *phrēn*' (*Il.* 22.475). In death *thumos* itself can 'leave the bones'
(as at *Il.* 12.386) or 'fly off' (as at *Od.* 10.163). We see then that the
presence of *thumos* is necessary for life. It can be temporarily absent
but not for long. It provides, it seems, the vital energy necessary for
consciousness and life in the limbs.

What is the relation of person and *thumos* in Homer? Of all psychic entities it emerges most distinctly from the person. As an active
agent within, it is particularly influential. Very often does it 'order',
'stir up', 'urge on', or 'drive' someone (as at *Il.* 10.534, *Od.* 14.246).
But more than this occurs: people speak to their *thumos*. This does
not occur with *noos* or *phrēn* but is found with *kradiē*.[89] Above, with
reference to intellectual activities, we heard of Odysseus speaking to
his *thumos* when stranded in battle (*Il.* 11.403). He does the same
twice when he is shipwrecked, at a loss about what action to take
(*Od.* 5.355, 406). Achilles likewise 'speaks to his great-hearted *thumos*'
when worried about the fate of Patroclus (*Il.* 18.5). The discussion
that takes place is then summed up by the phrase, 'while he pondered in *phrēn* and *thumos*' (18.15). These descriptions, found in formulaic expressions, emphasize the distinctness of person and *thumos*.

Thumos is very active within but a person also exerts considerable
control over it. One can 'restrain', 'conquer', 'delight', 'grieve', 'profit',
and 'satisfy' it.[90] These relationships too point to the distinctiveness
of person and *thumos*. But this psychic entity can also work in harmony with a person. It serves as a location of activity. It can be a
tool. It can accompany someone in activity, adding its own contribution. In all these instances person and *thumos* work in co-operation
and harmony. But even though distinct, *thumos* can often be the bearer,
to some degree, of an individual's qualities. In sum we can say of
thumos that it is a vibrant source of energy within, strongly influencing the person who may need to control it. It allows the individual
to stay alive and ever significantly affects behaviour.

---

[89] For *kradiē* see *Od.* 20.17–18 discussed below.
[90] See, for example, *Od.* 11.105, *Il.* 9.496, *Od.* 1.407, *Il.* 6.202, *Il.* 7.173, and *Od.*
8.98. See too Hes., *W. & D.* 315 and 335.

Lyric and Elegiac Poets

General Picture

Once again *thumos* is prominent and active.[91] It is found in over 130 passages. As always we deal in this poetry with specific themes, restrictive metres, and fragmentary evidence. But the first of these, which often focus upon human involvement in emotion, may partly explain the frequent appearance of *thumos*, so often concerned with emotion. As in Homer, *thumos* occurs always in the singular, whether spoken of as belonging to one or more persons.

Thumos shows in the lyric and elegiac poets the same broad range of activity as in Homer, the *Homeric Hymns*, and Hesiod. First, it acts as a seat of emotion; anger, joy, pain, grief, desire, courage, and endurance are found in it. It is frequently involved with love. Second, it is much concerned with thinking, pondering, and knowing and is a factor in the process of decision-making. Third, it is associated with volitional activities, such as desiring, choosing, and wishing. It can draw a person into different types of behaviour, not all admirable.

In the lyric and elegiac poets *thumos* has certain particular associations. It is often mentioned in relation to young people. It is much involved in friendship. In fighting and war its nature is of great importance. It can make the achievement of excellence possible. In moral choices it is very active. Death is still described in terms of the loss of *thumos* but rarely in the extant poetry we have. We still hear of the *thumos* of animals, namely that of pigeons and lions.[92]

We see *thumos* closely connected with the moral behaviour of individuals. This connection with moral action is strongly related to themes found in these poets, especially those in Pindar.[93] But the extent to which *thumos* can be a bearer of someone's qualities is significant. We hear it described by a range of adjectives. On the positive side, it can be 'courageous', 'gracious', 'gentle', 'kindly', 'moderate', and 'wise'. On the negative side it can be 'sinful', 'raging', 'pitiless', 'greedy', and 'sluggish'. It displays too a characteristic we observed of *noos*: 'it changes with the day'.[94]

---

[91] On *thumos* in the lyric and elegiac poets see Furley, Jarcho, Luck, Marg, Onians, Snell, *Tyrtaios*, *Der Weg*, Sullivan (note 3), and Treu.

[92] See Sa. 42, Tyr. 13, Sim., Epig. 83 (b), Pin., *Is.* 4.46, Bacch. 1.143.

[93] See in more detail the discussion of *thumos* in Pindar below.

[94] See Arch. 131; '*thumos* is such as Zeus brings on the day'. Cf. *Theog.* 966 where a '*thumos* suited to the day' is called for. On *noos* see above notes 28–9.

Thumos, as in earlier poets, is vulnerable to outside influences. Evil deeds, poverty, and cares can damage it. The gods can directly affect it, especially Aphrodite in situations of love. When *thumos* is thus affected, so greatly is overall behaviour.

In terms of the relationship of person and *thumos*, we see that, as in Homer and Hesiod, the two remain quite distinct. *Thumos* is very active as an agent within the individual. As in Homer, in the lyric and elegiac poets a person speaks directly to *thumos*.[95] It is called on to be strong, to endure, to behave in particular ways, or to be young. These passages show its independent activity and the ways in which a person tries to guide or influence it. In many passages a person directly affects *thumos*, often controlling it. Once again these passages suggest the vibrant activity of *thumos* within. *Thumos* can also prove a psychic entity useful to the person. It functions as a location, instrument, or accompaniment to action. Person and *thumos* in such instances act in harmony. In general *thumos* is a seat of energy, filled itself with desires and open to the influence of person or outside agent. It is ever distinct from the individual in whom it is found, able to affect conduct in a variety of ways.

Specific Passages
Certain poems from the lyric and elegiac poets present a vivid picture of *thumos*. Archilochus addresses his in 128:[96]

> *Thumos, thumos*, confounded by troubles without remedy,
> up, ward off your enemies, putting forth
> your chest and taking a stand near them
> firmly. And neither winning, boast openly,
> nor defeated, collapse at home giving way to grief.
> And do not rejoice excessively in joys
> nor be too vexed in troubles.
> Know what sort of constraint holds human beings.

Archilochus treats the changing fortunes that a person encounters

---

[95] See Arch. 128, Iby. 317b, Theog. 695, 877, 1029, 1070a, Pin., *Ol.* 2.89, *Nem.* 3.26, fr. 123.1, 127.4. See also discussion below on Arch. 128. In this context in Homer *thumos* did not appear in the vocative case but as an object of verbs of 'speaking to'. In these poets it now appears in the vocative.

[96] There are difficulties with the text in lines two and three but the sense seems somewhat clear. On the fragment see Burnett, pp. 48–9, Kirkwood, *Greek Monody*, p. 36, Podlecki, *Early Greek Poets*, pp. 43–5, and N.F. Rubin, 'Radical Semantic Shifts in Archilochus', *CJ*, 1981, vol. 77, pp. 1–8.

during life. It is *thumos* that is much involved with such changes. He addresses it twice, attracting, so to speak, its attention and drawing it away from some extreme reaction it may be showing. He urges restraint and resistance to any form of excessive response.

In this poem Archilochus uses the imagery of fighting. Life is to be seen as a battle which brings 'troubles without remedy'. *Thumos* at the moment is 'confounded' by these and must recover. Perhaps the first thing it must realise is that these problems are 'without remedy'. The challenge is not so much to solve them as to live through them with some perspective. As a soldier, *thumos* is to fight bravely. It is to take a firm stand against the foe, the troubles that assail it. Sometimes it may win; then it is not to exult too greatly. At other times, it will fail and on these occasions it is not to collapse and grieve excessively. It is not to be too happy in joy nor too distressed in sorrows. One truth it should recognise: a 'constraint' holds human beings.

This 'constraint' (*rhuthmos*) imposes limits to extremes for humans.[97] If one but wait, hardship will end. But joy too will not be boundless. Yielding to the positive and exulting too greatly is foolish and short-sighted. Such behaviour may make *thumos* unprepared for the opposite situation. But surrendering to the negative may be even more dangerous, since it removes initiative. Archilochus calls for this at the beginning of the poem. He urges *thumos* to pattern itself after the 'constraint' that objectively exists in human affairs. By imposing limits in response and behaviour, *thumos* will make existence more bearable and realistic for the person in whom it is found.

The range of function of *thumos* in this poem is very broad. First, it is connected with fighting. This association is frequent in Homer and Hesiod. So too Tyrtaeus (10.17) and Callinus (1.1) call for a 'valiant *thumos*' in war. Pindar speaks of a goddess urging on the warlike *thumos* of someone in battle (*Nem.* 9.37).[98] Second, this *thumos* suffers, 'confounded by troubles without remedy' (*amēchanos*). Theognis likewise describes someone 'stretched out in *thumos*' (646). Elsewhere he urges drinking for the person 'distressed in *thumos*' (989). Pindar

---

[97] On this meaning of *rhuthmos* see Jaeger, *Paideia*, pp. 123–6, R. Renehan, 'The Derivation of *Rhuthmos*', *CP*, 1963, vol. 58, pp. 36–8, and Rubin (note 96), p. 5.

[98] Cf. Arch. 98.16 where *thumos* is 'great' in battle, Tyr. 10.24 where a soldier dies, 'breathing forth his courageous *thumos*', and Mim. 14.1 where a person's 'strength and courageous *thumos*' in fighting are mentioned.

says that immediate concerns in particular 'disturb *thumos*' (*Nem.* 6.57). Bacchylides describes someone 'whose *thumos* the most trivial cares upset' (1.179).[99]

Third, *thumos* shares in joy. Semonides similarly speaks of a rich man 'delighting *thumos*' (7.70). Theognis several times associates *thumos* with happiness, especially in revelry (for example, 1070a, 1122). Pindar likewise talks of 'giving joy to *thumos*' (*Ol.* 7.43, *Is.* 7.2). Bacchylides asks 'what greater profit could be for human beings than to delight *thumos*' (fr. 20 B 20). But *thumos* is involved in pain too. Semonides suggests that we should not 'hold our *thumos* on evil pains' (1.24).[100] Theognis, in a passage echoing 128 of Archilochus, urges *thumos* to endure and not to increase 'its pain over things that cannot be accomplished' (1029–36). Elsewhere he speaks of a *thumos* in a 'painful state' (1091). In one poem Pindar describes himself as 'distressed in *thumos*' (*Is.* 8.52). Bacchylides says that there is 'one goal, one path of good fortune for mortals, if someone can pass through life, having a *thumos* without grief' (fr. 11.2).

Finally in this poem of Archilochus we see *thumos* connected with knowing or realising a truth. Theognis similarly speaks of one knowing or understanding in *thumos* (1247, 1305). He says also that one could not satisfy *thumos* with enough 'wisdom' (1160). Pindar speaks of people 'moderate and wise in *thumos*' (*Is.* 8.26).[101]

One important feature that *thumos* displays in 128 of Archilochus is that it is very capable of change. It can modify itself. By imposing limits on its own reactions, it can make life more endurable for the person in whom it is found. In so doing, it would match the 'constraint' present in human life. In this appeal to *thumos*, we see its great capacity for acting as an independent agent in the person.

In a second passage from the lyric and elegiac poets Simonides gives a negative picture of *thumos* (8.1–6).[102] He begins by referring to Homer:

> One very fine thing the man of Chios said: 'as is
> the generation of leaves, so too is that of humans'.
> Few mortals, hearing this with their ears,

---

[99] Cf. Alcaeus who suggests we should not 'entrust our *thumos* to troubles' (335). Mimnermus says that 'many evils take place in *thumos*' (2.11).

[100] See the discussion of this poem above in the section on *noos*.

[101] Cf. Alc. 129.22 where Pittacus fails to 'reckon in *thumos*' and Theog. 1050 where, as in Homer and Hesiod, information is to be placed in *thumos* and *phrenes*. Pindar describes the *thumos* of Pelias as 'shrewd' (*Pyth.* 4.73).

[102] I follow West in ascribing this poem to Simonides rather than to Semonides

place it in their breasts. For hope is present to each
    person and this grows in the chests of the young. As long
as some mortal possesses the very lovely flower of youth,
    having an empty *thumos*, this one thinks
many things that will not be brought to fulfilment.

Simonides continues in the poem (7–13), saying that such a person never expects to grow old or to die, or, being healthy, to face illness.[103] Those whose *noos* lies in this way are 'foolish'. They do not realise 'how brief is the time of youth and life for mortals'. He urges the reader to grasp these truths and to live to the end of life 'delighting *psychē* with good things'.

Simonides refers here to Homer's famous description of humans as resembling the 'generations of leaves' (*Il.* 6.146–8, cf. 21.464–6). The poem echoes Semonides 1, treated under *noos*. In that poem Semonides says that human beings, unlike Zeus, fail to have any grasp of the future: *noos* is lacking. Because of this they live on 'hope', assuming ever that blessings will appear. Such blessings do not, and troubles come instead. He suggests that we should live without letting our *thumos* be disturbed by evils.[104]

In the poem of Simonides we hear once again of how hope can delude. This time it is *thumos* that is 'empty' or 'fickle'. It devises plans that will prove impracticable because they are based on 'hope' for a life in which there are no ills. In such persons *noos* is foolish. Hope distorts the function of both *thumos* and *noos*. It keeps the young person from realising the shortness of youth and life. Simonides' advice, therefore, is to 'delight *psychē*' all during life.

This poem illustrates an important feature of psychic entities: the way they can overlap in meaning. As mentioned above, these entities often display similar characteristics and can function in similar ways. In our discussions thus far we have focused upon features that make them distinctive. In this poem we see that *thumos*, an 'empty' one, is first mentioned as thinking poorly because of hope. When the thoughts are specified, we hear that their source is *noos*. Clearly the two entities are closely connected with no clear distinction made between them.

(usually numbered 29). For a discussion of authorship see Adkins, *Poetic Craft*, p. 167, and West, *Studies*, pp. 179–80.

[103] On this poem see Adkins, *Poetic Craft*, pp. 166–73, and Campbell, *Golden Lyre*, pp. 213–14.

[104] Cf. similar advice given by Pindar in *Nem.* 3.59–60, treated above under *phrēn*.

Elsewhere we encounter *thumos* and *noos* mentioned together. In three passages Theognis describes these two entities as functioning equally in some situation.[105] But at 631 he suggests that *noos* should be stronger than *thumos* or else a person will always be 'in deceptions (*atai*) and helplessness' (*amēchaniai*). In this last instance *thumos*, it appears, can with its activity negatively affect a person's situation and capacity to cope. In the poem of Simonides, however, *thumos* and *noos* are equally misled by hope.[106]

This poem of Simonides gives interesting information about *thumos*. It is associated with hope.[107] It can be 'empty' or 'fickle'. *Thumos* is described thus only here in the these early poets but elsewhere we do hear of an 'empty *noos*' (see above, note 26). In this poem we see an association of *thumos* with youth; in them its state is negative. Theognis similarly speaks of a negative connection of these two, mentioning *noos* as well: 'youth and young impetuosity make *noos* empty and lift *thumos* into wrong-doing in many things' (629–30). Here he says that youth does not merely cause *thumos* to have bad judgement but leads it to immoral behaviour. In contrast, other passages in the lyric and elegiac poets suggest that in youth *thumos* can function in particular as a seat of joy.[108]

Simonides describes a *thumos* that functions poorly. Because it fails to grasp reality and to face the cruel aspects of existence, it forms plans that prove impossible. Its dreams and goals depend on the 'flower of youth' continuing without pause. Such cannot be. This poem complements in some ways the one of Archilochus we discussed above. Archilochus calls for hope when a situation is terrible and for restraint when all is flourishing. Thus, Archilochus suggests a positive role for hope; this hope does not mislead but takes into account change in human affairs, change that he regards as an objective reality. Things will eventually get better. On the other hand, just as Simonides too observes, excessive joy that is blind to the possibility of change simply misleads. In such a situation Archilochus calls for moderation. Then, as Simonides would agree, *thumos* will not be 'empty'. With some control over thought and response, it may be possible to live life 'delighting *psychē*'.[109]

---

[105] See Theognis 375, 630, and 1053. Cf. *Il.* 4.309 and *Od.* 14.490.

[106] Note that *phrēn* too is affected by hope: Pind., *Is.* 2.43 and Bacch. 20 B 8.

[107] See also Arch. 181 where *thumos* 'hopes' and Bacch. 10.45 where people express specific hopes in it.

[108] See Anac. 375, Theog. 877, 983, 1122, 1305, 1325 and Pin., *Pyth.* 4.295.

[109] On *psychē* see further in chapter 3.

Another feature of *thumos* is important in the lyric and élegiac poets: its connection with immoral behaviour. In line 630 of Theognis (quoted above), he says that youth leads *thumos* to 'wrong-doing' (*amplakiē*). At 386 he says that poverty does the same. At 733 he suggests that 'crooked deeds' should be what please evil people in their *thumos*. At 199 he says that if someone 'unjustly possesses wealth with greedy *thumos*', at first it may bring 'profit' but eventually it becomes an 'evil'. At 754 Theognis praises the person having 'a moderate *thumos* outside recklessness'.[110]

Certain passages in Pindar and Bacchylides likewise suggest the connection of *thumos* with moral behaviour. Pindar relates *thumos* to the achievement of excellence (*aretē*).[111] In *Ol.* 8.4–7 he says that people consult Zeus at Olympia to see

if he has any message about human beings
striving to take
great excellence with *thumos*,
and space to breathe after labours.

In the realm of athletic achievement *thumos* is involved. Elsewhere Pindar describes the sons of Aeacus as those 'willing to cherish a *thumos* familiar with contest' (*Nem.* 7.10). This *thumos*, pursuing excellence, will clearly display courage. Pindar describes the athlete Melissus as 'similar in *thumos* to the daring of loud-thundering lions' (*Is.* 4.46).[112] Bacchylides says that Theseus, when challenged, had a '*thumos* that did not bend back' (17.82). In *Nem.* 11.32 Pindar presents a contrast to this courageous kind of *thumos* that allows admirable behaviour. If someone has an 'unadventuresome *thumos*', it 'draws him back by the hand and deprives him of honours rightly his'. Heredity may give a person a rightful claim to high achievement but if *thumos* lack daring, it will discourage risk and prevent accomplishment.

Pindar also relates *thumos* to honesty (*Pyth.* 2.73–4):

Rhadamanthus fared well because he received
as his lot the blameless fruit of *phrenes*
nor did he delight
thumos within by deceits.

---

[110] Solon similarly remarks that Zeus always discovers the individual who has a 'sinful *thumos*' (47).

[111] On *aretē* see also below, chapter 4.

[112] Cf. *Is.* 6.47–9 where Heracles prays that his son have a *thumos* of a lion and Bacch. 1.143 who likewise mentions someone having 'the *thumos* of a lion'.

The judge in the underworld had *phrenes* that functioned well, especially in moral situations. He also had a *thumos* that resisted deceit. We see that *thumos* could take delight in such and perhaps does in many people. Rhadamanthus' *thumos* refused to do so.

In the case of Achilles, Pindar says of Chiron, the centaur who taught him: 'he nurtured the glorious offspring [of Thetis], increasing his *thumos* in all things fitting' (*Nem.* 3.58). Chiron did this so that Achilles might excel in fighting at Troy. In whatever was suitable for warlike endeavour, Chiron made *thumos* more ready, more eager, and more courageous. Its condition was an important factor in Achilles' being the best warrior at Troy.

Bacchylides suggests another moral association of *thumos*. At 3.78–84 Apollo says to Admetus:

> being mortal, you should foster
> two opinions, that you will see
>   only tomorrow's light of the sun,
> and that you will complete a life of
>   fifty years with much wealth.
> Doing holy acts, delight *thumos*, for
>   this is the highest of gains.

Although human beings are uncertain about the future, they should keep two possibilities in mind. If life is to be soon over, they should take time to 'delight *thumos*'. If life is to be long and prosperous, this itself will prove a cause of joy. However long the life, the happiness experienced in *thumos* appears to be of crucial importance; to have this will prove the 'greatest gain'. But such joy must be attended by a specific form of action: holy deeds. These deeds will keep a person in the right relationship with the divine. Then the act of delighting *thumos* can be free from any blame.[113]

These specific passages from the lyric and elegiac poets have demonstrated wide-ranging features of *thumos*. As a psychic entity within the person, its nature impressively influences behaviour. Archilochus urges it to adapt to the way change fashions human existence. Simonides suggests that it must not be misled by unrealistic hopes. Pindar describes it as a significant factor in the achievement of excellence. Bacchylides says that happiness in *thumos* during life is the

---

[113] Contrast this activity with Bacch. 17.23 where Theseus rebukes Minos for no longer 'guiding a holy *thumos* in *phrenes*'.

'greatest of gains'. *Thumos* is clearly an element to which the individual must carefully relate.

Presocratics

In the Presocratic philosophers *thumos* is mentioned rarely. The fragmentary nature of our evidence may be partly responsible for this situation but probably even more important is the focus upon rational thinking these philosophers show in their work. The rare appearance of *thumos* is significant since it suggests that for them this entity had probably become strongly associated with emotion. This emotional aspect will appear in four of the six passages where it appears. Nor is the picture of *thumos* we encounter there a positive one: in three of these passages it is negative. Let us look at what the Presocratics say.

Heraclitus in B 85 says:[114] 'it is difficult to fight *thumos*, for what it wishes it buys at the expense of *psychē*'. The meaning of *psychē* in Heraclitus will be discussed more fully in the next chapter. It is sufficient here to say that it is the soul of the individual, the source of life, and the seat of intelligence. This last function is of great importance for Heraclitus because associated with *psychē* is *logos*. As discussed above under *noos*, Heraclitus describes the divine principle as *logos*. Human beings, sharing in this capacity, partake in the divine nature, and are consequently able to understand how the universe works. What B 85 states is that *psychē* is vulnerable.

It is *thumos* that harms *psychē* by lessening it. Much discussion has taken place concerning the meaning of *thumos* in this fragment.[115] It is usually taken as 'anger' or 'desire'. As such, it is assumed to have become simply an emotion within *psychē* and to be no longer a separate psychic entity within the person. But the fragments of Heraclitus may be too early for *thumos* to have acquired such a role. It is true that *psychē* over the years does gradually become the most important

---

[114] For bibliography on Heraclitus see note 35. On B 85 see Conche, *Héraclite*, pp. 350–3, S.M. Darcus, '*Thumos* and *Psychē* in Heraclitus B 85', *RSC*, 1977, vol. 25, 353–9, W.K.C. Guthrie, vol. 1, p. 433, Kahn, *Art and Thought*, pp. 241–3, Kirk, Raven, and Schofield, p. 208 n. 2, J. Mansfeld, 'Heraclitus Fr. B 85 DK', *Mnemosyne*, 1992, vol. 45, pp. 9–18, Marcovich, pp. 383–6, T.M. Robinson, pp. 134–5, W.J. Verdenius, 'A Psychological Statement of Heraclitus', *Mnemosyne*, 1943, vol. 11, pp. 115–21, Wright, *Presocratics*, p. 73.

[115] See in particular Conche, *Héralcite*, pp. 351–2, Darcus (note 114), pp. 353–4, Kahn, *Art and Thought*, pp. 241–3, and T.M. Robinson, pp. 134–5.

psychic entity within the person, absorbing functions connected with
thumos, *noos*, and *phrēn* and other psychic entities (see next chapter).
But this change in *psychē* takes place slowly. It is also often the case
in this early literature, as pointed out at the beginning of this chapter, that the distinction between agent and function is not clearly
drawn. In B 85, therefore, *thumos* could be both an agent of emotion
and emotion itself. Consequently, to interpret *thumos* only as emotion
may be too narrow an approach.

Thumos, in other fragments of the Presocratics and also in other
passages of the lyric and elegiac poets, when it is mentioned with
psychē, appears still to be a separate psychic entity.[116] *Thumos*, then, in
B 85 may function in a similar way. It may act as a seat of emotion.
This emotion could be anger, but is more likely desire. *Thumos* 'buys'
what it wishes at the expense of *psychē*. The picture is one of *thumos*
wanting something and itself perhaps increasing as it achieves its
wishes.[117] It does so by diminishing *psychē*. In the thought of Heraclitus,
this may mean that, as *thumos* expresses emotion, *psychē* as seat of
intelligence (*logos*) is lessened. An emotional person, having more *thumos*
and less *psychē*, would not apparently show a high degree of rationality. Such an individual could not act according to *logos*, the divine
principle. This loss of rationality that occurs when *thumos* predominates may explain why Heraclitus in B 110 says that 'it is not better
for human beings to acquire whatever they desire'.

We see, therefore, in this fragment of Heraclitus a negative picture of *thumos*. By its activity within the person, it harms *psychē*, considered the more valuable entity. A person is called on to resist *thumos*
but this is said to be 'difficult'. Why? Apparently because *psychē* has
been lessened with the very activity of *thumos*. The latter dominates
the person who must try to resist it.

In our second passage from the Presocratics, a saying ascribed to
Democritus, though of questionable authenticity,[118] echoes B 85: 'it
is difficult to fight *thumos*, but to conquer it is the sign of a very
rational person' (B 236). Here *thumos* again may be an agent of emotion

---

[116] For *thumos* and *psychē* together in the lyric and elegiac poets, see Tyr. 10.13,
12.18, Theog. 910, and Bacch. 5.79–82.
[117] We heard of *thumos* increasing in earlier authors: *Il.* 17.226, *Od.* 2.315, Hes.,
Theog. 641, fr. 317, Pin., *Nem.* 3.58, Bacch. 10.45.
[118] See the discussion of the ethical fragments ascribed not to 'Democritus' but to
'Democrates' in W.K.C. Guthrie, vol. 2, pp. 489–97.

or emotion itself. Once again it appears to be a negative presence within, one that the rational person will master.

The other references to *thumos* in the Presocratics occur in Parmenides and Empedocles. Parmenides mentions it in the opening of his poem as he describes the journey he takes to receive the truth: 'the mares that bear me as far as my *thumos* aspires carried me on my way' (1.1).[119] Parmenides thus associates *thumos* with the desire he has to grasp the nature of the universe. In this case it expresses a positive emotion.

Empedocles mentions *thumos* three times.[120] Twice in the *Purifications* he refers to it as the 'seat of life', unknowingly removed from animals by those not understanding the transmigration of souls (B 128.10, B 137.6). They 'tear out *thumos*' and devour the flesh. In these fragments we see a connection of the loss of *thumos* with death, one that occurred often in Homer. In another fragment from the *Purifications* Empedocles says that people should avoid Strife, the destructive principle at work in the universe. He tells them that failing this: 'distressed by painful wickedness, you will never free your *thumos* from wretched grief' (B 145). Here *thumos* functions as a seat of sorrow that can mar the life of the individual. Clearly the opposite state of *thumos* would be desirable.

Overview of Thumos

In this section we have treated *thumos* from Homer to the Presocratics. As the most prominent psychic entity in the person in Homer, it strongly influences behaviour. Remaining distinct from the individual in whom it is found, it can be independent agent, location, instrument, or accompaniment to action. It can act separately from a person or in harmony and co-operation with the individual. More distinct within than *noos* or *phrenes*, it is directly addressed by different heroes. When it functions, it requires much attention. Sometimes it appears to need guidance or controlling. It endows the individual with vigour and energy. If it is lost, fainting or death result.

In the lyric and elegiac poets *thumos* functions with a similar broad range of activity. A person addresses it directly. Its nature and reactions dominate behaviour and direction for it seems necessary. It is

---

[119] On Parmenides in general, see above note 42.
[120] On Empedocles in general, see above note 39.

very much associated with emotional activity. It has too a strong involvement with moral action.

In the Presocratics *thumos* is rarely mentioned. No longer does it have a strong association with intellectual activity, as in Homer. Instead, it is seen as a seat of emotion, capable of beings at odds with rational thought.

Overall, *thumos* is a vital presence within the person. It can act with energy and strength and lead someone to great success. It can overact and bring about a negative state of the individual. One needs always to recognize its activity within, whether it is to be followed, directed, or controlled.

Kradiē, Ētor, and Kēr

Homer and Hesiod

We shall look briefly at the three terms that express 'heart' in early Greek poetry.[121] These are *kradiē* (or *kardiē*), *ētor*, and *kēr*. These psychic entities have a strongly physical aspect as the 'heart' within, endowing life by its activity. But each also is associated with a range of emotional functions. The activities of all three are very similar but some differences are also apparent among them. Of the terms, *ētor* is most frequent (101 times in Homer and the *Homeric Hymns*, 8 in Hesiod), then *kēr* (81, none in Hesiod), then *kradiē* (62, 6 in Hesiod).

These three terms for 'heart' are found referring to gods, human beings, and various animals.[122] Each as psychic entity serves as a location of different emotions, especially joy, grief, anger, and fear. What we can say in general of the different entities is that *kradiē* and *kēr* are more often active agents within the person than *ētor*. *Kradiē*,

---

[121] On *kradiē, ētor,* and *kēr* in Homer and Hesiod see Biraud, Böhme, A. Cheyns, 'Recherche sur l'emploi des synonyms *ētor, kēr,* et *kradiē* dans l'Iliade et l'Odyssée', *Rbph*, 1985, vol. 63, pp. 15–73, Claus, Furley, Gelzer (note 2), Harrison, Jahn, Krafft, Larock, Onians, Plambôck, G. Rose, 'Odysseus' Barking Heart', *TAPA*, 1979, vol. 109, pp. 215–230, Russo and Simon, Snell, *Discovery*, S.D. Sullivan, 'The Psychic Term *Ētor*: Its Nature and Relation to Person in Homer and the *Homeric Hymns*', *Emerita*, 1994, vol. 62, forthcoming, 'The Role of *Kēr* in Homer and the *Homeric Hymns*', *Parola del Passato*, 1995, vol. 150, forthcoming, 'What's There in a Heart? *Kradiē* in Homer and the *Homeric Hymns*', *Euphrosyne*, 1995, vol. 23, forthcoming, Vivante.

[122] *Kradiē*: lion, *Il.* 20.169. *Ētor*: lion, *Il.* 17.111, 20.169, wasps, *Il.* 16.265, fawns, *Il.* 11.115. *Kēr*: lion and boar, *Il.* 12.45, horses, *Il.* 23.284.

for example, quite often 'orders' a person to perform some action (*Il.* 13.784, *Od.* 8.204). *Kēr* is more often involved in thought than the other two (*Od.* 7.82, 18.344). *Kēr* too is related to love but *kradiē* and *ētor* are not (*Il.* 9.117, *Od.* 15.245). *Ētor* is 'loosed' as a person grows weak or is 'lost' in death (*Il.* 21.114, *Od.* 22.68); not so the other two.

Let us look at a few passages to see how these entities function. *Kradiē* appears prominently in *Od.* 20.5–23 when Odysseus grew angry as he heard the maidservants going to sleep with the suitors. As he pondered in his *phrēn* and *thumos* what to do, 'his *kradiē* barked within' (13). He has to calm this *kradiē*. He addresses it directly: 'endure, my *kradiē*', reminding it of earlier sufferings it faced. His *kradiē* settles down, obeying him.

Kradiē here is a seat of Odysseus' indignant rage. Its reaction, however, in urging Odysseus to rush out in attack, might have proved fatal for him. He was greatly outnumbered by the suitors. Thus he had to control this 'heart' and take action later at a more appropriate time.

Elsewhere *kradiē* is involved in a variety of emotions, especially anger, grief, and pain. It displays different qualities: 'throbbing', 'warlike', 'stout', 'eager', and 'unyielding'. It can also be 'senseless' and 'harder than stone'.[123] *Ētor* appears in a crucial situation in the *Iliad*. In the opening scenes, when Achilles grew angry with Agamemnon: 'grief came upon the son of Peleus and his *ētor* in his shaggy breast deliberated in two ways' (*Il.* 1.188). He wonders whether to kill Agamemnon or 'to stop his anger and to check his *thumos*' (192). Since *ētor* is rarely involved with thought, its appearance here seems somewhat significant. In this passage we do not encounter calm reflection but a raging anger that presents possibilities of action. As Achilles starts to draw his sword, Athena intervenes (194–5). His *ētor* has driven him, it appears, to attack Agamemnon. This psychic entity must be resisted.

In other very emotional situations we likewise hear of *ētor*. Andromache describes her reaction as she hears the clamour after Hector's death: 'her dear *ētor* leapt' to her mouth (*Il.* 22.452). In two passages of *Iliad* 24 the admirable courage shown by Priam in his willingness to go to ransom Hector is expressed in terms of *ētor*. Hecuba, trying to stop him, says: 'your *ētor* is of iron' (*Il.* 24.205). Achilles, astonished at his arrival, says the same (*Il.* 24.521).

---

[123] For specific references see Cheyns (note 121), p. 47 and Sullivan (note 121), 'Kradiē', App. Two.

Like *kradiē*, *ētor* is involved in several emotions: joy, grief, anger, fear, and pain. In nature it is often called 'dear', the adjective probably suggesting how precious it was within.[124] *Ētor* can also be 'of iron', like *kradiē* or 'firm', 'kindly', 'bold', or 'pitiless'.[125]

Kēr too appears as a 'dear' psychic entity (*Od.* 7.309, e.g., 16.274). At *Od.* 9.413 Odysseus' 'dear *kēr* laughed' when he saw the Cyclopes accept Polyphemus' explanation that 'no-one' was hurting him. Achilles has a far different emotion in *kēr*. At *Il.* 1.491 he 'wasted away his dear *kēr* as he longed for the war-cry and battle'. In the same book of the *Iliad* Apollo is 'angry at *kēr*' as he hears the prayer of his priest Chryses telling of the wrong done to his daughter.

Like the other two psychic entities signifying 'heart', *kēr* takes part in joy, grief, pain, and anger. It can be 'noble', 'fine', 'stubborn', or 'baneful'. It is sometimes given the description of 'shaggy', suggesting strength and endurance.[126]

Lyric and Elegiac Poets

In these poets psychic entities also function as 'heart'.[127] Their emotional range increases in this poetry. *Kradiē* (or *kardia* in Pindar and Bacchylides) is found thirty-one times, *ētor*, seventeen times, and *kēr* (usually *kear* in Pindar and Bacchylides), twelve times. The three are mentioned in gods and human beings but only once in an animal: in a cerylus bird (Alcm. 26). In general the range of emotion they experience is as follows: joy, pain, courage, love, fear, hope, and enthusiasm.

In some characteristics these psychic entities are as they were in Homer: 'dear', 'valiant', 'pitiless'. But many new qualities appear.[128] *Kradiē* or *kardia* can be 'black', 'sharp', 'upright', or 'unscathed'. *Ētor* can be 'tender', 'deceitful', or 'blind'. *Kear* can be 'most holy' or 'inspired'.

---

[124] This adjective has often been thought to indicate possession but should perhaps be taken in its more literal sense. See the persuasive article of D. Robinson, 'Homeric *philos*. Love of Life and Limbs and Friendship with One's *Thumos*' in *Owls to Athens, Studies Dover* (Oxford 1992), pp. 97–108.

[125] For specific references see Cheyns, (note 121), p. 23, and Sullivan (note 121), '*Ētor*', App. Two.

[126] 'Shaggy' (*lasion*): *Il.* 2.851, 16.554. See references to other adjectives in Cheyns (note 121), p. 35 and Sullivan (note 121), *Kēr*, App. Two.

[127] On these terms in this literature see Furley, Jarcho, Krafft, Marg, Onians, S.D. Sullivan, '*Kradiē*, *Ētor*, and *Kēr* in Poetry after Homer', *Rbph*, 1995, vol. 73, forthcoming, and Treu.

[128] See Sullivan (note 127), App. Two.

Some descriptions of the three psychic entities are vivid ones. Love 'twists its way under the *kardiē*' of Archilochus (191). A fighter keeps a 'bold *ētor* cooped' under his shield (Call. 1.10). Someone can 'drive anger into *kardia*' (Pin., *Pyth.* 8.9) or be 'forged in a black *kardia* with a cold flame' (Pin., fr. 123). In the latter description, Pindar is speaking of a person unresponsive to love.

The brave Cyrene has an '*ētor* above labour' (Pin., *Pyth.* 9.32) but most people have a 'blind *ētor*' (Pin., *Nem.* 7.24). Achilles is allowed to go with those most blessed to the Tower of Cronus after death when Thetis persuades the *ētor* of Zeus to let him (Pin., *Ol.* 2.79). In this life a person 'without pain in *kear*' would be a god (Pin., *Pyth.* 10.22). Cruel pain 'stings the *kardia*' of Theseus when he sees Minos behave in an unseemly way (Bacch. 17.18).

Presocratics

These terms for 'heart' are very rare. *Kēr* does not appear. Parmenides in the proem of his poem says that the goddess tells him: 'it is necessary for you to learn all things, both the unshaken *ētor* of well-rounded truth and the opinions of mortals, in which there is no true belief' (B 1.28–30). Parmenides is to grasp the essence of truth, an essence that will prove firm and unshaken. *Ētor* here indicates the core of truth.

Empedocles refers to the 'blood around the heart' (*pericardion haima*) as 'thought' (*noēma*) (B 105.3) but does not mention the three terms. Diogenes of Apollonia refers to *kardia* as the physical heart in his description of veins (B 6).

We are not surprised to find an absence of mention of the emotional range of these three entities in the Presocratics. Their interests lie elsewhere.

Summary

In this chapter we have treated in detail the nature of three psychic entities, *noos*, *phrēn*, and *thumos* and looked briefly at *kradiē*, *ētor*, and *kēr*. Giving Homeric background, we have focused in particular on the lyric and elegiac poets and Presocratic philosophers. It is apparent that *noos*, *phrēn*, and *thumos*, though often sharing a similar range of psychological activity, have distinctive features.

In this literature *phrenes* display some physical characteristics, *thumos*, fewer, and *noos*, generally none. All three emerge very much as psychic entities with many psychological functions within the person. They each remain distinct from the individual in whom they are found. They endow the person with a variety of capabilities and influence behaviour in many ways.

Noos is especially associated with inner vision and an ability to grasp the truth, even if it eludes the senses. To a great degree it acts as a seat of a person's true thoughts, emotions, and reactions. It unfortunately does not always function within and can also be concealed from other people. But if its nature becomes evident, it reveals most about a person or god.

Except in two instances, *noos* is not explicitly mentioned as present in animals.[129] In gods and human beings, its loss signifies an absence of its function. The individual considers *noos* a positive presence and wants it to function. When it does, person and *noos* act in harmony, the person wisely heeding it. *Noos* may be what puts humans on a continuum with the divine and what makes them what they are. Of all the psychic entities, it is perhaps the most important and most valued.

Phrēn is different in many ways from *noos*. Appearing usually in the plural, it displays some physical qualities. *Phrenes*, in this aspect, are best described as a composite of psychic entities found in the chest region. *Phrenes* are found in gods, human beings, and animals. In terms of activity, they are especially concerned with deliberation and decision. It is *phrenes* that a person often relies on in coping with problems. Perhaps *noos* might be able to see an instant solution but, if it fails to function, *phrenes* prove a valuable asset.

Most often *phrenes* are an instrument that an individual uses, a location where action takes place within, or an accompaniment with its activity to some action. They are subordinate to the person, acting in co-operation or harmony within. If they are damaged or lost, they cause foolish behaviour in someone as they fail to function or do so badly. *Phrenes* serve in particular as a tool the individual may frequently find indispensable.

Thumos is the most prominent of these three psychic entities. It is found in gods, human beings, and animals. It displays few physical

---

[129] See above note 20. Anaxagoras may also assume that it is present in living things (B 11), which may include animals.

characteristics. It functions most often as a seat of vital energy within the person. Of all psychic entities it has the broadest range of function for emotional, intellectual, and volitional activities. As an independent agent within, it has particularly strong influence, ordering, guiding, and inspiring different behaviour. But its activity may not always be positive and it itself may need direction and control. *Thumos* can, however, also prove, like *phrenes*, a useful instrument or accompaniment for an individual. In such instances it acts in harmony with someone.

Thumos is an important presence within. If lost, fainting or death results, not just loss of function as with *noos* and *phrenes*. The vital energy of this psychic entity, therefore, is considered necessary for full conscious life.

All three psychic entities can act as location of someone's qualities. All prove changeable, both *noos* and *thumos* 'with the day', but some aspects of them may be enduring over the lifetime of the person. If we can validly generalize about the three, we would say that *noos* acts as a seat of an individual's true thoughts or emotions. *Phrenes* are subordinate to the person, useful, obliging, accommodating. *Thumos* is an energetic psychic entity with which the person must cope, may heed, use or, on occasion, need to control.

The three terms, *kradiē*, *ētor*, and *kēr*, designate the physical heart within the person and also psychic entities engaging chiefly in emotion. This emotion includes joy, grief, pain, fear, and anger. The three are very similar but display some differences in their involvement in emotion.

In this chapter we have set out in detail the nature of psychological activity as found in authors of the Archaic Age. To a large extent psychological activity is seen in terms of several psychic entities active within the person. Individuals are very aware of these entities functioning within. They have different relationships to them. They may have some awareness of a 'self' apart from these psychic entities but how this awareness relates to that of their psychic entities remains unclear. It is to these psychic entities that they attribute psychological activity or in them that they carry it out. In their similar yet distinct natures, these entities richly endow individuals with different capacities. So valuable are they that certain early philosophers see them as a means of understanding the universe as a whole. In analysing them we can now answer the question posed in chapter 1: how did people in early Greek literature think, feel, and will?

CHAPTER THREE

SOUL

Background

In the previous chapter we discussed how the early Greeks viewed psychological activity. We saw that they considered several psychic entities responsible for it. Predominant among these were *noos, phrēn,* and *thumos*. Although often sharing many activities, these each display individual traits, matching facets of the psychological range that humans enjoy. With respect to intellectual activities, *noos* accounts for insight, *phrenes* for deliberation, *thumos* for energetic thinking that leads to action. All take part in emotion but particularly *thumos*. All are connected with volitional activities such as desiring, daring, wishing, or ordering. We saw too the way in which *kradiē, ētor,* and *kēr* functioned as 'heart'.

If we can imagine how early Greeks saw their inner nature, we would see them observing these different psychic entities functioning within. Each is distinct, similar to the others but possessing particular traits. These entities exist to be relied upon and to be used but they are not in any way simply submissive. On the contrary, they have their own independent activity and sometimes need to be checked or controlled. Nor do the early Greeks see a closed setting within. Instead, all the entities are open to the influence of outside forces. The gods can easily affect them in positive or negative ways. What would be apparent then to our observers would be a rich capacity for psychological activity deriving from sources with distinctive natures.

As we watch these early Greeks looking within, we note something pointed out frequently in chapter 2: they have an identity distinct from these psychic entities. In their entirety these entities do not simply compose what we would call someone's 'personality' or 'self'. It is true that individuals may find in each a seat of many of their deepest qualities but none adequately expresses the full person. Nor could any, since each proves vulnerable to many outside forces and itself frequently changes. As we mentioned also in chapter 2, this way of viewing psychological activities does not mean that the early Greeks did not have a sense of 'self'.[1] They clearly did. Achilles knows very well who he is. His whole future has been determined by a choice he himself has made, the choice of an early death. Agamemnon and Odysseus are also quite aware of who they are. But what these heroes do is to take a sense of self for granted. There is no examination or analysis of this concept and there is no one term to express it fully.

This situation, however, does not persist. What we can see in Greek literature is that by the late fifth century a particular term has come to designate the seat of personality or self. This term is *psychē*.[2] Some degree of unification too has taken place with reference to psychological functions. *Psychē* becomes the seat of emotion, intellect, and will.[3] Yet in Homer and much of early Greek literature it does not function at all in the living person as a psychic entity. A significant change has taken place in the meaning of this term. In this chapter we will trace some stages in its transformation.

Homer

In Homer *psychē* is mentioned over eighty-five times. In Hesiod it appears only once at *W. & D.* 686 but what is said of it here and in three fragments proves to be of interest. We shall focus mainly on Homer. In his poems *psychē* is mentioned in the living person only when death approaches or when a death-like condition, fainting, occurs. In the living person at these times *psychē* is not connected

---

[1] See chapter 2, note 2 for bibliography on this question.

[2] On *psychē* in Homer and Hesiod see Böhme, Bremmer, Burnet, Claus, Dihle, 'Totenglaube', Dodds, Fränkel, Furley, Garland, 'Causation', *Death*, Gelzer (ch. 2, note 2), Harrison, H.G. Ingenkamp, 'Inneres Selbst und Lebensträger', *Rh. M.*, 1975, vol. 118, pp. 48–61, Jaeger, *Theology*, Jahn, Krafft, M. McDonald, 'Terms for "Life" in Homer: An Examination of Early Concepts in Psychology', *Trans. and Stud., Coll. of Physicians of Philadelphia*, 1982, vol. 4, pp. 26–58, Nehring, Onians, Otto, Redfield, O. Regenbogen, '*Daimonion Psychēs Phōs*' in *Kleine Schriften*, Munich, 1961, pp. 1–28, Rohde, Rüsche, Schaufer, Snell, *Discovery*, S.D. Sullivan, 'A Multi-Faceted Term: *Psychē* in Homer, the *Homeric Hymns*, and Hesiod', *SIFC*, 1988, vol. 6, pp. 151–180, Vivante, J. Warden, '*Psychē* in Homeric Death-Descriptions', *Phoenix*, 1971, vol. 25, pp. 95–103.

[3] This role of *psychē* has been frequently noted. See in particular Adkins, *From the Many*, pp. 62–4, Burnet, Claus, pp. 1–7, Furley, *BICS*, 1956, p. 1, W.K.C. Guthrie, vol. 3, pp. 467–9, Havelock, *History*, pp. 197–200 (1963 ed.), F. Solmsen, 'Plato and the Concept of the Soul (*Psychē*): Some Historical Perspectives', *JHI*, 1983, vol. 44, pp. 355–67, and Snell, *Discovery*, p. 14.

with any psychological activity nor with a state of consciousness. Nor do we find it located in some specific part of the body. It does not, therefore, think, feel, or will. But its presence within is none the less critical for life. If it departs or is lost, the individual dies. It consequently becomes an object of concern in situations of danger or approaching death.

When someone does die, there is a portion that survives: *psychē*. All else is lost with the body including the psychic entities responsible for psychological activities. *Noos, phrēn, thumos, kradiē, ētor, kēr*: all fade.[4] *Psychē* itself flies off to Hades where it has an unenviable existence as a pale shade, lacking all the energy and vitality that the living person possesses. But however limited its range of activity in the underworld, it is recognisably the person and alone preserves the individuality that had been present in the living body.

If we examine the passages where *psychē* is mentioned in Homer, three meanings of the term emerge. First, it is connected with breath. The word *psychē* itself is likely derived from *psychō*, meaning 'to blow'.[5] This root suggests an association with air, in particular that which someone breathes. *Psychē* in fact appears to be the breath that endows the body with life. The necessity of such breath would have been universally recognised with its permanent loss evident as a sign of death. In their form as shades in the underworld, *psychai* are perhaps conceived of as 'portions' of air.

Second, *psychē* signifies the part of the individual that survives death. This *psychē* in the underworld is called an 'image' or 'likeness' (*eidōlon*) of the person. Its motion is like that of a 'shadow' (*skia*). It may be that the shadow which a living person cast was the image the early Greeks had of *psychē* in the underworld. This shadow would have been thought to be made of dark air. It also perfectly resembled the individual. It would not be that this shadow during life was thought to be *psychē*, but when the latter left at the moment of death, its nature outside the body would match this shadow.

Psychē as the 'shade' of the dead person varies in nature to some extent depending on whether the body has been buried or not. The 'unburied' shade appears to be capable of more activities than the 'buried' one. If 'buried' shades drink blood, as Odysseus allows them to do, they likewise acquire an extended range of activities not usu-

---

[4] Teiresias is the exception who keeps *noos* and *phrenes* (*Od.* 10.493–5).
[5] On the etymology see bibliography in Bremmer, pp. 21–2, and Claus, p. 93 n. 3.

ally possible for them. But even the 'buried' *psychē*, weak and fragile, enjoys some range of activity, however limited it may be.

The third meaning of *psychē* is that of 'life', apparently without specific reference to air or to the shade in Hades. It acts as an 'energy' or 'force' that makes a person live. Usually it is taken for granted but, when threatened, its importance and value receive mention.

Of these three meanings, none appears to be primary in Homer. As pointed out in chapter 1, the rich reservoir of formulaic oral poetry upon which Homer drew had a very long history. Over the centuries varying ideas, sometimes associated with the same term, appeared. An old meaning may have lingered as new ones were added. These ideas need not necessarily have been consistent with one another; they may even have been in conflict. As Homer repeated the formulas he had inherited, he would probably make no effort to offer a consistent or limited use of any terms in the language itself.

Such a variety in range of meaning seems to have been present for *psychē*.[6] In early times, when some formulaic expressions were being fashioned, it may have signified a specific physical entity, such as air or breath. As time passed, it came, in addition, perhaps to signify the sole surviving portion of the human being and also the vital, life-giving energy in the living person. In different passages, different aspects of *psychē* may be present, sometimes one more obvious than another.

With regard to *psychē*, as we mentioned above, one question is crucial: how did it become in later authors so prominent a psychological agent within the living person? A valuable suggestion has been made that *psychē* became such in imitation of *thumos*.[7] As we have seen in chapter 2, *thumos* functions in Homer and Hesiod as a seat of energy within the person and a psychic entity with a wide range of function. It is associated with many intellectual, emotional, and volitional activities. Already in certain passages of Homer *psychē* is linked with *thumos* where both appear to have the meaning of 'life'. Someone is 'deprived' of *thumos* and *psychē* at the same time (*Il.* 11.334, *Od.* 21.154, 171). Being thus associated with *thumos*, *psychē* gradually,

---

[6] Once again we point out that in the spoken language of the time *psychē* may have had a more extended range of meaning.

[7] See Harrison, p. 77, Jaeger, *Theology*, pp. 81–3, and Warden, *Phoenix*, 1971, pp. 95–103.

it may be, took on activities connected with it. This suggestion postulates some degree of identification of *psychē* with *thumos*. Such an identification could perhaps lead to the psychological activities later ascribed to *psychē*.

This suggestion explains one possible source of the range of activities that *psychē* came to enjoy. It does not explain, however, why *psychē* ever became a psychological agent in the living person at all. What seems to be of crucial importance in this regard is the role it had as shade of the dead. This *psychē*, it is true, was seen as a frail, feeble image of the living person, one having few powers or activities. But it was all that survived someone at death. Unlike psychic entities like *noos*, *phrenes*, and *thumos*, which perished with the body, it had a form of permanent existence, however unenviable in nature. In special circumstances its powers could be extended. The picture Homer gives of *psychai* in the underworld, each a recognisable person, speaking and acting as the individual might have done during life, probably proved a very strong influence on how *psychē* came to be seen in the living person. As a shade, if enhanced by blood, it could perform various functions. A transfer of this picture to its nature while in the body is one that could easily have been made. The rich and varied picture of *psychē* in the underworld that Homer gives, therefore, contains clues for understanding why *psychē* changed the way it did. Let us look in more detail at what he shows us about *psychē*.

Psychē in the Living Person

As we said above, *psychē* is referred to in the living individual only when death impends or a death-like state occurs. *Psychē* is not specifically placed in any region of the body. What we hear is that the 'throat' is the location for the 'swiftest destruction of *psychē*' (*Il.* 22.325). This placement suggests the association of *psychē* with the 'breath of life'. When it is mentioned in the living person, usually all three meanings of *psychē* are present. It is 'breath', 'life', and also the shade that will depart.

Within the living, *psychē* has a very high value. Achilles, refusing in Book 9 to return to fight, says that all the wealth of Troy and Pytho 'are not worth' his *psychē*. It is the case, he says, that once *psychē* 'has passed the barrier of teeth', it cannot be regained (*Il.* 9.401–9). It is by Achilles' '*psychē*, knees, and parents' that Hector requests the return of his body: these three are clearly judged most dear (*Il.* 22.338). When Odysseus meets him in the underworld, Achilles presents a very different picture of *psychē* outside the living body: better to be a 'hired labourer' in the world of the living than the 'king of the dead' (*Od.* 11.488–92).

Odysseus' whole long journey home with all its wanderings and hardships is described as a quest in which he sought 'to win his *psychē*' (*Od.* 1.5). When he tried to escape from Polyphemus, Odysseus 'wove all wiles and counsel, as in a situation concerning *psychē*' (*Od.* 9.423). When Achilles pursued Hector around the walls of Troy, it was not simply for prizes awarded to runners but 'for the *psychē* of Hector' (*Il.* 22.161). Elsewhere Achilles describes himself as ever 'staking' his *psychē* in fighting (*Il.* 9.322).[8] These passages show that people strive to keep *psychē*, being most precious, within the body.

In each person a single *psychē* is to be found. Of Achilles it is said: 'in him is one *psychē* and people say that he is mortal' (*Il.* 21.569). Even though Achilles may be a warrior terribly to be feared, he still has but one 'vital energy', one 'life' and only 'one' shade to fly to Hades. *Psychē* very much wishes to stay in the body. When Hector died, 'his *psychē*, flying from his limbs, went to Hades, bewailing her fate, leaving manliness and youth' (*Il.* 22.362).[9] *Psychē* laments its fate if it must leave. In some way it perceives its loss, when it departs, and its own feeble nature. One reason that Achilles may have prized his *psychē* so greatly, while it was in his body (*Il.* 9.401), is that there it enjoyed in his case too 'manliness and youth'. These had to be forfeited at death. *Psychē*, it appears, perceives in some degree the fragile and helpless state it will have in the underworld. It knows what it is losing and will never have again.

Sometimes *psychē* can leave for a short time and return. This happens in fainting.[10] At *Il.* 5.696–8 Sarpedon faints: '*psychē* left him and a mist was poured over his eyes. He breathed again and the North Wind . . . revived him, having breathed forth his *thumos* in an evil fashion.' Here Sarpedon's swoon is described in terms of the loss

---

[8] See too the description of the suitors 'who were fighting for their *psychē*' (*Od.* 22.245) and pirates who 'hazard' theirs (*Od.* 3.74). Hesiod says that for people who foolishly sail in the spring, 'money' has become *psychē* (*W. & D.* 686); usually *psychē* would be the treasure.

[9] The same description is given of Patroclus at *Il.* 16.856.

[10] On fainting see especially H. Nehring, 'Homer's Description of Syncopes', *CP*, vol. 42, pp. 106–21 and Schnaufer, pp. 191–201.

of both *psychē* and *thumos*. It illustrates the close association of the two. Recovery comes from 'breathing again': *psychē* is drawn back into the body. Andromache also 'breathes forth *psychē*' when she faints at the news of Hector's death (*Il.* 22.467). Her recovery takes place when '*thumos* is gathered into *phrēn*' (475).

At the moment of death, *psychē* leaves in different ways. It can 'speed away', 'hastening' through a 'stricken wound' (*Il.* 14.518). It can 'pass' through the 'barrier of the teeth' (*Il.* 9.409). It can 'fly' from the limbs (*Il.* 16.856). Or it can simply 'leave' (*Od.* 18.91) and 'go down' to Hades (*Il.* 7.330). All references are to *psychē* in a human being except for one where its departure results in the death of a boar (*Od.* 14.426). Animals too can have *psychē*, 'life', but the continued existence of this *psychē* after death seems unlikely.[11]

Within the living person *psychē* is vulnerable in different ways. At *Il.* 1.3 the 'anger' of Achilles 'cast many strong (*iphthimos*) *psychai* of heroes into Hades'. These *psychai*, present in the living, are clearly destined to become shades of the dead. In this passage Homer proceeds to contrast these *psychai* with the 'heroes themselves' whom Achilles left on the battlefield as prey for dogs and birds (1.4–5). This passage shows us that in Homer the body and various psychic entities are the location of someone's psychological activities, strength, and vigour; these stay with the hero on the battlefield.[12] *Psychē*, as we have heard, leaves behind 'manliness and youth'. While in the body, however, these *psychai* are 'strong' or 'powerful'.

It is unusual in Homer for *psychē* to be described by an adjective. We hear of 'one' *psychē* (*Il.* 21.569), or *psychē* alone (*Od.* 11.543), or 'other' *psychai* (*Od.* 11.541, 564) and, as we shall see below, several activities ascribed to *psychē* with participles ('grieving', e.g., or 'lamenting'). The adjective 'strong' (*iphthimos*), therefore, appearing with *psychē* at 1.3 is unique. Its meaning has been much discussed.[13] Another passage sheds light on its usage with *psychē*. At *Il.* 11.55 Zeus 'is about to cast many strong heads (*iphthimoi kephalai*) to Hades'. In contrast, in Hades, the dead are described as 'heads', but 'powerless' ones (*Od.* 10.521, e.g., or 11.29). Within the body, then, both '*psychai*'

---

[11] As we noted in chapter 2, *noos* is rarely found in animals but *phrenes* and *thumos* are. See in chapter 2 notes 20, 54, 86, and 94.

[12] On the nature of the body in Homer see especially R. Renehan, 'The Meaning of *Sōma* in Homer: A Study of Methodology', *CSCA*, 1979, vol. 12, pp. 269–82.

[13] See in particular Claus, pp. 61–2, and J. Warden '*Iphthimos*: A Semantic Analysis', *Phoenix*, 1969, vol. 23, pp. 143–58.

and 'heads' may have vitality and vigour, perhaps given by the body. This unique description of *psychē* suggests strength present in it; this description also points to the future when *psychē* within the body will have its own powers.

Finally, within the living, *psychē* is vulnerable to the actions of others. Hector hoped to 'take away' the *psychē* of Achilles (*Il.* 22.257) but Achilles instead 'took away' his 'with the long-edged bronze' (*Il.* 24.754). The bow of Odysseus can 'rob princes of *thumos* and *psychē*' (*Od.* 21.154, 171). *Psychē* is the one element that must be present for life. With its removal, death is inevitable. Thus, Odysseus says to Polyphemus: 'would that I, making you bereft of *psychē* and life (*aiōn*), could send you to the house of Hades' (*Od.* 9.523). Once a person is 'bereft' of *psychē*, existence is possible only as a shade in the underworld. It is as *psychē* that Polyphemus would go to Hades. In these lines we see an apparent identification of the pronoun 'you' and the form in which Polyphemus would appear among the dead. This identification seems quite natural and occurs frequently in passages describing the shades in Hades. Its significance lies in equating the person and the *psychē* that has been separated from the body. Later the two will become closely associated within the living person. This early identification may have been a crucial factor in the new role *psychē* was to have in the living. We shall discuss other instances of this phenomenon below.

Psychē After Death

How were the inhabitants of the underworld spoken of by Homer? We shall look in some detail at their nature as *psychai*. But other descriptions are given of them as well. In addition to being *psychai*, these inhabitants are also called 'shades', *skiai*, that 'flit about' (*Od.* 10.495). They are described too as an 'image' or 'likeness' (*eidōlon*) of the person (e.g., *Od.* 11.83). Individuals are thus recognizably themselves in their life apart from the body. These dwellers in Hades, as mentioned above, are also called 'powerless heads of the dead' (e.g., *Od.* 10.521). They are frequently referred to as 'dead bodies' (e.g., *Od.* 11.49) or 'senseless corpses' (*Od.* 11.475). Odysseus tries to embrace Anticleia, his mother, but she flies from his arms 'like a shadow or a dream' (*Od.* 11.206–8). What the dead lack is any 'firm strength or might' (*Od.* 11.393). Their powers are very limited and their condition, a negative one.

Turning now to *psychē*, we find more detail about its existence in Hades. Very important for this information will be Books 11 and 24 of the *Odyssey*, the First and Second Nekyia, in which a picture of the underworld is given. Serious problems exist concerning the composition of these portions of the *Odyssey*.[14] For our purposes, however, it will suffice to present an overview of the evidence as found in our texts.

Certain passages give a general description of the *psychai* of the dead.[15] *Psychai* are huge in number, including all categories of people (*Od.* 11.36–43). They are called the images (*eidōla*) of the dead (*Il.* 23.72, *Od.* 24.14). They are too insubstantial to be embraced (*Il.* 23.100). As it leaves for the underworld, *psychē* 'utters a shrill cry' (*Il.* 23.101). It moves 'like smoke' (*Il.* 23.100) or 'like a dream' (*Od.* 11.222).

These descriptions of the sound *psychē* makes and the way it moves very much point to its nature as breath or air. The verb expressing 'to utter a shrill cry' (*trizō*) is used as well in Homer to describe the sound of bats (*Od.* 24.6–8). What may be indicated is the shrill squeaking of air being forced out. We might hear this sound, for instance, from a balloon as it is gradually emptied. Motion 'like smoke' or 'a dream' suggests a composition of dark air, insubstantial, ethereal, and swift.

Of shades in general Achilles says: 'in the house of Hades in some way *psychē* and *eidōlon* are present, but *phrenes* are not there at all' (*Il.* 23.104). Here *psychē* and *eidōlon* are mentioned as parallel terms: 'breath' and the 'image' or 'likeness' of the individual remain after death. But *phrenes* are absent: the psychological activities a person enjoyed, namely, thought, emotion, will, are lost with the body. These *psychai* appear to be weak, fragile entities. They can be summoned; they can be led (*Od.* 24.100); they can be 'scattered' (*Od.* 11.385). But, however insubstantial they are, they are still individually recognisable as the person who once was alive. This feature will be significant in their later role as the seat of personality in the person.

Concerning these shades of the dead, we can speak of three categories; those 'unburied', those 'buried' but not having drunk blood,

---

[14] On the First and Second Nekyia see especially *A Commentary on Homer's Odyssey*, Oxford, 1988–92, vol. 2 (eds A. Heubeck and A. Hoekstra), pp. 73–7, and vol. 3 (eds J. Russo, M. Fernández-Galiano, and H. Heubeck), pp. 53–8, 356–9.
[15] On this topic see in particular Bremmer, pp. 70–124, Dihle, 'Totenglaube', pp. 14–20, Garland, *BICS*, 1981, p. 43, *Way of Death*, pp. 1–2, 68–9, and Schnaufer, pp. 58–124.

and those having drunk blood. In a category by themselves are the shades described in the opening of Book 24 of the *Odyssey* (the Second Nekyia). First, then, 'unburied' shades. These include Patroclus, Elpenor, and the suitors. At *Il.* 23.65–101, Patroclus appears to Achilles: 'there came the *psychē* of wretched Patroclus, like to himself in all things, size, fair eyes, and voice, and in such clothes about its skin was it clothed. It stood above his head and spoke a word to him'. The *psychē* of Patroclus resembles him as he was in body, shape, and dress. It sounds like him and can speak. When it does, it reveals more about its condition. Patroclus believes that Achilles has forgotten him (69–70). He apparently has no knowledge of the elaborate games being held in his honour. He tells how he has to wander outside Hades because his body is unburied (71–4). He retains his affection for Achilles and expresses sorrow and pity for their plight as mortals (75–9). He refers also to Achilles' death (80–1). He gives orders about how he himself is to be buried, recalling precisely details of his own life (82–92).

This *psychē* of Patroclus, however, lacks any substance that would allow Achilles to embrace him. When Achilles tries, *psychē* 'flies beneath the earth, uttering a shrill cry' (100–1). In its departure *psychē* no longer sounds like the person, but instead like the dark air that it is. Achilles sums up the behaviour of this shade of Patroclus: 'all night long the *psychē* of wretched Patroclus stood over me, lamenting and grieving, and he gave me orders on each thing and was wondrously like himself' (106–7).

Patroclus as *psychē* has a distinct range of activities missing in most other shades. Because his body is unburied, he can apparently draw upon it for some abilities. Other shades can move and express emotion. Patroclus can do more. He comes specifically to Achilles, recognising him. He speaks with a voice like his living voice. He knows that Achilles too is going to die. He expresses emotions of affection and sorrow with some intensity. He gives orders emphatically and clearly. He recalls details of his life exactly. Yet he has no knowledge of what Achilles has been doing to honour him after his death nor does he perceive why his body has not been buried. He has no substance that could make an embrace possible. His time with Achilles is short and, in his departure, he resembles other shades in movement and sound.

This picture of Patroclus is of great significance. His *psychē* possesses special characteristics because it is unburied. But these characteristics will come to be present in *psychē* as a psychological agent in the living person. It knows; it feels; it expresses its will. We have a clear foreshadowing of its later involvement in intellectual, emotional, and volitional activities.

Another unburied shade is that of Elpenor, who met his death falling from a roof in the house of Circe (*Od.* 10.552). Unlike Patroclus, he is not kept out of Hades by the other shades even though he too is unburied (*Od.* 11.51). This *psychē* of Elpenor is the first to meet Odysseus in the underworld and this may be so because he is still unburied. His *psychē* has a range of capacities. He recognises Odysseus (51) and is able to address him (59, 83). He feels sorrow (59). He wants burial, not in order to enter Hades, but to prevent any need to return to plague Odysseus (72–3). He makes requests of Odysseus (66) and asks him to remember him (71). He also gives Odysseus orders (73–8). He knows where Odysseus is going (69). This range of activities closely resembles that possessed by Patroclus. Once again, such capacities associated with *psychē* foreshadow how it will itself be described one day in the living person.

The suitors too, as they are led by Hermes down to Hades, retain certain abilities (*Od.* 24.1 f.) before their burial (417). Like Elpenor, they are allowed to enter the underworld. They 'follow' and 'go' with Hermes, 'uttering a shrill cry' (5, 9). They 'find' the shade of Achilles, apparently recognising him. One of their number, Amphimedon, is able to address Agamemnon's shade. Amphimedon vividly recalls details of the death of the suitors and knows that his body is still unburied. Once again we see capacities that *psychē* in the living person will come to exhibit.

In our treatment of *psychē* as shade of the dead, our second category includes buried *psychai* before they have drunk blood. In *Il.* 23.72 we hear of such shades that they keep the *psychē* of Patroclus away from the house of Hades and 'do not allow him to mingle across the river'. They apparently can recognise the unburied nature of Patroclus' *psychē* and exert some force in keeping it apart.

In *Od.* 11 (the First Nekyia), we see various characteristics of these shades. They can move about. They can gather together, sometimes around an individual *psychē* (36, 388). At 388 we find a picture of shades attending Agamemnon: 'other *psychai* were gathered around Agamemnon, however many died with him in the house of Aegisthus and met their fate'. Just as in life these shades attend their king whom they are still able to recognise. One inconsistency we find in the picture of shades given in Homer is that for some recognition is possible, for others the drinking of blood proves to be necessary first. In this description of Agamemnon such a capacity is present. Anticleia, the mother of Odysseus, gives a vivid description of these shades of the dead: 'for the sinews no longer hold flesh and bones, but the strong might of blazing fire overpowers them when first *thumos* leaves the white bones, and *psychē*, like a dream, flying away, flutters about' (219–22).

These *psychai* are capable of some emotion. Agamemnon's shade 'comes, grieving' (387). The *psychē* of Ajax stands apart by itself, 'angry' because Odysseus won the arms of Achilles (543). Odysseus too says of him that 'not even in death was he to forget his anger' (554) and calls on him 'to subdue his rage (*menos*) and proud *thumos*' (562). Without drinking blood, Ajax is able, it appears, to recognise Odysseus. He also nurtures his anger, so great that Odysseus applies terms used for the living person in referring to it, namely *menos* and *thumos*. Ajax, as a helpless shade, can harm Odysseus in no way but he can still remember just cause for anger and experience this emotion.

Another shade Odysseus meets is that of his mother: 'she sits in silence near the blood, nor does she dare to look at her son face to face nor to address him' (141–2). In this description we have the essence of the 'unburied' shade before drinking blood. It cannot speak. It does not recognise Odysseus.[16] It is frail and weak.

Our next category will be shades who have drunk blood. This blood gives back to *psychē* a portion of the body and the capacities the body was thought to have. What we see is the acquisition in particular of psychological activities usually connected with *noos*, *phrēn*, *thumos*, *kradiē*, *ētor*, and *kēr*. This blood gives the power of understanding and communication. It allows Teiresias to utter his prophecies (150). Even though Teiresias is a special case because, alone among the dead, he has 'steadfast *phrenes*' and '*noos*' (*Od.* 10.491–5), he still needs blood to share his knowledge of the future. This blood allows Achilles to recognise Odysseus and, with lament, to speak 'winged words' (471). In his speech he shows concern for his father and son (492–503). At Odysseus' praise of Neoptolemus, Achilles reacts with joy and departs 'with long strides over the fields of asphodel' (538–40). Other *psychai* likewise gain the power of speech from blood. They stand 'grieving' and 'ask' about those dear to them (541).

---

[16] We have noted, however, that some shades do have powers of recognition, as, for example, Ajax. Homer is not consistent about this capacity in the shades.

When they have drunk blood, *psychai* recall relationships on earth. They are filled with sorrow. They do not know what has happened to their relatives but they remember them and enquire about them. Once again we see *psychē* enhanced with powers that it will later have in the living person.

Our last category is made up of the *psychai* described in *Od.* 24 (the Second Nekyia). These are able to carry on some functions made possible only by blood in *Od.* 11 (the First Nekyia). Thus we hear that these *psychai* can 'address' each other (23, 35). In the speeches Agamemnon gives in the opening lines, he recalls with clarity Achilles' funeral (35–94), his own friendship with Amphimedon (114–19), and the evil deeds of Clytemnestra (199–202). These shades can also 'recognise' each other. Achilles and Agamemnon know who each other is and quickly perceive who the dead suitors are (101). These *psychai*, without reference to blood, have a somewhat extended range of activity. If the lines of the Second Nekyia come from the same rich reserve of formulaic epic tradition as the rest of Homer, we see *psychē* already capable of some breadth of activity, at least among the dead.

As mentioned above, Teiresias is a special case in the underworld since he still has *noos* and *phrenes* (*Od.* 10.492). Without drinking blood, he is able to recognise Odysseus and to speak to him (11.90–1). Once he has drunk blood, he prophesies. This picture of *psychē* with *noos* and *phrenes* may have influenced its later absorption of functions associated with these two psychic entities.

We have suggested above that the nature of each shade as recognisably the person probably had great importance in the emergence of *psychē* as the bearer of personality in living individuals. *Psychē* was the only part of the human being that continued to exist after death.[17] Even though its life in the underworld was one of deprivation of all the vitality, energy, and psychological range that presence in the body made possible, *psychē* lived on. Its very nature was 'life', 'breath', or 'air' and this did not cease to be. As the sole surviving portion of the person, *psychē* would later become in the living the principal bearer of traits of character.

Another important factor, as we suggested also above, in the emergence of *psychē* with psychological functions in the living person

---

[17] Certain fortunate individuals escape the fate of death. Menelaus is not to die but to go alive to the Elysian Fields where Rhadamanthus is also present (*Od.* 4.562–8). Heracles' *eidōlon* is in Hades but 'he himself' is among the gods (*Od.* 11.601).

is the identification Homer makes of *psychē* and person. He transfers
easily from noun to personal pronoun or to proper name. A few
examples will suffice. First, Anticleia. Once she has drunk blood, she
changes from the helpless *psychē* with no powers described above (*Od.*
11.141). Then it is 'she' who recognises her son Odysseus and speaks
to him, in grief (153–4). It is 'she' who knows of Penelope's loyalty
and sorrow, of Telemachus and his behaviour, and of Laertes and
his condition (180–96). Second, Agamemnon. It is 'he', having drunk
blood, who recognises Odysseus, who weeps, stretches forth his hands,
desiring to reach Odysseus, who answers, recalls his own death, and
asks about Orestes (11.390–456).

So too in Book 11 we encounter 'Minos' administering justice
among the dead who ask for judgements (11.569–70). 'Tityus', 'Tantalus', and 'Sisyphus' all pay in Hades for their crimes against the
gods (11.576–600). In each case it is the person himself who is described as carrying on these activities. The *eidōlon* of Heracles appears too in the underworld. But it is 'he' who 'glares terribly', speaks,
and goes back into Hades (11.606–8, 615–27). All these passages show
ways in which *psychē* and person could be identified in Hades, adum-
brating the role *psychē* came to have in the person when alive.

Summary of Psychē in Homer

We have looked at *psychē* in the living person and as a shade of the
dead. In the case of the latter, not surprisingly, we found some in-
consistencies in portrayal. The rich tradition of oral poetry, which
acts as a source for Homer, provided, it seems, varying ideas about
this entity that enlivens the human being and survives death.

Psychē has a wide range of activities in its different forms. Even in
the living person, where its importance is not emphasized except when
death threatens, it has different ways of leaving the person. As a
shade, its activities vary. Without blood it can move and experience
emotion. In the Second Nekyia (opening of Book 24), likewise, without blood, it can recognise other shades and speak. After drinking
blood, it can move, recognise others, speak, feel emotions, and proph-
esy. When its body has not been buried, *psychē* can show emotion,
speak, know, remember, express desires, and give orders. The body
and blood give *psychē* several powers. They may make it suitably
called 'strong' (*iphthimos*).

No one would deny that *psychē*, as shade of the dead, was generally regarded as a frail, feeble image of the living person, having few powers or activities. But only it survived death. Unlike *noos, phrenes, thumos, kradiē, ētor,* and *kēr,* that perished with the body, it had a form of permanent existence, however unenviable in nature. Its activities were not totally limited and, in special circumstances, its powers could be extended. When this happened, shades proved capable of intellectual, emotional, and volitional activities. A special individual like Teiresias, even as a shade, had *noos* and *phrenes* that made such activities possible for him.

Especially important in the Homeric picture of *psychē* are the indications it gives of how this entity could later become a psychological agent within the individual. When person and *psychē* are easily identified with regard to activities in Hades, we can see how *psychē* itself, when present within the living person, could also come to have a range of functions. Homer handed on to his listeners a general impression of what *psychē* was like. It was something insubstantial, dream-like, frail, and weak but able to become 'strong' in some circumstances. In later years *psychē* became 'strong' in yet a more vivid fashion, as a psychological agent in the living person.

Lyric and Elegiac Poets

In the lyric and elegiac poets we begin to see changes in the way in which *psychē* was viewed. In some passages, naturally enough, the Homeric sense of *psychē* is present. But an extended use of *psychē* appears in other instances and its role as psychological agent within the person starts to emerge. No longer is *psychē* mentioned only when death threatens or a death-like condition occurs. Instead a person relates in a more expanded way to *psychē* during life. What may be happening, as suggested above, is that *psychē*, capable of certain activities in the underworld and easily identified there with the person, begins to exhibit a similar range in the living. Perhaps in imitation of *thumos* and other psychic entities, it takes on functions long associated with them. In due course these come to include emotional, intellectual, and volitional activities. Such activities, of course, may have been long associated with *psychē* in the spoken language of early Greece. The evidence we examine is of a particular, restricted kind. But however old the wider sense of *psychē*, it becomes noticeable in the poetry of the lyric and elegiac poets.

There are only eighteen occurrences of *psychē* in these poets (apart from Pindar and Bacchylides, see below).[18] Several echo the Homeric usage with a particular emphasis on the meaning of 'life'. Archilochus in the seventh century, probably referring to sea-farers, describes those who 'hold their *psychai* in the arms of the waves' (213). These individuals choose to place their 'lives' in danger. Solon in the early sixth century also describes the sea-farer: he is one who 'places no sparing of his *psychē*' (13). The image here is of a person treating his *psychē*, his 'breath' or 'life', like an enemy. He shows no mercy to it as he takes bold chances.

Tyrtaeus in the seventh century urges soldiers to fight in his elegies. He twice mentions *psychē* as the 'life' to be expended, if necessary, in battle. He too uses the image of 'not sparing *psychē*' (10.14). Soldiers are not to 'love their lives' (*philopsycheō*) as they fight the enemy. 'Not to spare *psychē*' is to treat it within as the foe. 'Loving *psychē*' is to 'spare it', to protect life and play perhaps the coward. In 11.5 Tyrtaeus specifically calls on soldiers 'to treat *psychē* as the foe (*echthros*) and the black spirits of death as dear as the rays of the sun'. *Psychē* is to become 'hated' or 'hateful' and treated as the enemy. Tyrtaeus calls for a generous expenditure of 'life'. A reputation for courage and daring is to be considered of higher value than *psychē*.[19]

Theognis in the late sixth century likewise refers to *psychē* as 'life'. He speaks of 'cares that take hold of people, cares having variegated wings and weeping for *psychē* and *biotos*' (730). The two terms are close in meaning, *psychē* probably indicating the 'life-principle', *biotos*, 'physical sustenance' or 'livelihood'. People are harassed with different concerns, basically those related with helping them stay alive. Simonides in the early fifth century also too refers to *psychē* as 'life'. He speaks of a child 'breathing forth her sweet *psychē*' (553). Precious while in her body, this 'life' is sadly lost.

Only twice does *psychē* signify the 'shade of the dead' in the lyric and elegiac poets. At 710 Theognis describes 'the dark gates that restrain the *psychai* of the dead, even though they say no'. These shades do not wish to stay in Hades. They have some awareness, it seems, of their condition and long to leave. They 'say no' or 'refuse'

---

[18] On *psychē* in the lyric and elegiac poets see Adkins, *From the Many*, Claus, Dihle, 'Totenglaube', Furley, Jarcho, Onians, S.D. Sullivan, 'The Extended Use of *Psychē* in the Greek Lyric and Elegiac Poets (excluding Pindar and Bacchylides)', *Parola del Passato*, 1989, vol. 44, pp. 241–62, 'The Wider Meaning of *Psychē* in Pindar and Bacchylides', *SIFC*, 1991, vol. 4, pp. 163–83, Treu.

[19] At 12.15–18 Tyrtaeus again praises one who 'puts forth' *psychē* in fighting.

but no exit is available to them. Simonides in Epigram 70 P also refers to *psychai* as shades destined to dwell in Hades: 'alas, grievous disease, why do you begrudge *psychai* to abide in lovely youth?' *Psychai* prove vulnerable to disease which hastens their departure.

In other passages of the lyric and elegiac poets we encounter an extended meaning of *psyche*. In a humorous poem, 39, Hipponax, writing in the late sixth century, relates directly to his *psyche*: 'I will give my much-enduring *psyche* to evils'. He will do this, if he fails to receive ingredients to make up a potion that is a 'medicine for a miserable condition'. *Psyche* appears to be a seat of Hipponax's 'suffering'. In addition, it could also mean 'life'. Only rarely do adjectives appear with *psyche* in the lyric and elegiac poets. This one suggests an important role for *psyche* in the body. Either it is his 'life' marked with 'hardship' or it is an entity within acting as psychological agent that 'endures much'.

This poem is one of exaggerated humour but it reveals a new way of referring to *psyche* in the living person. *Psyche* can be a seat of awareness and endurance, one that can be given over to such 'evils'. Hipponax's mood will depend on whether he surrenders *psyche* to 'evils' or not. Either he will be in a bad state or, if he keeps *psyche* from 'evils', he will be in a better condition, helped by the potion he drinks. Alcaeus, writing earlier in the sixth century, in poem 335 speaks of 'not surrendering *thumos* to evil'. We see then a parallel usage. *Psyche* is beginning to be referred to like *thumos*. Its role in the living person is becoming apparent. When Homer speaks of someone 'giving *psyche*' (as at *Il.* 5.654 or 16.625), he refers to the moment of death. The living person now exerts control over *psyche* which abides within as a seat of emotion.

Anacreon in the sixth century likewise suggests an important role for *psyche* in the living person. In 360 he says: 'boy with virgin glance, you I seek but you do not heed, not realising that you are the charioteer of my *psyche*'. In this passage *psyche* may have the traditional Homeric meaning of 'life'. But it may be more, namely a seat of Anacreon's feelings of love and desire. The metaphor is a vivid one: the boy is a charioteer, *psyche*, the object of his control. In Homer a person could exert influence over the *psyche* of another but the effect was to inflict death. Here the boy exerts power over how Anacreon feels. His power is so great that *psyche*, the seat of 'life', becomes painfully involved.

Theognis relates *psyche* to inner qualities. At 529-30 he describes himself: 'never have I betrayed any friend or faithful comrade nor is there anything slavish in my *psychē*'. Theognis' moral nature is concerned. 'Nothing slavish' may imply intellectual, emotional, and volitional aspects. These are now thought to be found in *psychē*. No longer does *psychē* simply endow life; it has characteristics that can lead to admirable behaviour.

In another passage Theognis ponders a dilemma facing human beings. Since we do not know how long we shall live, should we spend much money or little? At 910–11 he describes his reaction to the problem: 'this situation has aroused great grief in me and I am bitten in my *psychē* and I hold my *thumos* in two directions'. *Psychē* serves as an entity within Theognis that acts as a location of pain. In this it resembles other psychic entities that were often affected by distress. Homer specifically speaks of *phrenes* 'bitten' by a word of Sarpedon (*Il.* 5.493). *Psychē* may, of course, retain too in this passage its association with 'life', appropriate in a context where the hidden nature of the human life-span is the topic discussed.

In this passage Theognis also 'holds his *thumos* in two directions'. In the lines that follow, he proceeds to say that he cannot decide whether to save or to spend his money; he decides at line 924 that living within one's means is best. *Thumos* here acts as a location of thought or deliberation and it is a 'divided' one. *Psychē* and *thumos* do not appear to be synonymous in this passage. The first is a seat of pain, the second, of thought. But, as happens elsewhere, the two are mentioned together.[20] Such linking may suggest that *psychē* gradually took on functions that *thumos* also could perform and thus came to act as a psychological agent in the living person.

Simonides too presents a picture of *psychē* that suggests that its role in the living person has become greater than in Homer or Hesiod. In poem 8 (discussed in chapter 2 under *thumos*), he speaks of the foolishness of young people who never imagine that death or old age will come. Instead, these people live on false hope, planning things that will not take place. He ends the passage by saying: 'nor do they know how short is the time of youth and life for mortals. But you, learning these things, endure to the end of your life (*biotos*), delighting your *psychē* with good things' (8.12–13).

In this passage *psychē* may have the traditional Homeric sense of

---

[20] See *Il.* 11.334, *Od.* 21.154, 171; Tyr. 10, 12.

'life'. Since the years human beings have are few, they should bring delight into 'life', if they can, because these years often prove also to be something to be endured. *Psychē*, however, may be more. It may indicate an entity that functions as a seat of pleasure in the person. It can affect how a person feels and reacts. In stark contrast to Tyrtaeus who consistently urges a generous expenditure of *psychē*, Simonides calls for an indulgence of it, one that will make the span of life, all too short, more enjoyable.

In these passages from the lyric and elegiac poets, we see *psychē* with traditional Homeric meanings. But we see too a change: *psychē* has become important not only when death approaches but during life. It is now associated with certain emotions: joy, love, pain. It is related to qualities in a person. It resembles in these agents some activities that we heard the shades of the dead carried on in Homer. It thus begins to have functions like those of other psychic entities, perhaps *thumos* in particular, with which it is mentioned three times.

One feature, however, of *psychē* seems especially prominent in these poets, one that may also set it apart from other psychic entities: its association with 'life'. Even as it comes slowly to express a full range of psychological activities, it strongly retains the sense of being that which endows a person with life. This was its role in the living person in Homer and Hesiod and may have been the same, perhaps, in the long epic tradition that preceded them. A person's natural instinct is to preserve *psychē*, to treat it well, since it is all too soon lost. When individuals must fight, they must also be encouraged to give up generously that which they might cherish and hold too dear. For them *psychē* must become 'hateful' and not to be 'spared'. In other circumstances the call is for *psychē* to be indulged since this will make days sweeter. *Psychē* thus appears to take on greater significance within the living person and to have a new capacity of affecting a person's nature and moods.

Pindar and Bacchylides

In these two epinician poets, we see the same pattern as in the other lyric and elegiac poets.[21] But even more does *psychē* emerge as a psychological agent within the individual. In particular we see an

---

[21] On *psychē* in Pindar and Bacchylides see above note 18.

association of it with moral behaviour. We have moved now into the fifth century and *psychē* within is a vibrant presence influencing strongly who a person is.

Among the twenty-four instances of *psychē* in these two poets several indicate the shade of the dead. This is particularly true in Bacchylides Ode 5 which treats Heracles' trip to the underworld. There he encounters Meleager who 'knows him well' (77) and can speak to him. He warns Heracles 'not to send in vain a cruel arrow against the *psychē* of the dead' (81). These *psychai* can do no harm nor threaten Heracles in any way. Meleager describes a battle in the upper world where 'blind weapons go from hands against the *psychai* of the enemy and bring death to whomever fate wishes' (133). Only in the living are *psychai* vulnerable.

Meleager tells also of his own death, caused by his mother's cruel burning of the log designating his life-span. 'My sweet *psychē* grew less and I knew, alas, that my strength was failing; wretched I wept as I breathed my last, leaving behind glorious youth'. We see here the association of *psychē* with 'life' and 'breath'. Meleager describes *psychē* as 'sweet'.[22] He views *psychē* as a precious entity in his youthful body. He mourns its loss as we heard in Homer the *psychē* of Patroclus and Hector doing as it bewailed its fate in losing 'manliness and youth' (*Il.* 16.856, 22.362). Its nature in the underworld differs greatly, being now weak and frail.

Pindar too speaks of *psychē* as the 'life' lost in death. He describes Achilles: 'by arrows losing his *psychē* in battle he, burning in fire, made lamentation arise from the Greeks' (*Pyth.* 3.102). He tells Megas that once *psychē* has left the body, 'it is not possible for one to bring it back again' (*Nem.* 8.44). In *Is.* 1.68 he gives a negative description of the person who nurtures a 'hidden wealth' while he is alive: 'he does not realise that he is paying tribute of his *psychē* to Hades without glory'. Each person must surrender *psychē*, 'life-soul', to Hades as 'tribute', but apparently has the choice of doing this with 'glory' or not. Because of a lack of generosity in using wealth, which should serve as a means of facilitating high achievement, this individual fails to achieve 'glory'.[23] He differs greatly from Achilles who always 'risked

---

[22] Simonides also calls *psychē* 'sweet' (553). Pindar describes *phrēn* as 'sweet to mingle among fellow-drinkers' (*Pyth.* 2.26). *Psychē* is thus spoken of in a way in which *phrēn* also is. This may likewise suggest an extended role for *psychē* in the living person.

[23] See too on *Nem.* 9.32 discussed below.

his *psychē*' in battle for the sake of a noble reputation (*Il.* 9.322). A person can control the way in which *psychē* can depart: with or without honour.[24] We hear in this instance the traditional Greek view that glory and high achievement are of great value since death and the unenviable existence of Hades await everyone (see further, chapter 4 below).

Another traditional sense of *psychē* we find in Pindar is his description of that in animals. As mentioned above, Homer refers to the *psychē* of a boar (*Od.* 14.426). References to the *psychē* of animals are not common in early Greek literature but the absence of these is probably due to the fact that few contexts treat them rather than to any assumption that *psychē*, 'life', was not to be found in them. No assumption of any continued existence, however, of the animal after death seems likely. Pindar refers twice to the death of snakes in terms of loss of *psychē* (*Ol.* 8.39, *Nem.* 1.47).

In other passages of Pindar and Bacchylides we find an extended role for *psychē* in the living person. At *Pyth.* 4.122 Pindar says of Aeson, father of Jason: 'he rejoiced about his *psychē*, seeing his exceptional son'. *Psychē* here functions as a seat of joy in the glad father. At *Nem.* 9.39 Pindar speaks in general of soldiers: 'few are powerful in hands and *psychē* to turn the cloud of carnage at their feet towards the ranks of the enemy'. *Psychē* serves as a centre of courage that allows daring in fighting. It is associated too with 'planning' that apparently permits some form of calm behaviour during battle. 'Powerful in *psychē*' suggests inner qualities, ones that serve well in a crisis.

At *Is.* 4.53 b Pindar describes Heracles as 'short in stature, unflinching in *psychē*'. Here again *psychē* serves as a seat of courage. 'Unflinching' suggests the presence of emotional, intellectual, and volitional aspects in *psychē*, ones that contribute to Heracles' brave actions. In this passage we find a contrast between Heracles' physical stature and the spirit within that drives him on, the latter apparently considered superior. In this case his relation to *psychē* proves to be the crucial factor in his behaviour.

At *Pyth.* 1.48 Pindar asks whether Hieron, king of Sicily, would

---

[24] Cf. fr. 123 where a possible reading of *psychē* would give a description of someone 'nurturing' it 'with womanly courage'. This person, interested chiefly in making money, guards *psychē*, never risking it. Pindar probably believes that this person too will give up this *psychē* to Hades 'without glory'.

recall 'in what battles, during wars, he stood his ground with steadfast *psychē*'. Elsewhere we hear of a 'steadfast *thumos*' (Hom., *Il.* 5.670, Tyr. 12.18). *Psychē* here functions like *thumos* in these earlier passages, acting as a seat of daring or courage. Hieron does not flinch; the spirit within remains firm.

In another passage we hear of the *psychē* of Apollo (*Pyth.* 3.41). As he rescues Asclepius from the funeral pyre of his mother Coronis, he says: 'no longer will I endure in my *psychē* to kill my child'. *Psychē* here may function as the seat of Apollo's deliberation concerning what to do. For a time it was the location of his determination to allow the death of his child. This changes and he saves his son. Here, within the god, *psychē* acts as the centre of resolve. It seems closely related to Apollo's character.

We heard above that failure to spend generously can cause a person to give *psychē* to Hades without honour (*Is.* 1.68). At *Nem.* 9.32 Pindar approves of a generous use of wealth. He describes the men of the house of Chromius as 'having *psychai* stronger than their possessions'. The love of gain does not hinder them from making sacrifices in order to win 'glory' (33–4). Again *psychē* appears to be a seat of inner qualities. This *psychē* is not overcome by greed but leads individuals to act with open hands. They vividly contrast those for whom Hesiod had said 'money is *psychē*' (*W. & D.* 686). In the living, *psychē* has become a centre of positive features of character.

Bacchylides too relates *psychē* to character. At 11.48 he describes the daughters of Proteus: 'with still girlish *psychē*, they went into the temenos' of Hera. There they boasted excessively about the wealth of their father. The adjective 'girlish' tells us of the ages of the young women and gives an explanation, or perhaps an excuse, for their foolish behaviour. This *psychē* is apparently one that can change. If the girls had been older, they might have acted more prudently. As a 'girlish' *psychē* matures, it evidently gains wisdom. *Psychē* functions prominently here in the girls in their youth. It strongly affects how they behave.

In one passage, Pindar addresses *psychē* in the vocative (*Pyth.* 3.61–2). He says: 'do not, dear *psychē*, hasten after immortal life but exhaust the means that can be done'. These lines follow other advice that Pindar gives: 'we must seek what is fitting from the gods with our mortal *phrenes*, knowing what is before our feet' (59–60).[25] In the

---

[25] See the discussion of this passage above in chapter 2.

same ode, he says of himself: 'I will be small among the small, great among the great. I will honour the divine spirit (*daimōn*) that follows my *phrenes*, and keep it according to my means.' In this ode Coronis and Asclepius both desired what they could not have. They failed to recall their human limitations or to show regard for the 'means' at their disposal. Asclepius, in particular, in returning to life a person already destined for death stepped outside the bounds of appropriate human behaviour.

Pindar tells his 'dear *psychē*' not to 'hasten after immortal life (*bios*)'.[26] Instead, it should turn its energies to what can be accomplished. What Pindar says is rich in meaning because *psychē* was traditionally associated with life. In some ways it might even be thought to have a form of 'immortal life' since it alone survived a person after death and never ceased to exist. But the 'immortal life' Pindar refers to here lies outside the range of *psychē*, even if it mistakenly should pursue it. This is a 'life', with its attendant powers, that only the gods have. *Psychē* then acts as an entity that can express desire, even excessive desires. It can apparently aim at what would be out of reach. In doing so, Pindar suggests, it could prove harmful to him.

In this passage, Pindar addresses *psychē* much in the same way as the lyric and elegiac poets address *thumos* and as he himself does in four passages.[27] Pindar also addresses *phrēn* directly (*Pae.* 4.50). Like these psychic entities *psychē* has come to occupy an important position in the living person. Individual and *psychē* remain distinct but *psychē* can exert considerable influence upon what someone does. It seems capable of independent action within. Opposition between person and *psychē* is apparently possible. In this passage it needs to be cautioned concerning the goals it may have.

In an unusual passage, Pindar mentions *psychē* in the context of the transmigration of souls.[28] We will discuss this topic more fully with the Presocratics in this chapter. *Olympians* 2, written for Theron of Acragas in Sicily, may indicate by its emphasis a great interest in

---

[26] Note that in earlier poets it is often *thumos* that is called 'dear' (see chapter 2). In this regard too *psychē* has come to resemble *thumos*, the most active of the psychic entities. It resembles *ētor* and *kēr*, likewise called 'dear'. Pindar also addresses *ētor* as 'dear' (*Ol.* 1.4, *Pae.* 6.12).

[27] See chapter 2, notes 56 and 88 and see *Ol.* 2.89, *Nem.* 3.26, frs 123.1, 127.4.

[28] On this passage see N. Demand, 'Pindar's *Olympian* 2, Theron's Faith, and Empedocles' *Katharmoi*', *GRBS*, 1975, vol. 16, pp. 347–57, W. Fitzgerald, 'Pindar's Second Olympian', *Helios*, 1983, vol. 10, pp. 49–70, G.F. Gianotti, 'Sull' *Olympica*

this particular topic in Sicily. As we heard in chapter 2, Empedocles, likewise from Sicily, expressed views on this subject. Pindar says: 'those who, remaining on the other side, have endured three times to keep their *psychē* entirely from unjust deeds travel the road of Zeus to the tower of Kronos' (70). The meaning of 'three times' is obscure but Pindar probably refers to three periods of existence on earth and three in Hades, 'the other side'. If people keep *psychē* from injustice during three lives on earth, they escape the cycle of rebirth and can travel to the 'tower of Kronos'. This 'tower' implies a location where *psychai* will have a favourable existence, very unlike the usual picture of the underworld.

Here we have elements of the traditional picture of *psychē*. It alone survives death and travels to Hades. But it has acquired new characteristics. It acts as the seat of someone's moral qualities. It comes under the control of the living person. Someone can help or harm *psychē* in the journey it must make depending on a choice or avoidance of 'unjust deeds'. If a person fails to keep *psychē* from such deeds, it must apparently return again and again to another earthly existence. The minimum this earthly existence appears to be is three lives, all marked by justice.

For someone alive, therefore, *psychē* acts as a seat of moral qualities, remaining distinct from the person. At death, this same *psychē* survives, alone preserving the person's individuality and identity. It retains too, it seems, a 'record' of the moral behaviour it has engaged in while in the living person. It goes through periods of existence and escapes transmigration only after three just periods of existence on earth.

In the living individual, person and *psychē* appear to be distinct. Yet in the picture of the final destiny awaiting humans, Pindar identifies person and *psychē*. He uses the pronoun 'they' in speaking of those destined to travel to the 'tower of Kronos'. 'They' achieve this destiny by the way in which they control *psychē* during life. Yet surely it must be *psychē* that makes this journey, since it alone survives death. As Homer did earlier, Pindar easily identifies individual and *psychē*. This identification may have influenced the range of activity that *psychē* came to have in the living person. This picture of the shade of the dead, of course, differs greatly from that of Homer. It has become the part of the human which eventually achieves, because of its moral condition, some ideal state, free from a body.

In another passage too Pindar mentions the transmigration of *psychai*.

Fr. 133.1–3 reads: 'from whom Persephone will receive a penalty of ancient grief and, into the upper sunlight, in the ninth year she gives back their *psychai* again'. The fragment proceeds to say that from these *psychai* arise 'holy kings, people powerful in strength, and those greatest in wisdom. For all time these individuals are called holy heroes by humans' (3–5). These *psychai* appear to have undergone some form of purification in the underworld. In their reincarnation, 'in the ninth year' (perhaps to be taken literally as a period of time, perhaps not), they return to earth as people particularly endowed with authority, power, and wisdom. As such, they are apparently in the final stages of reincarnation. What happens in the next stage is not indicated but their actions as human beings give them the permanent status of hero.

The exact role that these *psychai* have in the living person remains obscure. They have evidently become the bearers of moral excellence or lack thereof. They atone for the latter in the underworld and in time are reincarnated. Perhaps intellectual, emotional, and volitional aspects are present in these *psychai* while they are in those who are alive. They are likely responsible, after their return 'in the ninth year', for the actions that win individuals the status of hero for all time.

In Hades these *psychai* are subject to Persephone's control. She can return them to life on earth again. In Homer too Persephone affects *psychai*: she 'scatters' the shades of women (*Od.* 11.385). In Pindar's picture of *psychai* in fr. 133, the time in the underworld has a specific purpose, namely to allow some form of purification. No longer, it seems, are *psychai* to remain there forever. Hades has become simply a stage on a journey.

These passages from Pindar and Bacchylides show us *psychē* sometimes in the traditional Homeric sense but at other times with an extended meaning. *Psychē* now is an important factor in the living person, no longer attracting attention only when death approaches. It functions as a seat of emotion, endurance, and joy. It is associated with inner qualities. Someone can be 'powerful' in *psychē* or 'unflinching' in it. *Psychē* can prove generous or just.

In terms of relationship to person, three features of *psychē* appear. Addressed in the vocative, it shows itself capable of independent activity in the person that may need opposition. When Hieron fights with 'steadfast *psychē*', we see person and *psychē* acting in co-operation. When people 'pay tribute of *psychē* to Hades', 'care' for it, 'keep it

from unjust deeds' or maintain it 'stronger than possessions', *psychē*
appears to be subordinate to them and under their control. In the
two passages referring to transmigration of *psychai*, it has become in
the living person a seat of moral behaviour. As such, it may be associated with a wide range of psychological activities. In order to
achieve a desirable and purified state, it may face several incarnations.

One feature of *psychē* remains prominent in these two poets as it
did in the other lyric and elegiac poets: its connection with 'life'.
This feature may set *psychē* apart from other psychic entities that it
has come to imitate. *Psychē* has become a significant psychological
agent within the living person. Its emergence as the chief psychological agent has been clearly adumbrated in these poets.

The Presocratics

The Presocratic philosophers also provide us with important information about how the early Greeks viewed *psychē* and why it gradually became the chief psychological agent within the person. Traditional aspects of *psychē* persist, it is true, but new ones also appear.
Psychē is of central importance in the teachings of Anaximenes (followed later by Diogenes of Apollonia), the Pythagoreans, and Heraclitus. We shall focus upon their fragments. Other Presocratics refer
to *psychē* only rarely. Empedocles mentions it once in the traditional
sense of the 'life' removed by a weapon (B 138). Anaxagoras likewise refers to *psychē* as the 'life' (B 4) of living beings and says that
noos governs those having it (B 12). There are several references to
psychē in Democritus but the fragments involved are of questionable
authenticity.[29] By his time (late fifth century), *psychē* had become a

---

seconda di Pindaro', *RFIC*, 1971, vol. 99, pp. 26–52, H. Lloyd-Jones, 'Pindar and
the After-Life', in *Pindare* (Geneva 1985), pp. 245–83 (also in *Greek Epic* with Addendum, pp. 80–109), H.S. Long, *Metempsychosis*, D. McGibbon, 'Metempsychosis in
Pindar', *Phronesis*, 1964, vol. 9, pp. 5–11, F. Solmsen, 'Two Pindaric Passages on the
Hereafter', *Hermes*, 1968, vol. 96, pp. 503–6, Sullivan (note 18), pp. 172–4,
L. Woodbury, 'Equinox at Acragas: Pindar, *Ol.* 2.61–62', *TAPA*, 1966, vol. 97, pp.
597–616.
[29] See, e.g., B 37, 72, 159, 247, 264. Scholars differ in accepting or rejecting
these fragments. See W.K.C. Guthrie, vol. 2, pp. 489–97, C.H. Kahn, 'Democritus
and the Origins of Moral Psychology', *AJP*, 1985, vol. 106, pp. 1–31, esp. 3–5,
Kirk, Raven, and Schofield, pp. 431–3, and G. Vlastos, 'Ethics and Physics in
Democritus', *PR*, 1945, vol. 54, pp. 578–92 and 1946, vol. 55, pp. 53–64.

prominent psychic entity in the person and this role is present in these fragments. Suffice to say that he illustrates a stage not yet entirely evident in the earlier philosophers.

Anaximenes

Let us turn then to Anaximenes.[30] One of the earliest Milesian thinkers (late sixth century), Anaximenes suggested that 'all things' (the universe) were in essence air (A 5). This air was in constant motion (A 5–7). He explained differences among 'all things' as deriving from air's capacity for compression and dilation (A 5–7, B 1). Close-packed air appeared as earth and water; dilated air, as air itself and fire. This air was also the divine principle in the universe, encompassing all things, which it formed (A 4–7, 10).

We have just one fragment of Anaximenes which reads: 'Just as our *psychē*, which is air, controls us, so breath and air encompass the whole world-order' (B 2).[31] How much of the fragment contains authentic wording of Anaximenes is debated but for our purposes the fragment gives us important information about *psychē*. Its role is prominent. First, its nature is specified: it is made of air. Here we see again, as was the case in Homer, an association of *psychē* with the substance humans breathe and find crucial for life. We recall that the etymology of *psychē* may point to an origin related to 'breath'.

Second, in this fragment, the function of *psychē* is specified. The verb in the Greek (*sugkrateō*) has a broad meaning that includes 'holding together' and 'controlling'. These two activities are what Anaximenes sees air, *psychē*, as doing. It unites and 'holds together' the human body, giving life and movement. It also 'controls' that body. Anaximenes has apparently observed the effects of different forms of

---

[30] On Anaximenes see the Appendix and K. Alt, 'Zum Satz des Anaximenes über die Seele', *Hermes*, 1973, vol. 101, pp. 129–64, Barnes, vol. 1, pp. 38–56, C.J. Classen, 'Anaximander and Anaximenes: The Earliest Greek Theories of Change', *Phronesis*, 1977, vol. 22, pp. 89–102, Dumont, pp. 41–50, W.K.C. Guthrie, vol. 1, pp. 115–40, Hussey, pp. 11–31, Kirk, Raven, and Schofield, pp. 143–62, McKirahan, pp. 48–58, Mansfeld, pp. 82–97, A. Papanikolaou, '*Aer.* Anaximenes and Corpus Hippocraticum' in Boudouris, pp. 319–26, J.M. Robinson, pp. 41–8, J. Wubnig, 'Anaximander and the Opposites' in Boudouris, pp. 441–4, Wright, *Presocratics*, pp. xi–v. The treatments of Alt, Guthrie, and Kirk, Raven, and Schofield are especially helpful.

[31] On this fragment see W.K.C. Guthrie, vol. 1, pp. 131–2, and Kirk, Raven, and Schofield, pp. 158–62.

breathing. Heavy breathing alters movement and emotions. Light breathing brings less energy and sluggishness. Breathing, that is, air, determines to a large degree how a person behaves.

This wording in B 2 shows us how Anaximenes viewed *psychē* as air. First, a look backward. We have seen in Homer and the lyric and elegiac poets that *psychē* has two principal meanings. It is an entity that keeps a person alive, departing at death. It is also a shade preserving the identity of the person and having a continued existence in the underworld. Gradually it begins to act as a psychological agent within the living person. In this picture we see that *psychē* has a nature distinct and separate from the living person. It is identified with that person only after death and then simply as a pale, colourless image of the individual. Blood is usually needed for this shade to exhibit more of what the person was in the world above.

When Anaximenes speaks of *psychē* as 'holding us together and controlling us', he too regards it as something distinct from the person. In examining *psychē* he probably focused upon the nature of breathing. In doing so, he reveals that the early Greeks did not regard it as we might. It is not human beings who breathe, drawing in and expelling air. Rather, it is air, *psychē*, that moves in and departs, controlling in this fashion the person and bestowing life. As long as *psychē* continued its pattern of moving into the person and leaving the person, that individual remained alive. If it ceased to enter and leave in a constant rhythm, the person died.

This fragment of Anaximenes thus gives us evidence about the importance of air for the human being. Breathing demonstrated the presence of an entity, *psychē*, moving in its accustomed manner and vital for life. As long as this *psychē* continued its motion, 'holding together' and 'controlling', all was well. Battle brought the danger of the loss of *psychē* and during it care had to be taken to keep *psychē* safely within the body. In some degree this *psychē* was master of the individual. Anaximenes' wording helps us to see the crucial role he assigned to *psychē* in the living person.

Observing apparently that the one essential for life was air, Anaximenes considered it also the key for understanding the nature of the entire universe. The remainder of fragment B 2 concerns the 'whole world-order'. 'Breath and air encompass' this in the same way that *psychē* does the human body. In our discussion of *noos* above in chapter 2, we referred, in our treatment of Anaxagoras, to the theory of microcosm/macrocosm. This theory, common in the Presocratics, assumes that the microcosm, usually the human person, mirrors the macrocosm, the universe and the divine principle governing it. Anaximenes presents us with the first explicit statement of this view. On the level of the microcosm, air moves in and out of human beings, giving life and forming their substance. On the level of the macrocosm, the world-order (all things) is surrounded by air. This air, in constant motion, compresses, appearing then as earth and water, and dilates, appearing then as itself and fire. All things are essentially air, capable of manifesting itself in a variety of ways. We see a parallel between the two levels. As we have suggested, Anaximenes focused upon the phenomenon of breathing. Human beings breathe. So, he surmises, does the universe.[32] This breathing is the motion of air as it exhibits its own nature both in the living creature and in the universe as a whole.

Can we say more of the nature of air in Anaximenes? Is there within it the presence of intelligence? If so, this would be a feature as well of *psychē*. Anaximenes may have ascribed the function of 'governing' (*kubernaō*) to air, as Anaximander does to his divine principle (12 A 5). If he does, this might suggest some degree of intelligence within it. But our evidence is very slight and caution is needed in making any such assumption. *Psychē*, we can see, does not emerge in any obvious way as a psychological agent in the living person in Anaximenes' fragment, B 2.

Some years after Anaximenes another philosopher, Diogenes of Apollonia (mid-fifth century), very much echoed his views.[33] He too assumes that the primary substance of the universe is air (B 5). 'All things' are essentially air (B 2) and this element, ever moving, is the divine principle that governs them (B 5, 8). Diogenes explicitly ascribes intelligence to this air. 'Human beings and other living creatures live by means of air, by breathing it. And this is for them both *psychē* and intelligence (*noēsis*) ... if this is removed, then they die and intelligence fails' (B 4). 'For it would not be possible without

---

[32] See Jaeger, *Theology*, p. 80. Indirect evidence comes for this view when we hear that Xenophanes later (A 1) denies that his divinity 'breathed'. He may be rejecting Pythagorean views but perhaps also those of Anaximenes. See on this question W.K.C. Guthrie, vol. 1, p. 374, n. 2 and Kahn, *Anaximander*, p. 98, n. 2.

[33] On Diogenes see the Appendix and see Barnes, vol. 2, pp. 265–81, A.J. Cappelletti, *Los Fragmentos de Diógenes de Apolonia*, Caracas, 1975, Dumont, pp. 699–721, W.K.C. Guthrie, vol. 2, pp. 363–81, Hussey, p. 141, Kirk, Raven, and Schofield, pp. 434–52, A. Laks, *Diogène d'Apollonie*, Lille, 1983, McKirahan, pp. 344–52, J.M. Robinson, pp. 49–50. Guthrie's treatment presents his views well.

intelligence (*noēsis*) for it [air] so to be divided up that it has measures of all things—of winter summer, night day, rains, winds and fair weather' (B 3).

Air expresses itself in the rational ordering of the universe. This same air manifests itself as 'all things' and exists in a special way in living creatures. In human beings, it gives both life and intelligence and forms the soul (*psychē*). Diogenes does not locate intelligence within *psychē* but *psychē* itself, being identical to air, must exhibit this capacity. *Psychē* then has come to have a close association with thought. Its presence in the human person allows the ordering of an individual life and the understanding of how the universe works.

The views of Anaximenes and Diogenes are very similar but are somewhat different in focus. The earlier thinker, Anaximenes, concentrates on the mobility of air, its capacity for compression and dilation, and the consequences of this capacity. Diogenes, coming later, speaks of the role of air in the rational ordering of the universe. In relation to *psychē* we see in him a more explicit emphasis on its intellectual activity.

The picture we find of *psychē* in Anaximenes is of central importance because it probably had considerable influence later. He relates *psychē* in a fundamental way to his explanation of reality. He assumes that this *psychē* shares in the divine nature. Even though everything is essentially air, human beings in particular imitate and manifest the divine nature. We heard above (chapter 2) that *noos* could be considered the element that linked human and divine. Anaximenes makes it *psychē*. In so doing he ascribes *psychē* a role it would consistently have in later philosophers (the Pythagoreans, e.g., and Heraclitus). In Homer and the lyric and elegiac poets, *psychē* was a positive presence in the living person. Anaximenes continues that view but adds to the importance of *psychē* by defining it as a portion of divinity.

We do not know what Anaximenes considered the destiny of *psychē* after death. Since it was air, it may have become part of the divine air. No longer, it seems, does a negative existence as a shade in a dark, dreary underworld await individuals. Instead, a person would continue to exist simply as air, divine air. Homer had suggested that individuals survive as portions of dark air, the shades, in the underworld, all recognisably themselves. In Anaximenes this idea of individual survival seems to be missing. It is apparently replaced by a destiny for human beings of union with the divine air governing the

universe. Just as in Homer and other early poets, air never ceases to
exist. In Anaximenes it seems that *psychē* simply survives in its state
as air.

The Pythagoreans

A group of thinkers who had an enormous influence on how *psychē*
came to be regarded were the Pythagoreans. We know that Pythagoras
himself probably lived in the late sixth century and was associated in
particular with South Italy.[34] We know too that followers of his views
formed societies of some form that survived long after his death.
With the Pythagoreans, however, we face a major difficulty. Their
teachings were of a secret nature and were kept thus for a long
period. Our evidence about these teachings consequently comes from
a time long after Pythagoras and it is very hard to determine what
exactly he himself may have taught. But one view he seems to have
held is that the soul is immortal. It dwells for a time in living creatures, endowing them with life. It experiences transmigration.
Pythagoras probably adopted the second idea from traditions in the
East, where he is said to have travelled.[35] For our purposes one point
is crucial: the term Pythagoras used for this migrating soul was *psychē*.

We have a piece of early evidence that associates this theory of
migration of souls with Pythagoras. Xenophanes is said to have written the following lines to ridicule this idea (B 7). Coming upon someone beating a dog, he says: 'stop, do not beat the dog, it is clearly
the *psychē* of a dear friend, which I recognised as I heard it cry out.'
These lines show us features of *psychē*. It can migrate from human
being to animal. It can make sounds and feel pain. In some way its
'voice' is recognisable. Xenophanes is being humorous in this poem

---

[34] On Pythagoras see the Appendix and Barnes, vol. 1, pp. 100–20, Burkert,
Dumont, pp. 53–68, 217–28, 443–544, 556–612, K. Guthrie and T. Taylor (eds),
The Pythagorean Writings, London, 1986, R.S. Guthrie, W.K.C. Guthrie, vol. 1, pp.
146–340, Huffman, Hussey, pp. 60–77, C.H. Kahn, 'Pythagorean Philosophy be-
fore Plato' in A.P.D. Mourelatos, ed., *The Presocratics*, pp. 161–85, Kirk, Raven, and
Schofield, pp. 214–38, H.S. Long, McKirahan, pp. 79–115, Mansfeld, pp. 98–203,
Philip, R. Purtell, 'The Unity of Pythagorean Philosophy' in Boudouris, pp. 337–43,
Raven, J.M. Robinson, pp. 57–84, B.L. van der Waerden, *Die Pythagoreer, Religiöse
Bruderschaft und Schule der Wissenschaft*, Zurich and Munich, 1979. See also further
bibliography in L.E. Navia, *Pythagoras, An Annotated Bibliography*, New York and Lon-
don, 1990. The works of Burkert, Kahn, and Philip are particularly helpful.

[35] See evidence in Diels-Kranz 14 A 8–8a, 58 B 39–40. See too Herodotus 2.123
who suggests that the theory of transmigration of souls was originally Egyptian.

and not presenting these features in any serious way. But none the less in being stated, they show us some assumptions that can accompany the notion of a migrating *psyche*.

In looking at this *psyche* we can note some parallels to and differences from Homeric usage. The mention of a *psyche* in an animal is not unusual since Homer speaks of one in a boar (*Od.* 14.426). The *Homeric Hymn to Aphrodite* also refers to a *psyche* dwelling outside a human being, namely in a tree (272). Pindar similarly refers to the *psychai* of snakes (*Ol.* 8.39, *Nem.* 1.47). But in Xenophanes' poem *psyche* is a human one that has not gone to Hades but to a different living creature.

Present in the dog, this *psyche* 'cries out' in barking. The idea of *psyche* making sounds is not new. We heard above that the shades in the underworld utter shrill cries like bats (*Il.* 23.100, *Od.* 24.5,9). 'Unburied' *psychai* can speak; so can those that have drunk blood. That the *psyche* can utter sounds in a living creature is something different. Even though Xenophanes is joking, we may see in this capacity of *psyche* one similar to that possessed by *thumos* and *phren*. Both these psychological entities are said to speak or to sing.[36]

As the dog howls, Xenophanes says that he recognises the *psyche* it has. Being recognisable is again not a new association for *psyche*. Just as this *psyche* here in the dog, so in the underworld *psychai* prove to be recognisable to other shades and to Odysseus. They possess certain distinctive traits.

This *psyche* too in the dog experiences pain. Homer portrays the shades in Hades as entities feeling grief (*Od.* 11.387, e.g, and 11.542). In the underworld, therefore, *psyche* has a capacity for suffering. This now apparently accompanies it on its journey through other life-forms.

The poem of Xenophanes does not say why the *psyche* of this friend is currently in a dog. Xenophanes is making fun of the whole notion of the human *psyche* travelling in this way. If he had a specific friend in mind, he obviously did not have a high opinion of this person's *psyche* and its destiny. From the Pythagorean point of view this descent to a lower level of life is a serious issue. It must result from the need for purification in *psyche*[37]

---

[36] See for *thumos* Alc. 308, Theog. 826, and Pin., *Pyth.* 3.64 and for *phren*, Terp. 697, *Adesp.* 955.1, Pin., *Pyth.* 6.36 and *Pae.* 4.50.

[37] For this view of the reason for reincarnation see especially Burkert, pp. 98–142, W.K.C. Guthrie, vol. 1, pp. 186, 306, Kirk, Raven, and Schofield, pp. 235–8, H.S. Long, pp. 2–27, and Philip, pp. 156–71.

The impurity in *psychē* can apparently be removed by a series of incarnations. The Pythagoreans, therefore, present the picture of *psychē* as an entity that undergoes change. This change ideally is from impure to pure, if *psychē* moves upward through creatures. If, during some incarnation, *psychē* becomes worse, it may face reincarnation in a lower form. Such has happened to Xenophanes' friend. When *psychē* is in human beings, we may suppose that impurity in it was probably manifested in negative moral behaviour. We saw in our treatment of *Ol.* 2.70 of Pindar above that *psychē* needed to learn to be just. Our evidence about the exact nature of impurity in *psychē* is slight but it may involve some form of immorality.

What then is the final destiny of *psychē* once it is purified? Again our evidence for the Pythagoreans poses difficulties of knowing how early some views may have been. But we may perhaps assume that *psychē* very early on became associated with some notion of a divine or world soul. A similar notion emerged in the sixth century in what are called the 'Orphic' cults.[38] These cults too, like the Pythagoreans, were secret in nature. Both groups appear to have postulated that human beings possess a portion of divinity that is immortal in nature. This was akin to a divine being governing the universe. The term they chose to describe this portion was *psychē*. We can see in this view a parallel with Anaximenes' association of *psychē* with the divine air 'encompassing the universe'.

A possible early picture of the world-order of the Pythagoreans is in fact very similar to that of Anaximenes.[39] The universe appears as a living organism that 'draws breath from the infinite' (58 B 30). This cosmic breath may parallel the breath humans draw in. The source, the infinite, is likely the divine principle as it is in other early philosophers. We must, it is true, be cautious in these speculations on what the early Pythagoreans thought about the universe as a whole.

---

[38] On the Orphics in general and their relation to Pythagoras see W. Burkert, *Ancient Mystery Cults*, Cambridge, Mass., 1987, 'Craft versus Sect: The Problem of Orphics and Pythagoreanism' in Meyer, pp. 1–22, *Greek Religion*, trans. J. Raffan, Cambridge, Mass., 1985, pp. 296–304, A. Finkelberg, 'On the Unity of Orphic and Milesian Thought', *HThR*, 1986, vol. 79, pp. 321–5, W.K.C. Guthrie, *Orpheus and Greek Religion*, London, 1952, Kirk, Raven, and Schofield, pp. 21–33, J.M. Linforth, *The Arts of Orpheus*, Berkeley, 1941, Philip, pp. 137, 166–8, Zuntz.

[39] See evidence in Diels-Kranz 58 B 8, 22, 26–8, 30, 36–37a and 44 A 16–17, 19–21. See also Burkert, pp. 278–347 (German), W.K.C. Guthrie, vol. 1, pp. 272, 276–301, Kirk, Raven, and Schofield, pp. 339–45, and Philip, pp. 60–76. See further bibliography in Navia (note 34), pp. 215–77.

But if they conceived of it like Anaximenes, we can postulate that the destiny of the purified *psychē* was some kind of union with the divine principle.

Purification, however, takes a long time of travel through different life-forms. How the *psychē* becomes impure is not clear. But when it becomes such, it must experience rebirth. We find in the Pythagoreans the idea that life in the body is a punishment, the body being a 'tomb' for *psychē* (44 B 14). Why rebirth purifies is not clear but the presence of an immortal *psychē* in a mortal form is considered to be a negative condition. The suffering that *psychē* necessarily experiences from rebirth apparently acts to purify it. Only when *psychē* escapes the body and the process of migration does it truly begin to live. We see in this view a great difference from what Homer tells us of *psychē*.

For Homer, to have *psychē* within the body was the ideal. If there was danger of its loss, care had to be taken to preserve it. In the lyric and elegiac poets arguments had to be given to urge soldiers to risk their *psychai*. The state of *psychai* after death was lamentable, according to the traditional view. Pale squeaking shades having an existence that none would envy, they dwelt ever in darkness and sorrow. The Pythagoreans paint a different picture. *Psychē* in the body suffers. It has a destiny of joining the divine once it has escaped the body. Better by far its final condition than could ever be the case in a living creature. Thus, in their view, the time after death offers a positive goal for human endeavour.

But, just as with Anaximenes, one feature of the Homeric picture is lost, that of individual survival. Although the impure *psychē* may retain features of the person, as we saw with Xenophanes' poem, eventually the *psychē* appears to lose these as it joins the divine nature. This final union with divinity is seen as something totally positive.

The process of purification takes place while *psychē* is in living creatures. Our Pythagorean sources suggest that, when *psychai* have reached the stage of human beings, they become pure if people adhere rigorously to certain prescribed prohibitions (abstinence, e.g., from meat and beans) and to other external practices.[40] It is apparently a ritual purity that proves effective. Human beings can, therefore, actively affect what happens to *psychē*. This *psychē* is a portion of the

---

[40] For a list of these rules see evidence in Diels-Kranz 58 C. See too a discussion of them in W.K.C. Guthrie, vol. 1, pp. 183–91, Kirk, Raven, and Schofield, pp. 230–32, and Philip, pp. 134–50.

divine imprisoned in a person and desiring release. The individual can hinder or hasten its journey by chosen behaviour. The importance of *psychē* is that it is immortal, divine, and alone survives death. Somehow human actions affect its purity and individuals thus control the destiny of this portion of the divine. Although *psychai* in their migration may exhibit specific traits, it appears that in the purified state they are all the same.

From this necessarily tentative reconstruction of early Pythagorean ideas we can grasp the strong impact they had (along too with the appearance of Orphism) upon how *psychē* came to be viewed. Most important was the emphasis they placed upon *psychē* as a person's one valuable possession. It had distinctive features. As a portion of the divine, it demanded attention as it dwelt within the person. By its presence it gave life. It could be favourable or adversely affected by what someone did. It left at death, either travelling to another life-form or escaping the burden of migration and joining instead the divine principle, with which it was akin. From these features we can see how this *psychē*, with the passage of time, could gradually take on an expanded role in the living person. It could come to be associated with psychological activities. It could become too a bearer of someone's inner qualities.

Of equal importance is that the Pythagoreans emphasized the immortality of *psychē* and made it into something very positive. They taught that it was an entity to be guarded and treasured not merely at the moment of death but all though life. At the same time they presented a new perspective on the time after death. No longer did a dreary shadow-like existence await the human person. Instead, the options were two. On the one hand, *psychē* might face another existence in a living creature. This could be more or less positive depending on the state of its purity. Even if its next existence might be rather frightening (a dog?), there was always the knowledge that the journey of *psychē* would go on. Each particular life-form was only a stage in this journey. On the other hand, a state as 'purified *psychē*' could impend after death. This would involve union with the divine.

With their philosophy the Pythagoreans shifted the focus on this life as the source of happiness to another future one. Ironically, in so doing, they also encouraged people to concentrate on *psychē* during this life and to make its nature a chief concern. They took what had traditionally been the only part of the human to survive and altered its nature from undesirable to wonderful. Like Anaximenes they treated *psychē* as a positive entity. They thus greatly influenced its emergence as a crucial element within the living human person.

Heraclitus

The third philosopher in whose thought *psychē* has an important role is Heraclitus.[41] We have discussed some of his views above in chapter 2 while treating *noos* and *thumos*. We shall see in him the influence of earlier philosophical views of *psychē*, especially those of Anaximenes and the Pythagoreans. But we shall see too that he introduces new ideas about it that would prove very influential.

The interpretation of the nature of the universe that Heraclitus gives is of central importance to what he says about *psychē*. As mentioned in our treatment of B 114 in chapter 2, he postulates a divine principle which he terms *logos*.[42] What is immediately apparent from Heraclitus' choice of *logos* for the divine is an occurrence once again of the microcosm/macrocosm principle. Greeks knew that all human beings possessed *logos* and they would assume that this common term meant 'speech'. But for Heraclitus it meant much more. One reason then that he may have written his views in the obscure riddles he did was his wish to make his listeners perceive a deeper meaning in *logos*.[43] If he could encourage those who heard him to examine the very 'speech' both he and they used, he could share his views on the

---

[41] For bibliography on Heraclitus in general see above chapter 2, note 35. On *psychē* in Heraclitus see especially S.M. Darcus 'Logos of *Psychē* in Heraclitus', *RSA*, 1979, vol. 9, pp. 89–93, '*Thumos* and *Psychē* in Heraclitus B 85', *RSC*, 1977, vol. 25, pp. 353–9, 'What Death Brings in Heraclitus', *Gymnasium*, 1978, vol. 85, pp. 501–10 (each of these articles with earlier bibliography), Kahn, *Art and Thought*, pp. 126–30, 238–63, Kirk, Raven, and Schofield, pp. 203–8, J. Mansfeld, 'Heraclitus Fr. B 85 DK', *Mnemosyne*, 1992, vol. 45, pp. 9–18, M.C. Nussbaum, '*Psychē* in Heraclitus, I and II', *Phronesis*, 1972, vol. 17, pp. 1–16, 153–70, T.M. Robinson, 'Heraclitus on Soul', *The Monist*, 1968, vol. 69, pp. 305–14, M. Schofield, 'Heraclitus' Theory of Soul and its Antecedents' in S. Everson, ed., *Psychology*, Cambridge, 1991, pp. 13–34, T. Suzuki, '*Psychē* and *Logos* in Heraclitus' in Boudouris, pp. 375–83, W.J. Verdenius, 'A Psychological Statement of Heraclitus', *Mnemosyne*, 1943, vol. 11, pp. 115–21, 'Some Aspects of Heraclitus' Anthropology' in Bossier, pp. 29–35. See also bibliography in de Martino (chap. 2, note 35), p. 173. The article of Nussbaum is particularly valuable.

[42] See especially frs B 1, 2, 50, 72, 87 and 108. For bibliography on the nature of *logos* see above chapter 2, note 38, and in particular the work of Verdenius.

[43] See especially B 92 and 93. On Heraclitus' use of riddles see S.M. Darcus, 'Heraclitus the Riddler: B 101', *A&A*, 1978, vol. 24, pp. 40–2, D. Gallop, 'The Riddles of Heraclitus' in Boudouris, pp. 123–35, U. Hölscher, 'Orakelstil' in *Anfängliches Fragen*, Göttingen, 1968, and Kahn, *Art and Thought*, pp. 3–9.

role that this capacity, shared by all human beings, had in the universe. Thus he tells them in B 50 'not to listen' to him 'but to *logos*'.

Heraclitus saw that speech (reflecting thought) enabled humans to organise their world. He postulates that a divine principle exists that carries out on a cosmic level a similar activity. The divinity, by thinking and 'speaking' things, forms them. Humans, sharing in the same capacity, name these same objects, acting thereby in a manner similar to the divine. Heraclitus laments frequently that human beings fail to understand how their thought and speech works.[44] But even though they do not understand, they still in practice reflect what the divine *logos* does.[45]

The divine *logos* expresses itself always in opposites.[46] These opposites (cold/hot, e.g., dry/wet) exist as the bounds of a continuum of being. Though absolutely different, they none the less possess a unity.[47] In B 51 he illustrates this truth. He says that people fail to understand 'how being at variance it [the universe?] agrees with itself: there is a back-stretched connection (*harmoniē*) as in the bow and the lyre'. In the case of the bow, its components are a straight stick and a flexible cord, each quite opposite in form and shape. Apart they form distinct units. Together their opposition provides a tension making a unit filled with potential energy.

The microcosm/macrocosm theory in Heraclitus presents us with human beings expressing in language their thoughts about 'all things'. The divine *logos* does the same on a larger scale. It actually forms 'all things' by expressing them. Just as was the case with Anaximenes' principle of air, what this divine *logos* does is simply to display its own nature. In being itself, it speaks, makes, and sustains the universe. The nature of its thoughts becomes evident in the universe which is revealed as a unified series of opposites.

As mentioned above, human beings fail to grasp the significance

---

[44] Thus he says in B 1: 'although all things happen according to this *logos*, people are like those of no experience, even when they do encounter such words and deeds as I explain, as I distinguish each thing according to its constitution and declare how it is'. See frs B 1, 19, 34, 51, 72, and 108. Heraclitus criticises human beings in order to lead them to grasp the truth within themselves.

[45] Thus in B 72 Herclitus describes humans as being 'in continuous contact with *logos*'.

[46] See fr. B 67: 'god is day and night, winter and summer, war and peace, satiety and famine . . .'. See also frs B 60–1, 88, and 111.

[47] See fr. B 10: 'out of all things there comes a unity and out of a unity, all things'. See too frs B 54 and 123.

of their *logos*, even, as Heraclitus says, after they have heard him explain its importance (B 1). Instead of perceiving what happens when they think and speak, they fail to pay attention to *logos* at all. Thus he says of them: 'even though *logos* is common, the many live as though they had an individual way of thinking' (B 2). *Logos* is 'common', a capacity shared by all people.[48] But they imagine that their thoughts are their own, of a distinctive and private nature. Further- more when they consider the nature of the things they commonly name, they see them too as separate entities without relationship to one another and without any unity (B 51). This, of course, is natural enough. It is easy to observe things as opposites and difficult to grasp that they have some underlying unity.

Heraclitus must then meet the challenge of 'waking' human be- ings from their lack of perception (B 1). If with his riddles he can encourage his listeners to examine what they do when they speak, help them perceive how their minds function in their use of speech, and guide them to understand how the world they name has a ra- tional order underlying it, he will be able to present to them what he regards as the truth. He will thus make the value of *logos* clear and gradually lead people to realise that, in this capacity for thought and speech, a portion of the divine is also present. If people come to understand how they think and speak, they will perceive as well the divine principle.

Logos and its nature therefore are central to Heraclitus' thought. *Logos* is responsible for the amazing complexity that 'all things' mani- fest but also for their basic simplicity. All exist as manifestations of one organising principle that expresses itself in opposites while hold- ing them in unity. Heraclitus adds also another explicit feature of *logos*: in physical nature it is fiery. Thus he says of the universe (B 30): 'this cosmos, the same for all, no god or human being made, but it always was, is, and shall be, an everliving fire, kindling in measure and going out in measure'. At any instant, if a fire is observed, it is a bright, sparkling presence in constant motion. Heraclitus penetrates

---

[48] In B 114 Heraclitus probably refers to *logos* again as the common element on which people 'should base their strength'. (We discussed this fragment above in chapter 2 under *noos*.) He uses the same term 'common' for 'war' in B 80. Tension exists between the opposites, keeping them in existence. (See further on B 80 in chapter 5 on justice.) In B 103 he also uses this term 'common' of the beginning and end of a circle. In B 113 Heraclitus again uses the term: 'thinking' is 'common for all'.

its nature further to observe within it a perfect balance of life and death. In the 'measure' that it is extinguished, it is also kindled. The balance of these opposites makes the existence of fire possible.

Heraclitus says that in essence the universe is this fire. Like Anaximenes he assumes that the nature of the whole is a manifestation of one element, fire, ever displaying its own nature and able to appear as all other objects, especially the basic elements, earth, air, and water (B 30–1, 64). Thus is B 90 he says: 'all things are an exchange for fire and fire for all things, just as goods [are an exchange] for gold and gold for goods'. The divine principle then and the universe are a fire. This fire appears as a variety of opposites.

Within human beings, according to Heraclitus, there is an entity that is associated with the capacity for *logos* that they possess. This is *psyche*. Let us look at what he says about it.[49] B 36 reads: 'for *psychai* it is death to become water, and for water death to become earth. Water comes to be from earth and from water, *psyche*'. Speaking elsewhere of the world-picture, Heraclitus supposes that, although all things are essentially fire, this element undergoes a cycle of change. B 31 describes this cycle: 'the turnings (*tropai*) of fire: first sea but of sea half is earth, half lightning storm. Sea is poured forth from earth and is measured in the same proportion as existed before it became earth'. What has happened in B 36 is that *psyche* has taken the place of fire as described in B 31. This substitution suggests that the essential nature of *psyche* is fiery, like that of *logos* itself.

But Heraclitus intends in this fragment, B 36, as in so many others, to startle his listener. He speaks of the 'death' of *psyche*. Surely, it would seem, this is a contradiction in terms. Can *psyche*, normally assumed both to be 'life' and to be the portion of the human that never dies, experience 'death'? Heraclitus clearly does not refer to a total extinction of *psyche* but to a change in form that it can undergo. This change may seem a negative one but it may also be a necessary one if the universe is to continue as the balance of opposites that Heraclitus assumes it to be. At any moment Heraclitus believes that the universe is essentially a process of change in which fire 'turns', manifesting itself in measured form as the other elements (B 31, quoted above). As it becomes water, water becomes earth; earth becomes water and water, fire, all in equal proportions. This

---

[49] *Psyche* appears in frs B 36, 45, 77, 85, 98, 107, 115, and 117–18.

perfectly controlled cycle of change gives the illusion that the opposites are each separate and distinct. But in reality each one is actually one becoming another in balanced proportions.

Such too is the case with *psychē*. As it exists within the person, it also manifests itself as fire or water. But each of these elements is not static. Fire is water becoming fire in the same proportion as fire becomes water. So too water is fire becoming water in the same measure that water becomes fire. This process is the essence of *psychē*.

But in the case of *psychē* Heraclitus places a higher value on its manifestation as fire. He suggests that human beings have some control over the way *psychē* can appear within them. They should try to keep *psychē* as fiery as possible. He vividly illustrates the negative consequences of failing to do this in B 117. 'Whenever a person is drunk, he is led stumbling along by a beardless boy; he does not know where he is going because he has a wet *psychē*'. When *psychē* is wet, the person becomes foolish, gives up control of movement to another, and is led to an unknown destination. Wine, it appears, brings a partial death of *psychē*; it turns to water. What is lost is rationality and understanding. In contrast to this *psychē* Heraclitus asserts: 'a gleam of light is a dry *psychē*, wisest and best' (B 118). Heraclitus therefore appears to urge sobriety because it allows someone to keep *psychē* fiery. This condition is the preferable one for it to be in.

In these two fragments on *psychē* Heraclitus has assigned to it a significant new role: it is the seat of intellectual activity in the person. As such, it resembles *phrenes* and *thumos*. Like them it acts as a psychological agent within the person, a vital one connected with intelligence.

We see too in these fragments a range within which *psychē* moves. It varies from wise to foolish depending on its degree of dryness. At the same time it becomes more 'alive' or closer to extinction according to whether it is dry or moist. As in the traditional view, *psychē* is that which keeps human beings alive. When it is watery, it apparently fulfils this task less well than when it is fiery.

Within the living person, therefore, *psychē* is not something static. Thus far in other authors we have encountered *psychē* in the living as essentially 'breath' or 'air', having a single nature. This was true of its existence in Homer and the lyric and elegiac poets. As it emerged, however, as a psychological agent, its nature could vary. The Pythagoreans had introduced another new idea: *psychē* could become more or less pure. Like these Pythagoreans, Heraclitus too assumes change in *psychē* during the existence of the individual: it varies from fiery to watery.

Heraclitus urges that *psychē* be kept in its optimum state, like fire. But it is not easy for people to maintain it in this favourable condition. There are elements in the human being that act against its staying fiery. We heard above in chapter 2 on *thumos* that this psychic entity has an adverse effect upon *psychē*[50] In B 85 Heraclitus says: 'it is difficult to fight *thumos*, for what it wishes it buys at the expense of *psychē*'. We suggested in chapter 2 that *thumos* functions in this fragment as a psychological agent that opposes *psychē*. What it wants, it acquires by decreasing *psychē*. It is *psychē* that provides the 'money' for *thumos* and this 'money' is a portion of itself.[51] *Thumos* functions, it appears, primarily as a seat of desire. *Psychē* as we have seen in B 117 and 118 acts as a seat of intelligence. B 85 says that, once *thumos* gets the upper hand and *psychē* has been lessened, it is hard for the person to resist this *thumos*. *Psychē*, then, when it has not been diminished, could apparently help the person resist *thumos*. But once *thumos* predominates, an individual faces problems in resisting its force.[52] When *thumos* is active, *psychē* may still be fiery but its presence within the person does not seem to be very powerful.

Another fragment, though possibly not authentic,[53] may suggest too why *psychē* does not abide as a strong fiery presence in the individual or why a person may encounter resistance in keeping it thus. B 77 says: 'it is joy or death for *psychai* to become wet'. If *psychē* takes delight in becoming moist, it becomes clear why the person in whom it is found may find it difficult to keep it fiery. Yet 'delight' for *psychē* is also again termed 'death'. In its watery state *psychē* may gain enjoyment at the cost of both its rationality and its vitalizing influence.

Two other fragments of Heraclitus give us further information about *psychē*. They are especially important in that they specifically men-

---

[50] See also the discussion of this fragment above in chapter 2.

[51] Cf. Bacch. 5.151 (mentioned above) where Meleager describes the gradual lessening of his *psychē*. In Eur., *Andromache* 541, Menelaus says he lost a 'large portion of his *psychē*'.

[52] No wonder that Heraclitus says in B 110, as we noted in chapter 2, that 'it is not better for human beings to acquire whatever they desire'.

[53] B 77 is rejected by Kahn, *Art and Thought*, p. 245, Marcovich, pp. 354, 360, and T.M. Robinson, p. 130. It is accepted by Conche, *Héraclite*, pp. 330–2 and W.K.C. Guthrie, vol. 1, p. 433 n. 4.

tion the term *logos*. B 45 says: 'you would never discover the limits of *psychē*, even though you travelled along every road: so deep a *logos* does it have'.[54] B 115 says: 'the *logos* of *psychē* is one increasing itself'. In these passages *logos* is often interpreted as having a meaning different from that discussed above.[55] It is interpreted as 'measure'.[56] The reference then is to the 'measure' that *psychē* possesses, one that is boundless and ever increasing. These statements are significant in that they suggest that *psychē* has a capacity without limit. In the context of Heraclitus' philosophy we may assume that he defines this capacity in particular as one for wisdom, for understanding how the universe functions. This would be particularly true of *psychē* as a 'gleam of light' (B 118).

Heraclitus used language in a rich and varied way, appropriately so for the interpretation of reality that he presented. Since this is the case, it is possible that the references to *logos* in B 45 and B 115 relate also to it as 'speech reflecting thought', that is, to the capacity in humans that he considered a share in the divine principle.

We have heard in earlier authors that *psychē* as shade in the underworld could utter sounds. Xenophanes jokingly gives it this function in a living animal (B 7). Heraclitus too might be assigning the function of speech within the human being to *psychē*. The way he then refers to it is significant: the human capacity for thought and speech 'grows' and is 'deep'.[57] Always human beings can understand more, name more, speak more. They experience no limit in the ability of learning new words and expressions. Even foreign languages are accessible to them and consequently the experience that these languages embody.

The 'deep' *logos* that *psychē* possesses, then, may be a share in the divine nature. It too appears to be 'deep'. One description Heraclitus gives of the divine law governing the universe is that 'it has as much power as it wishes and suffices for all and is still left over' (B 114).

---

[54] This translation is based on that of T.M. Robinson, p. 32. 'Travelled every road' can also be translated as 'travelled the whole way'. Both translations suggest the extensive nature of *psychē*.

[55] See, e.g., Kahn, *Art and Thought*, pp. 129–30, 237, Marcovich, p. 367, T.M. Robinson, pp. 110, 157. See also Darcus (note 41) *RSA*, 1979, vol. 9, notes 8 and 17.

[56] This same meaning of *logos* occurs also in B 31.

[57] Cf. the reference to B 17 of Empedocles to 'learning (*mathē*) increasing *phrenes*' (discussed above in chapter 2). *Psychē* too may be 'expanded' by its capacity for *logos*.

If Heraclitus locates the capacity for *logos* in *psychē*, we can see how important *psychē* has become. With this speech/thought, human beings organise their world just as the divine principle forms the universe as a whole.

Another fragment may suggest that Heraclitus did associate *logos* in this meaning with *psychē*. B 107 says: 'poor witnesses for people are eyes and ears if they possess barbarian *psychai*'. Heraclitus uses an adjective for *psychai* clearly related to language. 'Barbarians' were those who did not understand the Greek language, even though they experienced the words that were uttered. 'Barbarian' *psychai* would, then, it appears, be those which do not grasp the meaning of the information that eyes and ears provide. The universe with its varied yet unified phenomena remains a foreign language to them. We may suggest that such *psychai* are perhaps 'moist', not 'fiery' in nature. What Heraclitus approves of are *psychai* that are not 'barbarian'. These would understand the 'language' of the universe. They would come to see that the universe itself is a language, *logos*, a divine expression varied and unified in nature.

Our picture of *psychē* in Heraclitus thus far is that of an entity which has emerged as an important psychological agent within the living person. Ideally, it will be fiery in nature, thus matching the divine principle that organises all things. In such a state it will be wise. Functioning as a seat of intelligence, it may act too as the location of *logos*, the capacity human beings have for thought and speech. But this *psychē* can unfortunately change in state and may even delight to do so. If it does and if it becomes watery, it loses its strength of rationality. It can also prove vulnerable to *thumos* when the latter becomes overly active in the person. *Psychē* thus ranges from positive to negative. Those in whom it is in a positive state, the fiery one, will be able, it seems, to respond best to Heraclitus' teachings about the universe and how it functions.

What happens to this *psychē* after death? Heraclitus provides us with little evidence. He has one fragment that states: '*psychai* have a sense of smell in Hades' (B 98). Heraclitus is obscure here as usual.[58] He may be referring to a traditional picture of *psychē* and suggesting that in the 'invisible' and dark land (the literal meaning of 'Hades'), it might be able to smell since it cannot see.

---

[58] See on this Conche, *Héraclite*, pp. 348–9, Darcus (note 41), Kahn, *Art and Thought*, pp. 256–9, and T.M. Robinson, pp. 145–6.

Heraclitus himself probably did not postulate a *psychē* surviving in Hades. Instead his views may be akin to what Anaximenes and the Pythagoreans taught. As mentioned above, Homer and the lyric and elegiac poets see the fate of *psychē* after death as essentially something negative. Anaximenes and the Pythagoreans make it positive, apparently postulating some form of union with the divine principle. Such seems to be the case too with Heraclitus. *Psychē*, capable of sharing the divine nature when it is fiery, may have an eventual destiny of joining the divine *logos*. But since *psychē* can also be watery, it may be that, if it is in this state at death, it will simply flow away as water. Such a range of possibility for *psychē* may be what Heraclitus refers to in B 25 when he says that 'greater deaths win greater destinies'.

Once again as with Anaximenes and the Pythagoreans the possibility of individual survival seems missing. Watery *psychai* would become water; fiery *psychai* would join the divine fire. Clearly this second destiny would be judged superior by Heraclitus.

Our evidence for what happens to *psychē* after death is slight. But whatever Heraclitus thinks happens to it at this stage, his interpretation of its role in the living person is of great importance. We see *psychē* functioning as a valuable psychological agent in the individual. It can provide the key for understanding reality and itself shares in the divine nature. It has become the seat of intellectual activity. Other authors of the fifth century will proceed to speak of the enhanced role of *psychē* in the living person, assigning to it a vital function in the person while alive, just as Heraclitus has done. It has emerged as a seat of intelligence in those who are alive.

Summary

In this chapter we have examined the Greek word *psychē* in Homer, the lyric and elegiac poets, and the Presocratics. This term, so vitally important in later philosophers, underwent a significant change in meaning during the Archaic Age. The authors we treated revealed important stages in its transformation. Gradually it was to designate in the living person the seat of personality. It was to function as the chief psychological agent within the individual, the centre of intellect, emotion, and will. But it did not appear to have these roles at all in our earliest evidence, early epic poetry.

In Homer, *psychē* proves important only when death impends or a death-like state, fainting, occurs. In the living person it signifies 'breath' and 'life'. The person places high value upon *psychē*. It proves vulnerable to various outside forces. In death it can leave through a wound or the teeth. When it does, it continues to exist in Hades as a pale shade, still a recognisable image of the person in whom it once lived.

The shades of the dead are utterly insubstantial. They make sounds like moving air. Their activities are severely limited. Until the body is buried, *psychē* retains some functions associated with it, but once it is buried, *psychē* becomes quite helpless. None the less, Homer's picture *psychē*, enhanced by the body's powers, foreshadows what it will later become in the living person.

Before they have drunk blood, *psychai* can move about and express a limited range of emotion. Agamemnon grieves (*Od.* 11.387); Ajax is angry (11.543). Some shades can recognise Odysseus, other do not. After blood, *psychai* can understand and communicate. They can remember and anticipate. They have received powers usually connected with psychological entities such as *noos*, *phrēn*, and *thumos*. This enhancement of *psychē* allowed it to be represented in ways that would probably influence a similar portrayal later in the living.

One significant feature of Homer's treatment of the shades of the dead is his casual shift from reference to *psychē* to that of person. Thus he easily mentions the *psychē* of Odysseus' mother, Anticleia, acting in some fashion, and then refers to Anticleia herself as the one who acts. Here we have an identification of person with *psychē* that foreshadows again the way in which *psychē* in those who are alive will function as a psychological agent.

With the lyric and elegiac poets, changes in *psychē* appear. *Psychē*, capable of a range of activities in Hades, now begins to demonstrate this same range in the living person. Perhaps too, in imitation of *thumos* and *phrēn*, it absorbs some of their functions. It has become an object of interest, not just at the time of death, but during life.

Psychē in these poets has in particular the meaning of 'life'. Situations have appeared in which individuals need encouragement to be willing to risk *psychē*. Tyrtaeus especially suggests that honour and glory exceed the value of *psychē* present within the body and therefore it should not be spared. Pindar likewise says that *psychē* should strive to enter Hades with 'glory'.

Several times *psychē* functions as a psychological agent in the person. It can be a seat of pain, love, desire, and courage. It can function as a location of inner qualities. We hear of someone 'unflinching in *psychē*' or having a 'steadfast *psychē*'. *Psychē* acts too as a seat of deliberation or resolve. Pindar addresses his own *psychē* directly, urging it not to pursue certain goals. He also in one passage refers to *psychē* in the context of the transmigration of souls and associates it with the justice of someone's deeds.

In the Presocratics we see new aspects of *psychē*. For Anaximenes it is air that 'holds together' and 'controls' the body. It gives life and movement. This same air is the divine principle that forms the universe and governs it. *Psychē* in human beings thus shares in the divine principle. Anaximenes does not make clear the destiny of this *psychē* after death but it probably is a positive one, consisting of union with the divine. The degree to which Anaximenes ascribed intelligence to air, *psychē*, in the person is likewise not clear. Later, Diogenes of Apollonia, very much repeating Anaximenes' ideas, makes *psychē*, being air, the seat of intelligence and thought. Anaximenes and Diogenes both present *psychē* as a positive entity, not only during life but after death as well.

The Pythagoreans viewed *psychē* as endowing the person with life. They saw it as an entity, divine in nature, that migrates from one life-form to another, gradually becoming more pure. When *psychai* enter human beings, they are apparently on the final stages of their journey. Humans have control over their destiny and, by ritual observances, can help to make *psychē* pure. They can fail to do so and may consequently face reincarnation into a lower life-form. But if *psychē* reaches a pure condition, it evidently needs to travel no farther and may experience union with the divine principle. Like Anaximenes, the Pythagoreans present a very positive picture of *psychē*. Its relationship to intellectual activity in the living person is still obscure but its role as sharer in the divine and its ultimate destiny as joining that divine being make it a possession to be highly valued.

Heraclitus thinks of *psychē* as an important psychological agent within the person. It is fiery in nature like the divine principle, *logos*. It is a seat of intelligence. It may be the location in human beings of *logos*, which is identical to the divine nature. This divinity speaks, forms, and organises the universe. With their *logos* humans can understand how this universe functions, speak about it, and also perceive the divine nature.

Within the living person Heraclitus assumes a variable state for *psychē*. It can be fiery, a positive condition in which it displays wisdom and rationality. It can, however, also become watery. When this happens, *psychē* functions badly, losing its intelligence. The destiny of *psychē* after death seems two-fold. Either it is a positive one in which a *psychē*, fiery at death, joins the divine fire. Or it is a negative one in which *psychē*, watery at death, simply flows away as this element. Like Anaximenes and the Pythagoreans, Heraclitus presents *psychē* as potentially a very positive entity. Its role within the living person is now prominent.

In this chapter we have traced some steps by which *psychē* gradually became a psychological agent in living human beings. Its first appearance is simply as the breath endowing life. After the individual dies, however, this breath continues to exist as a pale image of the person in Hades. Its very essence is 'life' that cannot be destroyed. In the underworld this *psychē* normally has a very limited range of activity. But under special circumstances, when it is given a portion of body again, it can display various functions. Gradually we see *psychē* taking on activities within the living person, activities connected with other psychological entities. We observe also that its destiny after death ceases to be negative. *Psychē* becomes associated with the divine principle, sharing it nature and destined to join it after death. In later authors *psychē* will become more and more important in the living person. Already its role has been clearly adumbrated in these early authors.

CHAPTER FOUR

EXCELLENCE

No question seems to have been more important to the early Greeks than this one: 'what makes a human being excellent?' The question is not a simple one and its complexity was already perceived, probably long before we encounter one treatment of it in Homer. For with the notion of excellence we are led to ask other questions. What is excellence itself? What makes it so? Who can attain it? Is there only one form? Will it change during an individual life? Will it alter from one century to the next?

What we find in Greek literature from our first poetry right through the fifth and into the fourth centuries is an enduring search for the essence of heroism. Heroes and heroines display excellence. But what one author considers heroic, another may not. Thus we encounter again and again an assessment and re-assessment of excellence. Always an assumption underlies the search. Human beings are capable of splendid feats that invite imitation. Among such admirable actions some take precedence over others. All present a challenge for those observing them. Which should be chosen? How can these be achieved by another?

In this chapter we shall examine the idea of excellence in early Greek authors. The term for 'excellence' is *aretē*. It is often translated as 'virtue', especially later when it appears in Plato. But this translation suggests too great a focus upon moral considerations. The term itself is more comprehensive: it includes, as we shall see, physical, intellectual, and volitional aspects as well.

Homer gives us one view of excellence; other writers will agree with this view, refine it, or disagree with it. These authors, acting as teachers of wisdom for their society, will speak of the ways in which human beings can excel. They may focus upon different capacities found in humans as the source of excellence. They may assume that one or more of these take precedence over others. All will summon their listeners to heed and, to the extent possible, to copy the ideal picture they present. Let us begin our treatment with Homer.

Homer

The *Iliad* and the *Odyssey* present us with our first picture of *aretē*. But the tradition from which these epic poems came, as we have said in chapter 1, was already centuries old by Homer's time. We have these two magnificent poems about heroes but many others were sung (the epic cycle), describing the exploits of different individuals. We cannot, therefore, simply generalize from Homer about the nature of early Greek ideas of heroism. Instead, we see in these two poems what Homer himself, assumed by long tradition to be the author of these poems, thought. And what Homer does is to show that he lived in a society where certain ideas about excellence prevailed. He responds to these ideas.

The early notion of *aretē* has been much studied.[1] The word itself is probably related to *aretaō*, meaning 'to thrive' or 'to flourish'.[2] The person exhibiting 'excellence' would clearly be thought to be someone 'thriving' or 'flourishing'. But even though the connection with the root of this verb may be the correct etymology of *aretē*, it appears that in practice the Greeks associated it more with *areiōn*, meaning 'better', and with *aristos*, meaning 'best'. The positive degree of 'best' (*aristos*) was the word '*agathos*', meaning 'good'. This term, like *aretē*, included moral aspects and also physical, intellectual, and volitional ones. *Aretē* signifies the 'highest' or 'best' quality possible. In its appearance in Homer we note a broad range of meaning of the

---

[1] For the idea of *aretē* see in particular A.W.H. Adkins, *From the Many, Merit, Moral Values*, 'Values, Goals and Emotions in the *Iliad*', *CP*, 1982, vol. 77, pp. 292–325, D.B. Claus, '*Aidos* in the Language of Achilles', *TAPA*, 1975, vol. 105, pp. 13–28, Donlan, 'Scale, Value, and Function in the Homeric Economy', *AJAH*, 1981, vol. 6, pp. 101–17, Dover, Ferguson, E.D. Francis, 'Virtue, Folly, and Greek Etymology' in Rubino, pp. 74–121, Jaeger, *Paideia*, vol. 1, K.C. King, *Achilles, Paradigms of the War Hero from Homer to the Middle Ages*, Berkeley, 1987, A.A. Long, *JHS*, 1970, Marg, G. Martano, '*Physis, aretē, dikē* nella cultura greca dell' eta arcaica', *Elenchos*, 1987, vol. 8, pp. 25–41, Nagy, *Best of Achaeans*, H. Patzer, 'Der archaische Aretē-Kanon im Corpus Theognideum' in G. Kurz, D. Muller, and W. Nicolai (eds), *Gnomosyne, Festschrift Marg*, Munich, 1981, pp. 197–226, Pearson, Podlecki, *CW*, 1969, *Early Greek Poets*, Prior, C. Rowe, W. Sale, 'Achilles and Heroic Values', *Arion*, 1963, vol. 2, pp. 86–100, M. Scott, 'Pity and Pathos in Homer', *A Class*, 1979, vol. 22, pp. 1–14, Snell, *Lexikon*, vol. 1, pp. 1229–1232, C. Spicq, O.P, 'Note de lexicographie: *aretē*', *RB*, 1982, vol. 89, pp. 161–76, C. Ulf, *Die homerische Gesellschaft*, Munich, 1990, pp. 1–49, Yamagata, pp. 184–208, Whitman. Of these Adkins, Jaeger, A.A. Long, Nagy, Sale, Yamagata, and Whitman prove most helpful.

[2] On the etymology see Chantraine, vol. 1, p. 107, and Snell, *Lexikon*, vol. 1, p. 1230.

term. Usually found in references to human beings, it is none the
less also said to belong to the gods (*Il.* 9.498) and to horses (*Il.* 23.276,
374).

The term suggests the presence of the highest quality of which
something is capable. In the case of horses, they exhibit speed in
running. This quality is the one most sought in these animals and
those exhibiting it are obviously best. *Aretē* in humans would evidently also be that quality which makes someone 'best', but its definition and essential nature are not always easy to define.

In his poems, Homer gives a rich and complex picture of *aretē* for
humans. In our discussion we shall focus upon two individuals, Achilles
in the *Iliad* and Penelope in the *Odyssey*. The details of the stories we
present may be quite familiar to some readers, less so to others. But
these will be given only to demonstrate how Achilles and Penelope
display *aretē*. What is especially interesting with these two people is
the way in which they show not only what might have been called,
already in Homer's time, a traditional *aretē* but also new forms of
aretē that he wished in particular to stress.

The Excellence of the Warrior: Achilles

In the *Iliad* we meet heroes at war and it is in this context that
Homer will describe what it is to be 'excellent'. Glaucus sums up the
essence of *aretē* when he says that his father urged him, on going to
Troy, 'always to be best and to be pre-eminent over all' (*Il.* 6.208).
Peleus gives the same advice to Achilles (*Il.* 11.784). The battlefield
would be the place of action. The challenge would be to fight in
single combat, to win, and to strip one's opponent of his armour. In
recognition of triumph, a fighter would win honour (*timē*), glory (*kleos*),
and recognition from other heroes. Practically he would receive prizes
from the common spoil, given with the consent of all (*Il.* 1.162, 368).
Hector describes the heroic code when he refuses to give up fighting
at Andromache's request: 'but I feel terribly ashamed before the Trojan
men and long-robed Trojan women, if like a coward I skulk apart
from battle. Nor does my *thumos* urge me to act thus, for I have
learned always to be noble and to fight in the front rank of the
Trojans, striving to win my father's great glory and my own' (*Il.*
6.442–6).

In the *Iliad* Odysseus too makes clear what is expected of heroes
when he debates with himself over what he should do when he is

caught alone on the battlefield. His choices are to flee or to stand and he considers both but then quickly asks: 'but why does my *thumos* discuss these questions with me? For I know that cowards depart from battle but he who is best in fighting must hold his ground firmly, whether he be struck or he strike another' (*Il.* 11.407–10).[3]

If a warrior fights valiantly, he will win glory (*kleos*) that will live after his death. It is because human beings are mortal and survive only as pale shades in Hades (see chapter 3) that they must strive to achieve something in life that will cheat death of all its prize. Sarpedon poignantly speaks of the human condition to Glaucus: 'my friend, if escaping from this battle we would be always ageless and immortal, neither would I myself fight among the first ranks nor would I send you into battle that brings men glory. But now, since fates of death in countless numbers, fates which no mortal can escape or avoid, stand over us, let us go. Either we will give a cause of boasting to someone or someone will give it to us' (*Il.* 12.322–8). Brave action in battle attracts notice. It illustrates what is splendid in the fighter and this 'excellence' has a chance to live on.

A warrior shows prowess in being able to defeat and kill his opponent. But he shows himself exceptional as well in how he treats the man he has slain. Hector challenging the Achaeans to send a champion against him says: 'if I kill him and Apollo gives me glory, I will strip him of his armour . . . but his corpse I will give back to the well-benched ships so that the long-haired Achaeans may give him burial . . . and perhaps some man of later generations will say as he sails by in his many-oared ship on the wine-dark sea: "this is the tomb of a man fighting at his best who died long ago whom glorious Hector killed." So perchance someone will say and my glory will never die' (*Il.* 7.81–91).

It is those living later who give immortality to heroes long dead. They do so by the telling and retelling of noble feats. So Hector prays before his death: 'but not without a struggle nor without glory let me die, but in achieving some great deed for those who are about to be to learn of' (*Il.* 22.304–5). The mouths of others will preserve the record of what heroes have done and one set of lips in particular will be of vital importance, that of the poet.

This heroic code found in Homer lays great importance upon the

---

[3] See also the discussion of this passage in chapter 2 on *thumos*.

opinions of others. It is not that the heroes do not have an inner sense of their own value and worth or that they do not act from convictions arising from within.[4] They clearly do.[5] But a large component of this *aretē* consists in public recognition. Thus Agamemnon urges on the Achaeans: 'my friends, be men and take a valiant heart. Have a sense of shame before one another in the mighty conflict. Of men showing a sense of shame more are saved than are killed. But in those who flee neither is glory called forth nor any valour' (*Il* 5.529–32). During life, the hero wishes to win praise from his peers who will likely honour him also with gifts. For the period after death, he must leave behind many instances of prowess that will give rise to stories to be retold.

Excellence is something that the hero both displays and achieves. However much noble birth may be a characteristic of the hero, excellence is not simply an inborn trait but comes to full growth only after long training. Thus Achilles in the *Iliad* receives Phoenix as a teacher. Phoenix urges: 'Peleus sent me on the day when he sent you [Achilles] from Phythia to Agamemnon, a mere child, not yet knowing of war in which men take part nor of assemblies, where they become distinguished. For this reason he sent me to teach you all these things, to be a speaker of words and a doer of deeds' (9.439–43). 'Speaker of words, doer of deeds' sums up the essence of *aretē*. The deeds, as we have made clear, will be glorious exploits on the battlefield. But the hero will also need to express his ideas with clarity as those who try to persuade Achilles to return to battle in *Iliad*, Book 9 illustrate. Achilles learned his lessons well from Phoenix, for he can answer in lucid and well-argued fashion these speeches in Book 9. Odysseus too, again and again in the *Odyssey*, will show versatility in argument and assessment of situations, excelling in choosing apt words.

This excellence then is built up by training. But a certain inherent capacity for it was probably assumed to be essential. Heroes are special

---

[4] These positions are much discussed in recent scholarship (see note 1) and are especially important in relation to *dikē* (see chapter 5). For useful general points see especially M.W. Dickie, '*Dikē* as a Moral Term in Homer and Hesiod', *CP*, 1978, vol. 73, pp. 91–101, and Lloyd-Jones, *Justice*.

[5] This will become clear in Achilles' response (see below). See also passages where people act from an inner sense of what is admirable or acceptable as, e.g., Odysseus at *Il.* 11.404–10 and Hector at *Il.* 6.442–6 (both treated above in the text). See also Odysseus' anger over the women sleeping with the suitors (*Od.* 20.10–21) and Agamemnon's dismay at Clytemnestra's behaviour (*Od.* 24.199–202).

individuals, endowed by birth with natures of great potential. These natures can be brought to flower and these people can then emerge as superior individuals. But the *aretē* that someone may have is vulnerable. Odysseus says that it is the gods who grant *aretē* and that, instead of giving this, they may send things that are 'baneful' (*Od.* 18.133–4). Eumaeus, the swineherd of Odysseus, tells him that Zeus removes 'half of someone's *aretē* when the day of slavery overtakes him' (*Od.* 17.322–3). Circumstances, therefore, and the intervention of the gods can bring to an end the flourishing of excellence. This fact probably put even more pressure upon the hero to strive for high achievement while it seemed within grasp.

We shall now examine *aretē* in relation to the hero of the *Iliad*, Achilles. His portrayal has absorbed the interest of readers, both ancient and modern. His character, an extremely complicated one, could be explored in wide-ranging ways. Our picture, focusing on *aretē*, will be a somewhat simplified one.[6]

Achilles is the swiftest of the Achaeans who came to Troy, the noblest fighter, and overall the best warrior. Justifiably he attracted, by his nature and deeds, the attention of a poet who made his name immortal. But the picture Homer presents of Achilles is not an entirely positive one. From its first word the *Iliad* focuses upon aspects of Achilles that veer far from what the heroic may have been assumed to be. 'Anger' (*mēnis*) begins the work and will prove an enduring presence throughout the epic. For book after book Achilles will not even fight. Instead, he will sit apart from his comrades, apart from the enemy, consoling with music a grievance that eats away at his heart. When he does fight again, it is violent, unrestrained hate that drives him on. His treatment of the warriors he meets is merciless and of his greatest enemy, Hector, appalling in its barbaric cruelty. The epic ends not with an account of his death or of his funeral but instead with a description of the rites paid to the one he treated so ruthlessly, Hector.

If we look in some detail at Homer's presentation of Achilles, we see two features that will prove to be very important in how *aretē* is considered during the centuries to follow. First, Achilles himself clearly accepts heroic code described above. Although his return to battle after the death of Patroclus is motivated by other causes, at the end of the *Iliad* he remains at Troy, fighting, as is expected of him, and

---

[6] On Achilles see in particular King, Nagy and Sale (note 1).

destined soon to meet his death. For as long as is given him he strives to be best, to win honour, and to claim immortality in song for his deeds. Second, in his picture of Achilles, Homer suggests that within the context of the heroic code certain factors are primary. He refines this code, showing ways in which it should not be pursued and emphasizing ways in which it should.

In coming to Troy Achilles makes a momentous decision: he knows that he will die there. As he says in Book 9: 'if I remain here and fight around the city of the Trojans, lost is my home-coming but my glory (*kleos*) will be imperishable. If I return home to my dear native country, my noble glory will be lost but my life will be long nor quickly shall the end of death come upon me' (412–6). Many warriors will die at Troy, it is true, but Achilles alone has himself chosen an early death in order to achieve 'glory'.[7] He thus acts according to the traditional code of honour. After nine years at Troy he can claim 'twelve sacked cities' (9.328) and large numbers slain, many from the family of Andromache (6.423) and Priam (24.205). He has fought for honour (*timē*) and won much more than anyone else: he displays the *aretē* of a warrior.

When Agamemnon arbitrarily removes a prize he received for this *aretē*, Achilles does not brook the insult. Rage (*mēnis*) swells in his heart as he sees the whole fabric of his quest for excellence threatened. Why die young for glory if another inferior individual can arbitrarily decrease it in a moment of time? This glory in its essence should be something impervious to time. It should be so stable that others will hasten to recognise it and speak of it. Agamemnon's action reveals instead that it could be fragile, subject to jealousy, and diminished with a word.

Achilles thus withdraws from battle. His reason is that 'there is no gratitude for fighting against the foe always, without ceasing. An equal portion awaits the one who remains [apart from the battle] and the one who fights vigorously. In equal honour stand the coward and the noble man' (9.318–20).[8] He therefore substitutes a new motive for engaging in conflict: self-preservation. He will fight again but only when the battle threatens his own hut and ship (9.650–5, 16.63).

---

[7] See Book 1, 415–18 where Thetis calls Achilles 'swift-footed and pitiable beyond all'.

[8] See too Book 16, 52–63 where Achilles explains to Patroclus why he refuses to fight.

Agamemnon soon understands how he has insulted this young warrior by reducing his *aretē*. Thus he sends an embassy to offer Achilles many gifts, not only returning the prize he took but adding many others in addition, including cities and his own daughter in marriage (*Il.* 9.121–56). But the Achilles this embassy meets has changed during his time away from fighting. Gifts, prizes, he says, now mean nothing to him (9.608). What he values at present is his *psychē* which, while still found in the living body, 'not all the wealth of Troy' could equal (*Il.* 9.401–3). And something else has occurred. The passion in Achilles' heart for *aretē* has been replaced by rage at Agamemnon (9.372–4, 426, 612, 646–8). One image alone is fixed firmly in his mind: that of Agamemnon insulting him. Ajax, the last speaker, after hearing Achilles reject all the gifts that were offered, sums up the condition of the young warrior: 'Achilles had made his great-hearted *thumos* fierce (*agrios*) in his breast' (9.629–30).

In terms of the heroic code, Achilles should have accepted the generous gifts he was offered (9.631–6). But Homer portrays him as no longer acting within the bounds of this code. Two other factors have taken precedence. One is positive: a re-evaluation of the preciousness of life. The second factor is negative: rage. This has grown so great in Achilles that it absorbs all his thinking and feeling. Ajax uses the term *agrios* for the state of his *thumos*: he resembles a 'wild beast' in his fury. As he abides apart from battle until Book 18, this rage grows greater and greater. Homer shows us in Achilles' reaction another greater threat to *aretē*: anger rising in the heart, anger beyond appropriate measure, blinding, weakening, consuming the hero in whom it is found.

Achilles' absence from battle brings many disasters to the Achaeans. At last Nestor urges Patroclus to ask to borrow Achilles' armour (11.665 f.). Both he and Patroclus, attempting to understand Achilles' behaviour, suggest that perhaps he 'is shunning some oracle' or that Thetis has brought him some command from Zeus (11.794, 16.36). But Achilles himself tells Patroclus that this is not so: he has simply been angry with Agamemnon (16.53–60) and determined to remain so until the fighting reached his own ships (16.60–3). After Patroclus borrows the armour and is killed by Hector, Achilles is overwhelmed with grief. He is eager to return to fighting, impelled now by one motive only: desire for revenge.

Homer at this point shows another Achilles. The hero realises that Zeus has answered his prayers, making the Achaeans need him desperately (18.73–9). Now, however, he asks his mother what 'pleasure' there could be for him in this situation since Patroclus is dead (80–2). Even though it will mean his death soon after, he is determined to slay Hector (87–93). He easily lays aside his anger with Agamemnon. He now asks the king to rouse the Achaeans for battle (19.56–73). Agamemnon gives a long apology for his behaviour (19.78–144), but Achilles' attention is already directed elsewhere. He tells Agamemnon to give all the gifts he is offering or to keep them (146–8). All he wants to do is to fight.

Achilles has stepped outside the heroic code once again. For him to accept Agamemnon's apology and the generous gifts he offers would restore and enhance his honour and glory. But no longer does this matter to Achilles. His motives are other now. Soon it becomes apparent that the anger consuming his heart is not dead. It has a new object and will blaze forth in unbounded fury. Hector is its object; desire for revenge, Achilles' driving impulse.

The death of Patroclus was one that Achilles might have prevented and failed to do so. His own death he now sees differently. As he laments, he thinks of how his own father, Peleus, is probably grieving for his son (19.322–37), destined to die young at Troy. Achilles' horse, Xanthus, reminds his master that death impends if he fights (19.407–17), but nothing curbs his eagerness for battle. Having experienced himself at first hand the grief of loss, he can think only of punishing Hector.

In Book 22 Achilles kills Hector. He totally ignores this hero's request that his body be returned for burial, and instead drags it by the rim of his chariot back to the Achaean camp (22.337–404). He tells the dying Hector that he wishes that he himself could devour his flesh. He promises him that dogs will eat his corpse and that no ransom of any size will persuade him to return his body (22.345–54). For eleven days Achilles daily drags Hector's body around Patroclus' tomb, vainly striving to make up to Patroclus for how he failed him. His fury is unabated. The gods gather, horrified by his behaviour. Of him Apollo says: 'his *phrenes* are not fitting, nor is the purpose (*noēma*) in his chest to be bent, but he acts wildly (*agria*) like a lion. . . . Achilles has lost pity nor in him is any sense of shame (*aidōs*)' (24.40–5).

Achilles has become like a wild animal in his anger. We hear an echo here of the way he was angry with Agamemnon: then his *thumos* was *agrios* (9.629–30). He has lost, as Apollo says, a 'sense of shame': he cares not what gods or humans think of his behaviour. Not from his lips comes the promise Hector made to the one the Greeks would choose for their champion that he would return his body for burial (7.84–91). Excessive rage has blinded Achilles to all sense of the appropriate. Hardly in him do we discern at this time a person in whom *aretē* shines forth.

Instead, another person will display *aretē* in the form of courage in this situation. The aged Priam, weak, old, heavy with grief, will venture forth to ransom Hector's body (24.253–328). Hecuba urges her husband to stay, saying of Achilles: 'if he will seize you and gaze on you with his eyes, so savage and untrustworthy a man is he, he will not pity you nor revere you in any way' (24.206–8).

Once again we hear of gifts in great supply for Achilles and once again, as events turn out, the gifts will prove unimportant. Priam approaches Achilles; he clasps his knees and kisses 'his hands, the terrible man-slaying hand which had killed so many of his sons' (24.478–9). The gesture, so humble, so revealing of an overwhelming love of father for son, strikes Achilles with astonishment. Priam urges Achilles to think of his own father, as he speaks of the fifty sons he himself has lost, Hector being the last. Pity replaces rage in the heart of Achilles and he treats Priam with compassion. He asks Priam how he dared so valiantly to come to the man 'who had killed so many of his sons' (24.520). He then echoes what Hecuba herself had said of Priam: 'truly of iron is your heart (*ētor*)' (24.205, 521).

The contrast between Achilles and Priam is clear. Thus far Achilles had been consumed with anger; he showed no pity. Priam displays courage beyond description. But Achilles changes. Recalling that his own father will lose his only son, he softens and shows compassion (24.522–51).

Yet Achilles' character has not altered. When Priam wishes to depart with haste, Achilles' anger begins to flare again and he curtly warns Priam to stay and not to provoke him (24.559–70). At this time also Achilles takes care, in the preparation of Hector's body for departure, to allow no cause for anger on either side to emerge (24.583–6). He asks Patroclus to forgive him for giving back Hector's body, saying that Patroclus will receive a share of the ransom (19.591–5). It was for his dead friend that Achilles raged.

Anger can still take hold of Achilles' heart but this heart has been softened by concern and pity. Of his own accord he offers to keep the Achaeans from fighting for the period during which Troy will mourn Hector (24.656–70). He himself has endured the suffering of grief and he can understand Priam's sorrow. Achilles had lost one dear friend and raged brutally against his slayer, showing no mercy to him when alive and attempting to dishonour him in death. Priam has lost fifty sons, many killed by Achilles. Instead of reacting with rage, he appeals as suppliant to the man responsible for these deaths, generously giving gifts, utterly motivated by love of his son. In this contrast of characters he presents, Homer underlines the importance he assignes to compassion as an element of *aretē*.

In the *Iliad* Homer presents a picture of what must have been the traditional code of honour that prevailed for centuries before his time. In the formulaic poetry from which he drew material, he probably frequently encountered the hero who trained well, fought magnificently, won victory after victory, and gained immortality in poetic song. It was in this very context that Achilles made his choice of an early death and travelled to Troy. But Homer, while providing details of the traditional picture, gives evidence of deep reflection about its demands. In his choice of theme, the anger of Achilles, in his portrayal of character, especially that of Achilles, Hector, and Priam, and in the actions of the heroes he focuses upon, Homer both presents and re-evaluates this code at one and the same time.

Achilles himself might have expected a very different poem from Homer. He might never have wished the focus on his rage, his absence from battle for eighteen books, and the description of his treatment of Hector's body. He might have wanted more attention on his exploits and perhaps his own death.

But Homer's purpose was different. Perhaps Achilles' anger always motivated him too greatly in his heroic encounters and was the great obstacle to his truly deserving glory. Not actions alone proclaim *aretē* but the way in which they are done. Only when Achilles had faced true courage in Priam and learned to show pity could he win the immortality he so greatly desired. Then it was appropriate for him to fight on. Then it was appropriate also, not to describe his death, but to leave the image of Achilles alive, about to continue in heroic endeavour.

Homer does not reject the heroic code by which the characters in his epic abide.[9] But he makes us aware of its demands. He shows us how vulnerable it could be, if arbitrarily broken, as Agamemnon broke

---

[9] With regard to Achilles, it is possible to see in his behaviour a rejection of the heroic code. See, e.g., Sale (note 1).

it in Achilles' case. He reveals that, within its broad demands, behaviour could conform but actions none the less could fail to be heroic. Achilles engages in fighting after Patroclus' death but his motive is negative (revenge) and his heart, consumed by rage, is distorted and ugly. Because human beings are mortal, they must fight to win some form of immortality. But Homer shows an awareness of mortality bringing forth a much nobler and more admirable quality: compassion. At the beginning of the *Iliad*, when honour is taken from Achilles, he reacts with great anger and seriously ponders giving up his quest for renown. At the end of the *Iliad*, of his own free will, he surrenders his greatest prize, Hector. He will fight on, but will do so now in a wider context, not merely for his own glory, but for his father, as son, as Hector had done, knowing pity in his heart. As he does so, he will deserve recognition from his peers and attention from a poet who will sing of him. What Achilles received was a poet who would choose to focus on the emergence of the hero in him, not simply upon his deeds of valour.

In the *Iliad* Homer's picture of *aretē* is thus many-faceted. What makes a hero excellent? Courage lies at the core and not just courage in fighting. Priam outshines everyone's courage in his willingness to confront Achilles. Nature of motivation and how it marks behaviour is of great importance: anger, rage, and fury are not what should drive a warrior on. And in all the ways that heroes can relate to one another, one shines brighter than the others: pity and compassion for shared suffering.

Female Excellence in the Odyssey: Penelope

In the *Odyssey* we shall look at what Homer says about excellence in women, in particular in Penelope.[10] Again we shall present details of the story of the *Odyssey* that may be familiar to readers but these are given only to focus upon excellence. Homer tells us about Penelope in detail. He contrasts her with other women mentioned in his poem, especially with Helen and Clytemnestra.

---

[10] On Penelope in the *Odyssey* see especially N. Felson-Rubin, 'Penelope's Perspective: Character from Plot' in Bremer, pp. 61–83, *Regarding Penelope: From Character to Poetics*, Princeton, 1994, P.W. Harsh, 'Penelope and Odysseus in *Odyssey* XIX', *AJP*, 1950, vol. 71, pp. 1–21, M. Katz, *Penelope's Reunion, Meaning and Indeterminacy in the Odyssey*, Princeton, 1991, L.A. MacKay, 'The Person of Penelope', *G. & R.*, 1958, vol. 5, pp. 123–7, M.-M. Mactoux, *Pénélope: Légende et Mythe*, Paris, 1975,

From the picture we find of Penelope, we can see that in a woman excellence manifested itself most strongly in fidelity.[11] Already other qualities that might be thought to be parts of or requirements for *aretē* are excluded, often explicitly so. Wealth does not seem essential. Nor does great beauty. In fact, this can be a positive detriment to the emergence of *aretē*, as proved to be true with Helen. What seems essential is the presence of 'good sense'. Frequently Homer will ascribe this to Penelope, making reference to her *phrenes*. In her case these are 'good' or 'noble' (2.117, 24.194). She 'excels in form, size, and *phrenes* well-balanced within' (18.249). She, 'beyond others, knows beautiful words, noble *phrenes*, and profitable things' (2.117). She is also often described by the stock epithets *periphrōn* and *echephrōn*, both compounds of *phrenes*, and meaning 'wise' or 'prudent' (1.329, e.g., 4.111, 17.36, 24.294).

Penelope is beautiful and excels others in appearance (18.249) but it is the way she conducts herself as wife of an absent hero that wins her praise. Her main focus is Odysseus and remains thus throughout the poem. When he left, Odysseus asked her to wait to remarry until Telemachus, then just a baby, reached manhood (18.269–70). This she does and soon after Telemachus grows up the suitors appear and begin their outrageous behaviour (1.226–9). For three or four years they remain, each vying for her hand (13.317, 24.141–2).

Through all the years of Odysseus' absence, Penelope's faithfulness endures. Other people refer to it (11.181–3, 13.379–81, 14.121–30). She herself says of her state: 'in longing for Odysseus I waste away in my dear heart' (19.136). On his return, as he speaks to her in his disguise as beggar, Odysseus can still make her shed tears for him (18.251–2).

When he departed, Odysseus left his household as a whole in charge of Mentor (11.177–9), but Penelope was to supervise domestic activities and the maidservants (1.356–8, 21.350–2). This task she performed with good sense. Her intention was clearly to carry on until

P. Marquardt, 'Penelope *polutropos*', *AJP*, 1985, vol. 106, pp. 32–48, J. van Nortwick, 'Penelope and Nausicaa', *TAPA*, 1979, vol. 109, pp. 269–76, S. B. Pomeroy, *Goddesses, Whores, Wives, and Slaves*, New York, 1975, H. Roisman, *Loyalty*, 'Penelope's Indignation', *TAPA*, 1987, vol. 117, pp. 59–68, A. Thornton, *People and Themes in Homer's Odyssey*, Dunedin, 1970, F. Wehli, 'Penelope and Telemachos', *MH*, 1959, vol. 16, pp. 228–37, J. Winkler, 'Penelope's Cunning and Homer's' in *The Constraints of Desire*, New York, 1990, pp. 129–61.
[11] See especially the treatment of Roisman, *Loyalty*.

she knew for certain that Odysseus was dead. When Eurymachus, one of the suitors, praises her for her beauty and intelligence, Penelope responds: 'all *aretē* I had, both in form and stature, the gods destroyed when the Argives embarked for Troy and my husband went with them' (18.251–3). She makes this same remark to Odysseus (in disguise), saying too that his return would increase and enhance her 'fame' (19.124–8). In this reference to *aretē*, we see Penelope revealing a traditional notion of its nature: beauty and intelligence attending a wife happily married and protected. Homer shows us that, in his view, it is the very behaviour of Penelope, still beautiful and wise, but with husband absent and unaccounted for, that constitutes her excellence.

Over the years Penelope has also acted admirably as mother. She is greatly distressed when she is not informed of Telemachus' departure from Ithaca (4.729). She worries much about his safety (4.828–30, 16.436). She has become accustomed to his being young and childish and is filled with astonishment at his more mature behaviour before his departure (1.360). On his return she is eager to 'win honour' in his eyes (18.162). She continues to be concerned for his well-being (18.166).

Once the suitors arrive, Penelope's intention not to remarry is not changed, even though Odysseus had told her to marry again. Telemachus too she has deceived to some extent because he says of her: 'the *thumos* in the *phrenes* of my mother ponders in two ways, whether she might abide here with me and manage the house, respecting the bed of her husband and the voice of the people or whether by now she should follow whoever is best of the Achaeans who woos her in the halls and offers her the most gifts' (16.73–7). But in fact this is not her frame of mind. Athena correctly describes Penelope's intentions to Odysseus: 'she, ever grieving over your return in her *thumos*, offers hope to all and makes promises to each man, sending them messages but her *noos* is set on other things' (13.379–81).

Antinoos, another suitor, criticizes Penelope with these same words, focusing upon her treacherous behaviour (2.90–2). He tells Telemachus that she is the one responsible for the long stay of the suitors in Ithaca. He mentions also her trick of weaving and unweaving the web after promising to marry on its completion (2.93–110). Penelope herself describes this device of weaving a shroud for her father-in-law, Laertes, saying that a divine spirit (*daimōn*) had given her the idea (19.138–56). The device succeeded for three years until Penelope was betrayed by her maidservants. Amphimedon, one of the suitors, after his death, once again repeats the same story about the web Penelope wove (24.128–46). He says of her as well: 'she neither refused the hateful marriage nor would she bring the situation to an end, devising for us death and black fate' (24.126–7). Penelope's tactics of delay proved effective because Odysseus arrived soon after she finished the shroud (24.149–50).

Single-minded in her devotion to Odysseus, Penelope proves instrumental in beguiling the suitors to their death. Inspired by Athena, she sets the bow of Odysseus before them, promising to marry the one who strung and used it successfully (21.1–79). It is not they but Odysseus who proves master of the bow (21.281–4, 404–9). But Penelope was not to see because Telemachus had ordered her to depart from the hall before the final contest (21.344–53).

In her slowness to accept Odysseus as her husband who had returned, Penelope again displays prudent reserve. As Agamemnon has advised him, Odysseus does not 'reveal all his thoughts' to Penelope (11.441–3). He conceals his identity, 'making trial', as Athena says, 'of his wedded wife' (13.336). In his disguise as beggar, he questions Penelope, testing her faithfulness (19.44 f.). Fitting then is her hesitation in accepting his claim to be Odysseus and her testing of him in turn. Her slowness to yield makes Odysseus exclaim of her: 'her heart (*ētor*) in her *phrenes* is of iron' (23.172). With the very words that Hecuba and Achilles had described the great courage of Priam (in *Il.* 24.205, 521 discussed above), Odysseus describes the resistance of Penelope. Yet this slowness to yield adds to her dignity. She has waited long and been untiringly faithful. Only with full assurance can she welcome the husband she had so long been faithful to and awaited (23.209–30).

In the *Odyssey* Homer offers two strong contrasts with Penelope, each too a wife. In Sparta we find Helen once again ensconced as the honoured wife of Menelaus (4.12, 121, 15.58, 100). As the gracious matron of the royal household, she shows special skills. She knows how to add a drug to wine that will remove sorrow from and soothe the hearts of her guests (4.219–33). It is she who can interpret correctly an omen that appears when Telemachus is about to depart (15.172–8). She also displays skill in embroidery, as other women excel in doing (15.104–5). She generously bestows the gift of a robe she has made upon Telemachus, to be kept for his bride by

Penelope (15.123–30). Because of his relationship to her we hear that Menelaus will receive a special and blessed fate after death, going not to Hades but to the 'Elysian plain' (4.560–9).

Homer presents the above picture of Helen as Telemachus arrives in Sparta, long after the Trojan War. Elsewhere we find different information about her in the *Odyssey*. Of her Odysseus says: 'for Helen's sake many of us perished' (11.438). The swineherd Eumaeus makes the wish: 'would that all the kindred of Helen had perished utterly, since she loosed the knees of many warriors' (14.68). Athena describes Odysseus as fighting 'for nine years for well-born Helen of the white arms' (22.228). Telemachus tells Penelope that he met Helen 'for whose sake Argives and Trojans laboured much by the will of the gods' (17.118–9).

Telemachus mentions an aspect of Helen's situation that Penelope and Helen herself will also focus upon: it was the gods who were responsible for her departure to Troy. In Book 4 Helen describes how she encountered Odysseus disguised as a beggar in Troy and helped his safe return to the Greeks. She says that at that time she was already 'lamenting the blind delusion (*atē*), given by Aphrodite', when she left 'country, child, bridal chamber, and husband, who lacked nothing either in *phrenes* or handsomeness' (4.260–4). What a contrast with Penelope who instead had to see her husband depart, then her son, knowing not if either would ever return. Helen regained all, at the same time forcing other women to lose the happy years of marriage she herself easily left behind.

Penelope makes this very point when, in her reunion with Odysseus, she says that the 'gods begrudged' that they should enjoy their youth together (23.210–11). She explains her slowness in accepting him as fear of beguilement by another (23.213–17). She then says of Helen that she would never have slept with a foreigner had she known she would return home, but in her case it was 'a god who prompted her to do this unseemly deed nor until then did she place in her *thumos* the blind delusion (*atē*), grievous delusion', that brought them all their sorrow (23.218–24).

Helen and Penelope differ remarkably in loyalty. Whatever the cause, Helen does leave her husband and give rise to the Trojan War. The two women differ too in their recognition of Odysseus. Homer presents Helen as seeing through his disguise as beggar (4.250–1). With Penelope, recognition will prove to be a long process (23.1–

204). Helen is somehow superior in this skill yet it occurs in a context where her whole situation lacks any cause for praise. When Penelope comes to recognise Odysseus, it is in the context of a marriage long honoured and cherished.

Both women end up the same; they have husband, child, home, and wealth. But it is Penelope who wins our admiration. She has been deprived of all that Helen freely gave up, even if under the influence of delusion. In Penelope, *aretē* has shone forth in the form of fidelity and loyalty. She probably was not as beautiful as Helen but in inner loveliness she is the one who excels.

The other wife in Homer who contrasts with Penelope is Clytemnestra. We meet her at the very beginning of the *Odyssey* when we hear that Aegisthus suffered pains 'beyond his fate' because he 'married the wife' of Agamemnon (1.35–6). Athena and Menelaus speak of the death of Agamemnon occurring because of the 'guile of Clytemnestra' (3.235, 4.92). But it is Agamemnon who twice speaks of the treachery of his wife.

In Book 11, as he meets Odysseus in the underworld, Agamemnon explains how he died at the hands of his wife in a merciless and cruel-hearted killing. He calls her 'treacherous' (*dolomētis*: 11.422) and 'sluttish' (*kunōpis*: 11.424). Her cleverness was not like that of Penelope in devising the trick (*dolon*: 2.292) of the web but in luring Agamemnon to a dinner where he would be killed. Her actions lead Agamemnon to say: 'for there is nothing more terrible or more vile than a woman who arranges such works with her *phrenes* just as she devised an unseemly deed, planning murder for her wedded husband. . . . she, making exceedingly grievous plans, has poured shame on herself and on women to come, even the one who does good deeds' (11.427–34).

In Book 11 also, Agamemnon envies Odysseus for his wife, Penelope. He warns him not to trust her completely but then adds that Penelope is too virtuous ever to harm her husband. In Book 24 he once again praises Penelope, saying that her name will be 'ever graced in song' (24.198). Clytemnestra, in contrast, will become a 'song of loathing' (24.200), since she has permanently harmed the reputation of all women.

At the end of the Trojan War Clytemnestra, like Penelope and Helen, acquired her husband again. But in her case infidelity, not loyalty, is what she displayed during his long absence. Very soon after his departure she wedded another. We do not hear of any 'delusion' sent by the gods or Aphrodite as an explanation to excuse her action, as happens with Helen. In hatred she kills her returning husband, showing no pity even to his corpse (11.425–6). By starkly contrasting Clytemnestra with Penelope, Homer emphasizes the latter's excellence revealed in long, patient suffering and unremitting loyalty.

Summary of Homer

The two great epics of Homer were to mould the Greek mind for centuries. In them we find our earliest notions of the heroic, notions that themselves had emerged over a long period of time. What we have seen is that Homer himself both presents traditional ideas of excellence and then offers, by his own stories, elements that he considers crucial for its presence in people. In the *Iliad* we see that birth, wealth, intelligence, handsomeness, and courage, however much they may be components of *aretē*, are not all important. Compassion for human suffering must also be present in the hero. In the *Odyssey* we see that, for women, birth, wealth, intelligence, and beauty do not suffice for *aretē*, although they may be aspects of it. A woman is expected to show good sense, to manage her household well, and to care for her children carefully. But most of all, she is to be loyal to her husband, no matter how much suffering this might entail. To the notion of excellence found in Homer later poets respond. Hesiod is generally more interested in justice than *aretē* but he does remark that it is achieved only with hard work.[12] The lyric and elegiac poets show various reactions to Homer. We shall look at the more important of these.

Lyric and Elegiac Poets

Archilochus

Archilochus, living in the seventh century, has little patience with some aspects of Homer's description of *aretē*. Being himself a mercenary soldier, he knew what it was like to face the enemy in battle and to risk his life again and again. Homer tells of heroes who found

---

[12] On justice, see chapter 5. His description of *aretē* occurs at *W. & D.* 289–92. We shall discuss these lines below with Simonides.

in single combat the very essence of excellence; fight, win, strip armour, and receive acclaim were the steps to be followed. The fame thus won and consequently immortalized in song was worth all the risks, even that of life itself.

Archilochus saw it otherwise. He says (5):[13]

> In my shield some Thracian is taking delight, a shield which
> in perfect shape, I left behind a bush, quite unwillingly.
> But I saved my *psychē*. What do I care about that shield?
> To hell with it! I can get another equally fine.

What behaviour is this? Instead of fighting bravely with his shield, Archilochus drops it and flees. Another item is more valuable to him: his *psychē*. A shield is replaceable; his soul/life is not.

We have here a stark contrast with Achilles and yet an echo too of his behaviour. Achilles comes to Troy knowing that he will forfeit his *psychē*, which he values more highly than 'all the wealth of Troy' (*Il.* 9.401–3). Once Agamemnon reduces his honour, he refuses to fight. At this time he says that his *psychē* is more important than fighting. But it is not the case that he places little value on the meaning of honourable combat (his shield), but rather a high one. Excellence in fighting is so valuable that it deserves glory that must be beyond any threat of arbitrary diminishment. When Achilles is engaged in fighting, he would never dishonour his shield. Later, Achilles too 'loses' his shield but not by choice. From his dearest friend it is stripped and will have to be replaced by a new, glorious shield made by Hephaestus. Not easily or casually would Achilles give this new shield up. Only death will separate him from it. After he dies the shield will cause the loss of life of yet another great hero of Troy, the mighty Ajax. The shame and injustice of not receiving the armour of Achilles will lead this hero through a series of events to commit suicide.

Archilochus gives a different message. Who cares about a shield? Why care if I play the coward? What matters is my *psychē* and that it is safe and sound within my body. Archilochus thus questions the whole system of values that Homer describes. Excellence could perhaps still be expressed in courage on the battlefield but this display of courage is not to be chosen over life itself.

---

[13] On this poem of Archilochus see Campbell, *Golden Lyre*, pp. 85, 208, Fränkel, *Dichtung*, pp. 152–5, and Podlecki, *Early Greek Poets*, pp. 40–1.

In another poem Archilochus expresses why this form of excellence is not worth dying for (133):[14]

> No one is respected among the citizens nor honoured
> after death. Instead we the living pursue the favour of
> the living. The worst evils always befall the dead person.

Glorious behaviour in battle does not, as Homeric heroes believed, attract the notice of the living, win their praise, and give a permanent memory for the future. Instead, citizens forget and pursue those who can bestow present advantages. Archilochus does not mention the possibility of fame given by a poet. His focus is a realistic one: in everyday life among the townspeople with whom a fighter may have lived, there is no honour for the dead and not even talk about them.

Archilochus was probably a good soldier who found the life of battle challenging and engrossing (2, 125). He calls himself a 'servant of Enyalios, lord of battle' (1). It may have been too that he died as a soldier in battle at a relatively young age.[15] What we find in his poems is a questioning of the absolute demands of *aretē* as described in the Homeric poems. In his view life and survival are more to be valued than excessive displays of courage. Death brings only silence, not honour; it should not, therefore, be hastened.

Callinus and Tyrtaeus

What a different message we hear in the elegy of Callinus of Ephesus, a contemporary of Archilochus. In a poem of his we encounter again the values Homer praises, set now in a wider context (1).[16] The poem opens with an appeal to young men to fight (1–4):

> How long will you hang back? When will you show courage, O young
> men? Are you not ashamed before your neighbours,

---

[14] See Campbell, *Golden Lyre*, p. 210, Fränkel, *Dichtung*, p. 155, and Podlecki, *Early Greek Poets*, p. 42.

[15] See Podlecki, *Early Greek Poets*, pp. 30–40.

[16] See on Callinus' poem Adkins, *Poetic Craft*, pp. 54–66, 'Callinus 1 and Tyrtaeus 10 as Poetry', *HSCP*, 1977, vol. 81, pp. 59–97, Campbell, *Golden Lyre*, p. 209, Fränkel, *Dichtung*, pp. 170–2, J. Latacz, *Kampfparänese, Kampfdarstellung und Kampfwirklichkeit in der Ilias, bei Kallinos und Tyrtaios*, Munich, 1977, pp. 229–38, Podlecki, *Early Greek Poets*, pp. 55–6, W.J. Verdenius, 'Callinus Fr. 1. A Commentary', *Mnemosyne*, 1972, vol. 4, pp. 1–8.

being so slack? You imagine you are in a
    time of peace but war holds the whole land.

These young people, apparently reluctant to fight, do not face the
reality of war. Callinus suggests that they should have a sense of
shame before others, specifically those who are their neighbours.

    Callinus proceeds to describe how the soldier should act and why
(5–13):

> Let someone as he dies throw his javelin one last time.
> For honourable is it and glorious for a man to fight
>   for his country, his children, and his wedded wife
> against the foe. Death will come at that time when
>   the Fates decree it. Come, let each one go straight,
> holding his spear high and under his shield preserving
>   a courageous heart, in the front where battle is joined.
> For not in any way is it fated for a man to escape death,
>   not even if one has ancestors among the immortal gods.

Callinus here in these lines answers objections that young men might
make. 'Why go to fight?' 'If we do not fight, we can avoid battle,
surely?' Callinus explains that honour and glory attend noble
behaviour, especially for those who have reasons to fight: land, children, wife. The time of death is outside everyone's control. The Fates
spin it for each person and decree its appearance. No one can avoid
it, no matter what his status. Achilles, he might have mentioned,
had Thetis for a mother yet he died young and by choice.

    Callinus then says in the poem what can befall the soldier (14–21):

> Often someone, fleeing the clash and sound of the spears,
>   comes away but at home the fate of death comes upon him,
> nor is this one at all dear to his people or missed by them.
>   But the one who stays both great and small lament, if he
> suffers at all. For all people long for the man
>   of staunch heart, if he dies. If he lives, he is treated
> almost like a god. They see him like a mighty tower.
>   For being one alone, he accomplished deeds worthy of many.

The soldier may save his life in battle (as Archilochus had done!) but
if his time to die has arrived, he will perish while safe at home. With
his cowardly behaviour, he has sacrificed much, especially respect
from his fellow citizens. They will not miss him when he dies, nor
grieve his passing. If he had died on the battlefield, he would have
won honour in their sight. If he had survived the battlefield, his future

would be bright as he received on-going regard for the courage he had displayed.

Callinus' message is clear. *Aretē* is summed up in courage which will bring, in its expression, respect and honour from others. Death comes only when it is fated. It is better, then, to act in a way that can bring advantages both during life and after it. Callinus has expanded the frame of reference of this form of *aretē*. It is not simply the family, one's peers, or poets who bestow honour. The city is now the setting for recognition or shame.

Tyrtaeus of Sparta, living also in the mid-seventh century, likewise gives a strong call for courage. In elegy 12 he shows that the question of what *aretē* is has been a topic for discussion.[17] As a poet he presents his own views (1–9):

> I would not remember nor put in my speech a man
>   on account of excellence (*aretē*) in running or wrestling,
> nor if he should have the size and strength of the Cyclops,
>   nor if he could outrun the Thracian North Wind,
> nor if he were more handsome than Tithonus,
>   more rich than Midas and Kinyras,
> more endowed with kingly power than Pelops, son of Tantalus,
>   and possessing the honey-sweet speech of Adrastos, nor if he should
> have all cause for esteem except spirited courage.

Carefully and precisely Tyrtaeus covers the range of activities for which individuals are praised and win a reputation among others. Outward appearance does not make someone excellent. Nor does wealth. Nor does speed of foot even though it brought Achilles fame. Nor does skill at wrestling and the ability to speak well. Only a 'spirited courage' qualifies.

War is the forum that counts in the question of excellence and for this courage is needed. Further in the poem Tyrtaeus says of courage (13–20):

> This is *aretē*, the best prize among human beings,
>   and fairest for a young man to win.
> Thus it is a common blessing for city and all people

---

[17] On Tyrtaeus fr. 12 see Adkins (note 16), Campbell, *Golden Lyre*, p. 210, Fränkel, *Dichtung*, pp. 384–6, Jaeger, *Paideia*, pp. 87–98, Latacz (note 16), Podlecki, *Early Greek Poets*, pp. 98–100, H.J. Shey, 'Tyrtaeus and the Art of Propaganda', *Arethusa*, 1976, vol. 9, pp. 5–28, Snell, *Tyrtaios*, T.A. Tarkow, 'Tyrtaeus, 9 D.: The Role of Poetry in the New Sparta', *AC*, 1983, vol. 52, pp. 48–69, G. Tarditi, 'Parenesi e areté nel *corpus* tirtaico', *RFIC*, 1982, vol. 110, pp. 257–76.

> when a man takes his stand and remains among the front
> ranks fearlessly, forgetting entirely shameful flight,
>> risking his *psychē* and bold *thumos*,
> and encouraging with words the soldier stationed next to him.

Fighting now occurs in the context of the city and the other soldiers with whom the battle-line is formed. It is no longer a situation in which individual combat occurs apart from others. Therefore the soldier must forget himself. He must not flee. He must endure and encourage others. He must be willing to 'risk *psychē*' and show forth a 'bold *thumos*'.[18] In this way he benefits the whole army and the city itself.

Tyrtaeus, much like Callinus, proceeds to say that, if a soldier dies on the battlefield, he 'brings honour to his father, people and city' (24) and 'all his city' mourns his loss (28). His tomb is remembered and his descendants share continually in his fame (29–30). 'Nor ever does his noble glory perish nor his name / but even though he is under the earth, he becomes immortal' (30–1). If he survives, he is likewise honoured throughout his life, ever treated with deference and respect (35–42). Tyrtaeus concludes his poem by saying (43–4): 'now let each man strive in *thumos* to come to the peak of *aretē*, not drawing back from battle'.[19]

Excellence, we see, for both Callinus and Tyrtaeus resembles that described by Homer, but differs in important aspects. A hero will be one who fights well but in a group and as part of that group. If he fights well, he will help fellow soldiers and city. But the rewards will be his alone. If he dies, he will receive individual honour. If he lives, he will, for the rest of his life, receive respect and esteem, again as an individual. As with Homer, this *aretē* promises a form of immortality: one's name will live on.

These two poets have considered the ideal expressed in the Homeric poems and still discovered in it the essence of what makes a person excellent. Clearly the need of the society for strong, fearless fighters has influenced their assessment. Because the type of soldier must differ from the single champion in Homer, new aspects of the expression *aretē* had to be introduced. But the message is essentially the same: bravery before the enemy, motivated by concern for honour, is the best quality someone can display.

---

[18] See discussion on this poem also in chapter 2 (*thumos*) and chapter 3 (*psychē*).
[19] See also Tyrtaeus poems 10 and 11 in which he makes strong appeals for courage.

Xenophanes

Another poet too will reassess what Homer has to say. Xenophanes,
living in the sixth and early fifth centuries, offers a new and different
definition of *aretē* in an elegiac poem.[20] Thus far in this book we
have treated Xenophanes among the Presocratics. As mentioned in
chapter 1, problems can sometimes exist with placing individuals of
the Archaic Age among either the lyric and elegiac poets or the
Presocratics. In some cases, especially with Xenophanes, there is overlapping in content. In the case of Xenophanes' poem on *aretē*, it fits
better here among these early poets than later with the philosophers.

In poem 2 W, Xenophanes first describes athletes (1–10):

> But if someone were to win a victory by swiftness of feet
>   or in the pentathlon, there where the precinct of Zeus
> stands in Olympia beside the river at Pisa, or in wrestling
>   or in the painful boxing-match
> or in that dreadful contest they call the pankration,
>   he would be full of glory for the citizens to gaze upon,
> and he would win a conspicuous front seat at festivals,
>   and he would be given meals at public expense
> from his city, and a gift for him to treasure, or winning
>   also with horses, he would take all these advantages.

Xenophanes shows us clearly by these lines that by his time the
successful athlete had acquired the status of hero in Greek society.
Tyrtaeus, as we heard, in the century before, also shows that athletics had become an acknowledged field for the expression of *aretē*. No
longer could an individual enter battle and find opportunities for
glory in single combat. Warfare had changed and Callinus and
Tyrtaeus, although still calling for courage, show that its expression
involves shared activity. The rewards of fighting may well bring individual recognition but the fighting itself is not of that nature.

Society, none the less, offered a field where one could still shine in
individual endeavour. Xenophanes lists the various contests: running,
wrestling, boxing, horse-racing or a combination of these. He describes the rewards offered: prestige, front seats at festivals, free meals,
and a special gift. Just like Homeric heroes, athletes had to train

---

[20] On Xenophanes 2 see Adkins, *Poetic Craft*, pp. 186–98, Campbell, *Golden Lyre*,
pp. 58–9, 265, Fränkel, *Dichtung*, pp. 375–6, and P. Giannini, 'Senofanes fr. 2 Gentili-
Prato e la funzione dell' intellettuale nella Grecia arcaica', *QUCC*, 1982, vol. 10, pp.
59–69.

carefully and diligently if they were to win. They were called upon
to demonstrate physical skill in many different contests. Success in
these contests was taken as an indication of *aretē* in the person.

Xenophanes has objections to this view, however commonly accepted it may have been. The person who acquires all these advantages because he has won in an athletic contest is (11–14):

> not as worthy as I am. For better than strength
>   of men or of horses is our wisdom (*sophia*).
> But this custom is practised very at random, nor is it just
>   to prefer strength to our good wisdom.

Xenophanes here rejects 'strength' as the standard for excellence.
Instead, he suggests that the wisdom he displays in his poetry is what
society should value most highly. This wisdom is the inspired information and knowledge that the poet shares with his listeners. It is
always 'more' than the person by whom it is uttered, its source being
the Muses or some divine inspiration. Xenophanes describes it as
'good' (*agathē*). Its content has intrinsic value.

Xenophanes proceeds in the poem to explain why he can make
this claim for *sophia* (15–22):

> For if among the people there should be a good boxer,
>   or one winning in the pentathlon or at wrestling,
> or by speed in running, which is most honoured
>   of all deeds of strength of men at a festival,
> not for that reason would the city have better government.
>   Small would be the joy for a city government if someone
> won an athletic competition by the banks of the Pisa.
>   For this one does not enrich the inner chambers of a city.

Xenophanes thus assigns to *sophia* an important role. It contributes
to 'good government', *eunomiē* (see also chapter 5). This term, already
prominent in the poetry of Solon (4.32), earlier in the sixth century,
suggests the ideal condition of a city: it has good laws (*nomoi*). The
poet's wisdom can help with the directives it gives, themselves assumed to be inspired. This wisdom can also 'enrich the inner chambers' (*muchos*) of the city. Xenophanes chooses an image here from
the home, the *muchos* being an 'inner room'. It is the every core or
essence of a city that a poet's wisdom can assist. From here advantage can flow out to the rest of the city.

We see here in this comparison of athletic skill and poetic wisdom
a criterion that Tyrtaeus also mentioned. *Aretē* should be something

that aids others. It should be useful. In the recognition it brings from society, athletic skill may bestow many personal advantages to the individual concerned. But in itself it does not help the city. It contributes nothing to good government and certainly has no 'riches' to provide in the way of counsel or direction. Xenophanes protests that the rewards offered to athletic skill belongs more properly to one who can help the city with *sophia*. Since athletic skill aids the city less than *sophia*, it is not 'just' for it to be more highly honoured. Things justly deserve their due (see further, chapter 5), and Xenophanes has detected an imbalance in what is offered to physical skill and wisdom.

At the end of the fifth century Plato will describe Socrates in his defense making the same claim for the activity in which he has spent his life (*Apologia* 37D–E). Like Xenophanes, he will suggest that he has served Athens better than the much-honoured athlete. It is he who should be given honour, free meals, and a front seat at festivals. For a person just found guilty and obliged to propose a penalty for himself, this was an outrageous request to make. But in it Socrates echoes the claim that Xenophanes already had made for *sophia*. In the essence and the usefulness of wisdom is to be found that most valuable. The one possessing it should therefore be recognised as showing excellence and should receive the time-honoured recognition accorded this achievement.

Theognis

Theognis of Megara, living in the late sixth and early fifth centuries, presents a different focus upon *aretē*[21] Theognis writes advice for Cyrnus, probably a young man of aristocratic birth in need of direction. Much like Phoenix in the case of Achilles, Theognis suggests how Cyrnus may best function in the society he encounters. And Theognis makes it clear that times have changed since the world of Homer. In so doing he shows us the importance of elements that formerly were taken as attendant upon *aretē* although not forming its essence.

---

[21] On Theognis see Campbell, *Golden Lyre*, *passim*, G. Cerri, 'La terminologia sociopolitica di Teognide: 1. L'opposizione semantica tra *agathos—esthlos* e *kakos— deilos*', *QUCC*, 1968, vol. 6, pp. 7–32, Figueira and Nagy, Fränkel, *Dichtung*, pp. 472–83, Jaeger, *Paideia*, pp. 194–204, G. Nagy, 'Theognis of Megara: The Poet as Seer, Pilot, and Revenant', *Arethusa*, 1982, vol. 15, pp. 109–28, Podlecki, *Early Greek Poets*, pp. 143–51, and Patzer (note 1).

It was a given that the heroes described in Homer were handsome, well-born, and wealthy. But in the Homeric picture also *aretē* involved much more: compassion, loyalty, or courage. Yet in the stories that were told of early great people *aretē* emerged, it seems, mainly in those having good birth and many possessions. In the poetry of Callinus, Tyrtaeus, and Xenophanes, these characteristics do not play a role since the first two call all soldiers to courage, rich or poor, well-born or not, the second focuses upon the gift given to poets. In his poetry Theognis looks back with longing to the aristocratic world of Homer.

Theognis himself, it appears, possessed noble birth. During his life, because of the injustice of people newly politically powerful and wealthy in his society, he became, at least for a time, poor.[22] This experience may have led him to focus upon what he felt were inherent differences between those who were good by nature and birth and those who seemed incapable of achieving this state. In the case of the latter, wealth could not be taken as a sign of *aretē*. In the case of those with good birth, poverty had to cease to be a sign of its absence. Thus the economic situation of dispossessed aristocrats caused Theognis to redefine elements of *aretē*. In his view birth remained of vital importance for its emergence; wealth, on the other hand, could no longer be taken as signalling its presence.

But even though good birth was of great importance, another factor was also important for the appearance of *aretē*. From Homeric times heroes, even with the highest birth, were assumed to need education and training. Thus Glaucus learned 'always to excel beyond others' (*Il.* 6.208). Cyrnus, it appears, needs the guidance of Theognis. But from his poem we see that Theognis believes that only one of noble birth was able to absorb teaching that would lead to admirable behaviour. No matter what the material wealth of those of lowly birth might be, it would not make possible what the aristocrat alone could learn and practise. It is thus only a restricted group that Theognis believes can attain *aretē*. This *aretē*, as we shall see, will also in its nature and expression be affected by those whom Theognis thinks are less valuable members of society. What then does he say of *aretē*?

At 149–50 he remarks:

---

[22] See Fränkel, *Dichtung*, pp. 454–83 and Podlecki, *Early Greek Poets*, pp. 148–51.

> A *daimōn* gives wealth even to one totally evil,
> Cyrnus, but a portion of *aretē* comes to few.

Here we see a separation of wealth from *aretē*. We also see that the acquisition of *aretē* is rare. In these lines and elsewhere Theognis probably refers to a *daimōn* as a person's 'guardian spirit'.[23] This can be either positive or negative in nature. The gift of wealth does not depend on the moral nature of a person and, as we shall see elsewhere, this gift may prove to be no blessing.

In two other passages, Theognis relates *aretē* to the manifestation of desires (335–6, 401–6):

1. Don't be over-zealous in anything. Mid-course is best.
   And thus, Cyrnus, you'll have *aretē*, difficult to acquire.
2. Don't be over-zealous in anything. Appropriateness is
   best for all activities of humans. Often one is
   eager for *aretē* as he pursues profit. His *daimōn*
   willingly leads him astray into great
   wrong-doing and easily makes him think that what is
   evil is good and what is useful is bad.

Theognis suggests that too great zeal can be counter-productive. Moderation is therefore preferable. Wealth appears to be the object of the endeavour described here. If a person is too eager for it, he can easily fall into confusion and make wrong choices. Yet this person has a noble goal: *aretē*. This, however, as he says, is not to be won by the 'pursuit of profit'. Few have *aretē*, in any case. But curbing of desire, the 'middle road of moderation', may prove more conducive to its acquisition.

What is the content of this *aretē* that Theognis is describing? At 465–6 he says:

> Busy yourself with *aretē* and let justice be dear to you,
> nor let shameful profit overcome you.

Again, we hear of the dangers of 'profit' that is not honourable. We see here an association of *aretē* with justice. Elsewhere Theognis explicitly identifies these two (145–8):[24]

---

[23] For a discussion of *daimōn* with bibliography see my article (Darcus), '*Daimōn* as a Force Shaping *Ēthos* in Heraclitus', *Phoenix*, 1974, vol. 28, pp. 390–407 (esp. n. 12). See also Inwood, pp. 53–65 and Wright, *Presocratics*, pp. 69–76, 273–4 for its use in Empedocles.

[24] The appearance of the word *dikaiosynē* for 'justice' in these lines has given cause

Choose to dwell as a holy person with few possessions
  rather than to be rich, having acquired wealth unjustly.
To put it briefly, all *aretē* is summed up in justice,
  and every good man, Cyrnus, is one who is just.

At line 255 he also describes 'the fairest thing' (*kalliston*) as that which
is 'most just'.[25]

In chapter 5 we shall treat the notion of justice more fully. Its
essence, we shall see, involves recognition of the rightful claims of
individual and others. Theognis, perhaps himself having been deprived of more than he thought fair while others gained more than
was their due, came to believe that having an attitude of respect for
what is right and fair constitutes excellence.[26]

This assumption, we can see, relates to his advice for Cyrnus (quoted
above) to pursue a path of moderation. Over-eager pursuit of wealth
must at some point lead to gaining more as other people lose. It will
thus prove to be unjust. Justice will always involve a consideration
not only of self but of other people as well. With a broader outlook,
goodness or excellence may well appear in someone's character. Thus
he suggests elsewhere that 'for the just person, nothing is better than
doing good' (547–8).

If *aretē* is justice, the person having it will probably show restraint
in the pursuit of profit. Thus he suggests that possessions that come
'from Zeus and with justice' abide (197–8). Theognis says elsewhere
that the manner of spending the wealth one already has likewise
relates to *aretē*. At 903–30 he treats the question of whether one should
spend little or much:[27]

Whoever watches the spending of his savings according
  to his means has the finest *aretē* in the eyes of the wise.

He then discusses the dilemma of human life: we do not know how
long we are going to live. If life is to be short, we may as well enjoy

---

for questioning their authenticity, since this term is usually found later. See B. van
Groningen, *Theognis, le premier livre*, Amsterdam, 1966, pp. 57–9. See futher discussion on these lines in chapter 5.

[25] Cf. also his statement that 'there is nothing better than a mother and father
for whom holy justice (*dikē*) is a concern' (131–2).

[26] See Theognis' views on the state of his city in 283–92. Cf. too 1135–50 where
he laments the state of human beings. See too his advice (discussed in chapter 2 on
phrēn) 'to delight *phrēn*, being just' (794–5).

[27] See the discussion of these lines (especially 910) also in chapter 3 (on *psychē*).

our savings; if not, we should take care to avoid poverty in our later
years. He thus remarks (924–5):

> Thus it is best of all to take care and
> to spend according to our means.

He concludes his thoughts on spending by saying (928–30):

> In this generation it is best to have money.
> For if you are rich, your friends are many; if poor, they are
> few and no longer is the same person still considered good.

Theognis in this section suggests a form of *arete* to be found in how
money is spent. His method involves what might be called a type of
justice. A person is to stay within the means available. It is not right
to save totally and deprive even oneself of any pleasure that money
can bring. On the other hand, to spend all lavishly and to become
a burden to others is not right either. As he ends these reflections,
he notes that in the generation in which he lives the lack of wealth
is attended by few friends. People are judged by what they have and
without wealth one forfeits a reputation also of being 'good'. We
thus hear Theognis claim that *arete* consists of intelligent spending.
In a world that still assumes that *arete* involves the presence of wealth,
this form of *arete* will also prevent one from losing the reputation of
being good.

Elsewhere Theognis speaks of another gift that is 'best for mortals'
(1171–3):

> Judgement (*gnōmē*), Cyrnus, is the best thing gods give
> to mortals; judgement holds the limits of everything.
> O blessed is the one who has it in *phrenes*.

With judgement, a person will know how to live, how to save, and
how to spend. *Gnōmē* involves insights into such things, and, in fact,
as Theognis claims, into 'all things'. In relation to the pursuit of
arete, such judgement will probably prove most valuable. As we heard
above, caution is needed as one 'hastens after *arete*, pursuing wealth'
(401–6), since divinity can intervene and cloud thinking. If *arete* involves justice, it is not surprising, in Theognis' view, that the evil
person cannot attain it (279–82):

> It is but likely that the evil person regards justice badly,
> showing no respect for retribution to come after.

For it is easy for a mortal to snatch up many useless things
   right at his feet and to think he disposes all things well.

This person shows no judgement concerning the value of justice and
will, without thinking, act rashly from moment to moment.

Theognis' view of *aretē*, as presented thus far, shows the following
features. It is summed up in just behaviour. It involves moderation
in the desire for wealth. It includes care in the spending of wealth.
Judgement and thoughtfulness will attend its pursuit and practice.

But human beings are not always in control of what happens to
them. Theognis thus at 653–4 makes the prayer:

May I be blessed with a good *daimōn* and dear to
   the immortal gods, Cyrnus; I desire no other *aretē*.

We heard above that a *daimōn* can lead a person astray as he pursues wealth (401–6). Theognis hopes that he has a good 'guiding
spirit'. It is important to be 'dear to the gods' since Theognis points
out (133–4):

No one, Cyrnus, is himself responsible for loss or gain,
   but the gods are givers of both of these.

He proceeds to say (135–41) that we do not know the outcome of
our ventures. They may seem good and turn out bad or the opposite may happen. He concludes by saying (141–2):[28]

We human beings think vain things, knowing nothing;
   the gods accomplish everything according to their *noos*.

Thus it can happen that poverty befalls the good person (1059–62):

Timagoras, it is difficult for someone, even if he is wise,
   to discern the character of many if he sees them from afar.
For some people keep badness hidden by wealth,
   others, virtue in destructive poverty.

At 173–4 he says of poverty:[29]

Poverty most of all overwhelms the good man,
   more than grey old-age, Cyrnus, or fever.

---

[28] See too on these lines in chapter 2 (on *noos*).
[29] See also 179–80, 181–2, and 373–406 for further comments on how terrible
poverty is.

The gods control all. As we heard, they can give wealth even to the evil person (149–50). They can also give poverty to the good person. Best then to be dear to them, if possible. Life will become very difficult if poverty befalls. A person may still be good, may 'conceal *aretē*' in a difficult situation but the world will believe that in this individual *aretē* is absent.

Even though hardship may befall a good person, Theognis believes that when it does, the intrinsic worth of that individual will emerge. Poverty reveals that the just man always has 'straight judgement (*gnōmē*) growing in his breast' (395–6). In the case of the evil person neither prosperity nor hardship shows him capable of restraining his evil ways (321–2). Theognis says (315–18):

> Many evil men are rich, and many good men are poor,
>   but we will not exchange our *aretē*
> for the wealth of these, since it is always enduring
>   whereas different people at different times have wealth.

Aretē, therefore, in Theognis' view is very much a question of noble character that is in no way to be acquired with the arrival of wealth.

Above we have heard Theognis describe *aretē* in terms of justice. He makes clear that many things are outside of human control. Success can come or failure. What he points out is that, whatever the circumstances, choice of behaviour is not outside of the range of humans. One can choose to be just and moderate. In his view only those who have the capacity for goodness will make this choice. But the good will do so and in their just actions the presence of *aretē* should be assumed to be present, regardless of whether they are rich or poor.

Within the long poem of Theognis we find as well what appear to be expressions of older views of *aretē*. At 933–4 he says:

> Excellence and beauty attend few human beings;
>   blessed is he who obtains both by lot.

He then says that such a person is treated with honour by all during his whole life, never 'harmed in respect and justice' (938). Beauty then seems an extra gift and is now named as something optimally attending *aretē*, not, as in Homer, assumed to be a component of it.

At 865–8 Theognis speaks of courage. He says first that the gods give prosperity to 'many useless people' (865) but 'the great glory of *aretē* never perishes./ For the man who is a fighter saves both land

and city' (867–8). Much like Callinus and Tyrtaeus, Theognis here recognizes the social value of the courageous soldier. Just like his definition of *aretē* as justice, this description of *aretē* focuses upon how an individual serves others. An individual or private attainment of glory does not in his eyes win the name of *aretē*.

Unfortunately, as mentioned above, the society in which Theognis lived focused mostly on external appearances and did not appreciate what Theognis perceives as the true essence of *aretē*. Of this society he says (699–700):

> To the majority of people there is this one *aretē*,
> to be rich; there is no use to all other things.

He proceeds to describe other forms of human achievement: wisdom, knowledge, swiftness in running. He concludes by saying that in effect these do not count since 'wealth for all people has greatest power' (718).

Because of this view of the majority of people Theognis does two things. He sets out for Cyrnus his own ideas of *aretē*, outlined above. He also gives him frequent advice on how to cope with the society in which he lives. One example of this advice occurs at 1071–4:

> Cyrnus, turn to all friends a varied disposition,
> mingling with the character which each has.
> Now imitate this person, then be different in character.
> For this skill (*sophia*) is better even than great *aretē*.

Both the lower standards of behaviour of others and their values cause Theognis to urge upon Cyrnus behaviour that is itself deceptive.[30] Theognis, it is true, urges Cyrnus not to behave in this way with himself, his teacher (87–92), but with others he should be cautious. Common opinion, then, has led Theognis to offer as advice a code of behaviour less noble than is found in Homer or in other poets. One cannot imagine either Achilles or various Homeric heroes being advised to act in this way. Achilles himself says firmly that he hates the person 'who thinks in one way and speaks in another' (*Il.* 9.313). Changes in society have altered ideas about excellence and made a simple call to heroism impossible. They have led Theognis to believe that the true expression of *aretē* will involve justice. But for survival, aristocrats, always assumed to be achievers of

---

[30] See too other such advice at 61–8, 73–6, 213–18, and 363–4.

aretē, are advised on occasion to dissemble, preserving only at a deep level the goodness Theognis assumes is rightly theirs.

In Theognis's poetry *aretē* is still highly valued but its presence, it seems, is rare and achieved by few. It is related now to a new form of behaviour that has a social focus. To some extent, *aretē* as justice could, it seems, be an achievement that all individuals might strive for. But Theognis believes that only those with an inherent capacity for goodness will be able to aim for it and to achieve it. Others may manage to acquire wealth, often taken as a sign of *aretē*, but it will be an exterior accomplishment only. If such individuals are tested by hard circumstances, they will reveal the lack of excellence that is in their character. The good person, in contrast, in poverty or in wealth, will emerge as one moderate and just. And in such an individual alone should *aretē* be thought to be present.

Simonides

Simonides of Ceos, living in the late sixth and early fifth centuries, likewise expressed ideas about *aretē*. In one poem he echoes Hesiod. At *W. & D.* 289–92, Hesiod says:

> In front of *aretē* the immortal gods have placed
> sweat; long and steep is the path to her
> and rough at first. But when a person reaches the top,
> then the path is easy, however difficult before.

The achievement of *aretē* calls for hard work that is arduous. Once a person attains it, however, the difficulty disappears. In his poem, Simonides says (579):[31]

> There is a story
> that *aretē* dwells on rocks hard to climb.
> Nor is she to be looked upon by the eyes
> of all mortals, but only by the one to whom
> *thumos*-eating sweat comes within,
> and he comes to the height of manliness.

The term here for 'manliness' is *andreia*, deriving from the same root as the word for 'man', *anēr*. In these lines, Simonides suggests that

---

[31] In the quotation line three, in which the reading is in question, is omitted. On this poem (579) see D Babut, 'Simonide moraliste', *REG*, 1975, vol. 88, pp. 20–62, Campbell, *Golden Lyre*, p. 238, and Fränkel, *Dichtung*, pp. 358–9.

individuals are capable of reaching the heights of 'manliness'. This
would consist, we can imagine, in the appearance in a person of
admirable traits. Certainly *andreia* would involve 'courage' but it probably would also include the whole range suggested by the Homeric
description of a hero: 'to be a speaker of words and a doer of deeds'
(*Il.* 9.443). The attainment of this *andreia*, this *aretē*, is not easy: effort
that 'eats away the *thumos*' must be exerted. Simonides in these lines,
like Hesiod, assumes that *aretē* can be attained but few, it would appear,
will 'make the climb' and reach the heights.[32]

In another poem Simonides suggests that human effort does not
suffice for the achievement of *aretē* (526):[33]

> no one without the gods
> achieved *aretē*, neither city nor mortal.
> God is all-wise; for mortals
> nothing is without sufferings.

The term for 'all-wise', *panmētis*, occurs only here in the Greek literature we have and focuses upon the type of wisdom that divinity
possesses. *Mētis* in Hesiod's *Theogony* (886–899) is the first wife of
Zeus. He swallows her down in order that he himself will never lose
his supreme power over the other gods and that he will produce
wise children. This *mētis* thus allows the chief divinity to rule the
universe. Among the Homeric heroes, one in particular is described
as being 'abounding in cleverness', *polumētis*. This is, of course, Odysseus[34] and once again the *mētis* involved allows mastery in different
situations.

Simonides says that in the question of *aretē* for human beings,
divinity is 'all-devising'. It can make possible what might otherwise
prove impossible. Humans must face everything with 'suffering'. This
will be the case too with *aretē* but divinity is capable of devising a
way for its attainment.

Thus far we have seen Simonides speak of *aretē* as a grand achievement, difficult to attain but available for the individual who is willing
to suffer and who is aided by divine help. In another poem he offers
an examination of goodness in human beings. Since we are not gods

---

[32] See also the reference to the 'height of *aretē*' in Pin., *Nem.* 6.23 (and discussion
below).

[33] On 526 see Campbell, *Golden Lyre*, p. 238 and Fränkel, *Dichtung*, pp. 258–9.

[34] See, e.g., *Il.* 1.311, 3.200 and *Od.* 4.763, 5.214 for descriptions of Odysseus as
'very wily'.

and cannot remain ever in favourable circumstances, the possibility of our always having *aretē* may not exist. But there may be other forms of goodness that could well qualify for admiration and praise. If this is so, some re-evaluation of how human behaviour is judged may prove necessary.

The poem we shall now consider is called the 'Scopas' poem, written by Simonides for his patron, Scopas of Thessaly. Plato quotes and paraphrases this poem in the *Protagoras* (339a to 346a). He does not quote it in full and we encounter missing lines. He offers literary and moral criticism of it for the purposes of his dialogue but we shall look at the poem outside of this context.

Simonides begins this poem as follows (542.1–3):[35]

> It is difficult for a man to be truly good
> in hands, feet, and mind (*noos*),
>   four-square, fashioned without fault.

The lines echo the description of Periphetes in the *Iliad* as 'son better in every form of *aretē*, in feet, fighting, or mind (*noos*)' (15.641–3). These lines also apparently borrow the image of 'four-square' from the Pythagoreans, the square indicating a perfect shape. Thus we see that a person standing with arms and legs spread widely apart might form this pattern. Add fine fashioning and admirable intelligence and the 'truly good' individual appears.

Some lines of the poem are here missing but as it continues what becomes evident is that the opening lines were a summary of a saying of Pittacus, one of the wise men of Greece (11–18):[36]

> Nor to me has this saying of Pittacus
> been uttered harmoniously, even though expressed
>   by a wise man. He said that it was difficult to be good.
> God alone has this privilege. It is not possible

---

[35] On the Scopas poem see Babut (note 31), Campbell, *Golden Lyre*, pp. 238–40, G. Christ, *Simonidesstudien*, Freiburg, 1941, pp. 13–26, M. Dickie, 'The Argument and Form of Simonides 542 *PMG*', *HSCP*, 1978, vol. 82, pp. 21–33, W. Donlan, 'Simonides, Fr. 4 D and P. Oxy. 2432', *TAPA*, 1969, vol. 100, pp. 71–95, Fränkel, *Dichtung*, pp. 352–6, B. Gentili, 'Studi su Simonide', *Maia*, 1984, vol. 16, pp. 274–306, H. Parry, 'An Interpretation of Simonides 4 (Diehl)', *TAPA*, 1965, vol. 96, pp. 297–320, E. des Places, 'Simonide et Socrate dans le *Protagoras* de Platon', *LEC*, 1969, vol. 37, pp. 236–44, Podlecki, *Early Greek Poets*, pp. 179–80, and L. Woodbury, 'Simonides on *Aretē*', *TAPA*, 1953, vol. 84, pp. 135–63.

[36] The interpretation of the first three lines is a debated question: see a summary of views in Parry (note 35), p. 77, n. 13. In our discussion they are taken as the statement of Pittacus.

> for a man not to be bad,
> upon whom irresistible misfortune has come.
> For when he is faring well, every man is good,
> but he is bad if he fares badly.

Pittacus, Simonides asserts, is wrong in saying that 'being good is difficult'. Instead, he takes this condition right out of the human range: only the god has this 'privilege'. Why? Because only upon divinity does 'irresistible misfortune' never fall. Human beings cannot maintain a state of perfection because they prove vulnerable to changes in condition. Unlike Theognis who suggests that in difficult circumstances the good person will none the less continue to show goodness, Simonides says that this will not occur.

In the earlier poems we quoted (526, 579), it seems that Simonides himself was echoing what Pittacus said: *aretē* is hard to achieve. It takes great effort and the help of the gods. In the present poem he focuses upon another aspect of human life. Misfortune makes all people equal. It will, it appears, most likely strip the person who has already achieved *aretē* of his accomplishment. 'Being good', 'remaining good', is outside of human control.

After another lacuna, this poem to Scopas continues (21–30):

> Therefore never will I throw away
> a portion of my life on an empty impracticable hope,
>   seeking what is impossible to be,
> the completely blameless person among us
>   who gather the fruit of the broad earth.
> But if I find such a one, I shall tell you.
> I praise and admire every person
> who willingly does
> nothing shameful (*aischron*). Against necessity
> not even the gods fight.

Since human beings are subject to misfortune and their *aretē* is vulnerable, it is pointless, Simonides says, to look for the perfect individual. Even if someone appears to be 'good' at some stage of his life, circumstances may bring about a reversal of fortunes and then his 'goodness' may cease to be so sterling. We are all mortal, dependent upon the 'fruits of the earth'. 'To be perfect' is an 'impracticable hope': it cannot be a state to be enjoyed for a whole lifetime. The completely blameless individual is not, it appears, to be found.

And yet Simonides says: 'if I find such a person, I'll tell you'. There could be someone endowed with zeal for goodness and favoured by circumstance and probably divine assistance who might merit the description 'all-blameless'. But the discovery of such an individual will not occur often and may never take place. Simonides therefore suggests that we should concentrate on different elements as we look for the good person.

The individual, he says, who does 'nothing shameful willingly' deserves praise and admiration. To the degree that people are free agents, in that degree only should their actions be judged. As free agents, human beings can make choices. If they choose to avoid the 'shameful', they are acting meritoriously. There may, however, be some circumstances in which such expression of choice becomes impossible. At such times, they will, as Simonides says at line 18, be 'bad' but in these circumstances they should not be negatively judged. Misfortune and calamity inevitably befall humans: this is the 'necessity' of their lives. No human being should be expected to 'fight against necessity' and win. Not even the gods, he says, are capable of that.

In these lines Simonides calls for a more gentle attitude on the part of human beings toward moral failure. First, we discern a call to be more understanding of others when they fail. Our expectations should not be impossibly high. Disaster makes humans victims of necessity and less desirable traits may emerge in their behaviour. Second, we can see a call for people to be more gentle with self. If calamity happens, one should not be surprised if negative behaviour results.

But Simonides in these lines also leaves open the possibility of a form of behaviour that merits praise. Perhaps even if people 'fare badly' (17), they can still choose to do 'nothing shameful' (29). Theognis was of the opinion that when individuals inherently good 'fared badly', their goodness would still emerge; in the case of those bad by nature this would not happen. Simonides does not expect this nobility of anyone. But it could appear. When it does, he suggests that what deserves recognition is the element of choice that is present.

Again after a lacuna, the last stanza of this poem speaks of an individual of whom Simonides can approve (34–40):

> nor too helpless and
> knowing justice that benefits the city,
> a sound (*hugiēs*) man. Nor shall I
> find fault with him. For of fools
> the generation is numberless.

All things are good (*kala*) in which
the shameful (*aischra*) has not been mingled.

In these lines we see perhaps an enhancement of the picture of the
person 'who does nothing wrong shamefully' (28–9). Simonides gives
characteristics of the individual with whom he will not 'find fault'.
He is not to be 'too helpless' (*apalamos*). This adjective, meaning literally 'without hands', echoes the reference in lines 2–3 to the person 'four-square in hands'. Simonides suggests that the person escaping blame may not manage to be 'four-square', but he cannot, in
contrast, be 'too helpless' either. Some strength, whether of body or
mind, will need to be present. This person too will have a specific
kind of knowledge: 'justice that profits the city'. His attitude, then, is
to be an out-going one, involving an awareness of the rights owed to
others.[37] With his knowledge of justice, this individual himself will
probably prove valuable for the city. In that setting he will display
justice.

Simonides terms the person with these two characteristics 'sound'.
He uses the adjective *hugiēs*, usually having a physical connotation of
'healthy' or 'vigorous'. Again Simonides echoes the physical description of the 'four-square' person at the beginning of the poem. 'Sound'
may not suggest perfection as 'four-square' does but it does imply
someone in whom parts are working together well with vigour and
energy present. Such a person can cope with life, even with disaster,
and will not prove 'too helpless'. He has regard for justice in the
social context of the city.

This individual may not be the greatest hero one could meet. He
will not strike another as 'totally blameless' (24). It may happen that
at a future time, if calamity or misfortune befalls, he will present a
poor image. But for the moment he deserves no blame and if he
'willingly does nothing shameful', he deserves praise and admiration.
Why should we be satisfied with such a person? Simonides answers:
there are many far worse. 'The race of fools is endless' (37–8).

In the closing lines of the poem Simonides suggests the way 'all
things' should be viewed. Instead of laying down impossible requirements for the ascription of the quality 'fair' or 'good' (*kalos*), we are
to check only that one thing is missing: the 'shameful' or 'bad' (*aischros*).
'All things are good with which the bad has not been mixed' (39–40).

---

[37] See further on justice in chapter 5.

Here Simonides uses the same term *aischra* as he did in describing the person who chooses 'nothing *aischron*' (29). If this element is present, things cannot be considered 'good'. If it is absent, behaviour can be taken as 'good', even though it may not be as glorious as that which a 'four-square' or 'all-blameless' person could achieve.[38]

In the poems of Simonides that we have treated we see an interesting treatment of *aretē*. In 526 and 579 he tells us two features of it: it is very difficult to attain and divine help is needed. In the Scopas poem (542), he essentially places the achievement of the standard notion of *aretē* in a special category. Pittacus is wrong in saying that 'it is difficult to be good'. It is instead impossible, if human beings encounter a disaster of great proportion. The 'necessity' that human beings face of suffering will make the 'four-square' individual, the 'entirely blameless' person, all but unknown.

But human beings can exhibit other positive qualities. One who 'does nothing shameful willingly' deserves praise. The person who is not 'too helpless' and 'knows justice profiting the city' merits no blame. The presence of the 'shameful' in behaviour removes it from being ever classified as 'good'. But the absence of this quality opens up many avenues of praise for what human beings choose to do. The 'sound' person, strong and vigorous, is the one to whom we can ascribe 'goodness'.

Simonides thus offers a challenge to a whole range of people to use their power of choice and to strive for goodness. Theognis and others before him might argue that without the correct birth or inherited qualities no goodness could emerge in individuals. Simonides says that the choice of 'nothing shameful', the knowledge of 'justice', and the condition of not being 'too helpless' mark the presence of goodness. Many people are capable of this, however many more fools there may be. If goodness is summed up by these characteristics, society will be more tolerant. It may too, ironically, exhibit more goodness than was present under impossible standards before. It may also prove to be the case that this 'lesser' form of *aretē*, like justice, will 'profit the city'. Simonides then speaks to a broader audience than some earlier analyses of goodness allowed. In so doing he offers a kind of excellence, *aretē*, more accessible to a range of individuals.

---

[38] For ideas similar to those expressed here see also 541, treated by Donlan (note 35), pp. 90–5 and Gentili (note 35), pp. 338–41.

Pindar and Bacchylides

We shall now treat Pindar and Bacchylides and their notion of *aretē*. We shall concentrate upon Pindar, for in many ways Bacchylides' poetry exhibits a system of values similar to his. But in one of Bacchylides' odes we hear views similar to those expressed by Theognis and Simonides when they connected *aretē* with justice. We shall glance at this ode first (14.8–11):[39]

> There are countless forms of human excellence
>   but one form stands in foremost place of all,
> the *aretē* of the person who guides affairs at hand
>   with just *phrenes.*

Bacchylides recognises that by his time many candidates had emerged claiming the title of *aretē*. In the poems we have treated, we have seen some of these claimants: courage, fidelity, compassion, wisdom, willing avoidance of the shameful, and justice. It is the latter that Bacchylides chooses as having the highest merit. In selecting it, he puts its appearance in a specific context: competence in handling tasks that face a person in the present moment. Thus, a person who acts recognising the rightful claims of others will manifest excellence. Once again, *aretē* has a social significance. It is not, in this ode of Bacchylides, a magnificent personal achievement having little bearing on or significance for others.

Most of Bacchylides' poems, however, like those of Pindar, show us *aretē* in a different context. Over the centuries the chance for a person to excel in single combat, like Achilles of old, had become rare. Warfare had changed and, as Tyrtaeus and Callinus showed us, a form of courage was called for that involved group activity. But, as Xenophanes also made clear to us, there remained a scene where an individual could display excellence: athletic competition.

As is well known, the Greeks had festivals in several cities where athletes could compete. In the odes of Pindar we encounter poems written to celebrate victories in various contests. These poems would usually be sung during the celebration in which the victor was welcomed home to his own city amid much joy and rejoicing.

Each poem, as Pindar constructs it, is an intricate work of art.[40]

---

[39] See also on this poem in chapter 2 (under *phrenes*). See too chapter 5 on justice.
[40] On the odes of Pindar bibliography is very rich. See especially the valuable

Pindar sees the specific victory and focuses upon it, but he also extends his vision far into the past and projects it as well into the future. To him the present triumph reveals an inherited strain of excellence that must have shone in earlier days and would be destined to shine again. Into the world of myth he reaches, not seeing it simply as a decorative parallel for the current victory but rather as evidence in the world of poetic truth of the existence of excellence re-emerging.

The victor would expect Pindar, Bacchylides, or any writer of this type of ode to include certain elements. His name, his family history, his earlier achievements, the identity of his city, victories won by other family members, any connections with heroes of old, and future aspirations—all were items that would need to be described. There were, then, conventions to be followed in the structuring of the ode. But Pindar consistently made the conventions of the victory ode his servant. In no way does he allow prescriptions on the poetic form he used to limit his role as poet, one which he assumed was lofty and inspired.

As poet, Pindar refers to himself as the 'divine bird of Zeus' (*Ol.* 2.88).[41] Early heroes had hoped that, if they achieved glorious feats, a poet would sing of them and bestow immortality upon their name. Pindar believes that he has the power to immortalize in song the presence in the individual of excellence. With his poetic gift he weaves an intricate tapestry in song with many threads masterfully woven together and creating a whole of varied richness. The ode is essentially a single creation. If particular elements are focused upon, the ode may appear to lack unity. But if gazed on as a whole, the elaborate pattern of an athlete's victory, family, city, and possible future triumphs becomes evident. The ode becomes a gift given to the victor and proves to be worthy in its nature of the victory.

Pindar took *aretē* and its appearance very seriously. He has definite ideas about what it consists of, how it can be brought forth, how it can be sustained, and how it can be lost. To achieve *aretē* is a glorious experience but ever a dangerous one. Pindar, as poet, must draw upon his wisdom not merely to praise a particular victory

---

work of D.E. Gerber, 'Pindar and Bacchylides 1934–87', *Lustrum*, 1989 and 1990, vols 31–2. On the style and structure of the Pindaric ode see this bibliography, 1989, vol. 31, pp. 124–38. See also Gerber's useful comments on trends in the treatment of Pindar, 1989, vol. 31, pp. 98–9.

[41] On the role of the poet see also bibliography in Gerber (note 40), *Lustrum*, 1989, vol. 31, pp. 130–6.

but also to advise the athlete how to be a winner. If a victor already shows signs of not knowing how to behave in his new role, Pindar believes that he must take steps to provide teaching in this matter. His odes, then, however greatly filled with praise and light, may also display sombre and dark tones.

What then does Pindar say of *aretē*? First, we shall treat descriptions selected from a variety of odes in order to establish a broad picture of his ideas of its nature. Then we shall focus upon one ode, *Olympians* 1, showing how he treats the *aretē* of a particular victor, Hieron of Syracuse.

For Pindar *aretē* is excellence manifested by different individuals. This *aretē* may be varied in nature. Its source is from the gods. Thus he says: 'from the gods come all means (*machanai*) for mortal *aretai* and individuals are by nature wise, powerful in hands, and eloquent' (*Pyth.* 1.41–2). In his poems Pindar concentrates on the middle category, 'powerful in hands', that is, evidence of physical capability. But he himself as poet clearly falls within the first and third categories, 'wise' and 'eloquent'. In these lines we hear once again an echo of what Achilles as hero was called to be, 'a speaker of words and doer of deeds' (*Il.* 9.443). In his odes Pindar will frequently describe examples of athletic *aretē*, revealing at the same time his own excellence in poetry.

Pindar strongly believes that for *aretē* to emerge in a person, there must be a capacity inherited by birth. The term he uses to indicate this capacity is *phuā*, 'nature'. The root of this noun is related to the verb *phuō*, meaning 'to grow'.[42] Pindar's view is that at the core of the individual there must be an essential natural ability; if this is not inherited, *aretē* will not be possible. Thus he says 'that which exists by nature (*phuā*) is ever the strongest' (*Ol.* 9.100). He praises an athlete who manifests '*aretē* not in any way inferior to his *phuā*' (*Is.* 7.22).[43] In his own case he says: 'whatever *aretē* fate, which is king, has given to me, I know well that time, as it comes, will bring to its destined perfection' (*Nem.* 4.41–3).

But an obvious objection arises to this view. Why is it that within families where an admirable *phuā* is to be found not all members exhibit *aretē*? Pindar remarks in one ode: 'ancient *aretai*, alternating,

---

[42] This word *phuā* is related also to *physis*, 'nature' or 'growth' which is the central focus of much of the thought of the Presocratics.

[43] See too *Is.* 2.44 and 3.13 where capacity for *aretē* is assumed to be an inherited trait.

reveal strength in generations of men' (*Nem.* 11.38–9). Capacity, therefore, is handed on but may not necessarily emerge in all family members or in all generations. He gives famous examples of *aretē* reappearing within a family, especially the excellence of Peleus (*Nem.* 3.32) and his son, Achilles (*Is.* 8.48).

Pindar, therefore, believes in 'inborn *aretai*' (*Ol.* 2.11). He contrasts people having these with those who have only training: 'an individual has great power by inborn valour. But the one who has only teachings dwells ever in darkness, attracted to one thing at one time, another at another, and never walks with a sure step. He tastes of countless forms of *aretē* with an ineffectual *noos*' (*Nem.* 3.40–2).[44] The person with simply teachings has no foundation on which to build. Although he may be attracted to *aretai*, he stays in the dark, trying this and that and never bringing his projects to completion.

Pindar is convinced that other elements too are necessary for the emergence of *aretē*. First, there must be training of inborn capacities. So he says that heroes can be grateful to their trainers. In one poem he makes Achilles thus to Patroclus, serving in this role: 'sharpening a person born for *aretē*, someone could, with the help of the god, drive him to achieve magnificent glory. For few individuals without toil have won joy that is a light for their lifetime in return for all labours' (*Ol.* 10.22–3). So also he says: 'if one is inclined in his whole character to *aretē*, both in expense and labours, when he has reached his goal, it is fitting with ungrudging thoughts to bring him noble praise' (*Is.* 1.41–5).[45] *Aretai* require challenge and dedication. Only those won with hardship and endeavour are deserving of their name. '*Aretai* without danger win no honour' (*Ol.* 6.9).

Second, training and *phuā* are not adequate by themselves. Divine help is also needed. Thus, continuing the quote given above, Pindar says: 'that which exists by nature (*phuā*) is ever the strongest: many men have striven to achieve glory by *aretai* acquired by teaching. But each thing achieved without the help of the god is none the worse for being left in silence' (*Ol.* 9.100–4). Elsewhere he says to Zeus: 'great *aretai* follow mortals from you' (*Is.* 3.4).[46] These then, in Pindar's view, are the three requirements for *aretē*: inherited capacity (*phuā*), training, and divine assistance.

---

[44] On this passage see also above in chapter 2 on *noos*.

[45] See also *Ol.* 5.15 and *Is.* 6.11–12 on the importance of training. At *Ol.* 8.6 individuals 'strive with *thumos* for *aretē*': it absorbs their whole attention.

[46] See too *Nem.* 1.9 where he speaks of '*aretai* given by the gods' (*daimonios*) and

The setting for the emergence of *aretē* on which Pindar concentrates is the athletic contest. He mentions different victories that are possible, specifically relating them to *aretē*: boxing, for example, and running (*Ol.* 7.89, *Is.* 1.22).[47] Deeds of *aretē* deserve recognition in song. This conviction was one long held. We saw Achilles choose to die young, convinced that his heroism would win an immortality in song, an immortality to be attained in no other way. Pindar sees victories as establishing the need for glorification. It is his role as poet to bestow required glory with song. Thus he says: '*aretē* lives long in splendid songs' (*Pyth.* 3.114). In speaking of his own role he says: 'some pray for gold, others for unlimited lands. But I, to lay my limbs in the earth, having pleased my fellow-citizens, praising that meriting acclaim and casting blame on wrong-doers' (*Nem.* 8.37–9). In this ode he continues by saying that *aretē* increases like a tree 'among men who are wise and just' (40–2). *Aretē* thus appears among people who are morally upright and it is their achievement that the poet praises. This praise of excellence brings joy to the living. Pindar suggests too that *aretē*, as it is sung on earth, may also perhaps be a topic heard in the underworld (*Pyth.* 5.98). By 'winning hymns' (*Pyth.* 1.80, 2.14, 2.62), *aretē* gives itself and the person in whom it appears lasting fame. Song, therefore, is the 'crown of *aretē*' (*Nem.* 3.7).[48]

Aretē is the great achievement for which humans should aspire. But just as its attainment is not easy, neither is its sustaining. Again and again Pindar urges athletes to consider carefully their behaviour in victory. As pointed out above, *aretē* is won only with the help of the gods. However much a person contributes by efforts and expenditure, the gift of achievement is a divine one. This fact must be ever central or the *aretē*, fought for so hard, may soon be lost. 'The honours,' he says, 'are diverse for human beings. On every man there lies envy for his *aretē*, but the head of the man of no achievement is hidden under dark silence' (*Parth.* 1.6–10). To achieve nothing means no recognition ever but *aretē* arouses envy in others. Thus Pindar says: 'envious delusions (*atai*) are warded off if someone, having taken the highest place, and tending it in peace, escape terrible pride (*hybris*)' (*Pyth.* 11.54–6). *Aretē* provides great blessing for the victor but if he begins to exult in it as his own achievement, giving way to pride (*hybris*), it will not endure. But if one avoid this pride, he may come

---

Is. 6.12 where he speaks of '*aretai* founded on the gods' (*theodmatos*).

[47] See also examples at *Nem.* 5.53 and 7.7.

[48] See also the relation of *aretē* and song at *Ol.* 11.5–6, *Pyth.* 9.76, and *Nem.* 9.54.

to death, 'leaving behind the grace of a good name, mightiest of possessions' (*Pyth.* 11.57–8).

Thought, then, must be taken not only for the winning of *aretē* but also for the manner of keeping it. 'Respect for forethought casts *aretē* and joys upon human beings' (*Ol.* 7.43). In ode after ode Pindar, fulfilling his role as poet and speaker of wisdom, warns athletes of the perils of success and the attention needed to approach it with the correct attitude. If pride and boasting are avoided and the essential nature of *aretē* as gift of the gods is appreciated, those who have attained excellence may well continue to exhibit this finest human quality for a long time.

Let us look briefly then at one splendid ode Pindar, tracing his thought and examining his notion of *aretē*. *Olympians* 1 was written for Hieron, king of Syracuse, to celebrate his victory of horse and rider at Olympia.[49] Hieron, as king, already by position showed that he possessed a form of excellence. By birth he was ruler, one having great wealth and power. On this occasion, at Olympia, being owner of the winning horse, he exhibited excellence in contest. What might the future not hold? Perhaps there would be someday for him another victory, one considered the highest, that in the chariot race.

Pindar begins the ode with a series of 'firsts' recognised by human beings. Of things, 'water is best', of valuables, gold, of elements, fire, of stars, the sun, of contests, Olympia, and of human conditions, that of king (1–11). This leads Pindar to Hieron, who is a king, and a description of his win with the horse and rider (12–23). It brings him also to recall the hero Pelops and to offer a new explanation of the disappearance, for a time, of this hero from among his fellow human beings. It was not because his father, Tantalus, had tried to serve him to the gods as food to test their foreknowledge, but because he, born with an unusual ivory shoulder, won the affection of Poseidon at birth and was later taken for a time to dwell with this god. Like Hieron, Poseidon too delights in horses and has power to help their victory (24–53).

But a dark shadow did exist in the family of Pelops. His father had done wrong, but in a different way from that usually supposed.

[49] On *Olympians* 1 see especially D.E. Gerber, *Pindar's Olympian One: A Commentary*, Toronto, 1982, G. Nagy, 'Pindar's *Olympian* 1 and the Aetiology of the Olympic Games', *TAPA*, 1986, vol. 116, pp. 71–88, C.P. Segal, 'God and Man in Pindar's First and Third *Olympian* Odes', *HSCP*, 1964, vol. 68, pp. 211–67. See also bibliography in Gerber (note 40), *Lustrum*, 1989, vol. 31, pp. 175–83.

Blessed excessively by the gods, he became proud, acted unjustly, and is ever, as a consequence, being punished (54–64). As a consequence too, his son, Pelops, was not allowed to remain for a longer time among the gods and was sent back to dwell among mortals (65–6).

Thus far in the ode we see Pindar's message for Hieron. Like Tantalus, he has been blessed by the gods. He has every good fortune a human being could hope for: wealth, power, and victory. But his situation is dangerous. The story of Tantalus acts as warning: bear your *aretē* well. Do not abuse your position. Be like Pelops, beloved by the gods, not like his father.

Pelops returns to earth and begs Poseidon to help him in a great enterprise: attaining Hippodameia as bride by winning a chariot race (67–81). He prays to Poseidon for help: 'great danger does not descend upon a mortal without courage. Since it is necessary to die, why should anyone pursue a nameless old age, sitting in vain in darkness, without share of all beautiful achievements? Thus to me this contest falls; may you give the welcome completion' (81–5). In these lines we find a detailed summary of *aretē*, as seen from the time of Homer. Human beings are mortal. As a consequence there seems no purpose in simply attaining a 'nameless old age'. Instead, glory should be sought, the contest attempted. With the help of the gods and with 'courage' in the heart 'beautiful achievements' can be won. Pindar then tells us that Pelops receives a 'golden chariot' and wins his bride, who then bear him six sons 'eager for *aretai*' (86–9). Pelops, after death, remains ever honoured at Olympia (90–9).

Again the lesson for Hieron is clear. If he behaves like Pelops, he too may win even more favour with the gods and find himself one day winner of the chariot race. But, as the ode continues, Pindar gives further words of warning to Hieron: he should appreciate 'the blessing that comes day by day' (99). If Hieron maintains this attitude, a god may grant him a 'sweeter victory' (109) for Pindar to celebrate, a win in the chariot race. Hieron 'walks now on the heights' (115); with care he may sustain his manifold *aretē*.

This ode shows us the elements of Pindar's notion of *aretē*. Hieron, as king, has inherited a capacity for *aretē*. As ruler, he has been trained and, as victor, he shows that the gods are favouring him. It is possible that, with all his blessings, he could go astray. He may overlook what he has been given as he desires too greatly a prize in the future. But, if he heeds Pindar's advice to bear victory with caution,

he may with divine assistance achieve even more success in the future and display the highest *aretē*. If he does, his name, like that of
Pelops, will be destined to live on, ever honoured and revered. In
this ode then Pindar in his role of poet celebrates a victory that
merits praise. As we heard above (*Nem.* 8.37–9), he considered it his
duty to give excellence glory in song but to give warning as well of
possible dangers. For Pindar that human beings can exhibit *aretē* is a
wondrous gift, one that he feels honoured to celebrate.

The Presocratics

In the Presocratics, as would be expected, *aretē* is not of central interest. For the later philosophers, Socrates and Plato, in contrast, the
nature of *aretē* was to be of great importance. The Presocratics are
more concerned about the role of human beings in the cosmos and
the nature of that cosmos than about their role in society. Once the
various questions concerning whether the universe is one or many or
a combination of these had been thoroughly examined, the focus
could shift to a more detailed examination of what the human being, as individual, consisted of and how this person should function
in society. In fifth century drama, of course, the evaluation of heroism is a consuming interest: in picture after picture different facets of
the human personality emerge. Heroes and heroines show the possible range of behaviour and response in individuals. The dramas
often suggested how these individuals were strong and admirable.

Two Presocratics do speak about *aretē*. Already above we heard
how one of them, often listed among the lyric and elegiac poets,
defines *aretē*.[50] Xenophanes in B 2 claims that his wisdom (*sophia*)
should properly be considered *aretē*. He rejects the common practice
of honouring athletes, pointing out in particular that their achievements do not help the city in the way that his wisdom does. He
claims that all he presents in his poetry, his 'wisdom', is actually
aretē.[51] In making this claim, Xenophanes makes one with which Pindar
and other Presocratics might well agree. Plato a century later certainly would come to do so. Xenophanes fully believes that his poetry, in presenting information valuable 'for the city', reveals excel-

---

[50] For bibliography on Xenophanes see above chapter 2, note 32.
[51] We shall discuss this poem of Xenophanes with its definition of *aretē* also in our
treatment of justice below (chapter 5).

lence, one that deserves recognition. We see here in an early philosopher intellectual activity being accorded first place in importance.

Another Presocratic also defines *aretē*. Heraclitus says the following
(B 112): 'to think well (*sophronein*) is the greatest *aretē* and wisdom
(*sophia*) is to speak and to perform the true, recognising it according
to nature'.[52] What is this 'thinking well' that Heraclitus refers to?[53]
In two other fragments he mentions *phronein* alone. In B 17 he remarks that 'most people do not think (*phronein*) things in the way that
they encounter them nor, learning them, do they understand them,
but they imagine that they do'. As we have discussed above in chapters 2 and 3, Heraclitus believed that the universe was a divine expression, a *logos*, ever revealing itself as a unity in balanced diversity.
Most human beings, however, fail to perceive the unity underlying
all things and perceive them instead as separate and often incompat-
ible entities.[54]

In another fragment Heraclitus refers to this tendency of humans
(B 2): 'although the *logos* is common, the many live as though they
had a private way of thinking (*phronesis*)'. The *logos* that on a divine
level expresses and forms the universe exists also in human beings as
their capacity for thought and speech. Human beings need to study
how *logos* works and come especially to realise that it is a shared
capacity. Thus in B 113 he says: 'thinking (*phronein*) is common for
all people'. The ability to think, therefore, like *logos*, belongs to all
human beings. In it is the key to understanding the nature of all
things.

In B 116 also Heraclitus refers to 'thinking', this time using the
verb *sōphroneō*: 'for all human beings it is possible to know themselves
and to think well'. In this echo of the saying inscribed at Delphi,
'know yourself', Heraclitus suggests that the key to truth is found
within each individual. It is possible to 'think well'. The prefix *sō-*
comes from 'safe' or 'sound' and suggests a particular form of thought.
Thus thought, in Heraclitus' view, is related to a grasp of the significance of *logos*. When people realise that they are expressions of a
divine *logos*, that they possess within the very capacity, *logos*, which is

---

[52] On Heraclitus in general see chapter 2, note 35. On B 112, whose authenticity
has been questioned, see Conche, *Héraclite*, pp. 234–6, Kahn, *Art and Thought*, pp.
120–3, and T.M. Robinson, pp. 153–4. All these accept the authenticity of B 112.

[53] The interpretation here takes only *sophronein* as composing *aretē* but other interpretations are possible. See further Kahn, *Art and Thought*, pp. 120–1, T.M. Robinson,
p. 154, and Sullivan in Gerber, pp. 296–8.

[54] See further on this balance of opposites in chapter 5 on justice.

a share in the divine nature, allowing them both to understand how the universe works and to order their lives accordingly, then they will truly 'know themselves'. In such a grasp of truth they will also 'think well' or 'soundly'.

In our first fragment quoted, B 112, Heraclitus describes this form of thinking (*sophronein*) as *aretē*. Excellence is summed up in an intellectual activity. The person who grasps the common nature of his thought-process, who relates it to the principle ordering the cosmos, shows precisely the special and exalted position that the human being occupies within the universe. It is this very capacity of 'thinking well' that sets humans apart from all other living creatures and at the same time constitutes, in Heraclitus' view, their highest achievement, *aretē*. Not surprising, then, in a philosopher we find that a form of intellectual activity is assumed to be the highest achievement of the human being.

Summary

In this chapter we have treated a topic that endlessly fascinated the Greeks: what is excellence (*aretē*) in the human being? In the *Iliad* Homer describes a heroic code in which courage is of great importance while handsomeness and wealth are taken as attendant factors. But in his treatment of Achilles, we see that it is compassion that makes Achilles truly great. In the *Odyssey* we see how, for women, fidelity is to be prized far more than beauty or any other characteristic.

In the lyric and elegiac poets we encountered reaction to or reformulation of Homer's ideas. Archilochus throws away his shield; life is more to be valued than any display of courage. Callinus and Tyrtaeus disagree. For them valour on the battlefield is most to be admired. The soldier, no longer concerned only with self-glorification, needs to show bravery along with others. His prize may be individual honour but it will be awarded by the city for service to that city.

In Greek society individuals continued to win glory by personal victory in athletic games. Pindar and Bacchylides praise this achievement highly, saying that it manifested *aretē*. But this *aretē*, Pindar assumes, depends on birth, training, and divine help. There are other forms of *aretē*, especially the gift of poetry that he himself enjoys.

Aretē, however splendid, is difficult to maintain and great care must be taken to recall ever the degree to which it is a gift.

With Theognis we encountered another picture of *aretē*. In essence, he says, it is justice. Wealth is not to be taken as a sign of its presence but the manner in which hardship is endured shows the inherent goodness of some individuals. In Theognis' view, it is only those with an inherited capacity for *aretē* who will achieve it. Society has become so corrupt that a lesser code of moral behaviour may be necessary for survival for such persons. But *aretē* essentially will consist in according all persons their due. Simonides recognises that the 'old' standard of *aretē* may be a splendid one. But the attainment of heroic excellence is difficult and dependent upon divine favour. He suggests that in the city a different form of goodness should be recognised as valuable: the willing avoidance of the shameful.

The philosophers rarely speak of *aretē* in the fragments we possess. With Xenophanes we hear of wisdom being described as *aretē*. With Heraclitus we learn that a form of thought, 'thinking well', expresses it. This way of thinking will grasp how the universe functions and will share, by its very nature, in the divine principle ordering that universe.

The Greeks recognise the strong human urge and zeal for greatness. With thoughtfulness they treat over the centuries what may be the essence of this greatness. The candidates that emerge in their thought, as constituting excellence, are several: physical prowess, beauty, wealth, courage, compassion, wisdom, justice, correct thinking. All of these will remain themes of later Greek literature, especially of the dialogues of Plato. These early treatments prove of great value both for their focus upon how human beings act and especially upon how they act well. Outstanding behaviour ever deserves praise and the summons to different forms of it, begun in the early Greek poets, continues to be heard in the years that follow.

CHAPTER FIVE

JUSTICE

Background

In this chapter we shall treat justice in the writers of the Archaic Age.[1] The topic, 'justice', is a complex one, especially since modern concepts of it differ greatly among themselves and sometimes differ markedly from those of earlier ages. 'Justice' too may be of different kinds: legal, political, moral, human, divine, cosmic. We find all these types present in Greek thought. What can we say of 'justice' in the Archaic Age? Can we correctly speak of a 'concept' of it? We do not encounter a concept consciously defined and expounded. But we do find a 'notion' of justice, 'notion' indicating a 'general sense' or 'awareness'. In the early fourth century we see in Plato's *Republic* a careful delineation of justice as a moral concept. No such clear definition of it exists in the authors we are studying.

In general the 'notion' of justice in the Archaic Age may have

---

[1] For bibliography on the idea of justice see in particular Adkins, *Merit, Moral Values*, R.J. Bonner and G. Smith, *The Administration of Justice From Homer to Aristotle*, I, Chicago, 1938, N. Bosco, '*Dikē* contro *themis*', *Filosofia*, 1967, vol. 18, pp. 309–46, 'Ne *Themis* né *dikē*', *Filosofia*, 1967, vol. 18, pp. 469–510, '*Themis* e *dikē*', *Filosofia*, 1967, vol. 18, pp. 131–79, M. Dickie, '*Dikē* as a Moral Term in Homer and Hesiod', *CP*, 1978, vol. 73, pp. 91–101, V. Ehrenburg, *Die Rechtsidee im frühen Griechentum*, Leipzig, 1921, Ferguson, H. Frisch, *Might and Right in Antiquity*, '*Dikē*' I: *From Homer to the Persian Wars*, trans. C. Martindak, Copenhagen, 1949, M. Gagarin, '*Dikē* in Archaic Greek Thought', *CP*, 1974, vol. 69, pp. 186–97, '*Dikē* in the *Works and Days*' *CP*, 1973, vol. 68, pp. 81–94, D. Gill, S.J., 'Aspects of Religious Morality in Early Greek Epic', *HThR*, 1980, vol. 73, pp. 373–418, W.C. Greene, 'Fate, Good and Evil in Pre-Socratic Philosophy', *HSCP*, 1936, vol. 47, pp. 85–129, G. Groffridi, '*Hybris* e *Dikē* nell' arcaismo greco', *SDHI*, 1938, vol. 49, pp. 331–6, E. Havelock, '*Dikaiosunē*: An Essay in Greek Intellectual History', *Phoenix*, 1969, vol. 23, pp. 49–70, *Greek Concept*, R. Hirzel, *Themis, Dikē und Verwandtes*, Leipzig, 1907, Jaeger, *Paideia*, pp. 1–184, Lloyd-Jones, *Justice*, D. Loenen, *Dikē*, Amsterdam, 1948, G. Martano, '*Physis, aretē, dikē* nella cultura greca dell' eta arcaica', *Elenchos*, 1987, vol. 8, pp. 25–41, Pearson, V.A. Rodgers, 'Some Thoughts on *Dikē*', *CQ*, 1971, vol. 21, pp. 289–301, C. Rowe, C.J. Rowe, 'The Nature of Homeric Morality' in Rubino, pp. 248–75, Snell, *Lexikon*, vol. 2, pp. 302–5, G. Vlastos, 'Equality and Justice in Early Greek Cosmologies', *CP*, 1947, vol. 42, pp. 156–78, E. Wolf, *Griechische Rechtsdenken I*, Frankfurt, 1950, Yamagata. Particularly useful are: Dickie, Gill, Havelock, *Greek Concept*, Lloyd-Jones, *Justice*, Vlastos, and Yamagata.

been something taken for granted. With time it would come to be consciously examined, its intricacies and difficulties appreciated, and its nature defined. But when authors come to do so, they can assume some understanding of justice present already in their audience. If the position they adopt is new or controversial, they can expect some reaction to what they say and perhaps a refusal to accept their views.

In the pages to follow we shall concentrate upon this 'notion' of justice. There has been disagreement among scholars concerning what the early Greeks thought about it. The chief questions are: what was its nature and at what stage did a moral element become discernible in it? Some of the disagreement surrounds the term commonly associated with justice in early Greek literature, *dikē*. Certain scholars suggest that it refers simply to legal process without moral implications; others argue that a moral element is present in it.[2] By the time of Plato a moral element is prominent in justice but he uses a different term: *dikaiosynē*.

In our discussion we shall suggest that the notion of justice in the Archaic Age has legal, political, and moral aspects. We shall see it operate on the human, divine, and cosmic levels. The moral aspect seems to be already present in Homer and to revolve around a sense of 'what is right'. With regard to the term *dikē*, we shall suggest that it has a basic meaning related to legal process (see discussion of its meaning below) but that already it contains moral aspects. The notion of justice, however, is not to be limited to this one word and its cognates. We shall look for the presence of this notion more generally in the literature we treat.

Our position will be that people appearing in the literature of the Archaic Age have a notion of 'what is right'. This they relate to 'what is just' or to 'justice' itself. The core of 'what is right and just' seems to be 'due share' or 'due portion'.[3] We see the idea of 'due share or portion' operative on both the divine and human levels. Gods have their claims, their rights, their due. So also do human beings. Among humans, however, the occurrence of imbalance and unequal distribution of shares is common. As expectations of or hopes

---

[2] For the first view see in particular Gagarin (note 1), both articles, Havelock, *Greek Concept*, and Rodgers (note 1). For the second see Adkins, *Merit*, Dickie (note 1), Gill (note 1), Jaeger, *Paideia*, and Lloyd-Jones, *Justice*.

[3] See especially Jaeger, *Paideia*, pp. 102–6. This aspect of justice will emerge clearly in the lyric and elegiac poets and the Presocratics.

for 'due portion' increase over time, obvious difficulties appear. What is someone's due share? How does the individual ensure reception of this? Who makes the allotment of shares? Who especially will make the distribution of shares equitable?

In this chapter we shall look at what Homer and Hesiod say of justice. We shall observe that the lyric and elegiac poets raise questions about its function in personal life and in society. We shall see certain Presocratics give it a central place in their thought. In this early literature, justice operates on the human level. On the divine level, it is assumed to be highly valued by the gods. The operation of justice on this divine level becomes the model for that in human society. In the Presocratics we encounter the notion of cosmic justice, analogical to that in human society. This justice is associated with the divine or ruling principle of the universe and, as with justice among the gods, acts as the ideal pattern for human justice. The passages we discuss will suggest legal, political, and moral elements in justice. These passages, rich and varied in themselves, provide background also for the magnificent discussions of justice that Aeschylus presents in the *Oresteia* and Plato, in the *Republic*. The interest in justice found so early in Greek literature was not to fade.

Before turning to our authors, we shall treat some terms related to the notion of justice. We have mentioned *dikē* above and it will be prominent in our discussion. But in Homer another word, *themis*, occurs almost interchangeably with *dikē*. Derived from the verb '*tithēmi*', it appears to be that which is 'laid down' as appropriate or right.[4] In Homer it can signify 'judgements' or 'rulings' (*themista*: e.g., *Il.* 1.238, 9.99), a 'way' or 'custom' (e.g., *Il.* 9.134, *Od.* 14.130), and occasionally a 'principle of right conduct' (e.g., *Od.* 16.91). Later, however, *themis* becomes more limited in meaning, referring especially to the relationship between gods and human beings.[5]

The etymology of *dikē* is not clear but it may derive from the verb '*deiknumi*', meaning 'to point out' or 'to show'.[6] *Dikē* becomes the

---

[4] See, e.g., *Il.* 2.206, 9.156, *Od.* 3.187, 11.451. *Themis* appears as a goddess at *Il.* 15.87, 93, 20.4, and *Od.* 2.68. On *themis* see Frisch (note 1), C. Groffridi, 'Su i concetti di *themis* e *dikē* in Omero', *BIDR*, 1962, vol. 65, pp. 69–75, Havelock, *Greek Concept*, pp. 134–6, Hirzel (note 1), Jaeger, *Paideia*, pp. 103–4, Pearson, p. 46, H. Vos, *Themis*, Assen, 1956, and Yamagata.

[5] See references in note 4, especially Jaeger.

[6] On the etymology of *dikē* see Chantraine, vol. 1, pp. 283–4, Gagarin (note 1), *CP*, 1973, p. 82, J. Gonda, *DEIKNUMI: Semantische Studie over den Indo-Germanische Wortel DEIK*, Amsterdam, 1929, Loenan (note 1), pp. 3–4, L.R. Palmer, 'The Indo-

way 'shown' or the direction 'indicated'. This way can be 'straight' (*itheia*) or 'crooked' (*skolia*). As a way pointed out and frequently taken, *dikē* apparently also became a 'custom' or 'manner of behaving'.

In legal contexts *dikē* displays several meanings. It is what judges 'point out', their 'decision'. Ideally this decision is 'straight' but it may be 'crooked'. *Dikē* can be the content of this decision, the 'penalty' to be paid. It can be a 'trial' or 'lawsuit'. More broadly, it can be a 'principle' for settling lawsuits. In these legal contexts, *dikē* displays moral aspects. It can signify 'lawful conduct'. It then appears to signify more broadly conduct that is 'right', that is, conduct including appropriate, fair, or righteous actions.

In our discussion we shall also frequently meet the opposite of *dikē*: *hybris*.[7] This term signifies the 'arrogance' or 'pride' that leads to a reckless disregard for the claims of others. In Homer we find this term often used to describe the behaviour of the suitors (see, e.g., *Od.* 1.368, 4.627, 15.329). These individuals do not do 'what is right'. They overstep the bounds of acceptable behaviour and take what is not their 'due share'. Thus too Achilles at *Il.* 1.203 describes the actions of Agamemnon in taking Briseis as *hybris*. He overstepped his bounds and deprived Achilles of his 'due'. *Hybris*, therefore, stands in contrast to 'right conduct.'

Homer

Dikē

We begin by looking at how Homer uses the term *dikē*. Then we shall turn to the opening of the *Odyssey*. The most common meanings of *dikē* in Homer are 'custom' or 'judgement'. First, 'custom'. At *Od.* 4.690–1 Penelope describes Odysseus as one 'who never did or said anything wrong (lit. "beyond fate") among the people, as is the custom (*dikē*) of divine kings'. She then says that the latter usually 'hate one person and love another' (692). *Dikē* indicates a usual pattern of behaviour, in this case one negative and different from

---

European Origins of Greek Justice', *TPhS*, Oxford, 1950, pp. 149–68, and Yamagata, p. 61, n. 2.

[7] On *hybris* see Dickie (note 1), p. 99, Groffridi (note 1), Jaeger, *Paideia*, pp. 103, 168, Fischer, Havelock, *Greek Concept*, pp. 85, 185–7, and Rowe (note 1).

Odysseus' fair treatment of others. At *Od.* 18.275–80 Penelope contrasts the behaviour of her suitors with the usual 'way of wooers' who would bring supplies and gifts to the prospective bride, not devouring the livelihood of another 'with no penalty'.[8] All through the *Odyssey* the suitors are portrayed as unjust. As noted above, Homer speaks often of their *hybris*. They arrogantly go far beyond their role as suitors, devouring Odysseus' livelihood, ignoring the claims of Telemachus, and imposing their authority over the household. Claiming more than their due, they eventually pay with their lives.

At *Od.* 11.570 we find the second common meaning of *dikē*, 'judgement'. In the underworld Odysseus sees Minos acting as 'law-giver for the dead' (*themisteuō*), while they asked him 'for judgements' (*dikai*). We may assume that he will allot to each what is fair, giving a due or proper share. In the *Iliad* we hear that Hephaestus, in the new shield of Achilles, fashions the scene of a disagreement between two individuals which is to be judged by elders (18.497–508). These, holding sceptres, 'gave judgement (*dikazō*) in turn'. Two talents of gold were also present to be handed over to the one 'who spoke in the straightest way judgement' (*dikē*). Here we see an association of *dikē* with a fair solution to a problem. The individuals are each making a claim and the 'best judgement' would apparently involve both what was right and what was most appropriate for each. The idea of 'due share', related to *dikē*, thus seems implicit here.

In four other passages in Homer the connection of *dikē* with a moral notion of right and with an idea of due share seems prominent. First, when Achilles wants to rush into battle after the death of Patroclus, Odysseus urges him to wait instead and to accept the gifts offered by Agamemnon (*Il.* 19.172–80). He suggests that Achilles should also take part in a feast in Agamemnon's hut so that he might lack nothing of 'his due' (*dikē*). He then says to Agamemnon: 'you hereafter will be more just (*dikaioteros*) to others. For in no way is it cause for blame if a king make amends to someone, when that one first became angry' (181–3). Here we see the retribution paid to Achilles being placed in a context of just and fair behaviour. Achilles was deprived of what was his by right. That must be returned; it is, with generous overpayment. This action allows healing of the relationship between the two. Agamemnon will have learned from his

---

[8] See also other instances of this meaning of *dikē*, 'custom', at *Od.* 11.218, 14.59, 19.43, 168, and 24.255.

experience with Achilles to show greater respect for what others may claim. Even as king, he must make sacrifices, if he has proved to be in the wrong.

Second, at *Od.* 3.224 Telemachus poses a question for Nestor, 'since beyond others he knows judgements (*dikai*) and wisdom'. Nestor's long life has brought him much experience. 'Knowing *dikai*' implies, it seems, making decisions that will prove both honourable and fair. Third, in another passage of the *Odyssey*, Eumaeus describes the attitude of the gods (14.83–4): 'the blessed gods do not love crooked deeds but they honour just behaviour (*dikē*) and the fitting (*aisima*) deeds of human beings'. He goes on to describe the insolent behaviour of the suitors in consuming Odysseus' wealth (85–108). 'They are not willing to woo justly' (*dikaiōs*)'; 'they consume possessions arrogantly' (*hyperbion*: 90–2). The suitors overstep the bounds of justice by their greedy and gluttonous behaviour. Their actions are not 'fitting' nor just. *Dikē* in this passage seems clearly to indicate moral righteousness, honoured by the gods and ignored by the suitors.

Fourth, this notion of *dikē* as moral justice is seen even more vividly in the description of Zeus at *Iliad* 16.384–93. There he pours forth a great storm on the earth, 'when, growing angry, he rages against men who by violence give crooked (*skoliai*) judgements (*themistai*) in the market-place and they drive out justice (*dikē*), not regarding the vengeance of the gods'. 'Crooked judgements' ignore the question of right or of what is fair for all individuals. What a situation may demand is overlooked and favouritism to some individuals is shown. When this happens, justice (*dikē*) is driven out: correct judgement and decision is absent. The gods, however, are not blind. Zeus punishes mortals with violent storms. We see in this passage a harsh event in nature interpreted as an act of retribution on the part of Zeus. The cause has been human behaviour and the neglect of fairness. In such a storm the innocent must suffer with the guilty. This should prove a source of caution for all. Zeus' anger is exceedingly great, showing the degree to which he reveres justice.

These four passages suggest that human beings should be just in their behaviour. Elsewhere, in another reference to *dikē*, Homer describes a group who are the opposites of what humans are urged to be: these are the Cyclopes (*Od.* 9.166–215). Polyphemus is one who 'knows lawlessness' (*athemistia*: 189), living apart by himself. Odysseus expects him to be 'wild, not knowing well judgements (*dikai*) or laws' (*themistai*: 215). The Cyclopes turn out to be arrogant (*hybristai*), wild (*agrioi*), and not just (*dikaioi*), quite opposite to those 'who love strangers and whose mind (*noos*) is god-fearing' (175–6).

This passage shows us elements of what injustice was thought to be. It is associated with those who are 'fierce' and 'arrogant'. Such people do not welcome strangers nor honour the gods. We may see in the last description a suggestion that justice is probably important to the gods and therefore to those respecting them. The Cyclopes, dwelling alone as they do, need not heed the rights of one another. Polyphemus certainly shows no pity for the suppliants and their claims for help (259–71). He explicitly says that he has no regard for Zeus and would not avoid killing suppliants to escape Zeus' anger (275–8). And he does not. The story of Polyphemus in particular illustrates behaviour humans are not to emulate. Odysseus punishes him for his cruelty and justice appears to be done when the Cyclops is struck blind. Human beings differ from the Cyclopes in being able to be 'god-fearing', 'kind to strangers', and 'just'. These features set them apart and make life in society possible.

The Opening of the Odyssey

A most important passage for the idea of justice in Homer is the opening of the *Odyssey* (1.1–79). Homer summons the Muse to tell of the 'versatile man' who encountered many 'bitter experiences' as he strove to go home. He begins his tale about Odysseus with a picture of a gathering of the gods, all except Poseidon, absent elsewhere. Zeus makes complaint to the other gods of the way mortals blame the gods for the evil that befalls them, even though it is their own 'blind folly' (*atasthalia*) that causes them 'pains beyond their destiny' (34). He describes how Aegisthus was warned by Hermes not to marry Clytemnestra nor to kill Agamemnon since Orestes would surely kill him in turn. But Aegisthus did not heed and 'paid for all in full' (43).

Homer thus in these lines speaks of the responsibility humans have for their actions. Human beings, even though forewarned, can choose to do wrong. When they do, they force the gods to bring punishment upon them, beyond what they would ever have suffered otherwise. The gods, then, punish such evil and see that justice is done. 'Evils' do not befall humans from any mere whim of the gods but from their own evil choices that demand punishment. One thus receives one's due in the form of some retribution. By exerting their will to do evil, people obviously infringe on the rights of others, causing them suffering. Sadly too the victims of evil may themselves be quite innocent. Evil can be the effect of freedom of choice and the gods will see that, when humans make such a choice, justice will follow. The suffering evil people will endure, therefore, is wholly deserved.

As he continues his story, Homer introduces a different type of suffering found among human beings: innocent suffering (44–79). Athena remarks that Aegisthus has received what he deserved. But what of Odysseus? What is his fault? 'Why', she asks, 'do you hate him so?' In her choice of the verb 'hate' (*odussomai*), Athena plays on the name of Odysseus ('the man people love to hate'),[9] suggesting perhaps that Zeus may somehow harbour a basic hatred for this hero. But Zeus' reply clarifies the situation and offers an explanation of innocent suffering. Poseidon, he says, hates Odysseus because of his blinding of Polyphemus and keeps him far from home. There is, therefore, a god who does 'hate' Odysseus and send evil upon him. Because Poseidon chooses to harass Odysseus, Zeus must yield before this exercise of will on the part of his brother and all the other gods must wait until Poseidon 'lets go his anger' (77). Innocent suffering, then, can result from the effect of different wills being exercised. In the case of the gods, Poseidon is acting from a personal grievance. The other gods, it seems, cannot prevent him and only by refusing to support him will gradually bring him to lay aside his rage (78–9). As long as Poseidon acts thus, Odysseus must suffer. But eventually help will come and 'in the year in which the gods had ordained he should return home' (17), he will surely do so.

This opening passage of the *Odyssey* suggests a deep concern for justice. We see that the gods do not want mortals to suffer. They send messages of warning. But human beings have freedom of choice and can choose a course of action that will bring 'evils beyond their fate' (33–4). The gods see in the case of 'blind folly' that the guilty party pays. Justice is done. But there is another form of justice they attend to as well: justice for the innocent sufferer. Even though the gods may be compelled for a time to honour the expression of free will of another divinity, they will not lend support to that expression and will see that in the end events will turn out well for the sufferer. However inexplicable and cruel the delay may seem, the gods are concerned for justice and will act. They will bring personal aid, as

---

[9] See the explanation of how Odysseus received his name and its meaning at *Od.* 19.400–12.

Athena does to Odysseus, and ensure that all turns out favourably. Such is the powerful picture given of justice in the opening of the *Odyssey*.

Homer speaks of justice on the divine and human levels. The gods appear to honour justice because of its intrinsic nature. It embodies 'what is right'. Human beings seem to be called on to do likewise and, if they fail to do so, will encounter divine disapproval. The approval or disapproval of the gods does not make actions just. They are so in themselves and receive divine approbation for that reason. In the *Iliad* we hear of Zeus using the forces of nature to punish a disregard for justice. In the *Odyssey* the whole story revolves around the unjust behaviour of the suitors and their eventual just punishment inflicted by Odysseus with Athena's help.

In Homer, therefore, we have seen the notion of justice among gods and human beings. We have seen that it has both legal and moral aspects. For centuries before Homer bards had sung the tales of gods and heroes. We cannot know how great a role justice played in their different stories nor how important it was in Homer's own time in contexts other than the poetic. Homer's poems, however, give us an inkling that this notion was recognised and valued. With time its importance was to grow.

Hesiod

Works and Days

In Hesiod's didactic epics, the *Works and Days* and the *Theogony*, justice occupies a central position.[10] It is vitally important on both the human and divine levels. It displays legal, political, and moral aspects. First, then, the *Works and Days*. Hesiod had a quarrel with his brother Perses over an inheritance. He addresses in this poem both

---

[10] On justice in Hesiod see in particular D. Blickman, 'Styx and the Justice of Zeus in Hesiod's *Theogony*', *Phoenix*, 1987, vol. 41, pp. 341–55, Dickie (note 1), H. Erbse, 'Die Funktion des Rechtsgedankens in Hesiods "Erga"', *Hermes*, 1993, vol. 121, pp. 12–28, Frisch (note 1), pp. 91–7, Gagarin (note 1), *CP*, 1973, 'The Poetry of Justice: Hesiod and the Origins of Greek Law', *Ramus*, 1992, vol. 21, pp. 61–78, Jaeger, *Paideia*, pp. 57–76, Pearson, pp. 55–83, F. Solmsen, *Hesiod and Aeschylus*, Ithaca, 1949, W.J. Verdenius, *A Commentary on Hesiod, Works and Days*, vv. 1–382, Leiden, 1985, M.L. West, Hesiod, *Theogony*, Oxford, 1966, Hesiod, *Works and Days*, Oxford, 1978, and Yamagata, pp. 79–92.

his brother and the kings who are to decide the suit. Perses had apparently taken more than his due share of the inheritance left to the brothers and courted the favour of the kings who would judge the case (*W. &. D.* 27–42). Hesiod writes his poem to present his views on the positive value of justice and also of hard work, which Perses likewise seems to have scorned. We do not know the outcome of the quarrel between the two but Hesiod's ideas about justice prove to be of great interest.

In the *Works and Days* we encounter the term for justice, *dikē*, used with a wider range of meaning than found in Homer. It again has the sense of 'judgement'. At 35–6 Hesiod says to Perses: 'let us settle our dispute again with straight (*itheiai*) judgements (*dikai*), which, being best, are from Zeus'. The ideal 'judgements' are those that are 'straight'. Elsewhere we shall hear of others that are 'crooked' (*skoliai*).[11] Another meaning of *dikē* is that of 'law-suit'. At 39 Hesiod mentions the kings (*basileis*) who 'are willing to judge (*dikaieō*) this case' (*dikē*).[12] A third meaning is 'atonement' or 'penalty'. Hesiod says that, if a friend has done or said 'something hateful' but wishes to return to friendship and is 'willing to make atonement', this person should be accepted again as friend (710–13). In this case *dikē* appears to be the 'portion' or 'due' owed to make recompense and to re-establish the balance of mutual regard and respect.

As in Homer, in several passages of the *Works and Days dikē* has the meaning of 'moral right' or 'righteousness'.[13] First, at 9 Hesiod asks Zeus to 'guide astraight our judgements with justice' (*dikē*). We see here that Zeus is assumed to be interested in justice and has the power to ensure that 'judgements' are straight ones. Even though it may be kings who make decisions, their actions ideally will reflect that of which Zeus would approve.

Second, in lines 106–201 Hesiod describes how human beings, once made of gold, have declined to a state of iron. In terms of moral behaviour, those of the golden race were superior but with the other races of silver, bronze, and iron great decline in this regard occurred. He describes those of iron: 'these people make violence their right (*cheirodikai*). One will sack the city of another. Nor will there be any

---

[11] See below on *W. & D.* 219, 221, 250, and 264.
[12] See also this meaning of *dikē* at *W. & D.* 249 and 269.
[13] On this aspect of *dikē* in Hesiod see Dickie (note 1), Frisch (note 1), p. 97, and Jaeger, *Paideia*, pp. 57–70. Contrast Gagarin (note 1), *CP*, 1973, who doubts its presence in Hesiod.

appreciation for the person who keeps his word nor for the just (*dikaios*) or good person but people will rather honour the doer of evil, the epitome of insolence (*hybris*). Justice (*dikē*) will lie in might of hand and a sense of shame before others (*aidōs*) will be gone' (189–93). Individuals will lie, cheat, and harm others until at last, all 'sense of shame' (*aidōs*) and 'public disapproval' (*nemesis*) will disappear from human society (200). Hesiod thus describes a gradual deterioration of human character. 'Justice' comes to be expressed only by violence. In due course, there will be neither regard or respect for others and their claims (*aidōs*) nor any fear of criticism from others for taking more than what is fair (*nemesis*).[14] Once these two attitudes disappear, Hesiod believes that society will not be able to exist.

We see here an association of *dikē*, *aidōs*, and *nemesis*, all seen as positive forces that make it possible for human beings to live together in harmony. *Dikē* implies an awareness of right and a recognition of the claims of others. *Aidōs* involves a sense of shame concerning one's own behaviour with others: these should be honourable. *Nemesis* describes the disapproval others may express of actions not considered admirable or just. The opposite of all three is *hybris*, arrogance that leads one to take far more than is fair or right and to exult in doing so.

Third, in another long passage, Hesiod sets out clearly his ideas about *dikē* (202–85). He begins here with a fable (202–11):

> Now I will tell a story for kings, who understand it well.
> Thus spoke a hawk to the speckled nightingale,
> bearing her high in the clouds, clutched in his claws.
> Pierced by his hooked claws, she wept: 'pity me'.
> But he, harshly victorious, addressed her:
> 'Foolish thing, why do you cry out? A much stronger
> Now holds you and you will go wherever
> I take you, even though you are a singer.
> If I wish, I shall make a meal of you or let you go.
> Foolish is the one who wants to strive against the stronger.'
> He loses victory and suffers pain in addition to shame.

Hesiod's story is an animal fable. In it he shows that in the animal world the principle of might being stronger is operative. Pity is unknown as is any concern for the rights of others. Hesiod tells this story to criticise the behaviour of the hawk. He suggests that human

---

[14] On the meaning of *aidōs* and *nemesis* see Cairns, Verdenius (note 10), pp. 115–16 and West, *Works and Days*, p. 204.

beings can and should be different from animals for whom strength is decisive. Kings could act like the hawk but such behaviour, in Hesiod's view, is not to be admired. Human beings are above animals and should not appeal to the right of the stronger. It may be their very capacity for justice that sets humans apart from animals. Humans can be like the gods who value justice highly.

Hesiod continues, urging Perses to 'listen to justice (*dikē*) and not to increase *hybris*' (213). As above, *hybris* appears as the opposite of *dikē*; it can lead to destruction (*atē*), even for the good person (216). In contrast, the 'road to justice' (*dikaia*) is a 'better' one: 'justice (*dikē*) emerges triumphant over *hybris* in the end' (218). Hesiod then goes on to describe (219–24) what happens when 'bribe-devouring individuals' drag Justice (*dikē*) away and 'pass verdicts with crooked judgements' (*dikai*). She returns, bringing harm to those who drove her away. If people are just, however, Zeus blesses them, and nature likewise favours them greatly (225–37). As we heard above in Homer, events in nature are related to the righteousness or lack thereof in human beings. 'Crooked judgements' attract Zeus' anger and then nature becomes a source of punishment.

Hesiod proceeds to describe what happens if *hybris* flourishes. Zeus marks out people in whom it is found for 'punishment' (*dikē*) and often the 'whole city' suffers because of one evil person (238–40). Nature becomes hostile and Zeus brings various calamities upon all (241–9). Hesiod points out that the gods are ever watchful over human activities, especially observing those who pass 'crooked judgements' (*dikai*). He says (252–7):

> For there are over the fertile earth thrice ten-thousand
> immortal guardians of human beings sent by Zeus,
> who watch over judgements and harsh deeds,
> clothed in air, travelling everywhere over the earth.
> There is the maiden Justice (*dikē*), born of Zeus,
> majestic, revered by the gods who hold Olympus.

Hesiod then explains that Justice, when treated with scorn by humans, sits by her father Zeus, describing 'the unjust mind (*noos*) of humans' (260). The result is that the whole people suffer for the deeds of unjust kings. Zeus observes whether a city is just or not and acts accordingly. If this were not the case, Hesiod ironically says, he himself would not care about justice (258–73).

Best then to 'heed justice' (275). Zeus has made it the 'natural order' of the universe that 'animals, birds, and fish should eat one

another, because justice does not exist among them. To human beings Zeus gave justice, which is by far the best' (277–80). To the just
person, Zeus sends 'prosperity'; to the evil person, who harms justice, disaster impends for himself and his family (281–5).

In this long portion of his poem we see Hesiod making several
important points. Justice is of great concern to Zeus. She is his daughter. He listens to reports of injustice, himself observing as well per-
verse human behaviour and sending many watchers to observe human beings. Zeus rewards those who are just and punishes the unjust
not only individually, but both as a family and as members of a city.
Many suffer for the crimes of one or of a few.

Human beings may be set apart from other living creatures in
their having a capacity for justice. This they should cultivate and
revere. But they prove capable too of abusing this gift and, on occasion, acting as though might were right. Justice brings prosperity to
person, family, and city. Nature acts favourably to the just. Even if
someone thinks it is possible to get away with injustice, in the end
justice always triumphs. As with Homer we see a recognition of the
intrinsic value and nature of justice. Because it is what it is, the gods
approve of it. Personified as *Dikē*, the goddess of justice, it is seen as
itself partaking of the divine nature. In relation to the chief god,
Zeus, this Justice is described as daughter: it is thus something, or
rather, 'someone' whom he will care for and heed. When wronged,
Justice can complain to Zeus and knows she will be heard. Zeus
himself guards her rights by carefully watching human beings himself and sending a 'myriad of watchers' to do likewise.

Why is justice so important to Hesiod? For him it has legal, political, and moral implications. On the human level, if present, it
allows society to function. If it is abused, discord inevitably follows.
If it is totally driven away, society collapses. On the divine level, the
gods honour and revere justice. Human beings incur punishment from
Zeus and the other gods if they violate it. This punishment may be
sent partly to be didactic: humans must learn to be just or the cost
to themselves will eventually be great.

The Theogony

In his other work, the *Theogony*, we find a different treatment of justice. In this poem Hesiod presents answers to some basic questions.
Where did this universe come from? Is it divine? Were the gods

always the same? If not, when did Zeus become chief divinity? What is Zeus actually like? In his careful description of how the complicated universe in which we live emerged, Hesiod assigns an important role to justice. On the divine level, it is the principle that ensures the continuance of the current universe. In this work we do not encounter the actual term, *dikē*, mentioned specifically very often, although we meet it personified as a goddess at 902. But the idea of justice is a crucial element in Hesiod's story.

Hesiod's view of the universe is that it is a family of gods. At the present time, it resembles in its variety and complexity some picture of a large family reunion at which several generations may be present. 'Great-grandfather and great-grandmother' may be there, seen by the youngest members as the 'cause of it all'. All the other parts of the family have some kinship of blood, however different their appearance and activities may be. So with the universe. Many parts are offspring of one pair of original parents, divine in nature. These partake in the divine nature which comes to express itself in myriad diversity.

The history of the universe is as follows. First there appeared Earth and Sky. Attracted by love, they produced many offspring, especially the Titans (116–53). But to the Sky his children 'were a source of annoyance from the beginning' (155). As they were born, he hid them all deep inside earth; he did not let any come 'into the light' (156). 'Sky took pleasure in this evil deed' (158). At the very beginning of the cosmos, therefore, Hesiod places an act of injustice. Sky denies his children their rights. He ignores their claims to separate existence, claims they can make because of their status as children. He acts unjustly as he preserves his own position of sole authority; he enjoys doing so.

But this situation does not continue. The 'youngest and cleverest' of Earth's children, Cronus (137–8), takes action. Earth devises a plan by which one of her children is to castrate their father; Cronus proves willing to do so and acts (160–210). Both mother and son in the planning stage make the point that Sky was 'the first to devise unseemly (*aeikea*) deeds' (166, 173). He has acted unjustly and therefore should suffer. Sky, after this act, warns that 'retribution would come later' upon his children because of what they had done (210). He thus points to their later defeat by Zeus. They suffer this defeat, however, only because they themselves choose to act violently.

Sky's injustice is put to an end with a drastic penalty. By castrating

Sky, Cronus had ended his father's productivity. In this event Hesiod may offer an explanation of why the universe in its cosmic form is 'just so big'. Many more offspring would be produced in the next generation of gods but this would occur now in a universe of established size. In the story of this first generation we see that justice was done to Sky.

His son, Cronus, however, has taken after his father in one respect: he too is unjust. True, he lets his children be born but he then immediately swallows them down (453–68). He does this because Earth and Sky informed him that 'it was fated (*peprōto*) for him to be conquered by his son' (464). We hear in this line of the strength of a force within the universe apart from the gods: that of fate. As in Homer, where fate (*Moira*) is a powerful element at work in the universe,[15] so here it decrees the ultimate destiny of Cronus. He may, for a time, delay its effect, but, ironically, by the very means he chooses to do that, he ensures his downfall.

In the next change of ruler, the god to act will be Zeus. He likewise overthrows his father. Instead of letting Cronus swallow down Zeus, as he had done all the other children, Earth gives him a stone to eat. She saves the life of Zeus, hiding him in Crete. After Zeus has grown up, Earth tricks Cronus into throwing up again. First he brings up the stone and then the other Olympian gods, learning thereby that he had been tricked. Zeus proceeds to remove him from office. He also frees the Cyclopes whom Sky had put in chains (468–501). The Cyclopes give Zeus 'thunder and the flashing lightning bolt'; these weapons allow him to continue to be master of the gods (501–6, cf. 141). Zeus inflicts punishment upon his father who had acted unjustly, by taking over as chief of the gods. The universe is now under Zeus' control.

The rest of the *Theogony* clarifies why Zeus can remain king. First, he is so wise that no one can deceive him. Even with Prometheus, it is only because he has plans of his own that he allows Prometheus to play a trick on him. His wisdom is endless (507–616). Second, Zeus shows that he is strongest. In a battle between the Olympians and the Titans, he leads the first group to victory. He imprisons the

---

[15] See, e.g., the story of Sarpedon (*Il.* 16.433–503). When 'it is fated' for him to die at the hands of Patroclus, Zeus ponders whether to save him, but Hera warns him that, if he does, the other gods will not approve (443). The gods, it seems, can go against fate but choose to respect it.

Titans in Tartarus where they remain under constant guard (617–735). Third, he proves a master of another monster who appears, Typhoeus, and also locks him in Tartarus (820–80). Thus in wisdom and strength he proves a match for any challenge. As in the past, so, it appears, he will remain the same for the future.

Hesiod brings the *Theogony* to a close with a description of the wives and children of Zeus. His first bride is Wisdom (*Mētis*), whom he devours. By so doing, he prevents her from having children who would threaten his power. More importantly, he keeps in his own being the very nature of this wife: acting within she advises him about 'good and evil' (886–900).

Zeus' second wife is Law (*Themis*). She bears for him the Seasons (*Horai*), identified with 'Good Order (*Eunomiē*), Justice (*Dikē*), and Peace (*Eirēnē*)'; these 'attend the works of mortals' (901–3). This second marriage summarises the nature of Zeus' rule. It is one attended by Law, which would seem to involve both the correct ordering of events in the universe and a recognition of the rightful claims of gods and humans.

The children of Law are three. They are called 'Seasons' and then specifically described. Why 'Seasons'?[16] It seems that these 'Seasons' are the ingredients of the life that unfolds in the universe with Zeus. In essence they express ideals, ones that human society at its best will reflect.

First of these is 'Good Order'. This term appears already at *Od.* 17.485–6: 'the gods, resembling strangers from different places, coming with various appearances, visit cities, observing the *hybris* and the good order (*eunomiē*) of human beings.' Here 'good order' is contrasted with *hybris*, as *dikē* is so often in Hesiod. *Eunomiē* probably indicates a respect for order and laws (*nomoi*) rather than the possession of these.[17] The word apparently became common later; in one of his poems Solon will characterize it in some detail (4: see below). It represents the attitude that humans should cultivate as they function in society.

The second 'Season' is 'Justice' (*Dikē*). As we have seen from the *Works and Days*, for Hesiod justice probably involves moral righteousness and a regard for the rights of all. And the third 'Season' is 'Peace'. This clearly indicates the ideal condition in which either divine

---

[16] See West (note 10), *Theog.*, p. 406 on the meaning of *Horai*.
[17] See West (note 10), *Theog.* p. 407 on this meaning.

or human actions can take place. Peace suggests harmony between individuals. It may partly be a consequence of the first two 'Seasons': respect for 'good order' and 'justice' allow for peaceful relationships.

These three 'Seasons attend the works of human beings' (903). The 'works' probably indicate the tilling of land and cultivation of crops among humans.[18] The Seasons, 'Good Order, Justice, and Peace', bring, it seems, prosperity. Being present with Zeus, they show what he values and what he wishes for mortals. The latter have the freedom to honour them or not. If they do honour them, the results will be favourable.

In Hesiod justice plays a central role both on the human and divine levels. In the *Works and Days*, when present in human society, it functions as the element that allows peaceful relations between individuals. On the divine level, it is much honoured by Zeus, who ensures that humans who violate it are punished. If human beings act unjustly, they cause dire consequences not only for themselves but also for innocent people in family and city. 'In the end justice always triumphs' (218): this is the truth human beings must recognise. In the *Theogony* Hesiod focuses on divine justice. The unjust behaviour of the first two rulers of the gods is checked and punished. Zeus is third and permanent ruler; he is married to 'Law' who produces 'Justice' as well as 'Good Order' and 'Peace'. These attend Zeus, where he dwells, and are ideal companions of human beings.

On both human and divine levels, justice involves a recognition of the rights and claims of others. Only when these are recognised and honoured do stability and peace become possible on either level. Hesiod has spoken of legal, political, and moral aspects of justice and accorded it first place in importance among gods and human beings.

Lyric and Elegiac Poets

In the lyric and elegiac poets we encounter further discussions of justice. These poets ponder its nature deeply. By so doing they suggest how important a topic this was in the society in which they lived and for which they wrote. As with the epic poets, we hear

---

[18] So West (note 10), *Theog.*, p. 406.

them speak of justice on the human and divine levels. They too mention legal, political, and moral aspects of it. The latter now have become particularly prominent in their poetry.

Archilochus

In one poem of Archilochus, a fox, having lost her cubs, exclaims to Zeus (177):[19]

> O Zeus, father Zeus, yours is power over the sky;
>   you oversee the works of human beings,
> both their crimes and lawful deeds. To you
>   the *hybris* and *dikē* of beasts are a care.

Here, as in Hesiod, we see Zeus as the watcher of what humans do. In this fable Archilochus extends the gods' watchfulness also to animals, ascribing to them the same capacity for *hybris* and *dikē* as humans have. In his tale of the hawk and the nightingale (*W. & D.* 202–11), Hesiod suggests that a capacity for justice, not present among animals, is what should set human beings apart from them. In his fable, in contrast, Archilochus says that animals are capable of both *hybris* and *dikē*. The fox in the story apparently had her cubs stolen by an eagle. In these lines she cries out for justice, which may have followed. The lesson for humans is clear: Zeus will punish acts of arrogance in which the rights of others are violated.

Solon

An Athenian poet was to ponder much on the nature of justice: Solon.[20] As an Athenian statesman and as archon in 594/3, he had extensive experience in political life. He speaks often about justice on the divine and human levels. He presents legal, political, and moral aspects of it. He considers it of the highest importance. He

---

[19] On this poem see Campbell, *Golden Lyre*, pp. 129–30, Fränkel, *Dichtung*, pp. 164–5, Gagarin (note 1), *CP*, 1974, p. 190, Kirkwood, *Greek Monody*, pp. 45–6, and West, *Studies*, pp. 132–4.

[20] On justice in Solon see A. Andrewes, '*Eunomia*', *CQ*, 1938, vol. 32, pp. 89–102, Anhalt, pp. 67–114, Fränkel, *Dichtung*, pp. 249–73, Gagarin (note 1), *CP*, 1974, pp. 190–2, Jaeger, *Paideia*, pp. 136–49, T.M. Linforth, *Solon the Athenian*, Berkeley, 1919, rep. New York, 1971, A. Masaracchia, *Solone*, Florence, 1958, Pearson, pp. 65–89, Podlecki, *Early Greek Poets*, pp. 117–43, G. Vlastos, 'Solonian Justice', *CP*, 1946, vol. 41, pp. 65–83.

also strives to understand why human beings so often fail to be just. We shall look at two of his poems, 13 (at length) and 4 (briefly).

Poem 13 is an elaborate poem.[21] Its thought sometimes seems difficult to follow: Solon moves into topics that do not immediately appear to be related. But they are. In this poem in particular he explains the presence and absence of justice in human society.

Poem 13 is a prayer to the Muses which Solon begins by expressing his desires. First, he asks for 'prosperity at the hands of the blessed gods' (3), which will allow him to be a boon to his friends and a source of fear to his enemies. With this request for 'prosperity' (*olbos*), Solon introduces the focus of his poem. He will go on to ponder in particular about one form of prosperity, wealth. What kind of wealth is best? How can one maintain it? What brings about its loss? As he answers these questions, we shall see that he is convinced that there is one force at work in human affairs that is inevitable: justice. This is of prime concern to the gods who will, sooner or later, enforce it. Human beings seem to be primarily preoccupied with growing rich. But in their actions they must take into account the workings of justice. Only if they do so will lasting prosperity become possible.

After his request for 'prosperity', Solon proceeds (7–13):

> Money I desire to have but to acquire it unjustly
> I do not wish; in every case justice comes later.
> The wealth which the gods give abides with a person,
> firm from its lowest foundation to its top.
> That which people honour from *hybris* comes in no
> orderly fashion, but trusting in unjust deeds
> it follows unwillingly, and is quickly mixed with delusion.

In these lines Solon points out that there is only one kind of desire for 'wealth' (*chrēmata*: 7) that is acceptable: one attended by justice. This is true because justice (*dikē*) always appears. We heard Hesiod say that 'justice flourishes over *hybris* in the end' (*W. & D.* 218). Solon shares the same conviction. This truth must regulate any desire for wealth that someone expresses. To the person having such a desire the

---

[21] On fr. 13 see A.W. Allen, 'Solon's Prayer to the Muses', *TAPA*, 1949, vol. 80, pp. 50–65, K. Alt, 'Solons Gebet zu den Musen', *Hermes*, 1979, vol. 107, pp. 389–406, Anhalt, pp. 11–65, Campbell, *Golden Lyre*, pp. 221–5, Fränkel, *Dichtung*, pp. 267–73, Lattimore, 'The First Elegy of Solon', *HJP*, 1947, vol. 68, pp. 161–79, G. Maurach, 'Über den Stand der Forschung zu Solons "Musenelegie"', *GGA*, 1983, vol. 235, pp. 16–33, Podlecki, *Early Greek Poets*, pp. 127–30, A. Spira, 'Solons Musenelegie' in *Gnomosyne, Festschrift Marg*, Munich, 1981, pp. 177–96, West, *Studies*, pp. 180–1.

gods, it seems, can give wealth, which abides as a steady possession.

But this type of desire is often absent. People can pursue 'wealth' (*ploutos*: 9) in a different way: from *hybris* (11). As in Hesiod, once again 'arrogance' or 'pride' is seen as the opposite of *dikē*. Individuals acting from *hybris* 'put their trust in unjust (*adikos*) deeds' (12). Wealth does not 'want' to attend such individuals. Reluctantly it 'follows' but is quickly mixed with 'delusion' or 'destruction' (*atē*). As often in Homer and Hesiod, *atē* is both the distorted thinking that leads to disaster and the disaster itself.[22] Acquiring wealth unjustly bears the seeds of the destruction of that very wealth.

Solon then describes what happens when wealth is obtained with *hybris* (14–24). Disaster grows like a fire, slowly at first and then in full blaze. Zeus 'oversees the end of all things' (17) and can strike like a sudden storm. Solon says further (25–32):

> Such is the punishment of Zeus nor over each
>   incident does he, like a mortal, become swiftly angry,
> but it never escapes him at all if someone has
>   a sinful *thumos*; completely in the end his view is clear.
> One person pays at once, another later. Those who escape
>   themselves, on whom the fate of the gods does not come—
> still it inevitably comes. Others not responsible pay for
>   their deeds, either their children or later descendants.

Solon sees misfortune befalling human beings as the working out of justice. As in Hesiod, Zeus, ever-watchful, brings punishment, sometimes right away, sometimes at a later date. Some people, it may seem, do escape but this is not really so. Their children or more distant descendants receive the punishment. Solon does not question whether the imposing of penalties upon the innocent can be just. He assumes that it is. Hesiod too believed that one person's injustice could harm both family and city. If this view is accepted, the call to justice involves assuming responsibility not merely for what might happen to oneself but also to others.

In the next part of the poem (33–42) Solon treats two questions. What keeps people from recognising the working of justice? If cause and effect are so clear, how can people still choose to be unjust? The cause, he says, lies in the hopes that people nurture within.[23]

---

[22] On the meaning of *atē* in Solon see Anhalt, pp. 61–3, H. Roisman, '*Atē* and its Meaning in the Elegies of Solon', *GB*, 1984, vol. 11, pp. 21–7.

[23] On negative aspects of 'hope' see also above chapter 2, Semonides 1 (under *noos*) and Simonides 8 (under *thumos*).

Until we 'suffer', each of us imagines that we are 'flourishing'. Then we grieve at our misfortune but still 'with our mouths gaping open, we take delight in light-weight (*kouphos*) hopes' (36). These hopes clearly are that the disaster that has befallen will soon change. The sick will become healthy, the coward, brave, the plain, beautiful, the poor, wealthy.

With these lines on hope Solon gives a partial answer to the questions he appears to have posed. Why do people not simply see that justice brings reward, injustice, punishment? It is partly because they refuse to understand the nature of the latter, even when it befalls. When they suffer, they may 'lament' (35) but very quickly they begin to hope for relief. What seems lacking is any reflection on the events that befall. The hopes they nurture are accompanied by desire. They exert their energies in overcoming the hardship. The desire they should cultivate, to act justly, is not a predominant one and may be altogether lacking. Solon has suggested that disasters come because of some exercise of injustice either recently or in the past. Human beings should, it seems, realise this and modify their own behaviour.

In his reference in line 42 to the poor hoping to be rich, Solon returns to his theme of wealth. He discusses different ways in which people can acquire it: sea-faring, farming, crafts, poetry, prophecy, and medicine (43–62). Humans may pour great energies into what they do. But there is another force at work in the universe that they need to recognise: that of fate and the gods (63–70):

> The fates bring for mortals either evil or good
>   and the gifts of the immortal gods are inescapable.
> There is danger in all endeavours nor does one know
>   where an undertaking, once begun, will end.
> But the person striving to act well, not foreseeing,
>   falls into great and difficult destruction.
> To another, acting badly, the god gives beyond all measure
>   great success, with deliverance from his foolish thinking.

In these lines Solon describes what happens to human beings, occurrences that make the effects of human endeavour unpredictable. What he mentions also helps to answer the question: why do people not simply choose to be just, if it brings rewards? Solon points out that the 'fates and the gods' bestow on people gifts that are 'inescapable'. And these gifts often seem mysterious. The person striving to act well meets with *atē* (68). The one acting badly, who is foolish, receives success. How can this happen? Surely the fates and the gods seem to act strangely.

In one line of this section Solon succinctly summarises the human condition: 'there is danger in all endeavours' (64). Human beings have to act as they live day by day, but they cannot do so with any sure confidence about the outcome. Our condition is one of 'not knowing' (65) and not 'foreseeing' (67). Yet despite all this, Solon believes that there is an explanation for all the unpredictable events that befall humans.

In ring-composition, linking the end with the beginning of his poem, Solon speaks again of wealth. In wealth and how people regard it, he finds the explanation of the events befalling human beings (71–6):

> Of wealth no end lies revealed for humans,
> since those of us who now have a plentiful livelihood
> hasten to double it. Who could satisfy all?
> Profits the immortal gods give to mortals
> but destruction can appear from them, and when
> Zeus sends it as a penalty, one person
> has it at one time, another at another.

Solon sees human desire for money as the key for understanding what happens to different individuals. His view, seen as a whole, appears to be as follows. (1) People who act with a desire for wealth obtained justly may receive it as a gift from the gods. This gift will last, provided the desire for wealth is kept moderate. Justice appears to involve an awareness of a larger situation in which other people too have rights. (2) Individuals who act from *hybris* and injustice may become rich for a time but inevitably *atē* will befall. These individuals may suffer themselves or their children and descendants will.

(3) On some people, who strive to act well, *atē* befalls. This must be a consequence of the working out of justice over time. Someone on some occasion must have been the ultimate source of this disaster. (4) For others, acting badly, undeserved good fortune comes. This event appears to be mysterious and inexplicable. But, Solon says, this happens by divine choice and we can only assume that the gods are working out a plan that will prove ultimately just.

In poem 13 we can see a similarity to the opening of the *Odyssey*. There human beings are described as sometimes forcing the gods to punish them because of their own evil choices. Their suffering is deserved. Another form of suffering, innocent suffering, can result from the expression of will of others; it has to be endured but, if the person afflicted acts heroically, in the end all will turn out well. In his poem Solon says that human greed forces Zeus to punish human beings. When this punishment comes, those not directly involved may also suffer. Greed thus brings deserved and innocent suffering. But for those guilty and for all others there is a proper hope that can be cultivated (unlike those described in 33–42). If individuals express a wish for wealth attended by justice, all may eventually turn out well.

Now a brief look at poem 4. In it Solon repeats some of his ideas found in poem 13 but he also explicitly relates justice to 'good order', *eunomië*.[24] This may even have been the title of this elegy. He thus suggests important political aspects of justice. He begins this poem by saying that it will not be the 'dispensation of Zeus' and the 'intentions of the gods' that will destroy Athens; Pallas is too strong a guard of the city (1–4). Instead, the citizens by their 'folly (*aphradia*) are willing to destroy the city as they trust in wealth (*chrēmata*). The *noos* of the leaders is unjust (*adikos*), who inevitably will suffer many pains from their great *hybris*' (5–8). What these leaders fail to do is to check 'excess' (*koros*: 9). We see again Solon's view that greed makes suffering inevitable.

He goes on to describe the failure of these nobles (14–17):

> They do not guard the holy fountains of Justice,
> who silently knows the present and the past,
>   and in time always comes to punish; this arrives
> as an inescapable wound for the whole city.

Solon then pictures how the overlooking of justice causes widespread suffering for the whole society (18–29). Slavery, civil strife, war result; citizens are forced into exile and into servitude. 'Evil' enters every home. Justice functions in these lines as the foundation stone of society. Regard for moral right and fairness to others is essential in leaders. If it is absent, the basic structure of society will collapse.

Solon calls the condition where justice is disregarded 'Bad Order' (*dusnomië*). He contrasts it with 'Good Order' (*eunomië*), whose nature he describes as follows (32–9):

> Good Order reveals all things well-ordered and fitting,
>   and often places bonds on the unjust.
> She smooths the rough, stops excess, dims *hybris*,

---

[24] On poem 4 of Solon see Adkins, *Poetic Craft*, pp. 107–25, Anhalt, pp. 67–114, Campbell, *Golden Lyre*, pp. 92–4, Fränkel, *Dichtung*, pp. 253–5, M. Halberstadt, 'On Solon's *Eunomia* (frg. 3D)', *CW*, 1955, vol. 48, pp. 197–203, W.J. Henderson, 'The Nature and Function of Solon's Poetry: Fr. 3 Diehl, 4 West', *AClass*, 1982, vol. 25, pp. 21–33, Podlecki, *Early Greek Poets*, pp. 124–6, E. Siegmann, 'Solons Staatselegie',

withers the flowers of *atē* as they grow,
straightens crooked judgements, and softens
    arrogant deeds. She stops the works of faction
and checks the anger of painful strife. It is due
    to her that all things among humans are fitting and wise.

In Hesiod we encountered *Eunomiē* as one of the 'Seasons' along
with '*Dikē*' and 'Peace' (*Theog.* 902). There it probably referred to
'respect for good order'. By Solon's time the term may have become
common, keeping, however, the same general sense.[25] Solon says that
in the city the power of *eunomiē* is very great. If 'good order' is present,
every cause for discord disappears. She prevents 'unjust' people from
having too much freedom of action. By her very presence *hybris* and
atē prove incapable of flourishing or growing. Judgements (*dikai*) that
are 'crooked' become straight.

In these two poems we see Solon's view of justice. On the divine
level, it is greatly revered by the gods. Their actions prevail and they
are just. The operations of justice are inevitable. In human society,
it is of primary importance. Human beings must honour it or they
will suffer. So will other innocent people. If individuals respect justice, they will curb their desires and be able to receive and to retain
prosperity as a divine gift. Justice lies at the root of 'good order', the
best condition for any city.

Solon thus presents us with justice on the divine and human levels. He shows us legal, political, and moral aspects of it. In poem 36
where he defends his actions while in office Solon speaks of 'fitting
together justice (*dikē*) and might (*biē*: 16)', and also 'fitting straight
justice' for every person (19). To act with justice was his strongest
motive; to have acted thus, he considered his greatest achievement.

Other Poets and Theognis

In this section we shall look briefly at what Xenophanes, Simonides,
and Bacchylides say of justice. Our focus, however, will be upon
Theognis. In his poetry we find political and, in particular, moral

---

Perspektiven der Philosophie, 1975, vol. 1, pp. 267–81, M. Stahl, 'Solon F. 3D', *Gymnasium*, 1992, vol. 99, pp. 385–408.
[25] On *eunomia* see Anhalt, pp. 100–14, Podlecki, *Greek Poets*, pp. 124–7 and West
(note 10), *Theog.* p. 407. An earlier poet, Tyrtaeus, may have related justice and
eunomia. Aristotle also mentions that one of Tyrtaeus' poems had the title '*Eunomia*':
this may refer to frs 2 and 4. In fr. 4, he says that the people 'ought to speak what

aspects of justice. On the divine level, it is revered by the gods. On the human level, it should likewise be pursued and honoured by human beings.

In chapter 4 we treated Xenophanes' poem 2 in which he claims that wisdom (*sophia*) is the highest form of *aretē*. In this poem he also makes two references to the idea of justice. At 13 he says that 'it is not just (*dikaios*) to prefer strength to our wisdom'. In analysing the claims of physical prowess and wisdom, Xenophanes feels those of the second are greater. At 19 he gives the criterion for this judgement: if athletes win contests 'not for that reason would the city be in the state of good order' (*eunomiē*). Xenophanes thus sees wisdom as contributing to 'good order'. With its insights into truth, it can help society know what is right and formulate laws that are fair. The social value of wisdom is higher than athletic prowess and therefore it deserves greater honour.

Like Hesiod and Solon, Xenophanes relates justice and 'good order'. Both are seen as positive forces in society and so important that judgements about excellence should be made in light of them.

Simonides too, as we heard in chapter 4, in the Scopas poem (542), introduces into his notion of an 'acceptable *aretē*' one essential ingredient: an awareness of justice. Simonides approves that person who is 'not too helpless, knowing justice that benefits the city, someone sound' (34-6). He makes social consciousness involving an awareness of the rights and claims of others a requirement for admirable behaviour. In this poem Simonides also speaks of the 'generation of fools being endless' (37): many there are who probably have no knowledge of justice that helps the whole community. An essential element of the 'good' (*kala*), therefore, which Simonides is describing, is justice.

In chapter 4 we encountered two other poets who related *aretē* to justice: Theognis and Bacchylides. We have just one brief passage where Bacchylides does this (14.8-11), which we discussed already in chapter 4. But in the long poem ascribed to Theognis, however much or little may be his own, much is said about justice.[26] Above in chapter

---

is honourable and to do all things just (*dikaia*) nor to plan anything crooked (*skolion*) for the city' (7-8). Once again we see how important these two ideas were. On these poems of Tyrtaeus see Adkins, *Poetic Craft*, pp. 68-75, Campbell, *Golden Lyre*, pp. 87-8, and Podlecki, *Early Greek Poets*, pp. 100-5.

[26] On justice in Theognis see Adkins, *Poetic Craft*, pp. 153-60, G. Cerri, 'La terminologia sociopolitica di Teognide: 1. L'opposizione semantica tra *agathos-esthlos*

4 on *aretē* we encountered Theognis placing great importance upon an inherent capacity for goodness. He is convinced that in some individuals inherited nature either makes the attainment of *aretē* possible or not. In light of this conviction, Theognis challenged several common standards, especially wealth, by which *aretē* was judged to be present. This same conviction affects as well what he has to say about justice.

First, at lines 145–8, as we heard also in chapter 4, he says:

> Choose to dwell as a holy person with few possessions
>   rather than to be rich, having acquired wealth unjustly.
> To put it briefly, all *aretē* is summed up in justice,
>   and every good man, Kyrnus, is one who is just.

We encounter here a reference to *dikaiosynē* 'justice', a term for justice very common later in Plato.[27] Like Solon, Theognis says that wealth with injustice is not to be desired. Excellence consists of justice. The good person will recognise the claims of others, will have a sense of moral right, and will act accordingly. Wealth is not to be taken as a sign of the presence of *aretē*. If someone acts unjustly to attain it, that one shows a lack of inner *aretē*. Justice is an essential ingredient of goodness.[28]

But who is capable of justice? At 53–60 Theognis expresses scepticism to Cyrnus over a capacity for it in all people:

> This city, though still a city, has different people.
>   Those who before knew neither judgement nor laws,
> who wore out skins of goats about their ribs,
>   and who lived outside this city like deer,
> even now they are the good men, Cyrnus. Those formerly
>   noble are now worthless. Who could endure this sight?
> Laughing at one another, they deceive each other,
>   knowing judgements of neither what is good nor bad.

---

e *kakos-deilos*', *QUCC*, 1968, vol. 6, pp. 7–32, A.I. Dovatur, 'Theognis von Megara und sein soziales Ideal', *Klio*, 1972, vol. 54, pp. 77–89, Fränkel, *Dichtung*, pp. 455–83, Figueira and Nagy, H. Patzer, 'Der archaische *Aretē*-Kanon im Corpus Theognideum' in *Gnomosyne Festschrift Marg*, Munich, 1981, pp. 197–226, Pearson, pp. 65–89.

[27] See above chapter 4, note 24 on the authenticity of these lines. The presence of this term for justice has made them open to question. We here treat them as authentic.

[28] Cf. also 255 where Theognis says that 'the fairest thing (*kalliston*) is the most just (*dikaiotaton*)', 465 where he urges: 'busy yourself with *aretē* and let just things (*ta dikaia*) be dear to you; let not gain that is shameful overcome you', and 548 where he says: 'for the just person there is nothing better than doing good'.

In these lines, we hear Theognis lamenting the social changes that have allowed a group, before quite uncivilized and unaware of 'judgements (*dikai*) and laws (*nomoi*)', to become identified with the 'good' (*agathoi*). The description of these individuals is reminiscent of that of the Cyclopes in the *Odyssey*. As with the Cyclopes, these newly powerful people appear to have no notion of justice. After they come to the city, their behaviour does not alter. The experience of living in the city does not teach them 'judgements' (*gnōmai*) of good and evil. Instead, they continue to mock and deceive one another. But those apparently who do know 'judgements and laws', the formerly 'good', are now deemed 'worthless' (*deiloi*).

Theognis speaks disparagingly of these people now honoured as 'good', probably because of their wealth and political power. He warns Cyrnus (61–8) to have few dealings with any of them since they cannot be trusted and their minds (*phrenes*) have 'wiles and deceits'. It is his conviction also (as we saw above in chapter 4) that such people lack any innate capacity for goodness or justice.

'It is likely', as he says in lines 279–282, that the evil person (*kakos*) thinks badly of just things (*ta dikaia*) and takes no thought for punishment (*nemesis*) to come'. Such a person acts in present circumstances, believing that 'all is fair'. But it is not so. The city can only suffer at the hands of such new 'good' persons.

In lines 197–208 Theognis expresses his views about the relationships between justice and wealth:

> Wealth that comes from Zeus both with justice and in
>   a pure way becomes for a person ever firm. But if,
> unjustly, contrary to what is appropriate, someone
>   acquires it with greedy *thumos* or takes it on oath,
> contrary to justice, at first it seems to bring some profit,
>   but in the end it again becomes evil. The mind
> of the gods prevails. But this deceives the mind
>   of humans. Not instantly do the blessed ones punish
> offenses. But one person himself pays his evil debt
>   nor over his dear children does he leave destruction
> hanging afterwards. Justice does not catch another, for
>   shameless death, bringing fate, sits upon his eyes.

In these lines we hear echoes of what Solon also says. Wealth that is 'given by Zeus' and acquired 'with justice' remains a 'firm possession'. The person who becomes rich with a 'greedy *thumos*' (200), acting 'unjustly' receives what seems to be an immediate blessing but it becomes an 'evil' (203).

The types of injustice that Theognis mentions are two: first, acting 'contrary to what is appropriate' and second, acting 'on oath, contrary to justice'. Describing the first, he uses the term *kairos*, which often means the 'appropriate moment' or the 'appropriate opportunity'. In each life instances of *kairos* appear and usually point to the actions individuals should take. The 'inappropriate' then involves what will not prove best for the person nor, in the context of justice, for others. Theognis' second instance of injustice involves giving an oath contrary to it. We can assume that this action involves falsehood and infringement in some way on the rights of others.

Theognis contrasts two 'minds' in these lines. The '*noos* of the gods prevails' (203). This statement tells us that the gods disapprove of injustice and that they have definite plans for those who commit it. Nor does their purpose fail. The *noos* of humans, however, is commonly deceived by what they see occurring. The gods do not punish wrong-doing at once but they wait. In some cases the individual may pay right away, saving his children from suffering later. But others appear to receive no punishment and die 'without shame'. Still, for them, the 'debt' (*chreos*: 205) incurred by the evil deed must be paid: 'destruction' (*atē*) awaits his descendants.

Like Solon, Theognis believes that justice will be done. The timing may not be what humans expect but the gods will act. The dangers of injustice are two-fold. One may have to pay for it right away or one fashions 'destruction' for future members of the family. The alternative is clearly to be chosen: to act 'with justice and in a pure way' (200). For the one who does, riches may come from Zeus and will abide.

In another set of lines in Theognis we find further reflection on why the wicked are ever allowed to have 'carefree wealth' (373–98). In these lines he looks more deeply into the nature of people who are rich and poor and suggests that this inner nature may be what is truly important. In a wonderfully familiar tone Theognis begins by addressing Zeus (373–80):

> I'm surprised at you, dear Zeus! For you rule all,
>   having yourself honour and great power,
> and you know well the *noos* and *thumos* of each human,
>   and your power is highest over all, O king.
> How, then, son of Cronus, can your *noos* endure to hold
>   the wicked and the just in the same fate,
> whether someone's *noos* is turned to moderation, or to
>   *hybris*, with trust placed in unjust deeds?

As humans survey other humans, it appears that the evil and good do not receive different treatment from the gods. Those choosing 'moderation' (*sophrosynē*) and *hybris* share alike what can happen to mortals.

Theognis proceeds to say that 'no one road' seems to have been laid out for mortals on which, walking, they can assuredly 'please the divine' (381–2). And the situation seems even more unfair. The wicked receive 'prosperity without pain' (383); those 'loving justice' (*ta dikaia*) and 'keeping their *thumos* from worthless deeds' (385) receive 'poverty'. The just do not get preferential treatment from Zeus; they are treated worse! The poverty they receive 'leads *thumos* astray into wrong-doing, harming the *phrenes* in the breast by strong necessity' (386–7). Theognis goes on to describe in detail what poverty can do to someone (388–91). It makes him endure 'much shame'. He can yield to 'want', he can learn 'lies', 'destructive deceits', 'quarrels', even though unwilling to do so. Poverty 'breeds grievous helplessness' (*amēchaniē*: 392). If poverty does this, why can it be that it befalls the good individual?

In the next lines Theognis provides an answer (393–8):

> In poverty the base man and the one much better
>   appear, when want is holding each fast.
> For in the one *noos* thinks just thoughts and in him ever does
>   straight judgement grow in the chest. In the other
> *noos* is present neither in good nor bad events but the good
>   person must endure boldly diverse circumstances.

Poverty clarifies the inner nature of individuals. The 'good person' will remain unchanged. He will still think 'just thoughts' and his 'practical judgement' (*gnōmē*) will be 'straight' (395–6). As in lines 197–208 and line 379, it is *noos* in the individual that forms opinions about justice and decisions to act. In the good individual this remains constant and even though it may appear that 'no road by which mortals can please the gods' has been laid out (381–2), one in fact has: the road of justice. Poverty can have terrible effects upon people (386–91) but cannot damage the good individual.

For evil persons, all is different. In them, no matter if circumstances are 'good or bad', '*noos* does not follow' (397). What the evil always lack is a mind that will prove an asset. The good, in contrast, show themselves to be flexible: they can bear diverse circumstances (398). The horrors that poverty bring will clarify the inner nature of people. Those who prove vulnerable to them will show that they are not just or good; those who bear them with attitudes unchanged will reveal that they are good.

Theognis began these lines (373–98) expressing astonishment at Zeus for apparently treating the good and bad alike. He proceeded to suggest that the situation with humans might be worse yet: the evil seem to prosper, the good, to suffer. But on reflection he sees that for good people external circumstances are to some extent irrelevant: these individuals themselves remain good. For evil persons circumstances cannot be irrelevant since they become totally victimized if poverty comes and even in good circumstances they lack understanding.[29] The distribution of wealth or poverty may remain a mystery for mortals but Theognis has come to see that his opening question was itself inappropriate: in no way are the good and evil ever 'in the same fate' (378). Even though poverty, an obvious evil, may befall the good, it cannot harm their intrinsic goodness. On an inner level they remain constant.

In another set of lines we find Theognis analyzing an aspect of the dispensation of justice that he accepted in lines 197–208 and that Solon also accepts: individual acts of injustice are paid for not only by oneself but also by one's descendants. Can payment by descendants be just? In lines 731–52 he says:

> Father Zeus, would that it might be dear to the gods
> that *hybris* please evil-doers, and this might be dear
> to their *thumos*, namely crooked deeds; whoever with *phrenes*
> does harsh deeds, with no regard for the gods, should
> then in turn himself pay for the evils, nor still after
> should the crimes of the father be evil for his children.
> Would that these children of an unjust father who think and
> do just deeds, son of Cronus, honouring your anger,
> loving from the beginning just deeds among the citizens,
> not pay for any crime of their father's.
> Would that these things were dear to the gods. But now
> the one acting escapes, another later bears the suffering.
> And how, O king of the gods, is this just,
> that the man being outside unjust deeds,
> having no crime nor sinful oath,
> but being just, should not experience justice?

---

[29] Cf. 279 (also referred to above) where Theognis says that 'it is likely that the evil man thinks badly of justice, showing no respect for punishment (*nemesis*)'. This person's focus lies only on the present and he imagines he is doing well (281–2).

Which other mortal, having what *thumos*, would
    look at this person and then honour the immortals,
when an unjust and evil man, avoiding the
    anger of neither man nor gods, acts with
insolence, satiated with wealth, but the just
    are worn away, wasted with grievous poverty?

Theognis says that if *hybris* pleases people and they want to act badly,
they have the freedom to do so but they should pay for their own
deeds. It should not be their children who pay, especially if those
children have acted justly.[30] As so often in Hesiod and Solon, *hybris*
is seen as the opposite of justice.[31] But those acting with *hybris* do not
pay: the innocent do. Theognis asks: if this kind of thing occurs,
who will bother to honour the gods?

In lines 197–208 Theognis had assumed that the descendants of
evil-doers would pay for crimes if those committing them did not. In
lines 373–406, he argued that poverty, however great an evil, could
not, at least, harm someone's intrinsic goodness. But here, in lines
731–52, he challenges the justice of the gods' behaviour: somehow
the innocent should not suffer. By letting them suffer, the gods en-
danger their own position because mortals may not take them seriously. But, as all humans know, the innocent do suffer. Theognis'
lines sow seeds of doubt that the usual explanation for it, namely
that the gods are punishing earlier crimes, may be adequate. How
then will this manifestation of injustice in the universe be explained?
Theognis himself gives no solution but the problem will be one that
later Greeks, especially Aeschylus and Plato, will treat.

Pindar

Pindar in his odes makes several references to justice. Like Solon
and Theognis, he mentions political aspects of it but focuses especially on its moral aspects. For him too justice is honoured by the
gods. Human beings, if they are to achieve and maintain *aretē*, will
need to hold justice in high regard. Pindar also suggests (*Ol.* 2) that

---

[30] It is understandable that in lines 131–2 Theognis says that 'there is nothing
better than the mother and father to whom holy justice is a care'. Their children
will not have to suffer.

[31] Cf. lines 291–2 where Theognis describes shamelessness (*anaideiē*) and *hybris* as
conquering *dikē*.

justice is the moral value that allows the soul eventually to escape the cycle of rebirth.

In some passages of Pindar we hear a clear echo of views expressed by earlier poets. This is especially true of some lines in *Ol.* 13 where Hesiod's *Theogony* 902 (treated above) is recalled. Pindar, speaking of Corinth, says (6–8):

> In her, a firm foundation of cities, *eunomiē*
> dwells and her sisters too,
> *Dikē* and *Eirenē*, nurtured with her,
> guardians of wealth for people,
> golden children of *Themis* of good counsel.

As in the *Theogony Eunomiē*, *Dikē*, and *Eirenē* are sisters, daughters of *Themis*. Hesiod says that their father was Zeus but Pindar does not mention this. These three sisters function in Corinth as 'guardians' or 'stewards of wealth for people'. We see here a connection between justice and wealth, one Pindar will mention also elsewhere. In this passage Pindar calls *Dikē*, 'daughter of *Themis*': it is born of law. When it is present, so ideally is 'good order' and 'peace'. These three allow a city to flourish. In another ode Pindar says that a daughter of *Dikē* herself, *Hesychia*, 'peace', 'makes cities great and holds the keys of councils and wars' (*Pyth.* 8, 1–4).[32] In *Ol.* 13, we can see, Pindar gives justice the role of bringing a society into the best condition.

Pindar relates justice to wealth in *Pyth.* 5.13 when he says of Arcesilas: 'you, walking in justice, much prosperity (*olbos*) surrounds'. Like Solon, Pindar suggests that prosperity can safely attend the just individual. Like Solon too, he believes that wealth without justice cannot last. At *Pyth.* 4.140 he says: 'the *phrenes* of mortals are quicker to praise crooked gain (*kerdos*) at the expense of justice (*dikē*), even though they come none the less to a bitter reckoning'. So too at *Is.* 7.48 he points out: 'that which is sweet, contrary to justice, a most bitter end awaits'. Justice must attend success or the latter turns to grief.

The justice Pindar refers to seems to involve a recognition of the rights or claims of others. At *Nem.* 4.12 he praises Aegina as a 'bulwark of justice for the stranger'.[33] He describes Neoptolemus at *Nem.* 7.48 as 'presiding over the procession of heroes for justice of fair

---

[32] On *hesychia* in this ode see especially M.W. Dickie, '*Hesychia* and *Hybris* in Pindar' in Gerber, pp. 83–109.

[33] He likewise praises the rulers of Aegina as 'never transgressing the right (*themis*) and justice (*dikē*) of strangers' at *Is.* 9.5.

name'. Neoptolemus apparently was to ensure the rights of all guests at the festivals. At *Pyth.* 9.96 Pindar says that Nereus advised that, no matter if someone is friend or enemy, his good deeds should be praised 'with all *thumos* and with justice (*dikē*)'. Excellence has its due and it is only just that this be rendered.

As we saw in chapter 4, the focus of Pindar's poetry is upon excellence as manifested in athletics. As he says in *Nem.* 8, 40–2: '*aretē* increases, as when a tree shoots up in refreshing dew, so it is carried to the aether among wise and just men'. The poet must be wise and fair in the praise he gives. As Pindar says also in *Nem.* 8.39, his prayer is to 'praise what deserves praise and to cast blame on those committing wrong'. The type of *aretē* that will last is one undertaken with justice: 'from labours which take place with youth and with justice comes a gentle life in old age' (*Nem.* 9.44). For this reason Pindar has high praise for individuals who act justly: '[Argos] united the fruit of *phrenes* with straight justice in the father of Adrastos and in Lyceus' (*Nem.* 10.12).[34]

But not all human achievement is necessarily just. In fr. 213 Pindar says: 'whether the race of men on earth raises a loftier wall by justice or by crooked deceits, my *noos* is divided in saying the exact truth'. At *Nem* 5.14 Pindar checks himself from speaking of some activities of the sons of Aeacus: 'I am ashamed to speak of a deed not dared in justice'. He also says that, when a more powerful person appears, 'he can destroy the justice present before' (*Nem.* 9.15). Justice appears to be the desired attitude with which one should act and the foundation for deeds that can last. But it does not prove to be always invulnerable.

In one ode Pindar assigns justice a vital role in human destiny. This is *Ol.* 2 which we shall discuss in some detail. As mentioned in chapter 3 on *psychē*, in this ode Pindar describes the soul as enduring through more than one earthly existence. He begins this ode for Theron of Acragas with high praise for his victory with the chariot. In athletic victories the win in a chariot race was the highest. Pindar says of Theron that he is 'just in his regard for strangers and bulwark of Acragas' (6). He then says that long suffering can be forgotten if prosperity follows: 'of deeds done in justice and contrary to

---

[34] Cf. also Amphiareus who deserves acclaim and whom Adrastus 'praises in justice' (*Ol.* 6.12). See too the praise of Hieron (*Pyth.* 1.86) and Battus (*Pyth.* 4.230) for being just.

justice not even time, the father of all, can undo the accomplished
end; forgetfulness can occur with fate that is favourable' (16–18). Deeds
done unjustly cannot be undone and neither can those done justly.
The first are clearly not desirable but in some cases a 'favourable
fate' can still follow.

In the myth he then presents in *Ol*. 2, Pindar speaks of the daughters of Cadmus who exemplify this truth. He says of humans: 'for
mortals the end in death has not in any way been clearly marked
out, nor when we shall complete a peaceful day, child of the sun,
with unimpaired blessing' (31–3). Fate changes, bringing good fortune or ill (35–8). 'Wealth adorned with *aretai* can be the truest light
for someone' (53), but people need to be aware of other truths about
human life.

At this point in the ode Pindar begins a description of the after-
life. He makes justice very important in this context (56–80):

> if one having [wealth] knows the future,
> that immediately here the helpless *phrenes* of the dead
> pay penalties—the sins committed in this realm
> of Zeus someone judges beneath the earth,
> speaking a judgement with hateful necessity.
> But with equal nights always,
> and having the sun equal in their days, the good
> receive a life without toil, not harassing
>   the earth with strength of hand
> nor the water of the sea
> for an empty livelihood. But by the honoured gods
> those who took delight in honouring oaths lead
>   a life without tears.
> The rest endure labour that none can look upon.
> However many endured three times,
> remaining on the other side, to keep their soul
> from unjust deeds have travelled the road
> of Zeus to the tower
>   of Cronus. There the ocean breezes
> blow around the
> island of the blessed. The flowers of gold blaze,
> some on the shore from glorious trees, others
>   nourished by water.
> With garlands of these they bind their hands and
> they fashion crowns according to the right decrees of
> Rhadamanthys, whom the great father has ready seated
> next to him, the husband of Rhea, who has
>   the highest throne.

Among these are numbered Peleus and Cadmus.
His mother carried Achilles there when she
persuaded the heart of Zeus with prayers.

These beautiful lines, frequently discussed, are somewhat obscure but
they appear to describe three fates that can await someone after
death.[35] First, if a person has committed 'sins' (59), someone judges
these sins beneath the earth and 'helpless *phrenes* pay penalties' for
them (57) here on earth. The image seems to be of souls judged
after death, found to have done wrong, and consequently facing rebirth
and a new human existence by 'hateful necessity' (60). We may relate the fate of these souls to what Pindar says earlier in the poem
that 'time cannot undo the accomplished end of deeds done justly or
unjustly' (16–18). For the latter, apparently, souls must pay. In some
cases the wrongs committed may have been especially terrible. For
people guilty of these, Pindar seems to assign a special punishment,
not on earth by rebirth, or at least not right away, but in the underworld: 'they endure labour that none can look upon' (68).

In this first group of souls, then, there appears to be those who
are punished by being sent back into life right away and those who
stay in the underworld suffering greatly. Pindar introduces this passage by saying that those with wealth should realise what the future
might hold for the soul. How humans use or abuse wealth may be
the source of their virtue or lack thereof.

Pindar suggests that there is a second group of souls who share a
different destiny after death.[36] These live in an area of 'equal nights
and days', an area of equinox. They carry on a life similar to one
on earth but of an idyllic nature (63–9). They need not farm or sail
the seas. They dwell with the gods. Their life is 'without tears'. They
are called 'good' (*esloi*) and are praised as ones 'who took delight in
honouring oaths'. In this description we hear an echo of the life of
the humans in the Golden Age of Hesiod (*W. & D.* 109–20) when

---

[35] On these lines of *Ol.* 2 see especially J. Bollack, 'L'or des rois: le mythe de la
Deuxième Olympique', *RPh*, 1963, vol. 37, pp. 234–54, J. van Leeuwen, *Pindarus' Tweede
Olympische Ode*, Assen, 1964, 2 vols, H. Lloyd-Jones, 'Pindar and the After-Life' in
Pindare Entretiens sur l'antiquité classique, 31, Genève: Fondations Hardt, 1985, pp. 245–
83 (=*Greek Epic*, pp. 80–109 with 'Addendum'), H.S. Long, pp. 29–44, F. Solmsen,
'Two Pindaric Passages on the Hereafter', *Hermes*, 1968, vol. 96, pp. 503–6,
L. Woodbury, 'Equinox at Acragas: Pindar, *Ol.* 2.61–2', *TAPA*, 1966, vol. 97, pp.
597–616.
[36] On this group see especially Woodbury (note 35). See also the reference to the
land of the equinox in Homer: *Od.* 10.80–6.

no one was 'touched by work or sorrow'. But even though 'good' souls may achieve this desirable destiny, it does not appear to be a permanent one. These souls too, it seems, must return to earth after absorbing the lesson of the place of equinox in which they have spent some time. This place of equinox teaches the essential nature of right: due shares allotted in equal measure. Once the nature of 'balance' has been impressed upon souls, they can carry this feature into their human existence.

The third group that Pindar describes achieves the fairest destiny and what appears to be the final one (69–80). What these individuals have managed to do is to 'keep their souls from unjust deeds' during three existences as human beings. Here Pindar explicitly mentions the crucial value of justice. Only when the soul has acted fairly, consistently so during three lives, can it hope to escape rebirth in human form. If it does escape, it can travel to the 'tower of Cronus', to the 'island of the blessed' (70). This place is filled with the golden light that Pindar so often associates with divinity.[37] Here souls perform idyllic deeds, abiding by the 'right decrees' (*orthai boulai*) of Rhadamanthys, ever the just judge in the underworld. Zeus is present with Rhea and three heroes are also present: Peleus, father of Achilles, Cadmus, ancestor of Theron, and Achilles himself.

Just behaviour is what allows eventual escape from transmigration. Those who do not know it either face terrible punishment in the underworld (68) or pay for their sins here on earth (57). In an oblique way Pindar may be offering an explanation of what humans commonly see as innocent suffering. People receive the fate they have merited. Their soul is paying now itself for what it did in a former life. Even though there may not be evidence of wrong-doing in the current existence, it must have been present in a former one. Thus it is not that the innocent pay for the crimes of their ancestors but they suffer the consequences of their own earlier actions. Such payment is clearly just and removes the seeming injustice of innocent suffering. We saw Theognis questioning whether the gods could be just in punishing the 'innocent' (731–52). Pindar suggests that the 'innocent' are not really so.

Those who could be described as 'good' during their earthly life may face a better destiny. For a time, after death, they will dwell in

---

[37] See on this topic in particular Fränkel, *Dichtung*, pp. 555–7.

'the land of equal nights and days', absorbing the essence of this place itself. These souls have the gods as companions and a life of ease. They are rewarded for 'honouring oaths' and made ready, it seems, to live with justice in their next human existence.

Those who have managed to live three times in a just fashion are rewarded with a wonderful existence. They dwell amid 'flowers of gold blazing forth', with Zeus and Rhea for companions (73, 77). On the isle of the blessed they meet great heroes: Peleus, Cadmus, Achilles. According to Pindar's description these heroes, in the stories so often sung of them, were in fact completing their 'third' existence, 'keeping their souls from unjust deeds'. Achilles, we know from the *Iliad*, learned to give Hector his due, his right to burial, after his heart softened with compassion. Pindar, earlier in *Ol.* 2, mentions that Achilles killed 'Hector, Cycnus and Ethiop' (81–2). His mother's prayers proved effectual in winning him entrance to the 'tower of Cronus' (80).

In *Ol.* 2 Pindar appears to be offering Theron the hope that he too belongs to the group of souls who will escape rebirth. At line 6 he says that Theron is 'just in his regard for strangers'. It is true, Pindar points out, humans do not know, since we are mortals, when 'we shall complete a peaceful day, child of the sun, with unimpaired blessing' (31–3). But this description of death seems to apply best to those who will no longer need to dwell in human form. This 'day' may not come soon for some souls but lines 56–86 have shown that perhaps for every soul it will eventually arrive. There may be many existences before it comes but finally death will prove a blessed event. Before then fate may change greatly (35–8) but what happens to humans is strongly related to what they did in a former life. Ultimately even negative fortune is understandable. Former mistakes or sins are being paid for. Even though time cannot undo unjust deeds (16–18), when a more favourable fate arrives, 'forgetfulness can occur'.

Theron in his present existence is very rich and wealth can be someone's 'truest light' (53). Pindar shows, however, that justice is the key to eventual bliss. Theron has been blessed by fate: he is king; he is wealthy; he is victor in the chariot race. But, most important, he is 'just' (16). As the ode comes to an end Pindar says of him: 'for one hundred years no city has given birth to a man more generous in heart to his friends nor ungrudging in hand' (94–6). 'Envy, not joined to justice' may attack those who do good (95). In Theron's case 'no one can number the joys he has given others' (95–100).

Theron, therefore, has used the favourable situation in which fate has placed him to act with generosity, kindness, and justice. Surely the tower of Cronus awaits this king.[38]

Pindar in his odes, therefore, considers justice very valuable in the city. He relates it, like Hesiod and Solon, to 'good order' (*eunomiē*). For humans striving to excel, justice must be practised. Wealth is to be generously shared; just actions, with recognition of the claims of others, are to be chosen. For people longing to escape the fate of transmigration, justice is crucial. Three times they must 'keep their souls from unjust deeds' during life on earth. Then they will escape rebirth. 'Justice of fair name' (*Nem.* 7.48), therefore, Pindar thinks to be of great importance.

The Presocratics

In the poets treated thus far we have seen justice become more and more prominent as a factor in human behaviour. Justice became the key for ensuring 'good order' in the city and, in private life, for acquiring and sustaining prosperity and excellence. In Hesiod's *Theogony* we saw how important justice was on the divine level. Its absence caused the downfall of the first two rulers of the gods. Zeus finally had the wisdom to marry 'Law' (*Themis*); he then produces a daughter, 'Justice' (*Dikē*). His reverence for justice would prove to be one reason that he could continue as ruler of the universe.

Certain Presocratics place great emphasis upon justice. They see in it the force that ensures that the universe stays in existence. As they examine the mystery of 'all things' (the universe) they seem to have posed one question again and again: why do 'all things' continue to exist? Some too seem to have asked: why does an ordered, predictable pattern of change take place among them? Something makes this happen. Although their theories about the nature of 'all things' may vary, we see in three Presocratics in particular—Anaximander, Heraclitus, and Parmenides—the conviction that at the core of the universe there is justice at work. Only if this is so can the assumption that the universe will abide be confidently stated. With the Presocratics, we shall be focusing on justice mainly in its cosmic aspect but we shall encounter it also in human society.

---

[38] Cf. fr. 159 where Pindar says that 'time is the best saviour of just men'.

Anaximander

First, let us look at Anaximander, of whom we have one fragment written in prose (about 600 B.C.).[39] From other sources we learn that he thought that the source of the universe was a divine principle which he called the *Apeiron*, the 'Infinite' or the 'Boundless'. The term '*apeiron*' signifies that which is '*apeiras*', 'without limit' or 'without bounds'. This *Apeiron* apparently lacked all the 'bounds' or 'limits' that other things were subject to. It was, it seems, unlimited in time and space; it was unlimited in quality in that it displayed no qualities (A 9, 11, 15). Anaximander describes it as a 'divine thing' (*theion*), as 'surrounding' the universe, and as 'guiding' it (A 15). Within this *Apeiron* 'all things' were formed, beginning from a set of basic opposites, 'hot' and 'cold' (A 9, 10). First a 'seed' (*gonimon*) of these two was broken off from the *Apeiron*. This began to spin, to grow, and gradually, still within the *Apeiron*, the universe that we know came to be (A 10).

Anaximander appears to have seen this universe, being 'all things', as essentially composed of a number of opposites. Each opposite expressed and could only express its own nature, which was a limited one. 'Hot', for example, is always hot and consistently and only expresses 'hotness'. But why does Anaximander speak of 'hot', instead, perhaps, of 'fire'? In his thought, as in that of other Presocratics, we see what we call 'qualities' being treated instead as 'things'.[40] 'Hot' has a separate existence as does 'cold'. Anaximander, therefore, would say that 'hot' is in fire, in the sun, in living creatures, in all manifestations of warmness. 'Cold' likewise is in water, in the earth, in

---

[39] On the philosophy of Anaximander see the Appendix and Barnes, vol. 1, pp. 19–37, C.J. Classen, 'Anaximander and Anaximenes: The Earliest Greek Theories of Change', *Phronesis*, 1977, vol. 22, pp. 89–102, Conche, *Anaximandre*, Dumont, pp. 24–40, J. Engmann, 'Cosmic Justice in Anaximander', *Phronesis*, 1991, vol. 36, pp. 1–25, A. Finkelberg, 'Anaximander's Conception of the *Apeiron*', *Phronesis*, 1993, vol. 3, pp. 229–56, G. Freudenthal, 'The Theory of the Opposites and an Ordered Universe. Physics and Metaphysics in Anaximander', *Phronesis*, 1986, vol. 31, pp. 197–228, H.B. Gottschalk, 'Anaximander's *Apeiron*', *Phronesis*, 1965, vol. 10, pp. 37–53, W.K.C. Guthrie, vol. 1, pp. 72–114, U. Hölscher, 'Anaximander and the Beginnings of Greek Philosophy', *Hermes*, 1953, vol. 81, pp. 255–77, Hussey, pp. 11–31, Kahn, *Anaximander*, 'Anaximander's Fragment: The Universe Governed by Law' in A.P.D. Mourelatos (ed.), *The Presocratics*, pp. 99–117, Kirk, Raven, and Schofield, pp. 100–42, McKirahan, pp. 32–47, Mansfeld, pp. 56–81, Robinson, pp. 195–236, Vlastos, *CP*, 1947, Wright, *Presocratics*, pp. xi–xv. Particularly helpful are Conche, Guthrie, and Kahn.

[40] See on this point W.K.C. Guthrie, vol. 1, pp. 78–9.

every instance of coldness. So too with all other opposites which may exist in different measure in the same or separate objects. Each opposite, therefore, manifests itself and is limited to itself. 'All things', the universe, is a composite expression of these opposites.

The *Apeiron*, acting as a source for all the opposites, is itself unlimited in nature. It is unlimited because it is not composed of only one opposite or only a few opposites. Instead, it is source of all the opposites manifested in our universe. These opposites are limited both in number and quantity of each. The *Apeiron* acts as their origin, being sufficient for their number and all their quantity. The *Apeiron*, as *apeiron*, like the opposites, manifests its own nature and only its own nature. It lacks all limitation. As source of all that is and of all that could ever be, its existence and nature, if accepted, both explain where the universe in which we dwell came from and guarantee its continued existence.

Having postulated, probably primarily on the observation of phenomena, that 'all things' were made up of opposites, Anaximander seems also to have noted difficulties. If there are, for example, two opposites, and each of these can express only its own nature and consistently does so, how do the two, opposed to each other, stay in existence? Are they in perfect balance? Anaximander observed that they clearly were not. Instead, each one, expressing itself, appeared also to threaten and to challenge the expression of the other. But somehow the two did remain in existence. How?

Concerning this problem, Anaximander offered an explanation in the one fragment we have of his work (B 1). These words occur in a sentence found in Simplicius, a sixth century A.D. commentator on Aristotle (B 1): 'into those things from which existing things have their coming into being, their passing away also takes place "according to what must be (*to chreōn*). For they pay penalty (*dikē*) and reparation (*tisis*) to one another for their injustice (*adikia*) according to the assessment of time (*taxis chronou*)", as he describes it in these rather poetical terms'.[41]

What does Anaximander say in this fragment? First he states that 'existing things' come into being from certain 'things' and pass away again into those 'things'. The 'things' acting as source and return are the opposites. The picture Anaximander gives, therefore, is that

---

[41] The words actually ascribed to Anaximander are within the double quotation marks.

of an opposite growing from its opposite and likewise being absorbed again into that opposite. Why does this happen? Anaximander speaks of it occurring 'according to what must be (*to chreōn*)'. Here he introduces a force present in the universe somewhat like that of fate (*moira*) found in Homer. Homer describes 'fate' as a mighty power determining events. It is apart from the Olympian gods and in practice they revere it. Anaximander likewise places a 'necessity' in the universe. 'It must be', for some reason, that the opposites grow into and wane from one another.

The reason for this Anaximander provides in the next clause of his fragment. The opposites 'pay a penalty and reparation to one another for their injustice according to the assessment of time'. The opposites, it appears, are guilty of injustice in the way they relate to one another. For this 'injustice' (*adikia*), they must pay a 'penalty' (*dikē*). This reference to *dikē* suggests a situation in which the rights of one opposite were violated by the other and retribution was made in the form of a 'penalty'. But the opposites also do more: 'they make reparation (*tisis*)'. This description suggests surrendering something to which one may have a perfect right. What establishes this relationship between the opposites? Anaximander speaks of the 'assessment of time'. Time, as it passes, evaluates how the opposites are relating to one another and makes those guilty of injustice pay their due.

In this fragment Anaximander has apparently drawn imagery from a feature of his society to explain how the components of the universe relate. This feature is the law-court. When an opposite 'misbehaves', it is brought before the judge, 'time'. Time, as judge, assesses the injustice committed, imposes a 'penalty' and suggests the 'reparation' due. The opposites then leave the 'court' and carry on their activities, abiding by the orders of the court. If similar injustice and infringement of rights occur again, future visits to the courts will prove necessary.

Let us look at an example of the process Anaximander discerned. At the beginning of spring, we see, perhaps, a balance of hot and cold. As far as this pair of opposites is concerned, we encounter justice. But this condition does not last. Hot grows greater and greater, increasing at the expense of cold which slowly disappears. Soon there is only hot with no trace of cold left. Hot has been guilty of injustice, dominating and removing all trace of cold. This cold has 'passed away' into its opposite, hot. Summer has appeared. At this stage, a visit to court proves necessary. Time faces the opposites and orders that hot 'pay penalty and make reparation' to cold. It must yield place to cold and allow balance to exist once more.

As the year continues, hot proves to be obedient to time's judgement and gradually lessens. Now cold 'comes into being' from hot. In the fall we encounter a balance of hot and cold once more. But cold then proves capable of the same injustice as hot has shown. It increases greatly, causing hot to fade and to disappear. Hot 'passes away' into cold and by winter no trace of hot remains. Once again a 'visit to court' must occur. Time acts as arbiter between the opposites. Cold must yield and allow hot to grow once again. Slowly hot makes a reappearance and spring returns.

In this fragment of Anaximander we have an analysis of how opposites in the universe relate. In their essential nature, these opposites are unjust. Each one can express only its own nature and does so aggressively. Injustice, then, appears to be at the core of the behaviour of the components of the universe. We see in this assumption of Anaximander a parallel with Hesiod's view that the first gods, Sky and Cronus, likewise were unjust as they attempted to hold complete sway and to deny other parts of the divine family their rights or due.

But, as in Hesiod where a sense of justice motivates action and leads to the kingship of Zeus, so in Anaximander's universe the opposites grow and wane 'according to what must be'. 'What must be' is the action of time in imposing justice. No opposite can prove unjust forever. It is forced to recognise the rights and claims of its opposite. What will occur with the opposites will be a pattern of balance and imbalance, balance and imbalance. But because balance is always restored, the universe as we know it will continue. Justice proves to be the key to the existence of the universe as a composite of opposites, ever in a varying relationship.

Time never allows one opposite to become permanently dominant. We can compare this idea to the one of 'restraint' (*rhuthmos*) that we encountered in Archilochus 128.[42] He urges his *thumos* neither to rejoice too much in good circumstances nor to grieve too much in painful situations because a 'restraint' is operative in human affairs. Neither joy nor pain will be permanent since a 'restraint' limits both. As in Anaximander, the operation of this 'restraint' occurs in time.

---

[42] See above chapter 2 on Archilochus 128, under *thumos*.

What is not clear in Anaximander is the relationship among time, necessity, and the *Apeiron*. In a mysterious way time proves to be instrumental in imposing what necessity demands. The pattern of change among the elements takes place within the *Apeiron* which acts as source of all the opposites. This *Apeiron*, as we noted, 'surrounds' and 'guides all things' (A 15); it is divine in nature. We may perhaps assume that what the *Apeiron* guides is the very way that opposites are forced to relate under time. It thus probably acts as the source of justice within the universe.

We see in Anaximander a two-fold role of justice. Using its presence in human society, Anaximander postulates its working on a cosmic scale. As in other Presocratics, we encounter here a microcosm/macrocosm view of the universe.[43] The microcosm acts as a pattern for a principle assumed to be operative as well in the macrocosm. The large thus mirrors the small. When both microcosm and macrocosm are studied further, the macrocosm proves to be the model for the microcosm. Anaximander saw the principle of justice at work in human courts. He assumed that it was operative also in the universe as a whole. Its existence on the cosmic scale proves to be most important. Justice keeps the cosmos in existence just as it allows human society to function. Its importance is therefore vital.

Heraclitus

A second Presocratic in whose thought justice plays a dominant role is Heraclitus.[44] We shall discuss several fragments, focusing our discussion on his notion of cosmic justice. We shall see that justice is operative in the very nature of the divine principle Heraclitus introduces and also in 'all things', the universe as a whole. In his notion of justice certain elements will prove important: balance, tension, and measure.

As we described in chapter 3 (on *psychē*), Heraclitus believes that the universe is the expression of a divine principle which he identifies as *logos*. This *logos* is a thought-process that manifests itself in a series of opposites, each balancing the other. When the divine principle, *logos*, expresses itself and speaks, it forms 'all things' as these opposites. Human beings possess a capacity for thought reflecting

---

[43] On this principle see under Anaxagoras in chapter 2.
[44] For bibliography on Heraclitus see chapter 2, note 35.

itself in speech, namely *logos*; in this way they share in the divine nature. With this capacity they can identify the opposites composing 'all things'. Those using *logos* correctly perceive that these opposites are related to each other in a basic way. They are not discrete or separate entities.

The divine nature, *logos*, reveals in the formation of 'all things' its own nature. These 'things' are its 'thoughts' or 'words'. The relationship between a pair of opposites ('life', for example, and 'death' or 'good' and 'evil') is an important aspect of divine thinking and speaking. What Heraclitus proposes is that this relationship is one of balance. It is a just relationship, with each member having its appropriate rights. When the divine *logos* thinks and expresses one opposite, it equally thinks and expresses the other. All opposites, then, as they compose 'all things', are equal and balanced.

Two fragments make clear the relationship of the divine *logos* to the opposites.[45] First, B 32: 'one thing, the only wise, is unwilling and willing to be spoken of by the name of Zeus'. Heraclitus is probably referring to the divine principle, *logos*. It is partly willing to be identified with the 'name of Zeus', which means 'life'. But it is also unwilling, because this name is limited in nature. Its opposite, 'death', is missing. The essence of divinity expresses itself in opposition and the whole range of possibilities must be found in its name. Second, B 67: 'god is day, night, winter, summer, war, peace, satiety, and famine'. Here we have an explicit list of opposites with which the divinity is identified. As we have seen, the one term that Heraclitus found adequate to express the full nature of divinity was *logos* (B 1, B 2, B 50). All things continue in existence in perfect balanced tension because divinity expresses them in that way and only in that way. This way is a perfect reflection of its own nature, *logos*.

In three other fragments Heraclitus emphasizes the importance of the balance existing between the opposites. He wishes to counter a view that people might have that the opposites have little relationship to one another and that some are positive in value, others negative. Such an assumption could easily be made, for example, about peace and war, justice and injustice, or life and death. Heraclitus, therefore, boldly states (B 80): 'it is necessary to understand that war

---

[45] On these and other fragments discussed in this chapter see in particular Conche, *Héraclite*, W.K.C. Guthrie, Kahn, *Art and Thought*, Kirk, Raven, and Schofield, and T.M. Robinson. See also Vlastos (note 1) on justice.

is common, and justice (*dikē*) is strife (*eris*), and that all things come into being according to strife' (*eris*).[46]

We heard in chapter 2 that one description given of *logos* in the universe is that it is 'common' (B 2). Heraclitus uses the same word, *xunon*, to describe 'war' in this fragment, B 80. He selects one of a pair of opposites and states that it is pervasive, as pervasive as the divine principle itself. This opposite is 'war', not apparently a 'common' presence that would prove attractive to human beings. But people might be willing to accept that it is often a dominant presence. Heraclitus' next assertion, however, is even more startling: 'justice is strife'. He states too that 'all things (the universe) come into being according to strife'.

How is 'justice', 'strife'? For Heraclitus we can suppose that justice will be related to the opposites making up the universe. 'Strife' describes the relationship of these opposites. They are ever in contention. But in their very 'strife' justice is to be found. The opposites fight constantly. Each opposite may strive to get the upper hand but no opposite can. The battle is equally engaged. The very balanced tension of opposites keeps the universe going. Therefore, 'according to strife all things come into being'. 'War', thus, is 'common'. It produces a balanced universe. It is ever present and necessary.[47]

Here we see a view of the universe that differs from Anaximander's. The latter, as we observed, assumed that injustice was at the core of the universe. One opposite, constantly expressing its own nature, causes imbalance as it dominates the other. Time must 'step in' to restore balance between the two and to impose justice. Heraclitus, in contrast, thinks that the opposites are never out of balance. By being ever in a balanced tension, they allow the universe to continue. Heraclitus assumed, it appears, that if the opposites did get out of balance, one would predominate and balance could never be reimposed. Thus, in his view, justice, being strife, is ever present in the universe.

In Heraclitus' view, therefore, no one opposite in the universe can overstep its bounds in the way that Anaximander describes the

---

[46] The end of the fragment is corrupt and is here omitted. See Kahn, *Art and Thought*, p. 207 and T.M. Robinson, p. 132.

[47] Compare A 22 where Heraclitus is said to have rebuked Homer for having Achilles pray: 'would that conflict might vanish from gods and human beings' (*Il.* 18.107). If this happens, Heraclitus claims, it would mean the 'destruction of the whole'.

opposites as doing. He explicitly denies this possibility (B 94): 'the sun will not overstep its measures. If it does, the furies, the servants of justice (*dikē*), will find it out'. Heraclitus draws here on an image from myth. The furies were depicted as pursuing those who transgressed justice. Heraclitus says that it probably could not happen that one element, fire, the 'sun', could overstep the limits of its range. But if it tried to do so, there is a force in the universe that would right the situation and it would be just for this to happen.[48]

In B 53 we hear further of this tension or 'war' (*polemos*) in the universe: 'war is the father and king of all. Some he shows forth as gods, others as human beings. Some he makes slaves, others free'. Again Heraclitus startles his listeners. Zeus, perhaps, would be the expected 'father and king of all'. Instead, Heraclitus speaks of 'war'. What this 'war' does is to reveal opposites: gods/humans and slaves/free. Each group could stand as extremes on a continuum of being. Gods and humans cover the range of conscious beings in the universe. 'Slaves' and 'free' describe the possible conditions of human beings. War 'shows forth' these different groups; in so doing, it produces a balanced universe.

Thus far we have suggested that Heraclitus' view of justice is closely related to the nature of the divine principle and the way it expresses itself in opposites. Other fragments tells us more about this relationship. In B 102 he says of the divine *logos*: 'to the god all things are fair and just (*diakaia*), whereas human beings have supposed that some things are unjust (*adika*) and others are just (*dikaia*)'. The divine *logos* expresses itself in all the opposites that compose 'all things'. Its 'thoughts' and 'words', which become all things, are by nature 'fair and just'. When human beings encounter these things, they appear as opposites. Therefore, they label them as distinct. They assign a positive value to some, calling them 'just' and a negative value to others, calling them 'unjust'. But, in so doing, they fail to grasp that each in a pair of opposites is necessary and that all opposites exist in perfect balance.

Most important of the opposites are the elements: earth, air, fire, and water. With one of these, as was pointed out in chapter 3, the

---

[48] Note that in the philosophy of Anaximenes, who asserts that all things are air, one opposite has become dominant. Anaximenes may not have thought that there was a problem of imbalance or injustice since essentially the universe was simply an embodiment of one element, air. See further on Anaximenes in chapter 3.

divine *logos* is identified: fire. In B 64 Heraclitus says that 'thunderbolt steers all things'. Zeus, it seems, is not chief ruler in the universe but his weapon is. And this weapon is the divine *logos*. At B 30 Heraclitus describes the cosmos as 'an everliving fire, being kindled in measures (*metra*) and extinguished in measures (*metra*)'. What this fire does in the cosmos is to 'die' into all things and 'live' again as itself. Thus at B 90 Heraclitus says: 'all things are an exchange for fire and fire for all things'. What is important for the question of justice in these fragments is that the change that fire undergoes occurs 'in measures'. It is a balanced change and, being such, ensures both the existence of itself and of 'all things'.

We hear further of this 'fire' in its appearance as one of the elements. Heraclitus says (B 76a): 'for fire lives the death of earth and air lives the death of fire; water lives the death of air and earth that of water'. Fire is always living and dying, as are all the elements. When one dies, another element lives. But the exchange among the four elements appears to be stable. Why? Heraclitus tells us in another fragment, B 31b: 'earth is dispersed as sea and is measured out in the same proportion (*logos*) as before it became earth'. As the elements alter, they do so in strict 'measure'. We encounter here another meaning of the term *logos* (see also chapter 3), namely 'measure'. The elements remain balanced in the universe because their change into each other is precisely regulated. They are equally balanced. For Heraclitus their relationship is both strife and justice.

Finally, we find in two fragments of Heraclitus specific references to justice (*dikē*) with regard to human beings. At B 23 he says: 'if these things did not exist, people would not even know the name of justice (*dikē*)'. As ever, the saying is puzzling but we may suppose that the 'things' mentioned are instances of injustice. It is the very presence of one opposite that allows the 'name', the nature of the other, to be recognized. The two are ever related to one another. At B 28b Heraclitus remarks: 'justice (*dikē*) will catch those who devise lies and those who act as witnesses for them'. Here we have clear reference to justice within the system of courts in human society. 'Lies and false witness' harm the rights and fair claims of others. But there is a force, justice, at work that will stop this situation. Those who may be attacking others will themselves be caught. Both on the cosmic and human levels justice preserves balance.

With Heraclitus, as with Anaximander, justice is very important, especially on the cosmic level. It is closely related to the nature of the divine principle. Three elements are important in Heraclitus' view of justice: balance, tension, and measure. The presence of justice among 'all things' allows them to stay in existence. The opposites engage permanently in strife with one another but the conflict is equal. They change into each other in perfect measure. Because their strife is equal and will ever be so, the world-order will endure, ever changing yet ever stable. Justice is balanced tension and its maintenance in the universe.

Parmenides

In our next Presocratic we meet an old and new idea of justice. As we pointed out in chapter 2, Parmenides thought that reality existed as one Being, unchanging, unmoving, and complete.[49] Human beings, endowed with *noos*, can grasp this truth. In so doing, they will learn to reject the evidence of their senses which suggest, in contrast, that the universe is made up of a multiplicity, 'all things', that come into being, pass away, change, and move. In one part of his poem Parmenides treats what he postulates as the correct view of reality: this is the 'Way of Truth' or 'Way of Being'. In another part he presents the incorrect view mortals hold: this is the 'Way of Opinion'. But he prefaces both parts of his poem with a significant proem.

We shall discuss this proem, concentrating on its relation both to the correct and incorrect views of reality that Parmenides presents in the rest of his poem. Since the proem is an allegory, other interpretations are possible. Ours will focus on Parmenides' picture of justice as a cosmic one.

In his proem, (B 1), Parmenides describes the journey by which he travelled beyond the world of the senses. He was led by the daughters of the sun who 'left the home of night, hastening into the light' (9–10). They come in their travels to the double 'gates of the ways of night and day' (11); over these 'Justice (*dikē*), much avenging, holds alternate keys' (14). The daughters of the sun persuade her to open the gates and allow them through. She does so. Parmenides and the maidens then travel on, meeting a goddess who tells Parmenides that it was 'law (*themis*) and justice (*dikē*)' that sent him to her (28). What he is to learn is 'all things', both the Truth and the 'opinions of mortals', which prove misleading (29–32).

The picture Parmenides presents in this proem gives important

---

[49] On Parmenides in general see bibliography in chapter 2, note 42. See also the treatment of justice in Vlastos (note 1).

information about his view of justice. Parmenides arrives at the 'gates of the ways of night and day' (11) over which Justice presides. When Parmenides comes to describe the 'opinion of mortals', he says that they err essentially in assuming that reality can be multiple in form. What they do is to postulate two principles, 'fire and night' (8.56–9), instead of one alone. What we can surmise from the proem is that the 'world of mortals' through which Parmenides journeys on his way is very much one of opposites. We have encountered this world already in the philosophy of Anaximander and Heraclitus. It is a world that Parmenides needed to get beyond if he was to grasp the truth.

The Justice 'who holds the alternating keys' of the doors of the 'ways of night and day' can be seen then as preserving the balance of 'night' and 'day' and presumably all other opposites (14). She is 'much avenging': she apparently punishes severely occurrences of injustice or imbalance. Anaximander and Heraclitus, we can suppose, would have approved of this description of justice. But Parmenides leaves this notion of justice behind.

He travels to a goddess who assures him that 'law' (*themis*) and 'justice' (*dikē*) have led him on his journey. What are these? Surely they must be related to his new grasp of 'truth' (29), which he proceeds to describe in the 'Way of Being'. There we encounter a new idea of justice. In the context of the journey Parmenides describes, he is being assured (and his listeners too) that it is right and proper for him to grasp reality in the way in which it will soon be revealed.

What is the new notion of justice that Parmenides introduces? In terms of function it resembles the role assigned to it by Anaximander and Heraclitus. As in them, so in Parmenides it is that which sustains reality in the condition it must be in so that it can endure. In the case of the earlier philosophers, this justice involved the maintenance of balance between the opposites. For Parmenides, in contrast, it is the force that makes Being have the qualities it does. As he gives his long description of Being in B 8, he specifically mentions Justice (*dikē*): 'therefore Justice does not loosen her fetters so as to allow it [Being] to come into being or to pass away but holds it fast' (8.13–15).

In the proem we saw Justice guarding the double 'doors of night and day' (11). She evidently keeps control over each opposite, ensuring that neither usurps the rights of the other and proving to be 'much avenging' in the case of unfairness. In the picture of reality given to Parmenides when he passes beyond these doors, Justice is again presented as a 'locking force'. She no longer deals with two entities but one only. It is she, the inherent force of right, that makes Being exist in the only way that it can. Being must only 'be' and all its characteristics flow from that one necessity. Parmenides at 8.13–15 refers specifically to Justice in the context of Being lacking all beginning or end. We may assume that this Justice was operative in other characteristics of Being as well.

When speaking of other necessary qualities of Being, we discover Parmenides also using other terms. In 8.26–33 he argues that Being is motionless and totally complete in itself. 'For strong Necessity (*Anankē*) keeps it in the bonds of limit, which holds it on every side since it is not right (*themis*) for it to be incomplete' (30–2). In these lines the force imposing characteristics upon Being is 'Necessity' (*Anankē*). Being cannot be anything other than still and complete. 'Right' (*themis*) is involved in this situation. Any other condition for Being would be 'wrong'.

At 8.34–41 Parmenides says again that there can be only Being. 'Nothing exists or will exist except for Being, since Fate (*Moira*) has fettered it to be whole and immovable' (36–9). In these lines, Fate (*Moira*) is the power constraining Being, making it complete and motionless.

In these three passages where 'Justice', 'Necessity', and 'Fate' are mentioned, the image is the same: that of 'fettering' or 'binding'. These powers, which are probably related and may even in Parmenides' view have been thought to be one, function to make Being what it is. Because they do so, reality exists as it does and will ever do so.

In the part of his poem treating the mistaken view of mortals, the 'Way of Opinion', Parmenides likewise assigns a role to justice. As mentioned above, human beings err in accepting that reality is two: 'fire and night' (8.56–9). In accepting the possibility of opposites, mortals apparently believe that they are somehow balanced. This at least seems to be the case when Parmenides gives his description of the 'two forms they name' (8.54–61) and also when he speaks of the 'ways of night and day' in the proem. In a fragment from this part of the poem, B 9, he speaks of 'light and night' as the two basic opposites in the universe, 'both equal' with all other things sharing in them.

What Parmenides apparently did in the 'Way of Opinion', of which we have only a few fragments, was to develop a consistent picture of the universe based on an assumption of two realities instead of one. This picture, of course, does not correspond to truth but he shows that it could be logical in itself. In speaking of this world of duality, Parmenides once describes 'Necessity' (*Anankē*) as fettering the sky so that it keeps the 'limits of the stars' (B 10). Here we see a function of Necessity similar to the one it had in the 'Way of Truth': it compels behaviour that ensures existence and continuance.

Elsewhere, in a description given of the universe as presented in this part of Parmenides' poem (A 37), we encounter an elaborate picture of rings of fire and darkness, sometimes mixed, at other times alternating with each other.[50] 'The most central of the mixed rings is the source and cause of movement and generation for them all and he calls the goddess who steers, holder of the keys, Justice and Necessity'. We have a clear echo here of the role of these two forces in the 'Way of Truth' (8.14, 30). In a universe where two forms are accepted, they function as they do for Being: they ensure the essential nature of what they control. Here, of course, in stark contrast to their effect upon Being, they allow 'movement' and 'generation', the very things denied to Being itself.

In his poem as a whole, Parmenides, therefore, presents both an old and new idea of justice. The 'old' idea is that found in Anaximander and Heraclitus that there are opposites in the universe that justice controls and balances. Parmenides, refuting their ideas and those of all who accept duality, nonetheless shows in the 'Way of Opinion' that justice correctly has this role if opposition is assumed.

In the proem Parmenides shows that he 'went beyond' this notion of justice, leaving a realm where this force balanced opposites. In the realm of Being justice has a similar method of acting and yet a different role. It still 'fetters' and 'controls' but it makes Being manifest itself as only itself: one, unmoved, unchanging, complete reality. By constantly exerting control over Being, justice ensures that it ever exists. This justice, also termed, it seems, 'necessity' and 'fate', operates outside the realm of plurality or opposition. It has the same function as the 'old' justice, ensuring continuance of the cosmos, but its activity in the realm of Being is new.

---

[50] This description comes from the doxographic tradition on Parmenides and is not one of his fragments. See W.K.C. Guthrie, vol. 2, pp. 61–6.

Summary

In this chapter we have examined the notion of justice in the Archaic Age. We have seen it operative on the human and divine levels. We have observed legal, political, and moral aspects of it. In the Presocratics we encountered different views of cosmic justice. In Homer justice is valued highly, probably reflecting already a long tradition of honour for it in Greek society. In the *Iliad* and the *Odyssey* the term *dikē* commonly has the meaning of 'custom' or judgement'. In some passages it signifies 'moral right'. Zeus honours *dikē* and is angry at its absence. The opening of the *Odyssey* shows that guilty people were thought deserving of punishment, which they often brought upon themselves. For victims of injustice, caused by the expression of free will in others, right would prevail in the end, as it did for Odysseus and Telemachus.

In Hesiod we see a dominant role assigned to justice. It is the foundation of human society, setting human beings apart from animals. Even though there may be a delay in its appearance, it always 'flourishes' in the end. Justice is the opposite of *hybris*, 'arrogance', that infringes upon the rights of others. Zeus and nature bless those who are just; they both punish the unjust. In the *Works and Days*, justice is the 'majestic daughter of Zeus', who carefully guards her claims. In the *Theogony*, justice is again daughter of Zeus but also of Law (*Themis*). Associated with her as sisters are 'Good Order' (*Eunomiē*) and 'Peace' (*Eirenē*). In the history of the universe injustice appears early and leads to a change in who is king of the gods. Zeus, by marrying Law and producing Justice, ensures that he will remain king. Hesiod's view is that the universe is under the sway of justice which will ever prove victorious, whatever the behaviour of human beings.

In the lyric and elegiac poets justice continues to be of great importance. Xenophanes, Simonides, and Bacchylides relate *aretē* to justice. Solon, like Hesiod, finds in justice the foundation of human society. He identifies human greed as the cause of most unjust behaviour of humans. Only wealth that is won justly with divine approval can last. The desire for more and more, however, usually leads people to overstep their bounds and to infringe upon the rights of others. Zeus, however, watches human action and, although he may delay, eventually inflicts punishment either on the individuals who committed injustice or upon their descendants.

Solon also believes that a society founded on justice and 'good order' (*eunomiē*) will flourish. Justice is blessed both by Zeus and by nature. Cities which honour fairness and right have it in their power to prevent innocent suffering in future generations.

In Theognis we encounter several reflections upon justice. He is convinced that the 'worthless' (*deilos*) or 'evil' (*kakos*) person is incapable of justice. He assumes that only the 'good' (*agathoi*) are capable of *aretē* which is summed up in 'justice'. Wealth that comes from Zeus with justice will last; riches attained unjustly will eventually be lost as the 'mind of the gods prevail'. The gods, especially Zeus, are guardians of justice and ensure its triumph.

Theognis has questions about justice in the world he lives in. He sees that the distribution of poverty and wealth often seems unjust. The evil have wealth but the good do not. But he suggests that, even though this distribution may be mysterious, for the good and just person, the presence of wealth proves in some way irrelevant. Their inner goodness remains intact. For evil persons the absence of wealth proves to be all important; they have no inner resources to cope with poverty.

Theognis also wonders whether it can be just for innocent descendants to pay for the crimes of their ancestors. He had observed, as Solon had also done before him, that the guilty appeared to escape punishment and that their children paid later. Theognis does not find an answer to this dilemma but his questioning shows a concern about an apparent lack of fairness in the course of events and an assumption that this should not be so.

Pindar echoes Hesiod in speaking of Justice as daughter of *Themis* and sister of *Eunomiē* and *Eirenē*. He too believes that wealth can be stable if attained justly. He relates justice to the distribution of due shares or rights. In his focus upon *aretē*, he assumes that only those who honour justice will be able to preserve *aretē*. He also believes that excellent performance makes claims for praise that the poet justly fulfils. In *Ol.* 2, Pindar sees justice as the key for escape from rebirth for souls. He describes three possible fates for souls after death. If they have committed serious sins, they may be punished with great toil in the underworld or face immediate rebirth on earth. If they have been relatively good and just, they will be sent to an area of 'equal nights and days' and carry on a life similar to one on earth. Here, apparently, souls will absorb from this very setting the notion of balance and justice. If souls have managed, during three earthly lives, to refrain from 'unjust deeds', they escape rebirth altogether and travel to the Isle of the Blessed, about to enjoy the company of heroes. These souls, who have become entirely just, can enter the realm of light where 'flowers of gold blaze'.

What is significant about the treatment of justice in Homer, Hesiod, and the lyric and elegiac poets is the common acceptance of its value without attempts to analyse its specific nature. Justice has worth. Its effects, when present, are valuable. Its absence lead to problems. Its violation causes disasters. With *arete* we saw specific attempts to identify its essence: courage, for example, justice, or wisdom. With *dike*, we do not find these poets asking: what is its exact nature? Instead, what we see is justice being associated with the fair distribution of rights and the recognition of the appropriate claims of others. These poets may not specifically describe it as such but all seem to assume that its nature is something like that. In their 'silent' acceptance of the value of justice, they may carry on a tradition where this value was long recognised. Justice, it seems clear, was in their view well worth praising and speaking of to others.

The Presocratics assign an important role to justice, especially cosmic justice. They see in it the force that allows the universe to continue in existence. Without it the opposites which compose all things would quickly show disarray. Anaximander sees these opposites as constantly falling into imbalance as one asserts its nature at the expense of another. But time acts as judge over the opposites and constantly reestablishes balance. Heraclitus, in contrast, believes that the opposites remain ever in an equally-posed tension, their conflict ensuring that no one opposite becomes predominant. The universe is a 'war' but a just one.

Parmenides describes one form of justice, accepted by mortals whose ideas, however, are misleading. This justice, similar to that of Anaximander and Heraclitus, ensures the balance of the opposites in the universe. Parmenides describes these opposites as 'night' and 'light'. With regard to the true understanding of the universe, justice relates to Being, making it have the range of characteristics it must have. Being must be one, unchanging, unmoving, and complete. It is just that it be so and it cannot be otherwise. In referring to this justice, Parmenides relates it to 'necessity' and 'fate'. All three forces ensure both the existence and exact nature of 'what is'.

Justice, we see, was a subject of great interest to these early Greeks. They do not define it exactly as a concept but they have a clear notion of varying kinds of it. Justice was to become in the fifth century a theme of the *Oresteia* of Aeschylus and in the fourth century the topic of one of Plato's greatest dialogues, the *Republic*. All those who treated justice after the writers we have considered would discover in them valuable assumptions and penetrating questions. With this chapter we have considered some of the questions posed at the end of chapter 1. What makes human society possible and able to function? In what sort of universe do human beings live and why does it continue to exist? In the answers provided justice has played a key role.

CHAPTER SIX

OVERVIEW OF THE IDEAS

The focus of this book has been upon human beings in certain specific contexts. We selected ideas that played a dominant role in early Greek poetry and philosophy and studied how a variety of authors treated them. These writers included the epic poets, Homer and Hesiod, the lyric poets, and the Presocratic philosophers. In terms of time we began in the seventh century and covered authors until the end of the fifth century. The ideas chosen were consciousness, soul, excellence, and justice. In chapter 1 we listed a number of questions that the book would undertake to answer. A summary of these answers is as follows.

What is the Nature of Human Consciousness?

In chapter 2 we treated principally three terms that appear frequently in early authors to express aspects of human consciousness: *noos*, *phrēn*, and *thumos*. Although there are several other terms that likewise express psychological activity in human beings, these three are most important. In all cases the psychic entities discussed are thought to be present within as something distinct from the persons themselves. Psychic entity and individual relate in some way.

First, *noos*. From early times this entity was associated with 'insight' or 'inner vision'. It functioned too as a seat of someone's disposition or character. But *noos*, however much it could grasp the truth of a situation, had the unfortunate characteristic of being hidden. It operated at a deep level that could elude the person having it. On the other hand, with others, people might intentionally conceal *noos*, that is, what they were actually thinking or feeling. *Noos*, thus, could be useful for protecting one's real nature. Nor was *noos* ever the same: it proved to be a variable entity that 'changed with the day'.

The philosophers assign *noos* a very central role. For Parmenides, it is the faculty that allows a grasp of truth. For Xenophanes, it is the divine thought that directs the universe. For Anaxagoras, it is divinity itself. Of the psychic entities, *noos* was probably considered the most valuable. This faculty may also be that which determines the essence of human beings, allowing them alone to ponder the nature of the universe and to understand what it is.

The second psychic entity that we treated was *phrēn*. This faculty, usually referred to in the plural, differs in several ways from *noos*. *Phrenes* serve frequently as the location of other psychic entities. Their main activity is intellectual and involves pondering and deliberation. It may be that, when *noos* fails to function, *phrenes* must act. Although they might not always grasp the truth, *phrenes* could prove to be a very valuable tool for the individual. If *phrenes* were 'lost', people acted foolishly; if they were present, people showed prudence.

Within the person, *phrenes* are subordinate in nature. They do not function as an active agent but instead serve as an instrument or tool used by a person. Person and *phrenes* co-operate in activity and work in harmony. In the lyric poets we saw that *phrenes* became more active in the person and began to serve more as a seat of character. In the Presocratics *phrenes* function to understand the universe. Empedocles makes *phrēn* the essence of the divine nature. In range, then, *phrenes* prove to be flexible and diverse.

The third psychic entity we examined was *thumos*. In Homer and Hesiod this faculty figures most prominently in the human being. It does not have an 'inner vision' of the truth, like *noos*, but covers a wider range of intellectual, emotional, and volitional activities than *phrenes*. It often functions as an independent agent in the individual. The two, remaining ever distinct, can be in harmony or in tension. People address *thumos* directly and sometimes need to control it. *Thumos* is the psychic entity that fills a person with vigour and energy. If *thumos* is lost, the individual either faints or dies. Ever a vital presence within, it frequently commands the attention of the person in whom it is found.

In the lyric poets *thumos* continued to play an important role, especially with regard to emotional activity. But in the Presocratics it is rarely mentioned, probably because it has become very strongly associated with emotion.

In studying these psychic terms, we observed that human consciousness in early Greek poetry and philosophy is complicated in nature. Several different psychic entities function within and thus form its range. Individuals probably have some notion of 'self', ill-defined perhaps and not subject to scrutiny. But this 'self' is not composed of the various psychic entities. Instead, they are distinct from it. The person relates in various ways to the faculties present and active within. These faculties show an amazing range of function which takes place within the person. Nor do they simply act. Often they can be affected from without by gods and other people. In the early Greek poets and philosophers consciousness is presented as complicated in nature. The inner working of the human person proves to be both mysterious and complex.

What Keeps People Alive?

In chapter 3 we turned to the notion of *psychē*. By the time of Socrates and Plato this term had come to denote the personality of the individual. It functioned as the seat of intellect, emotion, and will. But this was not always the case. In Homer and Hesiod *psychē* is simply the 'breath' or 'air' that keeps a person alive. It has no psychological function in the living person. *Psychē*, then, undergoes a dramatic change in relation to the living person by the end of the fifth century.

In this chapter we surveyed the role *psychē* had in the living. From being simply 'breath', it comes to act as a seat of different psychological functions. First, in the lyric poets it becomes involved with emotion. It suffers pain. It feels love. Also in these poets, it becomes associated with moral traits and character. But as its range extends, it still remains closely connected with 'life' or the 'life-principle' within.

In the Presocratics *psychē* takes on new significance as well as the portion of the living person that shares in the divine nature. In Anaximenes, retaining a close association with 'breath', it functions to keep the person alive just as the same 'breath' or 'air' maintains the universe as a whole in existence. For Heraclitus, *psychē* acts as the seat of *logos* which, as divine principle, also governs the cosmos. In his fragments we see *psychē* acting as a seat of intelligence and wisdom. It can prove vulnerable to the impulses of *thumos* and calls for attention on the part of the person to keep it in a 'fiery', rational state.

What Happens to People After Death?

We saw too in chapter 3 that *psychē* alone survives the individual at death. Flying forth from the body, this 'shade' travels to Hades where

it continues to exist. *Psychai* are pale 'images' of the people from
whom they came, all being recognisable as the individuals they were
on earth. This characteristic of being the only part of the person to
survive death probably profoundly influenced the major role *psychē*
came to have later in the living person.

Homer shows us the shades as Odysseus meets them in Hades
(*Od.* 11). Once they have drunk blood, they take on functions associated with the body and with other psychological entities. These
shades begin to act very much as the people they were on earth. We
suggested that this picture of *psychai* in the underworld probably significantly influenced the range of functions that *psychē* came to exhibit
in the living.

The traditional picture of *psychē* as shade that survives after death
continues to be found in the lyric poets. In the Presocratics it takes
on new characteristics in this role. For Anaximenes and Heraclitus it
may be that the *psychē* found in the living person was thought at
death to join the divine principle. Xenophanes and the Pythagoreans
(echoed also by Pindar in *Ol.* 2) refer to the notion of the transmigration of *psychai*. According to this idea, a *psychē* could experience
several human life-times, undergoing positive change in the form of
purification and moving toward some enviable destiny.

In chapter 3, therefore, we saw the existence of human beings
after death painted in two ways. It could be negative, as Homer
showed it to be and as poets would continue to suggest. It could be
positive, as the philosophers postulated. In both cases its nature was
ever considered worthy of discussion and analysis.

What Do People Value in Human Behaviour?

Our next two chapters (4 and 5) treated the answer to this question.
As we examined early Greek poetry and philosophy, we saw people
making some basic assumptions. These Greeks were essentially opti-
mistic in outlook. There existed in human beings elements worthy of
high praise or admiration. It might not be that these elements were
always present or perhaps even frequently present. But within the
human character the potential for greatness was there.

At first this literature presupposes that there are a few and only a
few who can show forth human greatness. Heroes and heroines stand
apart from the rest of humanity. They compel our praise, wonder,

and even astonishment for their deeds. They act as models for other human beings, who perhaps lack the same range because no parent of theirs was divine. But these people are none the less able to understand the deeds that heroes accomplish and to imitate them in some degree.

As time passes, more and more ordinary people with ordinary parentage become the focus of poetry and philosophy. The range of these individuals, even though abbreviated perhaps in comparison to that of heroes and heroines, itself appears as a cause for wonder. The early philosophers will suggest that all human beings within the universe share in some way in the divine nature. They believe that once people grasp how this is so, they will prove able to modify their behaviour, as the heroes of old did, and act at a very high level.

These early Greeks believe that no human being could ever be capable of splendid behaviour on the basis of birth alone. Training, education, and guidance over a period of time was always necessary. In some, who received these aids, human character would emerge in ways deserving of praise. In others, even though these advantages had been received, such an emergence would not take place. Why this should be so would appear a source of mystery and cause yet further consideration of how admirable features of character could be made to appear.

Chapters 4 and 5 discussed ways in which different authors detected such positive elements within human beings and clarified the nature of these elements. These chapters also showed how various writers differed in their assessment of the worth of various elements, selecting among those already recognised or introducing new ones. Chapter 4 treated 'excellence' (*aretē*), as a whole. Chapter 5 focused upon justice, sometimes seen as part of *aretē* but at other times standing apart with a powerful role of its own.

What Makes Someone Excel?

As we saw in chapter 4, the early Greek poets showed a great and enduring interest in this question. Homer, as he draws upon a poetic tradition with a long history, presents a heroic code in which courage played a significant part. The heroes he describes in the *Iliad* are to aspire to greatness by fighting in single combat, defeating their opponent, and receiving deserved recognition from their peers. The hero of the *Iliad* accepts this code, convinced that this behaviour will attract the attention of a poet who can bestow the only type of immortality possible, fame in song. But Homer in this epic also showed that such excellence would not suffice. Achilles came to deserve his praise, not for military prowess alone, but for learning to show compassion to one more courageous than he, Priam, his greatest enemy. Homer thus enriches an early view of excellence by placing importance upon an admirable inner range of the human person.

In the *Odyssey* we discussed Homer's presentation of Penelope. Excellence in women requires much more than beauty. Penelope wins praise for her intelligence and good sense but, beyond all else, for her steadfast loyalty to Odysseus. Unlike Helen and Clytemnestra, who lack the quality of fidelity, Penelope proves herself to be unwavering in this regard, subjecting even Odysseus to severe testing before accepting him as her husband who had returned.

When we studied the lyric poets, we found several reassessments of the earlier notions of excellence. Callinus and Tyrtaeus praise courage but it is now to be displayed in group, not individual, effort. Pindar and Bacchylides extol athletic achievement, carefully showing the contribution of birth, training, and divine help. Theognis gives a detailed treatment of *aretē*, ascribing great importance to the role of inherited character. Without this ingredient, he assumes that the highest form of *aretē*, justice, cannot be displayed.

Xenophanes, explicitly rejecting athletic accomplishment as *aretē*, says that poetic wisdom (*sophia*) has much higher value. Heraclitus places importance on a mode of thought: he suggests that 'thinking well' (*sophrosynē*) will involve a grasp of the way the universe functions; it thus constitutes in human beings their highest capacity.

All these different views of *aretē* show an unfailing confidence among the early Greek poets and philosophers that human beings can excel. What manifestation of the human range should be thought most valuable proves a challenging question for them. Their answers would continue to influence Greek thought for a long time to come.

What Makes Human Society Possible?

In chapter 5 we turned our attention to the nature of justice. We saw that already in Homer justice was valued by the gods for its intrinsic value and recognised as something human beings must strive to practise. When people fail to be just, they bring punishment upon themselves and deservedly so. It may be that human beings endure injustice in the form of innocent suffering but eventually right will triumph and evil persons will be punished.

Hesiod sees justice as the force that separates human beings from animals. When people are unjust, they will be punished or, if there is a delay, their descendants will. Zeus and nature honour justice and punish its absence. Solon makes justice the foundation of human society and, like Hesiod, assumes that its presence will bring blessing and its absence, eventual punishment.

Several of the lyric poets relate justice to *aretē* as the highest manifestation of human capacity. Theognis assumes that only a few people with the appropriate birth are capable of it. Simonides, on the other hand, suggests that all individuals who exhibit justice should be treated as praiseworthy.

Pindar in *Ol.* 2 makes justice the one mode of behaviour that can save a person from the need for rebirth. If manifested during three lifetimes, justice allows someone to travel to the 'island of the Blessed', to dwell forever in light.

What we saw in the various selections we studied was a frequent association of justice with 'due share' or 'appropriate portion'. Gods and human beings have just claims and if these are ignored or violated, negative consequences result. Justice, involving 'balance' or 'correct distribution', is seen as allowing human beings to act together in a group. No one should take more at the expense of another. 'Imbalance', unfortunately, proves to be very common but at the core of the universe the divine powers honour justice and ensure its eventual presence.

In What Sort of Universe Do Humans Live?

In the different chapters we encountered poets and philosophers offering explanations of the universe. Hesiod saw it as a large family of gods deriving from two original parents and manifesting great complexity by the diverse natures of its members. Within this universe human beings dwelt and related to the gods. This relationship between human and divine could be harmonious or marked by discord.

Different philosophers explained the universe in different ways.

Anaximander saw it as a limited structure deriving from an unlimited and divine source. In essence it was composed of opposites. Anaximenes viewed it as the expression of divine air, ever compressing and dilating itself. Heraclitus focused upon the constantly changing nature of the cosmos. He saw it as a manifestation of a divine fire, ever kindling and being extinguished, in perfect balance.

Parmenides changed philosophical thought by showing that reality could be only one, unmoving, and unchanging. Empedocles insisted, in contrast, upon multiplicity in the form of four elements and upon motion caused by two divine principles, Love and Strife. Anaxagoras likewise argued for multiplicity in the universe. He said that all natural substances, existing as seeds, were real and functioned as the building blocks of reality. Democritus finally discovered the two actual components of which the universe is made up: atoms and space.

Why Can Humans Understand the Universe?

In the various chapters we saw different responses to this question. Chapter 2 on consciousness showed us the basic tools that human beings possess to cope with their world. The early poets and philosophers did not question the means by which they formed opinions: they simply proceeded to do so. If challenged about this, they would probably have responded that *noos* was most trustworthy for grasping truth. If it did not function, then *phrenes* would prove useful.

With the Presocratics of the fifth century, we see thinkers focusing upon the capacities that humans possess as the key to why they can, or even would want to, explain the cosmos. Heraclitus concentrates upon speech/thought (*logos*), Parmenides, upon *noos*, Empedocles, upon the human capacity for loving and hating, and Anaxagoras, again on *noos*. With these tools humans can search for the truth.

What Makes the Universe Continue to Exist?

To this question we found an amazingly consistent answer: justice. Hesiod thought that injustice marked the behaviour of the earliest rulers of the gods but the third ruler, Zeus, learned justice. He thus ensured that his own rule would continue and also that the universe, as we know it, would endure. Anaximander sees the constant reimposition of balance between the opposites, in time, as the reason that the universe remains stable, even though it changes.

Heraclitus assumes that justice is ever operative, keeping the components of the universe perfectly poised. Parmenides rejects the notion of justice as a balance of opposites. Instead, he argues that, in relation to Being, justice is the force that makes this Being what it is: one. Empedocles echoes the earlier thinkers in believing that the overall balance of Love and Strife explains why the universe goes through the complicated changes it does.

Conclusion

This book has focused upon the Archaic Age, slightly extended to include the later lyric poets and Presocratics. It has, for the ideas discussed, looked first at Homer and Hesiod. It has then turned to the lyric poets and the Presocratic philosophers, in all cases including selections from available poems or fragments. Although the lyric poets and Presocratics often treated themes divergent in nature and in some instances used different genres, they lived in the same period of time. Sometimes they approached questions quite differently but at other times we see in them a remarkable similarity in focus and opinion. This proved to be especially true in the case of the idea of justice. By bringing these poets and philosophers together, we hope that some ideas of the Archaic Age were delineated in more breadth and detail than could happen if they were treated separately.

Consciousness, soul, excellence, justice—these ideas we have examined. In the Archaic Age they had an important role. In later times this role was to grow. We have looked at human beings in specific contexts, illustrated by the questions discussed above. We well know that the early Greek poets and philosophers asked many other questions. We have concentrated on only a few. But these questions later authors also would pose and answer in a variety of ways. In so doing these later thinkers, whether poets, dramatists, historians, or philosophers, would act within a framework of time. Ever would they glance back to the Archaic Age to see what had been said, to consider its value, and, in light of it, to respond. A portion of the legacy of ideas to be found in early Greek poetry and philosophy has filled these pages. Its richness, we believe, always merits study.

AUTHORS DISCUSSED IN CHRONOLOGICAL ORDER
(WITH BIOGRAPHICAL NOTES)

NAME   ABBREVIATION   DATE

A. Epic, Lyric and Elegiac Poets

HOMER   Hom.   mid-8th century (?)

The date of Homer is obscure but he is usually placed in the mid-eighth century. His place of origin was also disputed in ancient times but he is best known as the 'blind poet of Chios', an island in Ionia. To him traditionally the *Iliad* (=*Il.*) and *Odyssey* (=*Od.*) were assigned. The present work treats him as the author of each of these narrative epic poems written in dactylic hexameter verse.

The Homeric Hymns: these are a collection of thirty-three hymns dedicated to different gods. They were ascribed to Homer but were probably written by different authors, some in the eighth century, some later. Like the Homeric epics, these poems draw upon the reserve of formulaic hexameter verse. They may have served as preludes in the recitation by bards of longer epic poems. References will be made to the *Hymns to Apollo, Venus, Hermes, and Demeter* (abbreviated *H. Ap., H. Ven., H. Mer., H. Cer.*).

HESIOD   Hes.   mid-8th-7th centuries (?)

The date of Hesiod is in question. Whether he was earlier than, contemporary with, or later than Homer has been disputed, although usually he has been thought to be later than Homer. He himself tells how his father left Aeolian Cyme in Asia Minor to travel to Ascra in Boeotia (*W. &. D.* 633–40). Like Homer he writes in dactylic hexameter but composes didactic epic. The present work treats his poems, the *Theogony* (=*Theog.*), the *Works and Days* (*W. &. D.*), and also the fragments of his poetry.

ARCHILOCHUS   Arch.   mid-7th century

Born on the island of Paros, Archilochus lived perhaps from 680–640 B.C. He was a mercenary soldier who took part in the colonisation of Thasos, off the coast of Thrace. He composed iambic and trochaic verses, epodes, and elegiacs. He wrote on personal topics including war, love, hate, and adventure.

CALLINUS   Call.   mid-7th century

Callinus was from Ephesus in Asia Minor. Little is known of him. He was involved in resistance to Cimmerian attacks on Ionia. He wrote elegiac verse treating martial themes.

TYRTAEUS   Tyr.   mid-7th century
Tyrtaeus lived in Sparta during the Second Messenian War (670–630 B.C.) and was a general in this war. He wrote elegiac poetry with martial and political themes. His poems were gathered into five books.

SEMONIDES   Sem.   2nd half of 7th century
Born on the island of Samos, Semonides was connected especially with the small island of Amorgos. He composed elegiac and iambic poetry. His themes include the nature of women and of human life in general.

ALCMAN   Alcm.   2nd half of 7th century
Alcman may have been from Sardis in Lydia but he lived in Sparta. He wrote hymns and choral lyrics for girls' choirs in Sparta. His poems were collected into six books.

MIMNERMUS   Mim.   2nd half of 7th century
Mimnermus may have been from Smyrna and perhaps Colophon in Asia Minor. He composed elegiac poetry, collected into two books. He wrote on love, youth, old age, and mythological subjects.

SAPPHO   Sa.   c. 630–?
Sappho was born at Eresus or Mytilene on the island of Lesbos. She wrote short lyric poems on personal topics, especially love. Her poems were collected into nine books.

ALCAEUS   Alc.   c. 630–?
Alcaeus was born at Mytilene on Lesbos, a contemporary of Sappho. He too wrote short lyric poems on personal topics, especially politics, drinking, and love. His poems may have been collected into ten books.

SOLON   Sol.   fl. 594
Athenian Statesman, who was archon in 594/3, Solon wrote elegiac poetry as well as iambic and trochaic verse. His themes include politics, wealth, law, and war.

STESICHORUS   Stes.   c. 630–556
Stesichorus, 'leader of the chorus', is said to have been born in Mataurus in South Italy and to have lived at Himera in Sicily. He wrote long narrative poems, treating epic themes and intended perhaps for choral performance. His poems were collected into twenty-six books.

IBYCUS   Iby.   fl. 535–522
Ibycus was born at Rhegium in South Italy. He visited the court of Polycrates

on the island of Samos. Like Stesichorus, he wrote lyrical narratives of a choral nature.

ANACREON   Anac.   c. 570–?
Born in Teos in Asia Minor, Anacreon travelled to Thrace, then to Polycrates' court in Samos, and also to Athens. He wrote lyric poetry and some elegiacs and satire. His themes include love, hate, drinking, and war. His poems may have been gathered into five books.

PHOCYLIDES   Phoc.   fl. 544
Phocylides was from Miletus in Asia Minor. He composed *Maxims* (*Gnōmai*) in short hexameter poems; he may have written epigrams in elegiac verse. His themes include the training of children, the golden mean, and politics.

THEOGNIS   Theog.   c. 550–480 (?)
Theognis came from Megara. About 1400 lines of elegiac verse (300–400 poems) are ascribed to him but he is probably not the author of them all. These poems may have been an anthology of several poets from the seventh to fifth centuries with some being the verse of Theognis himself. For convenience the present work refers to all these lines as 'Theognis'. Written from an aristocratic point of view, the poems give advice to Cyrnus on morals, politics, and survival in a world of changing values.

HIPPONAX   Hipp.   2nd half of 6th century
Hipponax was born in Ephesus and lived in Clazomenae in Asia Minor. He composed iambic verse with some epodes, trochaics, and hexameters. He wrote on personal themes with some strong invective. His poems were gathered into two or three books.

SIMONIDES   Sim.   c. 556–468
Simonides was born on the island of Ceos but lived mostly in Athens. He travelled widely and became very well known. He wrote several types of choral lyric, including victory odes, as well as lyric monodies and elegies. He composed famous epitaphs, commemorative poems and epigrams.

PINDAR   Pin.   518–438
Pindar lived in Thebes in Boeotia. He wrote choral poetry of varying kinds and became very well known. He treated in particular the achievements of athletic victors. We have four books of victory odes and many fragments of other poems. These odes are named after the places of different victories: *Olympians* (=*Ol.*), *Pythians* (=*Pyth.*), *Nemeans* (=*Nem.*), and *Isthmians* (=*Is.*). We shall also quote from *Paeans* (=*Pae.*), poems of praise.

BACCHYLIDES   Bacch.   c. 517–452 (?)
Bacchylides was born on the island of Ceos, a nephew of Simonides. He wrote choral poetry of different kinds. Like Pindar, he often celebrates athletic victories.

B. Presocratic Philosophers

THALES — fl. 585, prose?
Thales was the first Presocratic. He lived in Miletus in Asia Minor. Although we have evidence about him, we have no fragments of his own words and he will, therefore, not be explicitly treated in this book. He had wide-ranging interests including geography, astronomy, and mathematics. Chief points: All things are made of water. The earth floats on water. All things are 'full of gods'.

ANAXIMANDER Anaxd. c. 610–540 (?), prose
Anaximander lived in Miletus in Asia Minor. He wrote in prose; we have one fragment of his work. His interests included astronomy and geography. He drew the first map of the earth. Chief points: The universe ('all things') is guided by a divine principle called the 'Infinite' (*Apeiron*). The universe is made up of opposites in conflict. These opposites are regulated by Justice that imposes balance between each opposing pair.

ANAXIMENES Anaxs. mid-6th century, prose
Anaximenes lived in Miletus in Asia Minor. He wrote in prose, of which we have one fragment. Chief points: The universe is guided by a divine principle which is Infinite Air. The universe is itself a manifestation of air in different forms. The soul is composed of air.

XENOPHANES Xen. c. 570–470, poetry
Xenophanes was born in Colophon in Asia Minor. He travelled widely in the Greek world, coming to Sicily and perhaps to Elea in South Italy. He wrote poetry in hexameters, iambics, and elegiacs. We possess several fragments of his poems. His subject matter leads him to be treated as a Presocratic and an elegiac poet. His philosophical views are presented in hexameters. Chief points: Anthropomorphic views of the gods are incorrect. Divinity is 'one', unlike mortals in form and thought. Human beings can form opinions of the truth but never know it. Philosophical wisdom is of more value than athletic excellence.

PYTHAGORAS Pyth. late 6th century
Pythagoras is an obscure figure of whom we have no writings. Evidence suggests that he came from Samos to Croton in South Italy. There Pythagorean groups were founded whose teachings were kept secret. Pythagoras evidently had wide interests, especially in music, mathematics, astronomy, and metaphysics. His chief importance for the present work is his teaching on the transmigration of the soul.

HERACLITUS Her. c. 540–480, prose
Heraclitus lived in Ephesus in Asia Minor. He dedicated his book in the Temple of Artemis in 500 B.C. He wrote in prose, presenting obscure riddle-like statements that won him the reputation of being the 'obscure'. Chief

points: The key to understanding the universe is to be found in a divine principle called *Logos* that is fiery in nature. The universe is made up of opposites kept in perfect balance. The tension of these opposites keeps the universe in existence. The human soul, fiery in nature, is the seat of intelligence.

PARMENIDES   Par.   c. 515–?, poetry
Parmenides lived in Elea in South Italy. He wrote a didactic poem in hexameters presenting his view of truth and his rejection of false views. His ideas were very compelling and strongly ˙influenced the thought of later Presocratics. Chief points: Only 'Being' exists. It is one, unchanging, unmoving, and imperishable. Plurality is impossible. Mortals are in error accepting two principles, Light and Dark.

EMPEDOCLES   Emp.   c. 492–432, poetry
Empedocles lived in Acragas in Sicily. He wrote two poems in hexameter verse, *On Nature* and *The Purifications*. Chief points: The universe is made up of the four elements, earth, air, fire, and water. It goes through cycles of change caused by two divine principles, Love and Strife. The soul is a divine spirit that undergoes transmigration.

ANAXAGORAS   Anaxg.   c. 500–428, prose
Born in Clazomenae in Asia Minor, Anaxagoras came to Athens to live. He wrote in prose. Chief points: The universe is composed of tiny seeds, each containing 'a portion of everything'. The ruling principle is Mind (*nous*) which initiates motion among the seeds and separates them out.

DIOGENES   Diog.   fl. 440–430, prose
Diogenes live in Apollonia in Asia Minor. He wrote in prose. He followed the Ionian tradition, especially the ideas of Anaximenes. Chief points: The universe is composed of air as the one underlying substance. Air is divine and intelligent. The soul is made of air and is the seat of intelligence.

DEMOCRITUS   Dem.   c. 460–?, prose
Democritus lived in Abdera in Thrace and travelled widely, going also to Athens. He wrote in prose. He followed the views of Leucippus, who introduced the idea of atoms and space. Chief points: The universe is made up of atoms and space. Atoms are solid, homogeneous, unchanging, infinite in number, differing in size and shape. Space is infinite in extent. Atoms and space in combination form compounds that display secondary characteristics. The soul is composed of fine, round atoms.

SELECTED BIBLIOGRAPHY

I. Sources and Numbering of Fragments = [N]

Homer

Allen, T.W., *Homer's Odyssey*, Oxford, 2nd edn, 1917, 2 vols. [N]
Allen, T.W., Halliday, W.R., Sikes, E.E., *The Homeric Hymns*, Oxford, 2nd edn, 1936. [N]
Monro, D.B., Allen, T.W., *Homer's Iliad*, Oxford, 3rd edn, 1920, 2 vols. [N]

Hesiod

Solmsen, F. (ed.), *Hesiodi Theogonia, Opera et Dies, Scutum*, with Merkelbach, R. and West, M.L. (eds), *Fragmenta Selecta*, Oxford, 3rd edn, 1990. [N]
Merkelbach, R., West, M.L., *Fragmenta Hesiodea*, Oxford, 1967. [N]

Lyric and Elegiac Poets

Davies, M., *Poetarum Melicorum Graecorum Fragmenta*, Oxford, 1991, vol. 1. [N]
Gentili, B., Prato, C. (eds), *Poetarum Elegiacorum Testimonia et Fragmenta*, Leipzig, 1979, 1985, 2 vols.
Page, D.L. (ed.), *Epigrammata Graeca*, Oxford, 1975. [N]
—— *Poetae Melici Graeci*, Oxford, 1962. [N]
—— *Supplementum Lyricis Graecis*, Oxford, 1974, [N]
West, M.L. (ed.), *Iambi et Elegi Graeci*, Oxford, vol. 1, 2nd edn, 1989, vol. 2, 1971. [N]
Voigt, E.-M. (ed.), *Sappho et Alcaeus Fragmenta*, Amsterdam, 1971. [N]

Pindar and Bacchylides

Maehler, H. (ed.), post Snell, B., *Pindari Carmina cum Fragmentis*, Leipzig, Part 1, 1971. [N]
—— *Pindari Carmina cum Fragmentis*, Leipzig, Part 2, 1989. [N]
—— *Bacchylidis Carmina cum Fragmentis*, Leipzig, 1970. [N]
—— post Snell, B., *Die Lieder des Bakchylides*, Leiden, 1982, Parts 1 and 2.

Presocratics

Diels, H., *Die Fragmente der Vorsokratiker*, ed. by Kranz, W., Berlin, 10th edn, 1960. [N]

II. Criticism

Adkins, A.W.H., *From the Many to the One*, Ithaca, N.Y., 1970.
—— *Merit and Responsibility: A Study in Greek Values*, Oxford, 1960.
—— *Moral Values and Political Behaviour in Ancient Greece*, New York, 1972.
—— *Poetic Craft in the Early Greek Elegists*, Chicago, 1985.
Anhalt, E.K., *Solon the Singer*, Lanham, Md., 1993.
Anton, J. and Kustas, G.L. (eds), *Essays in Ancient Greek Philosophy*, Albany, 1971, 1983, 2 vols.

Atchity, K., *Critical Essays on Homer*, Boston, 1987.

Aubenque, P. (ed.), *Etudes sur Parménide*, Paris, 1987, 2 vols.

Austin, N., *Archery at the Dark of the Moon*, Berkeley, 1975, 2nd edn, 1982.

Austin, S., *Parmenides, Being, Bounds and Logic*, New Haven and London, 1986.

Barnes, J., *The Presocratic Philosophers*, London, 1979, revised in one volume, 1982. [References are to 1st edn.]

Ben, N. van der, *The Proem of Empedocles' Peri Physios*, Amsterdam, 1975.

Biraud, M., 'La conception psychologique à l'epoque d'Homère: les "organs mentaux". Étude lexicale de *kēr, kradiē, thumos, phrenes*', *Cratyle*, 1984, vol. 1, 27–49, 1984, vol. 2, 1–23.

Boehme, R., *Die verkannte Muse, Dichtersprache und geistige Tradition des Parmenides*, Bern, 1986.

Böhme, J., *Die Seele und das Ich im Homerischen Epos*, Leipzig and Berlin, 1929.

Bollack, J., *Empédocle*, Paris, 1965–9, 4 vols.

Bollack, J. and Wismann, H., *Héraclite ou la séparation*, Paris, 1972.

Bona, G., *Il 'Noos' e i 'Nooi' nell' Odissea*, Torino, 1959.

Bormann, K., *Parmenides*, Hamburg, 1971.

Bossier, F. and others, *Images of Man in Ancient and Medieval Thought, Studies Verbeke*, Louvain, 1976.

Boudouris, K. (ed.), *Ionian Philosophy*, Athens, 1989.

Bowra, C.M., *Greek Lyric Poetry*, Oxford, 2nd edn, 1961.

—— *Pindar*, Oxford, 1964.

Bremer, J.M., de Jong, I.J.F., Kalff, J., *Homer: Beyond Oral Poetry, Recent Trends in Homeric Interpretation*, Amsterdam, 1987.

Bremmer, J., *The Early Greek Concept of the Soul*, Princeton, 1983.

Burkert, W., *Weisheit und Wissenschaft. Studien zu Pythagoras, Philolaus und Plato*, Nuremberg, 1962.

—— *Lore and Science in Ancient Pythagoreanism*, trans. E.L. Minar, Jr., Cambridge, Mass., 1972 (trans. of previous entry).

Burn, A.R., *The Lyric Age of Greece*, London, 1960.

Burnet, J., 'The Socratic Doctrine of the Soul', *Essays and Addresses*, London, 1929, 121–62.

Burnett, A.P., *Three Archaic Poets*, Cambridge, Mass., 1983.

Cairns, D.L., *Aidōs: The Psychology and Ethics of Honour and Shame in Ancient Greek Literature*, Oxford, 1993.

Campbell, D.A., *The Golden Lyre: The Themes of the Greek Lyric Poets*, London, 1983.

—— *Greek Lyric*, Cambridge, Mass., vol. 1: 1982, vol. 2: 1988, vol. 3: 1991, vol. 4: 1992.

Capasso, M., de Martino, F., Rosati, P., *Studi di filosofia preplatonica*, Naples, 1985.

Carey, C., *A Commentary on Five Odes of Pindar*, New York, 1981.

Carne-Ross, D.S., *Pindar*, New Haven and London, 1985.

Caswell, C.P., *A Study of Thumos in Early Greek Epic*, Leiden, 1990, *Mnem. Suppl.* 114.

Chantraine, P., *Dictionnaire étymologique de la langue grecque*, Paris, 1968, 2 vols.

Cheyns, A., 'La notion de *phrenes* dans l'*Iliade* et l'*Odyssée*, I', *Cah. Inst. Ling. de Louvain*, 1980, vol. 6, 121–202.

—— 'Le *thumos* et la conception de l'homme dans l'épopée homérique', *RBPh*, 1983, vol. 61, 20–86.

Claus, D.B., *Toward the Soul, An Inquiry into the Meaning of Psyche before Plato*, New Haven and London, 1981.

Cleve, F.M., *The Philosophy of Anaxagoras*, The Hague, 1973.

Cole, T.A., *Democritus and the Sources of Greek Anthropology*, Cleveland, 1967.

Conche, M. (ed.), *Anaximandre, Fragments et témoignagnes*, Paris, 1991.

—— *Héraclite, Fragments*, Paris, 2nd edn, 1987.

Cordero, N.-L., *Les deux chemins de Parménide*, Paris, 1984.

Coxon, A.H., *The Fragments of Parmenides*, Assen, 1986.

Crotty, K., *Song and Action: Odes of Pindar*, Baltimore, 1982.

Darcus, S.M., '*Noos* Precedes *Phrēn* in Greek Lyric Poetry', *AC*, 1977, vol. 46, 41–51.

Davison, M.A., *From Archilochus to Pindar*, London, 1968.

Dihle, A., *The Theory of Will in Classical Antiquity*, Berkeley, 1982.

—— 'Totenglaube und Seelenvorstellung im 7. Jahrhundert vor Christus' in Klauser, T., Dassmann, E., Thraede, K. (eds), *Jenseitsvorstellungen in Antike und Christentum*, *JbAC Ergzbd.* 1982, vol. 9, 9–20.

Dodds, E.R., *The Greeks and the Irrational*, Berkeley, 1951.

Donlan, W., *The Aristocratic Ideal in Ancient Greece*, Lawrence, Kansas, 1980.

Dover, K., 'The Portrayal of Moral Evaluation in Greek Poetry', *JHS*, 1983, vol. 103, 35–48.

Duchemin, J., *Pindare, Poète et Prophète*, Paris, 1955.

Dumont, J.-P., *Les présocratiques*, Paris, 1988.

Edwards, M.W., *Homer, Poet of the Iliad*, Baltimore and London, 1987.

Ferguson, J., *Moral Values in the Ancient World*, London, 1958.

Figueira, T.J. and Nagy, G., (eds), *Theognis of Megara: Poetry and the Polis*, Baltimore, 1985.

Finkelberg, A., 'On the Unity of Orphic and Milesian Thought', *HThR*, 1986, vol. 79, 321–35.

Fisher, N.R.E., *Hybris: A Study in the Values of Honour and Shame in Ancient Greece*, Warminster, 1992.

Fogelmark, S., *Studies in Pindar*, Lund, 1972.

Fowler, R.L., *The Nature of Early Greek Lyric: Three Preliminary Studies*, Toronto, 1987.

Fränkel, H., *Dichtung und Philosophie des frühen Griechentums*, Munich, 2nd edn, 1962. English edn: *Early Greek Poetry and Philosophy*, trans. M. Hadas and J. Willis, Oxford, 1975. [References are to German edn.]

—— *Wege und Formen frühgriechisches Denken*, Munich, 2nd edn, 1960.

Freeman, K., *Ancilla to the Pre-Socratic Philosophers*, Oxford, 1946.

Fritz, K. von, *Grundprobleme der Geschichte der antiken Wissenschaft*, Berlin, 1971.

—— 'Der *Nous* des Anaxagoras', *ABG*, 1964, vol. 9, 87–102 and 594–622.

—— '*Nous, Noein* and their Derivatives in Homer', *CP*, 1943, vol. 38, 79–93.

—— '*Nous, Noein* and their Derivatives in Pre-socratic Philosophy', *CP*, 1945, vol. 41, 223–42.

Furley, D.J., *Cosmic Problems: Essays on Greek and Roman Philosophy of Nature*, Cambridge, 1989.

—— 'The Early History of the Concept of the Soul', *BICS*, 1956, vol. 3, 1–16.

—— *Two Studies in the Greek Atomists*, Princeton, N.J., 1967.

Furley, D.J. and Allen, R.E. (eds), *Studies in Presocratic Philosophy*, London, vol. 1: 1970, vol. 2: 1975.

Gallop, D., *Parmenides of Elea*, Toronto, 1984.

Garland, R., 'The Causation of Death in the *Iliad*: A Theological and Biological Investigation', *BICS*, 1981, vol. 28, 43–60.

—— *The Greek Way of Death*, London, 1985.

Gentili, B., *Poetry and its Public in Ancient Greece*, Baltimore and London, 1988.

Gentili, B. and Cerri, G., *History and Biography in Ancient Thought*, Amsterdam, 1988.

Gerber, D.E. (ed.), *Greek Poetry and Philosophy, Studies Woodbury*, Chico, Calif., 1984.

Gianotti, G., *Per una poetica Pindarica*, Turin, 1975.

Griffin, J., *Homer on Life and Death*, Oxford, 1980.

Guthrie, R.S., *The Pythagorean Sourcebook and Library*, Grand Rapids, 1987.

Guthrie, W.K.C., *A History of Greek Philosophy*, Cambridge, vol. 1: 1962, vol. 2: 1965, vol. 3: 1969.

Hamilton, R., *Epinikion: General Form in the Odes of Pindar*, The Hague, 1974.

Harrison, E.L., 'Notes on Homeric Psychology', *Phoenix*, 1960, vol. 14, 63–80.
Havelock, E.A., *The Greek Concept of Justice*, Cambridge, Mass., 1978.
—— *A History of the Greek Mind, I: A Preface to Plato*, Oxford, 2nd edn, 1978.
Hölscher, U., *Anfängliches Fragen, Studien zur frühen griechischen Philosophie*, Göttingen, 1968.
—— *Parmenides: vom Wesen des Seienden*, Frankfurt am Main, 1969.
Hubbard, T.K., *The Pindaric Mind*, Leiden, 1985.
Hudson-Williams, T., *Early Greek Elegy*, London, 1926.
Huffman, C.A., *Philolaus of Croton: Pythagorean and Presocratic*, Cambridge, 1993.
Hussey, E., *The Presocratics*, London, 1972.
Inwood, B., *The Poem of Empedocles*, Toronto, 1992.
Irwin, J., *Classical Thought*, Oxford, 1989.
Jaeger, W., *Paideia: The Ideals of Greek Culture*, trans. G. Highet, Oxford, 1945, 2 vols.
—— *The Theology of the Early Greek Philosophers*, Oxford, 1947.
Jahn, T., *Zum Wortfeld 'Seele-Geist' in der Sprache Homers*, Munich, 1987, *Zetemata*, 83.
Jarcho, V.N., 'Zum Menschenbild der nachhomerischen Dichtung', *Philologus*, 1968, vol. 112, 147–72.
Kahn, C.H., *Anaximander and the Origins of Greek Cosmology*, New York, 1960.
—— *The Art and Thought of Heraclitus*, Cambridge, 1979.
—— 'Pythagorean Philosophy before Plato' in Mourelatos, A.P.D. (ed.), *The Presocratics*, Garden City, 1974, 161–85.
Kegel, W.J., *Simonides*, Groningen, 1962.
Kirk, G.S., *Heraclitus: The Cosmic Fragments*, Cambridge, 1954.
Kirk, G.S., Raven, J.E., Schofield, M., *The Presocratic Philosophers*, Cambridge, 2nd edn, 1983.
Kirkwood, G.M., *Early Greek Monody*, Ithaca, N.Y., 1974.
—— *Selections from Pindar*, Chico, Calif., 1982.
Krafft, F., *Vergleichende Untersuchungen zu Homer und Hesiod*, Göttingen, 1963, *Hypomnemata* 6.
Lamberton, R., *Hesiod*, New Haven and London, 1988.
Lambridis, H., *Empedocles*, Alabama, 1976.
Larock, V., 'Les premières conceptions psychologiques des Grecs', *Rbph*, 1930, vol. 9, 377–406.
Latacz, J. (ed.), *Zweihundert Jahre Homer-Forschung: Rückblick und Ausblick*, Colloquium Rauricum Band 2, Teubner, 1991.
Lefkowitz, M.R., *The Lives of the Greek Poets*, London, 1981.
—— *The Victory Ode: An Introduction*, Park Ridge, N.J., 1976.
Lesher, J.H., 'Perceiving and Knowing in the *Iliad* and the *Odyssey*', *Phronesis*, 1981, vol. 26, 2–24.
—— *Xenophanes of Colophon: Fragments*, Toronto, 1992.
Lloyd, G.E.R., *Magic, Reason, and Experience. Studies in the Origin and Development of Greek Science*, Cambridge, 1966.
—— *Methods and Problems in Greek Science*, Cambridge, 1991.
Lloyd-Jones, H., *Greek Epic, Lyric, and Tragedy: The Academic Papers of Sir Hugh Lloyd-Jones*, Oxford, 1990.
—— *The Justice of Zeus*, Berkeley, 2nd edn, 1983.
—— 'Modern Interpretation of Pindar: The Second Pythian and Seventh Nemean Odes', *JHS*, 1973, vol. 93, 109–37.
Long, A.A., 'Morals and Values in Homer', *JHS*, 1970, vol. 90, 121–39.
—— 'Thinking and Sense-Perception in Empedocles: Mysticism or Materialism?', *CQ*, 1966, vol. 16, 256–76.
Long, H.S., *A Study of the Doctrine of Metempsychosis in Greece from Pythagoras to Plato*, Princeton, 1948.
Luck, G., 'Der Mensch in der frühgriechischen Elegie' in Kurz, G., Muller, D., and Nicholai, W. (eds), *Gnomosyne, Festschrift Marg*, Munich, 1981, 167–76.

Lynch, J.P. and Miles, G.B., 'In Search of *Thumos*: Toward an Understanding of a Greek Psychological Term', *Prudentia*, 1980, vol. 12, 3–9.

McKirahan, Jr., R.D., *Philosophy Before Socrates*, Indianapolis, 1994.

Mansfeld, J., *Die Vorsokratiker*, Stuttgart, 1987.

Marcovich, M., *Heraclitus*, Merida, 1967.

Marg, W., *Der Charakter in der Sprache der frühgriechischen Dichtung*, Wurzburg, 1938, repr. Darmstadt, 1967.

Meyer, B.E. and Sanders, E.P., *Jewish and Christian Self-Definition*, III, London, 1982.

Molyneux, J.H., *Simonides, A Historical Study*, Wauconda, Ill., 1992.

Mourelatos, A.P.D. (ed.), *The Presocratics*, Garden City, 1974.

—— *The Route of Parmenides*, New Haven and London, 1970.

Mulroy, D., *Early Greek Lyric Poetry*, Ann Arbor, Mich., 1992.

Nagy, G., *The Best of the Achaeans: Concepts of the Hero in Archaic Greek Poetry*, Baltimore, 1979.

—— *Pindar's Homer: The Lyric Possession of an Epic Past*, Baltimore and London, 1990.

Nehring, A., 'Homer's Descriptions of Syncopes', *CP*, 1947, vol. 42, 106–21.

North, H., *Sophrosyne*, Ithaca, N.Y., 1966.

O'Brien, D., *Empedocles' Cosmic Cycle*, Cambridge, 1969.

—— *Theories of Weight in the Ancient World*, Paris, 1981, 2 vols.

O'Brien, M.J., *The Socratic Paradoxes and the Greek Mind*, Chapel Hill, 1967.

Onians, R.B., *The Origins of European Thought*, Cambridge, 2nd edn, 1954.

Osborne, C., *Rethinking Early Greek Philosophy: Hippolytus of Rome and the Presocratics*, London, 1987.

Ostenfeld, E., *Ancient Greek Psychology and the Modern Mind-Body Debate*, Aarhus, Denmark, 1987.

Otto, W.F., *Die Manen*, Darmstadt, 2nd edn, 1962.

Owen, G.E.L., 'Eleatic Questions', *CQ*, 1960, vol. 10, 84–102.

Page, D.L., *Sappho and Alcaeus*, Oxford, 1955.

Paquet, L., Roussel, M., Lafrance, Y., *Les Présocratiques: Bibliographie analytique (1879–1980)*, Paris, 1988.

Parry, A.A., *Blameless Aegisthus, a Study of Amumōn and Other Homeric Epithets*, Leiden, 1973, *Mnem. Suppl.* 26.

Pearson, L., *Popular Ethics in Ancient Greece*, Stanford, 1962.

Philip, J.A., *Pythagoras and Early Pythagoreanism*, Toronto, 1966.

Plamböck, G., *Erfassen, Gegenwartigen, Innesein, Aspekte homerischer Psychologie*, Kiel, 1959.

Podlecki, A.J., *The Early Greek Poets and their Times*, Vancouver, 1984.

—— 'Three Greek Soldier-Poets, Archilochus, Alcaeus, Solon', *CW*, 1969, vol. 63, 73–81.

Prier, R.A., *Archaic Logic: Symbol and Structure in Heraclitus, Parmenides and Empedocles*, The Hague-Paris, 1976.

Prior, W.J., *Virtue and Knowledge: An Introduction to Ancient Greek Ethics*, London and New York, 1991.

Ramnoux, C., *Héraclite, ou l'homme entre les choses et les mots*, Paris, 1959.

Rankin, H.D., *Archilochus of Paros*, Park Ridge, N.J., 1977.

Raven, J.E., *Pythagoreans and Eleatics*, Cambridge, 1948.

Reale, G., *A History of Ancient Philosophy, I. From the Origins to Socrates*, trans. J.R. Catan, New York, 1987.

Redfield, J.M., *Nature and Culture in the Iliad: The Tragedy of Hector*, Chicago, 1975.

Reinhardt, K., *Parmenides und die Geschichte der griechischen Philosophie*, Frankfurt am Main, 2nd edn, 1959.

Renehan, R., 'The Meaning of *Sōma* in Homer: A Study of Methodology', *CSCA*, 1979, vol. 12, 269–82.

Ricken, F., *Philosophy of the Ancients*, Notre Dame, Ill., 1991.

Robb, K. (ed.), *Language and Thought in Early Greek Philosophy*, La Salle, Ill., 1983.

Robinson, J.M., *An Introduction to Early Greek Philosophy*, Boston, 1968.
Robinson, T.M., *Heraclitus, Fragments: A Text and Translation with a Commentary*, Toronto, 1987.
Rohde, E., *Psyche*, trans. W.B. Hillis, London, 8th edn, 1925.
Roisman, H., *Loyalty in Early Greek Epic and Tragedy*, Hain, 1984.
Romilly, J. de., *'Patience, mon coeur.' L'essor de la psychologie dans la littérature grecque classique*, Paris, 1984.
Rosenmeyer, P.A., *The Poetics of Imitation: Anacreon and the Anacreontic Tradition*, Cambridge, 1992.
Rowe, C., *An Introduction to Greek Ethics*, London, 1976.
Rowe, C.J., *Essential Hesiod*, Bristol, 1978.
Rubino, C.A. and Shelmerdine, C.W. (eds), *Approaches to Homer*, Austin, 1983.
Russo, J. and Simon, B., 'Homeric Psychology and the Oral Epic Tradition', *JHI*, 1968, vol. 29, 483–98.
Rüsche, F., *Blut, Leben und Seele*, Paderborn, 1930.
Sambursky, S., *The Physical World of the Greeks*, London, 1956.
Sansone, D., *Aeschylean Metaphors for Intellectual Activity*, Wiesbaden, 1975, *Hermes Einzelschr. 35*.
Schadewaldt, W., *Von Homers Welt und Werk*, Stuttgart, 4th edn, 1965.
Schein, S.L., *The Mortal Hero: An Introduction to Homer's Iliad*, Berkeley, 1984.
Schmitt, A., *Selbständigkeit und Abhängigkeit menschlichen Handelns bei Homer*, Mainz, 1990.
Schnaufer, A., *Frühgriechischer Totenglaube*, Hildesheim, 1970, *Spudasmata 20*.
Schofield, M., *An Essay on Anaxagoras*, Cambridge, 1980.
Schofield, M. and Nussbaum, M.E. (eds), *Language and Logos, Studies Owen*, Cambridge, 1982.
Segal, C.P., *Pindar's Mythmaking: The Fourth Pythian Ode*, Princeton, 1986.
Shiner, R.A. and King-Farlow, J. (eds), *New Essays on Plato and the Presocratics*, Guelph, 1976.
Sider, D., *The Fragments of Anaxagoras*, Meisenheim, 1981.
Snell, B., *Die Entdeckung des Geistes*, Göttingen, 4th edn, 1975. English edn: *The Discovery of the Mind*, trans. T.G. Rosenmeyer, Oxford, 1953. [References are to English edn.]
——— *Tyrtaios und die Sprache des Epos*, Göttingen, 1969, *Hypomnemata 22*.
——— *Der Weg zum Denken und zur Wahrheit*, Göttingen, 1978, *Hypomnemata 57*.
Snell, B. and others, *Lexikon des frühgriechischen Epos*, Göttingen, 1955–, in progress.
Solmsen, F., 'Antecedents of Aristotle's Psychology and Scale of Beings', *AJP*, 1955, vol. 76, 148–64.
Spariosu, M.I., *God of Many Names*, Durham, 1991.
Stanley, K., *The Shield of Homer: Narrative Structure in the Iliad*, Princeton, 1993.
Stallmach, J., *Ate*, Meisenheim, 1968.
Stokes, M.C., *One and Many in Presocratic Philosophy*, Wash. D.C., 1971.
Sullivan, S.D., 'The Nature of *Phrēn* in Empedocles' in Capasso, M., Rosati, P. (eds), *Studi di letteratura preplatonica*, Rome, 1985, 89–106.
——— *Psychological Activity in Homer: A Study of Phrēn*, Ottawa, 1988.
——— 'To *Sophon* as an Aspect of the Divine in Heraclitus' in Gerber, D.E. (ed.), *Greek Poetry and Philosophy, Studies Woodbury*, Chico, Calif., 1984, 285–301.
Taplin, O., *Homeric Soundings: The Shaping of the Iliad*, Oxford, 1992.
Tarán, L., *Parmenides: A Text with Translation*, Princeton, 1965.
Teodorsson, S.T., *Anaxagoras' Theory of Matter*, Göteberg, 1982.
Thalmann, W.G., *Conventions of Form and Thought in Early Greek Epic Poetry*, Baltimore and London, 1984.
Treu, M., *Von Homer zur Lyrik*, Munich, 1955.
Tsagarakis, O., *Self-Expression in Early Greek Lyric, Elegiac and Iambic Poetry*, Wiesbaden, 1977.

Untersteiner, M., *Parmenide*, Florence, 1958.

Verdenius, W.J., *Commentaries on Pindar*, Leiden, 1987, 1988, *Mnem. Suppl.*, 97, 101, vols. 1 and 2.

—— *Parmenides, Some Comments on his Poem*, Amsterdam, 2nd edn, 1964.

Vivante, P., 'Sulle designazioni Omeriche della realtà psichica', *AGI*, 1956, vol. 41, 113–38.

Vlastos, G., 'Equality and Justice in the Early Greek Cosmogonies', *CP*, 1947, vol. 42, 156–78.

—— 'Theology and Philosophy in Early Greek Thought', *PQ*, 1952, vol. 2, 97–123.

Voigt, C., *Überlegung und Entscheidung, Studien zur Selbstauffassung des Menschen bei Homer*, Berlin, 1933, repr. Meisenheim, 1972.

Walsh, G.B., *The Varieties of Enchantment*, Chapel Hill and London, 1984.

Warden, J., 'The Mind of Zeus', *JHI*, 1971, vol. 32, 3–14.

—— '*Psyche* in Homeric Death-descriptions', *Phoenix*, 1971, vol. 25, 85–103.

West, M.L., *Early Greek Philosophy and the Orient*, Oxford, 1971.

—— *Greek Lyric Poetry*, Oxford, 1993.

—— *Studies in Greek Elegy and Iambus*, Berlin, 1974.

Wheelwright, P.W., *Heraclitus*, Princeton, 1959.

Whitman, C.H., *Homer and the Heroic Tradition*, Cambridge, Mass., 1965.

Wilamowitz-Moellendorf, U. von., *Der Glaube der Hellenen*, Berlin, 1931, 2 vols.

Will, F., *Archilochos*, New York, 1969.

Woodbury, L.E., *Collected Papers*, Atlanta, Georgia, 1991.

Wright, M.R., *Empedocles: The Extant Fragments*, New Haven, 1981.

—— 'Presocratic Minds' in Gill, C. (ed.), *The Person and the Human Mind: Issues in Ancient and Modern Philosophy*, Oxford, 1989, 207–25.

—— *The Presocratics*, Bristol, 1985.

Yamagata, N., *Homeric Morality*, Leiden, 1994, *Mnem. Suppl.* 131.

Young, D.C., *Three Odes of Pindar. A Literary Study of Pythian 11, Pythian 3, and Olympian 7*, Leiden, 1968.

Zuntz, G., *Persephone*, Oxford, 1971. [Bk 2 on 'Empedokles' *Katharmoi*'.]

THE AEGAEAN

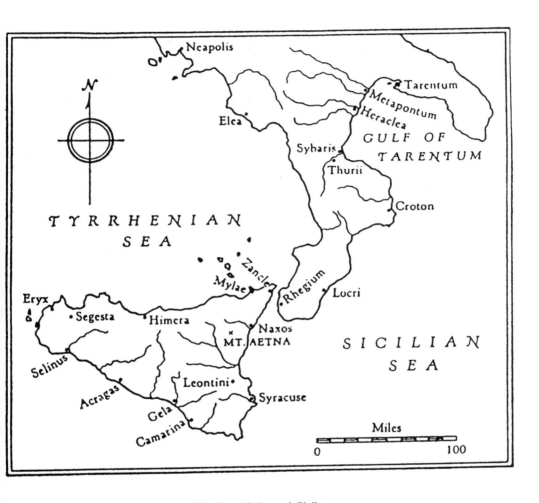

Southern Italy and Sicily

INDEX OF PASSAGES DISCUSSED

GENERAL INDEX

(Entries in **bold** indicate chief discussions.)

SUPPLEMENTS TO MNEMOSYNE

EDITED BY J. M. BREMER, L. F. JANSSEN, H. PINKSTER,
H. W. PLEKET, C. J. RUIJGH AND P. H. SCHRIJVERS

4. LEEMAN, A.D. *A Systematical Bibliography of Sallust (1879-1964).* Revised and augmented edition. 1965. ISBN 90 04 01467 5
5. LENZ, F.W. (ed.). *The Aristeides 'Prolegomena'.* 1959. ISBN 90 04 01468 3
7. McKAY, K.J. *Erysichthon. A Callimachean Comedy.* 1962. ISBN 90 04 01470 5
11. RUTILIUS LUPUS. *De Figuris Sententiarum et Elocutionis.* Edited with Prolegomena and Commentary by E. BROOKS. 1970. ISBN 90 04 01474 8
12. SMYTH, W.R. (ed.). *Thesaurus criticus ad Sexti Propertii textum.* 1970. ISBN 90 04 01475 6
13. LEVIN, D.N. *Apollonius' 'Argonautica' re-examined.* 1. The Neglected First and Second Books. 1971. ISBN 90 04 02575 8
14. REINMUTH, O.W. *The Ephebic Inscriptions of the Fourth Century B.C.* 1971. ISBN 90 04 01476 4
16. ROSE, K.F.C. *The Date and Author of the 'Satyricon'.* With an Introduction by J.P.SULLIVAN. 1971. ISBN 90 04 02578 2
18. WILLIS, J. *De Martiano Capella emendando.* 1971. ISBN 90 04 02580 4
19. HERINGTON, C.J. (ed.). *The Older Scholia on the Prometheus Bound.* 1972. ISBN 90 04 03455 2
20. THIEL, H. VAN. *Petron. Überlieferung und Rekonstruktion.* 1971. ISBN 90 04 02581 2
21. LOSADA, L.A. *The Fifth Column in the Peloponnesian War.* 1972. ISBN 90 04 03421 8
23. BROWN, V. *The Textual Transmission of Caesar's 'Civil War'.* 1972. ISBN 90 04 03457 9
24. LOOMIS, J.W. *Studies in Catullan Verse.* An Analysis of Word Types and Patterns in the Polymetra. 1972. ISBN 90 04 03429 3
27. GEORGE, E.V. *Aeneid VIII and the Aitia of Callimachus.* 1974. ISBN 90 04 03859 0
29. BERS, V. *Enallage and Greek Style.* 1974. ISBN 90 04 03786 1
37. SMITH, O.L. *Studies in the Scholia on Aeschylus.* 1. The Recensions of Demetrius Triclinius. 1975. ISBN 90 04 04220 2
39. SCHMELING, G.L. & J.H. STUCKEY. *A Bibliography of Petronius.* 1977 ISBN 90 04 04753 0
44. THOMPSON, W.E. *De Hagniae Hereditate.* An Athenian Inheritance Case. 1976. ISBN 90 04 04757 3
45. McGUSHIN, P. *Sallustius Crispus, 'Bellum Catilinae'. A Commentary.* 1977. ISBN 90 04 04835 9
46. THORNTON, A. *The Living Universe. Gods and Men in Virgil's Aeneid.* 1976. ISBN 90 04 04579 1
48. BRENK, F.E. *In Mist apparelled. Religious Themes in Plutarch's 'Moralia' and 'Lives'.* 1977. ISBN 90 04 05241 0
51. SUSSMAN, L.A. *The Elder Seneca.* 1978. ISBN 90 04 05759 5
57. BOER, W. DEN. *Private Morality in Greece and Rome.* Some Historical Aspects. 1979. ISBN 90 04 05976 8
61. *Hieronymus' Liber de optimo genere interpretandi (Epistula 57).* Ein Kommentar von G.J.M. BARTELINK. 1980. ISBN 90 04 06085 5
63. HOHENDAHL-ZOETELIEF, I.M. *Manners in the Homeric Epic.* 1980. ISBN 90 04 06223 8
64. HARVEY, R.A. *A Commentary on Persius.* 1981. ISBN 90 04 06313 7
65. MAXWELL-STUART, P.G. *Studies in Greek Colour Terminology.* 1. γλαυκός. 1981. ISBN 90 04 06406 0
68. ACHARD, G. *Pratique rhétorique et idéologie politique dans les discours 'Optimates' de Cicéron.* 1981. ISBN 90 04 06374 9
69. MANNING, C.E. *On Seneca's 'Ad Marciam'.* 1981. ISBN 90 04 06430 3

70. BERTHIAUME, G. *Les rôles du Mágeiros*. Etude sur la boucherie, la cuisine et le sacrifice dans la Grèce ancienne. 1982. ISBN 90 04 06554 7

71. CAMPBELL, M. *A commentary on Quintus Smyrnaeus Posthomerica XII*. 1981. ISBN 90 04 06502 4

72. CAMPBELL, M. *Echoes and Imitations of Early Epic in Apollonius Rhodius*. 1981. ISBN 90 04 06503 2

73. MOSKALEW, W. *Formular Language and Poetic Design in the Aeneid*. 1982. ISBN 90 04 06580 6

74. RACE, W.H. *The Classical Priamel from Homer to Boethius*. 1982. ISBN 90 04 06515 6

75. MOORHOUSE, A.C. *The Syntax of Sophocles*. 1982. ISBN 90 04 06599 7

77. WITKE, C. *Horace's Roman Odes*. A Critical Examination. 1983. ISBN 90 04 07006 0

78. ORANJE, J. *Euripides' 'Bacchae'*. The Play and its Audience. 1984. ISBN 90 04 07011 7

79. STATIUS. *Thebaidos Libri XII*. Recensuit et cum apparatu critico et exegetico instruxit D.E. HILL. 1983. ISBN 90 04 06917 8

82. DAM, H.-J. VAN. *P. Papinius Statius, Silvae Book II*. A Commentary. 1984. ISBN 90 04 07110 5

84. OBER, J. *Fortress Attica. Defense of the Athenian Land Frontier, 404-322 B.C.* 1985. ISBN 90 04 07243 8

85. HUBBARD, T.K. *The Pindaric Mind*. A Study of Logical Structure in Early Greek Poetry. 1985. ISBN 90 04 07303 5

86. VERDENIUS, W.J. *A Commentary on Hesiod: Works and Days*, vv. 1-382. 1985. ISBN 90 04 07465 1

87. HARDER, A. *Euripides' 'Kresphontes' and 'Archelaos'*. Introduction, Text and Commentary. 1985. ISBN 90 04 07511 9

88. WILLIAMS, H.J. *The 'Eclogues' and 'Cynegetica' of Nemesianus*. Edited with an Introduction and Commentary. 1986. ISBN 90 04 07486 4

89. McGING, B.C. *The Foreign Policy of Mithridates VI Eupator, King of Pontus*. 1986. ISBN 90 04 07591 7

91. SIDEBOTHAM, S.E. *Roman Economic Policy in the Erythra Thalassa 30 B.C.-A.D. 217*. 1986. ISBN 90 04 07644 1

92. VOGEL, C.J. DE. *Rethinking Plato and Platonism*. 2nd impr. of the first (1986) ed. 1988. ISBN 90 04 08755 9

93. MILLER, A.M. *From Delos to Delphi*. A Literary Study of the Homeric Hymn to Apollo. 1986. ISBN 90 04 07674 3

94. BOYLE, A.J. *The Chaonian Dove*. Studies in the Eclogues, Georgics and Aeneid of Virgil. 1986. ISBN 90 04 07672 7

95. KYLE, D.G. *Athletics in Ancient Athens*. 2nd impr. of the first (1987) ed. 1993. ISBN 90 04 09759 7

97. VERDENIUS, W.J. *Commentaries on Pindar. Vol. I. Olympian Odes 3, 7, 12, 14*. 1987. ISBN 90 04 08126 7

98. PROIETTI, G. *Xenophon's Sparta*. An introduction. 1987. ISBN 90 04 08338 3

99. BREMER, J.M., A.M. VAN ERP TAALMAN KIP & S.R. SLINGS. *Some Recently Found Greek Poems*. Text and Commentary. 1987. ISBN 90 04 08319 7

100. OPHUIJSEN, J.M. VAN. *Hephaistion on Metre*. Translation and Commentary. 1987. ISBN 90 04 08452 5

101. VERDENIUS, W.J. *Commentaries on Pindar. Vol. II*. Olympian Odes 1, 10, 11, Nemean 11, Isthmian 2. 1988. ISBN 90 04 08535 1

102. LUSCHNIG, C.A.E. *Time holds the Mirror. A Study of Knowledge in Euripides' 'Hippolytus'*. 1988. ISBN 90 04 08601 3

103. MARCOVICH, M. *Alcestis Barcinonensis*. Text and Commentary. 1988. ISBN 90 04 08600 5

104. HOLT, F.L. *Alexander the Great and Bactria*. The Formation of a Greek Frontier in Central Asia. Repr. 1993. ISBN 90 04 08612 9

105. BILLERBECK, M. *Seneca's Tragödien; sprachliche und stilistische Untersuchungen*. Mit Anhängen zur Sprache des Hercules Oetaeus und der Octavia. 1988.
     ISBN 90 04 08631 5
106. ARENDS, J.F.M. *Die Einheit der Polis. Eine Studie über Platons Staat*. 1988.
     ISBN 90 04 08785 0
107. BOTER, G.J. *The Textual Tradition of Plato's Republic*. 1988. ISBN 90 04 08787 7
108. WHEELER, E.L. *Stratagem and the Vocabulary of Military Trickery*. 1988.
     ISBN 90 04 08831 8
109. BUCKLER, J. *Philip II and the Sacred War*. 1989. ISBN 90 04 09095 9
110. FULLERTON, M.D. *The Archaistic Style in Roman Statuary*. 1990.
     ISBN 90 04 09146 7
111. ROTHWELL, K.S. *Politics and Persuasion in Aristophanes' 'Ecclesiazusae'*. 1990.
     ISBN 90 04 09185 8
112. CALDER, W.M. & A. DEMANDT. *Eduard Meyer*. Leben und Leistung eines Universalhistorikers. 1990. ISBN 90 04 09131 9
113. CHAMBERS, M.H. *Georg Busolt. His Career in His Letters*. 1990. ISBN 90 04 09225 0
114. CASWELL, C.P. *A Study of 'Thumos' in Early Greek Epic*. 1990. ISBN 90 04 09260 9
115. EINGARTNER, J. *Isis und ihre Dienerinnen in der Kunst der Römischen Kaiserzeit*. 1991.
     ISBN 90 04 09312 5
116. JONG, I. DE. *Narrative in Drama*. The Art of the Euripidean Messenger-Speech.
     1991. ISBN 90 04 09406 7
117. BOYCE, B.T. *The Language of the Freedmen in Petronius'* Cena Trimalchionis. 1991.
     ISBN 90 04 09431 8
118. RÜTTEN, Th. *Demokrit — lachender Philosoph und sanguinischer Melancholiker*. 1992.
     ISBN 90 04 09523 3
119. KARAVITES, P. (with the collaboration of Th. Wren). *Promise-Giving and Treaty-Making*. Homer and the Near East. 1992. ISBN 90 04 09567 5
120. SANTORO L'HOIR, F. *The Rhetoric of Gender Terms*. 'Man', 'Woman' and the portrayal of character in Latin prose. 1992. ISBN 90 04 09512 8
121. WALLINGA, H.T. *Ships and Sea-Power before the Great Persian War*. The Ancestry of the Ancient Trireme. 1993. ISBN 90 04 09650 7
122. FARRON, S. *Vergil's Æneid: A Poem of Grief and Love*. 1993. ISBN 90 04 09661 2
123. LÉTOUBLON, F. *Les lieux communs du roman*. Stéréotypes grecs d'aventure et d'amour. 1993. ISBN 90 04 09724 4
124. KUNTZ, M. *Narrative Setting and Dramatic Poetry*. 1993. ISBN 90 04 09784 8
125. THEOPHRASTUS. *Metaphysics*. With an Introduction, Translation and Commentary by Marlein van Raalte. 1993. ISBN 90 04 09786 4
126. THIERMANN, P. *Die* Orationes Homeri *des Leonardo Bruni Aretino*. Kritische Edition der lateinischen und kastilianischen Übersetzung mit Prolegomena und Kommentar. 1993. ISBN 90 04 09719 8
127. LEVENE, D.S. *Religion in Livy*. 1993. ISBN 90 04 09617 5
128. PORTER, J.R. *Studies in Euripides' Orestes*. 1993. ISBN 90 04 09662 0
129. SICKING, C.M.J. & J.M. VAN OPHUIJSEN. *Two Studies in Attic Particle Usage*. Lysias and Plato. 1993. ISBN 90 04 09867 4
130. JONG, I.J.F. DE, & J.P. SULLIVAN (eds.). *Modern Critical Theory and Classical Literature*. 1994. ISBN 90 04 09571 3
131. YAMAGATA, N. *Homeric Morality*. 1994. ISBN 90 04 09872 0
132. KOVACS, D. *Euripidea*. 1994. ISBN 90 04 09926 3
133. SUSSMAN, L.A. *The Declamations of Calpurnius Flaccus*. Text, Translation, and Commentary. 1994. ISBN 90 04 09983 2
134. SMOLENAARS, J.J.L. *Statius*: Thebaid VII. A Commentary. 1994.
     ISBN 90 04 10029 6
135. SMALL, D.B. (ed.). *Methods in the Mediterranean*. Historical and Archaeological Views on Texts and Archaeology. 1995. ISBN 90 04 09581 0
136. DOMINIK, W.J. *The Mythic Voice of Statius*. Power and Politics in the *Thebaid*.
     1994. ISBN 90 04 09972 7

137. SLINGS, S.R. *Plato's Apology of Socrates*. A Literary and Philosophical Study with a Running Commentary. Edited and Completed from the Papers of the Late E. DE STRYCKER, S.J. 1994. ISBN 90 04 10103 9

138. FRANK, M. *Seneca's* Phoenissae. Introduction and Commentary. 1995. ISBN 90 04 09776 7

139. MALKIN, I. & Z.W. RUBINSOHN (eds.). *Leaders and Masses in the Roman World*. Studies in Honor of ZVI YAVETZ. 1995. ISBN 90 04 09917 4

140. SEGAL, A. *Theatres in Roman Palestine and Provincia Arabia*. 1995. ISBN 90 04 10145 4

141. CAMPBELL, M. *A Commentary on Apollonius Rhodius* Argonautica III 1-471. 1994. ISBN 90 04 10158 6

142. DeFOREST, M.M. *Apollonius'* Argonautica: *A Callimachean Epic*. 1994. ISBN 90 04 10017 2

143. WATSON, P.A. *Ancient Stepmothers*. Myth, Misogyny and Reality. 1995. ISBN 90 04 10176 4

144. SULLIVAN, S.D. *Psychological and Ethical Ideas*. What Early Greeks Say. 1995. ISBN 90 04 10185 3

145. CARGILL, J. *Athenian Settlements in the Fourth Century B.C.* 1995. ISBN 90 04 09991 3

146. PANAYOTAKIS, C. *Theatrum Arbitri*. Theatrical Elements in the *Satyrica* of Petronius. 1995. ISBN 90 04 10229 9

147. GARRISON, E.P. *Groaning Tears*. Ethical and Dramatic Aspects of Suicide in Greek Tragedy. 1995. 90 04 10241 8

148. OLSON, S.D. *Blood and Iron*. Stories and Storytelling in Homer's *Odyssey*. 1995. ISBN 90 04 10251 5